Take the Next Step in Your IT Career

Save
10%
on Exam Vouchers*

(up to a $35 value)

*Some restrictions apply. See web page for details.

CompTIA.

Get details at
www.wiley.com/go/sybextestprep

To get the discount code, you'll need to register and
bank. Then go to Resources.

CompTIA® Network+®
Practice Tests
Exam N10-008
Second Edition

Craig Zacker

SYBEX®
A Wiley Brand

About the Author

Craig Zacker is the author or co-author of dozens of books, manuals, articles, and websites on computer and networking topics. He has also been an English professor, a technical and copy editor, a network administrator, a webmaster, a corporate trainer, a technical support engineer, a minicomputer operator, a literature and philosophy student, a library clerk, a photographic darkroom technician, a shipping clerk, and a newspaper boy.

About the Technical Editor

George "Buzz" Murphy, CISSP, SSCP, CASP, is a public speaker, corporate trainer, author, and cybersecurity evangelist who has instructed thousands of cybersecurity professionals around the world over the past 25 years with courses, seminars, and consulting presentations on a variety of technical and cybersecurity topics. A former Dell technology training executive, he has addressed audiences at Comdex, Networld, and the National Computer Conference as well as major corporations and educational institutions such as Princeton University. Buzz has earned more than 29 IT and cybersecurity certifications from such prestigious organizations as ISC^2, CompTIA, PMI, and Microsoft, and other industry certification organizations. He is an ISC^2 Authorized Instructor and recently served as technical editor for the ISC^2 CCFP - *Certified Cyber Forensics Professional Certification Guide* (McGraw-Hill, 2014). During the past year, he served as technical editor on five cybersecurity textbooks for both McGraw Hill Education as well as Sybex, an imprint of Wiley and Sons, which includes technical editor for the recent publication *CASP+: CompTIA Advanced Security Practitioner Study Guide* by Jeff T. Parker and Michael Gregg (Sybex, 2019).

Having held a top-secret security clearance in both U.S. and NATO intelligence, he has trained network and cybersecurity operators for the U.S. Army, various U.S. government security agencies, and foreign military personnel across CONUS and EMEA, and has been involved with facilitating such course subjects as Critical Site Nuclear EMP Hardening, International Cryptographic Methodology, and Computer Forensic Sciences, as well as cybersecurity topics. Buzz can be reached at buzz@buzzmurphy.com.

Contents at a Glance

Contents

Introduction

Welcome to *CompTIA® Network+® Practice Tests: Exam N10-008*. This book gives you a focused, timesaving way to review your networking knowledge and prepare to pass the Computing Technology Industry Association (CompTIA) Network+ exam. The book combines realistic exam prep questions with detailed answers and two complete practice tests to help you become familiar with the types of questions that you will encounter on the Network+ exam. By reviewing the objectives and sample questions, you can focus on the specific skills that you need to improve before taking the exam.

How This Book Is Organized

The first five chapters of this book are based on the five objective domains published by CompTIA for the N10-008 Network+ exam. There are approximately 200 questions for each objective domain, covering each of the suggested topics. The next two chapters each contain a 100-question practice test covering all of the objective domains. Once you have prepared for each of the objective domains individually, you can take the practice tests to see how you will perform on the actual exam.

Objective Map

The following table gives you the extent, by percentage, that each domain is represented on the actual examination, and where you can find questions in this book that are related to each objective.

Objective	Percentage of Exam	Chapter
1.0 Networking Fundamentals	24%	1
2.0 Network Implementations	19%	2
3.0 Network Operations	16%	3
4.0 Network Security	19%	4
5.0 Network Troubleshooting	22%	5

Who Should Read This Book

CompTIA recommends, but does not require, that candidates for the Network+ exam meet the following prerequisites:

- CompTIA A+ certification or equivalent knowledge
- At least 9 to 12 months of work experience in IT networking

CompTIA's certification program relies on exams that measure your ability to perform a specific job function or set of tasks. CompTIA develops the exams by analyzing the tasks performed by people who are currently working in the field. Therefore, the specific knowledge, skills, and abilities relating to the job are reflected in the certification exam.

Because the certification exams are based on real-world tasks, you need to gain hands-on experience with the applicable technology in order to master the exam. In a sense, you might consider hands-on experience in an organizational environment to be a prerequisite for passing the Network+ exam. Many of the questions relate directly to specific network products or technologies, so use opportunities at your school or workplace to practice using the relevant tools. Candidates for the exam are also expected to have a basic understanding of enterprise technologies, including cloud and virtualization.

How To Use This Book

Although you can use this book in a number of ways, you might begin your studies by taking one of the practice exams as a pretest. After completing the exam, review your results for each Objective Domain and focus your studies first on the Objective Domains for which you received the lowest scores.

As this book contains only practice questions and answers, the best method to prepare for the Network+ exam is to use this book along with a companion book that provides more extensive explanations for the elements covered in each objective domain. Todd Lammle's *CompTIA® Network+® Study Guide: Exam N10-008* provides complete coverage of all the technology you need to know for the exam.

After you have taken your pretest, you can use the chapters for the objective domains in which you need work to test your detailed knowledge and learn more about the technologies involved. By reviewing why the answers are correct or incorrect, you can determine if you need to study the objective topics more.

What's Next

The next step is to review the objective domains for the Network+ N10-008 exam and think about which topics you need to work on most. Then, you can turn to the appropriate chapter and get started. Good luck on the exam.

Chapter

1

Networking Fundamentals

THE COMPTIA NETWORK+ EXAM N10-008 TOPICS COVERED IN THIS CHAPTER INCLUDE THE FOLLOWING:

✓ **1.1 Compare and contrast the Open Systems Interconnection (OSI) model layers and encapsulation concepts.**

- OSI model
    - Layer 1 – Physical
    - Layer 2 – Data link
    - Layer 3 – Network
    - Layer 4 – Transport
    - Layer 5 – Session
    - Layer 6 – Presentation
    - Layer 7 – Application
- Data encapsulation and decapsulation within the OSI model context
    - Ethernet header
    - Internet Protocol (IP) header
    - Transmission Control Protocol (TCP)/ User Datagram Protocol (UDP) headers
    - TCP flags
    - Payload
    - Maximum transmission unit (MTU)

✓ **1.2 Explain the characteristics of network topologies and network types.**

- Mesh
- Star/hub-and-spoke
- Bus
- Ring

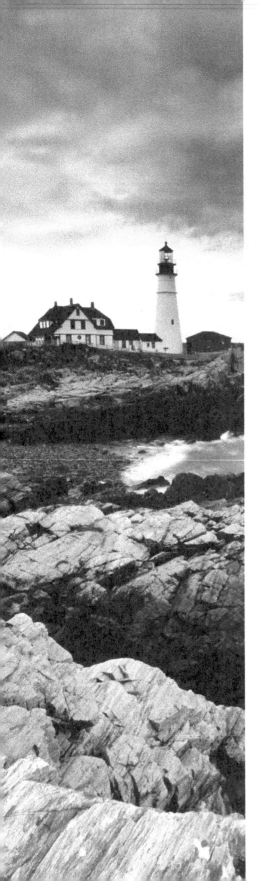

- Hybrid
- Network types and characteristics
    - Peer-to-peer
    - Client-server
    - Local area network (LAN)
    - Metropolitan area network (MAN)
    - Wide area network (WAN)
    - Wireless local area network (WLAN)
    - Personal area network (PAN)
    - Campus area network (CAN)
    - Storage area network (SAN)
    - Software-defined wide area network (SDWAN)
    - Multiprotocol label switching (MPLS)
    - Multipoint generic routing encapsulation (mGRE)
- Service-related entry point
    - Demarcation point
    - Smartjack
- Virtual network concepts
    - vSwitch
    - Virtual network interface card (vNIC)
    - Network function virtualization (NFV)
    - Hypervisor
- Provider links
    - Satellite
    - Digital subscriber line (DSL)
    - Cable
    - Leased line
    - Metro-optical

✓ **1.3 Summarize the types of cables and connectors and explain which is the appropriate type for a solution.**

- Copper

- Twisted pair
  - Cat 5
  - Cat 5e
  - Cat 6
  - Cat 6a
  - Cat 7
  - Cat 8
- Coaxial/RG-6
- Twinaxial
- Termination standards
  - TIA/EIA-568A
  - TIA/EIA-568B
- Fiber
  - Single-mode
  - Multimode
- Connector types
  - Local connector (LC), straight tip (ST), sub-scriber connector (SC), mechanical transfer (MT), registered jack (RJ)
    - Angled physical contact (APC)
    - Ultra-physical contact (UPC)
  - RJ11
  - RJ45
  - F-type connector
  - Transceivers/media converters
  - Transceiver type
    - Small form-factor pluggable (SFP)
    - Enhanced form-factor pluggable (SFP+)
  - Quad small form-factor pluggable (QSFP)
  - Enhanced quad small form-factor plugga-ble (QSFP+)

- Cable management
  - Patch panel/patch bay
  - Fiber distribution panel
  - Punchdown block
    - 66
    - 110
    - Krone
    - Bix
- Ethernet standards
  - Copper
    - 10BASE-T
    - 100BASE-TX
    - 1000BASE-T
    - 10GBASE-T
    - 40GBASE-T
  - Fiber
    - 100BASE-FX
    - 100BASE-SX
    - 1000BASE-SX
    - 1000BASE-LX
    - 10GBASE-SR
    - 10GBASE-LR
    - Coarse wavelength division multiplexing (CWDM)
    - Dense wavelength division multiplexing (DWDM)
    - Bidirectional wavelength division multiplexing (WDM)

✓ **1.4 Given a scenario, configure a subnet and use appropriate IP addressing schemes.**

- Public vs. private
  - RFC1918

- Network address translation (NAT)
- Port address translation (PAT)
- IPv4 vs. IPv6
  - Automatic Private IP Addressing (APIPA)
  - Extended unique identifier (EUI-64)
  - Multicast
  - Unicast
  - Anycast
  - Broadcast
  - Link local
  - Loopback
  - Default gateway
- IPv4 subnetting
  - Classless (variable-length subnet mask)
  - Classful
    - A
    - B
    - C
    - D
    - E
  - Classless Inter-Domain Routing (CIDR) notation
- IPv6 concepts
  - Tunneling
  - Dual stack
  - Shorthand notation
  - Router advertisement
  - Stateless address autoconfiguration (SLAAC)
- Virtual IP (VIP)
- Subinterfaces

✓ 1.5 Explain common ports and protocols, their application, and encrypted alternatives.

Protocols	Ports
File Transfer Protocol (FTP)	20/21
Secure Shell (SS)	22
Secure File Transfer Protocol (SFT)	22
Telnet	23
Simple Mail Transfer Protocol (SMTP)	25
Domain Name System (DNS)	53
Dynamic Host Configuration Protocol (DHCP)	67/68
Trivial File Transfer Protocol (TFTP)	69
Hypertext Transfer Protocol (HTTP)	80
Post Office Protocol v3 (POP3)	110
Network Time Protocol (NTP)	123
Internet Message Access Protocol (IMAP)	143
Simple Network Management Protocol (SNMP)	161/162
Lightweight Directory Access Protocol (LDAP)	389
Hypertext Transfer Protocol Secure (HTTPS) [Secure Sockets Layer (SSL)]	443
HTTPS [Transport Layer Security (TLS)]	443
Server Message Block (SMB)	445
Syslog	514
SMTP TLS	587
Lightweight Directory Access Protocol (over SSL) (LDAPS)	636
IMAP over SSL	993
POP3 over SSL	995
Structured Query Language (SQL) Server	1433
SQLnet	1521
MySQL	3306
Remote Desktop Protocol (RDP)	3389
Session Initiation Protocol (SIP)	5060/5061

- IP protocol types
    - Internet Control Message Protocol (ICMP)
    - TCP
    - UDP
    - Generic Routing Encapsulation (GRE)
    - Internet Protocol Security (IPSec)
        - Authentication Header (AH)/Encapsulating Security Payload (ESP)
    - Connectionless vs. connection-oriented

✓ **1.6 Explain the use and purpose of network services.**

- DHCP
    - Scope
    - Exclusion ranges
    - Reservation
    - Dynamic assignment
    - Static assignment
    - Lease time
    - Scope options
    - Available leases
    - DHCP relay
    - IP helper/UDP forwarding
- DNS
    - Record types
        - Address (A)
        - Canonical name (CNAME)
        - Mail exchange (MX)
        - Authentication, authorization, accounting, auditing (AAAA)
    - Start of authority (SOA)
    - Pointer (PTR)
    - Text (TXT)

- Service (SRV)
- Name server (NS)
- Global hierarchy
  - Root DNS servers
  - Internal vs. external
  - Zone transfers
  - Authoritative name servers
  - Time to live (TTL)
  - DNS caching
  - Reverse DNS/reverse lookup/forward lookup
  - Recursive lookup/iterative lookup
- NTP
  - Stratum
  - Clients
  - Servers

✓ **1.7 Explain basic corporate and datacenter network architecture.**

- Three-tiered
  - Core
  - Distribution/aggregation layer
  - Access/edge
- Software-defined networking
  - Application layer
  - Control layer
  - Infrastructure layer
  - Management plane
- Spine and leaf
  - Software-defined network
  - Top-of-rack switching
  - Backbone

- Traffic flows
    - North-South
    - East-West
- Branch office vs. on-premises datacenter vs. colocation
- Storage area networks
    - Connection types
        - Fibre Channel over Ethernet (FCoE)
        - Fibre Channel
        - Internet Small Computer Systems Interface (iSCSI)

✓ **1.8 Summarize cloud concepts and connectivity options.**

- Deployment models
    - Public
    - Private
    - Hybrid
    - Community
- Service models
    - Software as a service (SaaS)
    - Infrastructure as a service (IaaS)
    - Platform as a service (PaaS)
    - Desktop as a service (DaaS)
- Infrastructure as code
    - Automation/orchestration
- Connectivity options
    - Virtual private network (VPN)
    - Private-direct connection to cloud provider
- Multitenancy
- Elasticity
- Scalability
- Security implications

1. At which of the following layers of the Open Systems Interconnection (OSI) model do the protocols on a typical local area network (LAN) use media access control (MAC) addresses to identify other computers on the network?

   A. Physical

   B. Data link

   C. Network

   D. Transport

2. Which of the following organizations developed the Open Systems Interconnection (OSI) model?

   A. International Telecommunication Union (ITU-T)

   B. Comité Consultatif International Télégraphique et Téléphonique (CCITT)

   C. American National Standards Institute (ANSI)

   D. Institute of Electrical and Electronics Engineers (IEEE)

   E. International Organization for Standardization (ISO)

3. Which layer of the Open Systems Interconnection (OSI) model is responsible for the logical addressing of end systems and the routing of datagrams on a network?

   A. Physical

   B. Data link

   C. Network

   D. Transport

   E. Session

   F. Presentation

   G. Application

4. On a TCP/IP network, which layers of the Open Systems Interconnection (OSI) model contain protocols that are responsible for encapsulating the data generated by an application, creating the payload for a packet that will be transmitted over a network? (Choose all that apply.)

   A. Physical

   B. Data link

   C. Network

   D. Transport

   E. Session

   F. Presentation

   G. Application

5. What layer of the Open Systems Interconnection (OSI) model is responsible for translating and formatting information?

   A. Physical

   B. Data link

- **C.** Network
- **D.** Transport
- **E.** Session
- **F.** Presentation
- **G.** Application

6. Which of the following devices typically operates at the network layer of the Open Systems Interconnection (OSI) model?
   - **A.** Proxy server
   - **B.** Hub
   - **C.** Network interface adapter
   - **D.** Router

7. Which layer of the Open Systems Interconnection (OSI) model provides an entrance point to the protocol stack for applications?
   - **A.** Physical
   - **B.** Data link
   - **C.** Network
   - **D.** Transport
   - **E.** Session
   - **F.** Presentation
   - **G.** Application

8. Which layer of the Open Systems Interconnection (OSI) model is responsible for dialogue control between two communicating end systems?
   - **A.** Physical
   - **B.** Data link
   - **C.** Network
   - **D.** Transport
   - **E.** Session
   - **F.** Presentation
   - **G.** Application

9. Some switches can perform functions associated with two layers of the Open Systems Interconnection (OSI) model. Which two of the following layers are often associated with network switching? (Choose all that apply.)
   - **A.** Physical
   - **B.** Data link
   - **C.** Network
   - **D.** Transport

    E. Session

    F. Presentation

    G. Application

10. At which layer of the Open Systems Interconnection (OSI) model are there TCP/IP protocols than can provide either connectionless or connection-oriented services to applications?

    A. Physical

    B. Data link

    C. Network

    D. Transport

    E. Session

    F. Presentation

    G. Application

11. Which of the following layers of the Open Systems Interconnection (OSI) model typically have dedicated physical hardware devices associated with them? (Choose all that apply.)

    A. Physical

    B. Data link

    C. Network

    D. Transport

    E. Session

    F. Presentation

    G. Application

12. At which layer of the Open Systems Interconnection (OSI) model is there a protocol that adds both a header and footer to the information that is passed down from an upper layer, thus creating a frame?

    A. Physical

    B. Data link

    C. Network

    D. Transport

    E. Session

    F. Presentation

    G. Application

13. Identify the layer of the Open Systems Interconnection (OSI) model that controls the addressing, transmission, and reception of Ethernet frames, and also identify the media access control method that Ethernet uses.

    A. Physical layer; Carrier Sense Multiple Access with Collision Detection (CSMA/CD)

    B. Physical layer; Carrier Sense Multiple Access with Collision Avoidance (CSMA/CA)

    C. Data link layer; CSMA/CD

    D. Data link layer; CSMA/CA

14. At which layer of the OSI model do you find the protocol responsible for the delivery of data to its ultimate destination on an internetwork?

    A. Data link

    B. Network

    C. Session

    D. Application

15. Which of the following is *not* a protocol operating at the network layer of the OSI model?

    A. IP

    B. ICMP

    C. IGMP

    D. IMAP

16. Ed is a software developer who has been given the task of creating an application that requires guaranteed delivery of information between end systems. At which layer of the Open Systems Interconnection (OSI) model does the protocol that provides the guaranteed delivery run, and what type of protocol must Ed use?

    A. Data link layer; connectionless

    B. Network layer; connection-oriented

    C. Transport layer; connection-oriented

    D. Application layer; connectionless

17. Which of the following devices operates only at the physical layer of the Open Systems Interconnection (OSI) model?

    A. Hub

    B. Bridge

    C. Switch

    D. Router

18. Alice is a network administrator designing a new Local Area Network (LAN). She needs to determine the type of cabling and the network topology to implement. Which layers of the Open Systems Interconnection (OSI) model apply to cabling and topology elements?

    A. Physical and data link layers

    B. Data link and network layers

    C. Network and transport layers

    D. Transport and application layers

19. Which layers of the Open Systems Interconnection (OSI) model do not have protocols in the TCP/IP suite exclusively dedicated to them? (Choose all that apply.)

    A. Physical

    B. Data link

    C. Network

    D. Transport

    E. Session

    F. Presentation

    G. Application

20. The protocols at which layer of the Open Systems Interconnection (OSI) model use port numbers to identify the applications that are the source and the destination of the data in the packets?

    A. Application

    B. Presentation

    C. Transport

    D. Network

21. Which of the following is a correct listing of the Open Systems Interconnection (OSI) model layers, in order, from top to bottom?

    A. Physical, data link, transport, network, session presentation, application

    B. Application, session, presentation, transport, network, data link, physical

    C. Presentation, application, transport, session, network, physical, data link

    D. Session, application, presentation, transport, data link, network, physical

    E. Application, presentation, session, transport, network, data link, physical

22. At which of the Open Systems Interconnection (OSI) model layers do switches and bridges perform their basic functions?

    A. Physical

    B. Data link

    C. Network

    D. Transport

23. On a TCP/IP network, flow control is a function implemented in protocols operating at which layer of the Open Systems Interconnection (OSI) model?

    A. Presentation

    B. Session

    C. Transport

    D. Network

24. Which layer of the Open Systems Interconnection (OSI) model defines the medium, network interfaces, connecting hardware, and signaling methods used on a network?

    A. Physical

    B. Data link

    C. Network

    D. Transport

    E. Session

    F. Presentation

    G. Application

25. Which of the OSI model layers is responsible for syntax translation and compression or encryption?

    A. Data link

    B. Network

    C. Session

    D. Presentation

    E. Application

26. Which layer of the Open Systems Interconnection (OSI) model is responsible for transmitting signals over the network medium?

    A. Physical

    B. Data link

    C. Network

    D. Transport

    E. Session

    F. Presentation

    G. Application

27. Specify the layer of the Open Systems Interconnection (OSI) model at which the Internet Protocol (IP) operates and whether it is connection-oriented or connectionless.

    A. Network; connection-oriented

    B. Network; connectionless

    C. Transport; connection-oriented

    D. Transport; connectionless

28. An Ethernet network interface adapter provides functions that span which two layers of the Open Systems Interconnection (OSI) model?

    A. Physical and data link

    B. Data link and network

    C. Network and transport

    D. Transport and application

29. Which of the following protocols operate at the application layer of the Open Systems Interconnection (OSI) model? (Choose all that apply.)

    A. HTTP

    B. SNMP

    C. ICMP

    D. IGMP

    E. UDP

30. Which layer of the Open Systems Interconnection (OSI) model would be responsible for converting a text file encoded using EBCDIC on the sending system into ASCII code, when required by the receiving system?

    A. Application

    B. Presentation

    C. Session

    D. Physical

31. Which of the following protocols operates at the network layer of the OSI model, but does not encapsulate data generated by an upper layer protocol for transmission over the network?

    A. IP

    B. UDP

    C. ARP

    D. ICMP

    E. TCP

32. A client on a TCP/IP network is attempting to establish a session with a server. Which of the following correctly lists the order of the TCP flags raised in the Transmission Control Protocol (TCP) session establishment messages?

    A. SYN, ACK, SYN, ACK

    B. SYN, SYN, ACK, ACK

    C. SYN/ACK, SYN/ACK

    D. SYN, SYN/ACK, ACK

33. Which of the following is the Maximum Transmission Unit (MTU) size for an Ethernet frame?

    A. 512

    B. 1024

    C. 1500

    D. 1518

34. Which of the following Transmission Control Protocol (TCP) control bits is set to 1 to initiate the termination of a session?

    A. SYN

    B. URG

    C. FIN

    D. END

    E. PSH

35. An electrician installing a new light fixture accidentally severs one of the LAN cables running through the dropped ceiling space. With which topology would the severed cable cause the greatest amount of disturbance to the network?

    A. Bus

    B. Star

    C. Logical ring

    D. Mesh

36. Which of the following statements about a wired Local Area Network (LAN) is true?

    A. Wired LANs support only the star topology.

    B. Wired LANs support only the star and bus topologies.

    C. Wired LANs support only the star and ring topologies.

    D. Wired LANs can support ring, bus, or star topologies.

37. Which of the following is an example of a hybrid topology?

    A. A workstation with two network interface cards, one of which is connected to a star network and one to a bus network

    B. Four Ethernet switches connected using a bus topology

    C. Four workstations, each with a separate network connection to each of the other three

    D. Four Ethernet switches, each with a separate network connection to each of the other three

38. Which type of network is typically confined to a small area, such as a single room, floor, or building?

    A. WAN

    B. LAN

    C. MAN

    D. CAN

39. Which type of network connects Local Area Networks (LANs) in distant locations?

    A. WAN

    B. LAN

    C. MAN

    D. CAN

40. Which of the following topologies requires the installation of terminating resistors at two locations?

    A. Bus

    B. Star

    C. Ring

    D. Mesh

41. Which of the following topologies is used by the majority of new Ethernet networks installed today?

    A. Bus

    B. Virtual ring

    C. Mesh

    D. Hierarchical star

42. Alice has constructed a five-node failover cluster in which all five servers are connected to a hard disk array using a dedicated Fibre Channel network. Which of the following terms describes this network arrangement?

    A. SAN

    B. PAN

    C. WAN

    D. MAN

43. Which of the following is not a technology typically used for a personal area network (PAN)?

    A. Bluetooth

    B. Z-Wave

    C. NFC

    D. SDWAN

44. Which of the following network topologies are used by Wireless Local Area Networks (WLANs)? (Choose all that apply.)

    A. Ad hoc

    B. Bus

    C. Infrastructure

    D. Star

45. Which of the following cabling topologies was used by the first Ethernet networks?

    A. Bus

    B. Ring

    C. Star

    D. Mesh

46. On an Ethernet network using the star topology, which of the following devices can function as the cabling nexus that forms the figurative center of the star? (Choose all that apply.)

    A. Hub

    B. Router

    C. Switch

    D. Access Point

47. Which of the following cabling topologies provides the greatest number of redundant paths through the network?

  A. Star

  B. Ring

  C. Mesh

  D. Bus

48. Which of the following Ethernet physical layer options does not use the star topology?

  A. 10Base2

  B. 10Base-T

  C. 100Base-TX

  D. 1000Base-T

49. Which of the following network types are typically wireless? (Choose all that apply.)

  A. WAN

  B. PAN

  C. SAN

  D. WLAN

50. Dense Wave Division Multiplexing (DWDM) is a signaling technology that has become a popular choice in the construction of which of the following types of provider links?

  A. Digital Subscriber Line (DSL)

  B. Metro-optical

  C. Satellite

  D. Cable

51. Which of the following statements is true about the differences between a peer-to-peer network and a client-server network?

  A. Peer-to-peer networks are inherently less secure than client-server networks.

  B. Peer-to-peer networks are illegal, while client-server networks are legal.

  C. On peer-to-peer networks, every workstation is capable of authenticating users.

  D. On a peer-to-peer network, all workstations must share their resources.

52. Why does DSL (Digital Subscriber Line) technology support faster data transmissions than a standard Public Switched Telephone Network (PSTN) modem connection?

  A. DSL uses a separate control circuit that provides clear channels for data.

  B. DSL does not perform Cyclic Redundancy Check (CRC) functions and therefore has less overhead.

  C. DSL performs only a single analog-to-digital conversion.

  D. DSL uses a higher frequency range.

53. Which DSL (Digital Subscriber Line) technology can adjust its transmission speed based on line conditions?

    A. HDSL

    B. IDSL

    C. RADSL

    D. VDSL

54. Which of the following Wide Area Network (WAN) technologies uses broadband signaling?

    A. Digital Subscriber Line (DSL)

    B. Synchronous Optical Network (SONET)

    C. Integrated Services Digital Network (ISDN)

    D. Cable television (CATV)

55. Ed has been hired by a private company to connect two remote sites with a Wide Area Network (WAN). Each of these sites has more than 200 users, and they all need to constantly transfer files across the WAN. One of the sites has a customer database that is accessed by both sites at all hours of the day. Access to the database and other information is time sensitive and constant. The company estimates that their aggregate bandwidth needs to be approximately 40 Mbps. Management says that they need to guarantee access to this information and that money is not a factor in the WAN implementation. Which WAN technology should Ed recommend for this scenario?

    A. A standard modem-to-modem connection

    B. A T-3 dedicated leased line

    C. A cable television (CATV) connection

    D. An ADSL (Asymmetrical Digital Subscriber Line) connection

56. Ralph is an employee of a company that offers the option to telecommute from home. As a telecommuting employee, he needs to connect to the company network to access client information, transfer files, and send email through a Virtual Private Network (VPN) connection. Ralph is investigating the different Wide Area Network (WAN) services available for the remote connection before he implements one. His home is over 30 years old; the existing telephone wiring was not run through conduit, and the wiring seems to be deteriorating. Ralph has cable television (CATV) service, and his home is also approximately 20,000 feet from the nearest telephone central office. He wants to implement the fastest remote connection service possible, but cost is a factor in the decision. Which WAN technology should Ralph implement?

    A. A dedicated leased line (fractional T-1)

    B. A standard modem-to-modem connection

    C. A DSL (Digital Subscriber Line) connection

    D. A broadband CATV connection

57. Which of the following Wide Area Network (WAN) connection technologies uses analog signaling?

    A. Public Switched Telephone Network (PSTN)

    B. Cable television (CATV)

    C. Digital Subscriber Line (DSL)

    D. Synchronous Optical Network (SONET)

58. If you want to allow both voice and data traffic to be transmitted across the same Digital Subscriber Line (DSL) connection, what type of device is required at the customer site?

    A. A signal terminator

    B. A Digital Subscriber Line Access Multiplexer (DSLAM)

    C. A coder/decoder (CODEC) device

    D. A splitter

59. What are the two main factors that affect DSL (Digital Subscriber Line) transmission rates?

    A. Signal termination

    B. Distance to the nearest central office

    C. Line conditions

    D. Line reflection

60. Which of the following best describes the function of a demarcation point or demarc?

    A. The vertical cross-connect that links horizontal networks together

    B. The place where an outside service enters the building

    C. A switch or hub that connects the computers in a particular work area together, forming a horizontal network

    D. The place in a telecommunications room where a patch panel is located

61. Which of the following broadband WAN services provides equal amounts of upstream and downstream bandwidth?

    A. ADSL

    B. SDSL

    C. Satellite

    D. Cable

62. Which of the following hardware components is typically found at the demarcation point of a leased line, such as a T-1 or T-3?

    A. Terminator

    B. Punchdown block

    C. 110 block

    D. Smartjack

    E. CSU/DSU

63. Which of the following remote access connection technologies can support the simultaneous transmission of voice and data traffic over the Public Switched Telephone Network (PSTN)? (Choose all that apply.)

 A. Dial-up modem connection

 B. Integrated Services Digital Network (ISDN)

 C. Digital Subscriber Line (DSL)

 D. Synchronous Optical Network (SONET)

 E. Cable television (CATV) network

64. A company is moving their entire operation to a new building, and part of the plan is to increase the speed of their Internet access by installing a leased T-3 line to replace their existing broadband connection. The service provider they have selected sends a technician to install the leased line. Which of the following is the correct term for the location in the new building where the technician will terminate the T-3?

 A. Patch panel

 B. Switch

 C. Firewall

 D. Demarc

65. A T-3 leased line connection runs at 44.736 megabits per second (Mbps). How many separate channels does a T-3 provide?

 A. 24

 B. 64

 C. 128

 D. 512

 E. 672

66. A T-3 leased line connection is the equivalent of how many T-1 connections?

 A. 7

 B. 14

 C. 28

 D. 112

67. Which of the following is the U.S. standard for synchronous data transmissions that defines data rates designated by optical carrier levels, such as OC-3, OC-12, OC-48, and OC-192?

 A. SDH

 B. SONET

 C. ISDN

 D. DSL

68. Which of the following is a wide area networking mechanism that assigns labels to packets and forwards them based on those labels, rather than addresses?

    A. Frame relay

    B. MPLS

    C. ATM

    D. PPPoE

    E. SDWAN

69. Which two of the following constructs provide roughly the same function? (Choose two that apply.)

    A. SIP trunk

    B. CSU/DSU

    C. VoIP gateway

    D. Smartjack

    E. VPN concentrator

70. Which of the following is the European equivalent of the Synchronous Optical Networking (SONET) standard in the United States?

    A. SDH

    B. OC-3

    C. E-3

    D. ATM

71. Which of the following is the device that provides the interface between a Local Area Network (LAN) and a Wide Area Network (WAN)?

    A. QSFP

    B. CSU/DSU

    C. SIP trunk

    D. IDS/IPS

72. Which of the following terms describes a leased line subscription that provides access to only part of a T-1?

    A. E-1

    B. B channel

    C. OC-1

    D. Fractional T-1

73. Multiprotocol Label Switching (MPLS) is sometimes said to operate between two layers of the Open Systems Interconnection (OSI) model. Between which two layers is it usually said to function?

    A. Physical and data link

    B. Data link and network

C. Network and transport

D. Transport and Session

74. Which of the following Wide Area Network (WAN) services provides the fastest transfer rate?

A. T-1

B. E-1

C. T-3

D. OC-1

75. To which of the following Internet connection types does a specification called DOCSIS apply?

A. Dial-up modem

B. DSL

C. Cable broadband

D. ISDN

76. Which of the following are types of circuits offered by frame relay services? (Choose all that apply.)

A. SRV

B. PVC

C. SVC

D. UPC

77. Which of the following types of Wide Area Network (WAN) connections commonly use Point-to-Point Protocol over Ethernet (PPPoE)? (Choose all that apply.)

A. Leased lines

B. SONET

C. Cable broadband

D. Digital Subscriber Line (DSL)

78. Which of the following devices often provides diagnostic testing capabilities at the demarcation point of a leased line Wide Area Network (WAN) service?

A. SIP trunk

B. Media converter

C. Smartjack

D. AAAA server

79. Which of the following Wide Area Network (WAN) services typically uses a switched fabric that was called a *cloud* long before the term came into general use?

A. ATM

B. Fractional T-1

C. SONET

D. Frame relay

80. Ralph has been contracted to consult for a company that wants to update its legacy Ethernet network to Gigabit Ethernet. On examining the site, he discovers that the network is still using coaxial-based Thin Ethernet. What change in network topology must occur to upgrade the existing network to Gigabit Ethernet using Unshielded Twisted Pair (UTP) cable?

A. Bus to Ring

B. Ring to Star

C. Star to Bus

D. Bus to Star

E. Star to Ring

81. Which of the following best describes the function of a vSwitch (or virtual switch)?

A. A vSwitch is a software product that enables a computer with multiple network adapters to function as a switch.

B. A vSwitch is a feature in layer 3 switches that enables VLANs on the same switch to communicate with each other.

C. A vSwitch is a feature in layer 3 switches that enables VLANs on different switches to communicate with each other.

D. A vSwitch enables virtual machines (VMs) running on the same hypervisor to communicate with each other internally.

82. Which of the following statements best describes the difference between Type I and Type II virtualization?

A. Type II virtualization requires the host computer to have a processor that supports hardware virtualization assistance; Type I virtualization does not.

B. In Type I virtualization, the hypervisor runs directly on the physical computer hardware, whereas in Type II virtualization, a host operating system runs on the computer hardware and the hypervisor runs on top of the host OS.

C. Type I virtualization supports up to 256 virtual machines, whereas Type II virtualization supports only 8.

D. Type I virtualization requires a separate processor for each virtual machine, whereas in Type II virtualization, the VMs all share a single processor.

83. On which of the following virtual networking components can you create VLANs?

A. Virtual NIC

B. Virtual switch

C. Virtual router

D. Virtual firewall

84. On an unmanaged network, which of the following virtual networking components have media access control (MAC) addresses assigned to them?

A. Virtual switches

B. Virtual NICs

C. Hypervisors

D. Virtual firewalls

85. Which of the following components is responsible for providing a virtualized hardware environment and running virtual machines?

A. Hypervisor

B. Virtual server

C. vSwitch (virtual switch)

D. VPN concentrator

86. Which of the following is the proper term for a computer with a hypervisor on which you can create virtual machines and other virtual components?

A. Guest

B. NAS

C. Host

D. SAN

87. In which of the following ways does a vSwitch (virtual switch) differ from a physical switch?

A. Virtual switches have an unlimited number of ports, whereas physical switches have a specific number.

B. Physical switches typically support the creation of VLANs, whereas virtual switches do not.

C. Virtual switches cannot forward traffic to the host server running them, whereas physical switches can forward traffic to all connected computers.

D. Physical switches always include layer 3 functionality, whereas virtual switches do not.

88. In which of the following components can a virtual firewall be implemented?

A. On a host operating system

B. On a guest operating system

C. In a dedicated virtual machine

D. In a virtual switch

E. All of the above

89. Which of the following technologies can replace leased lines, such as T-1s, by multiplexing signals as packets switched through virtual circuits in a cloud?

A. E-1s

B. Frame relay

   C. ATM

   D. PPP

90. Which of the following is not a protocol that uses tunneling to establish secured links between TCP/IP systems?

   A. L2TP

   B. IPsec

   C. MGRE

   D. NAT

91. Which of the following is not one of the primary components of the Network Function Virtualization (NFV) framework?

   A. VNF

   B. NFV ISG

   C. NFVI

   D. NFV-MANO

92. Which of the following best describes the function of the network medium?

   A. The network medium provides the physical connection between networked computers.

   B. The network medium provides the protocol used to transmit data between end systems.

   C. The network medium passes data packets between two routers.

   D. The network medium processes electrical or light signals and converts them to data.

93. Which of the following signal types is carried by copper cable?

   A. Fiber optic

   B. Microwave

   C. Infrared

   D. Electrical

94. Identify the organizations that developed the general cable type standards for voice and data communications that are currently in use and identify the document name.

   A. ANSI/TVA, document C568

   B. TWA/ANSI/EIA, document T530-A

   C. EIA/ANSI/TWA, document 802.2

   D. TDA/EIA/TIA, document 802.11

   E. ANSI/TIA/EIA, document T568b

95. Which of the following cable types and connectors are used to attach a television set to a cable television (CATV) network?

   A. A fiber-optic cable and a Straight Tip (ST) connector

   B. A coaxial cable and a Bayonet-Neill-Concelman (BNC) connector

   C. A twisted pair cable and an RJ-45 connector

   D. A coaxial cable and an F-type connector

   E. An AUI cable and a vampire tap connector

   F. A twinaxial cable and a Bayonet-Neill-Concelman (BNC) connector

96. Which of the following cable types is used for Thick Ethernet network segments?

   A. RG-8

   B. RG-58

   C. RJ-45

   D. RJ-11

97. Which of the following cable types is used for Thin Ethernet network segments?

   A. RG-8

   B. RG-58

   C. RJ-45

   D. RJ-11

98. Which of the following telecommunications components is all but obsolete and is found only in old, analog telephone installations?

   A. 66 block

   B. 110 block

   C. Patch panel

   D. Smartjack

99. Which of the following is a common European alternative to the 110 punchdown block used in U.S. telecommunications installations?

   A. 66 block

   B. mGRE

   C. Krone LSA-Plus

   D. BIX

100. Which of the following coaxial cable types are still in general use? (Choose all that apply.)

   A. RG-6

   B. RG-8

   C. RG-58

   D. RG-59

101. Which of the following statements about the differences between fiber-optic Angled Physical Contact (APC) and Ultra-Physical Contact (UPC) connectors are true? (Choose all that apply.)

   A. APCs should only be joined to other APCs.

   B. APCs generate more insertion loss that UPCs.

C. UPCs generate more return loss than APCs.

D. UPCs use a green connector boot or body.

102. Which of the following is not a type of fiber-optic connector?

A. SC

B. MTRJ

C. ST

D. BNC

103. Which of the following physical layer transceiver module standards is the oldest and therefore the most obsolete?

A. SFP

B. SFP+

C. GBIC

D. QSFP

E. QSFP+

104. Which of the following cable types is typically configured in a star topology, uses eight copper conductors arranged in four pairs, and uses RJ-45 connectors?

A. RG-8

B. Twisted pair

C. RG-58

D. Fiber optic

105. Which of the following statements explains the purpose of the twists in twisted pair cabling?

A. The twists prevent collisions.

B. The twists completely eliminate crosstalk and electromagnetic interference (EMI) in adjacent wire pairs.

C. The twists prevent crosstalk in adjacent wire pairs and limit the effects of EMI on the signals carried over the cable.

D. The twists extend the bend radius allowance of the cable.

106. Which of the following tools do cable installers use to add connectors such as RJ-45 and RJ-11 to twisted pair cabling?

A. A crimper

B. A splicer

C. A pigtail

D. A patch

107. Which of the following combinations of attributes describes the cable used for a Thin Ethernet network?
   A. RJ-45, 50-ohm, 0.270-inch, coaxial cable with BNC connectors
   B. RG-59, 75-ohm, 0.242-inch, coaxial cable with F connectors
   C. RG-58, 50-ohm, 0.195-inch, coaxial cable with BNC connectors
   D. RG-8, 50-ohm, 0.405-inch, coaxial cable with N connectors
   E. RJ-6, 75-ohm, 0.242-inch, coaxial cable with BNC connectors

108. Which of the following connector types are typically associated with Ethernet networks? (Choose all that apply.)
   A. F-type
   B. BNC
   C. RJ-45
   D. DB-9
   E. N-type

109. Which of the following connector types was typically associated with a T-connector attached to the computer?
   A. RJ45
   B. MT-RJ
   C. 8P8C
   D. BNC
   E. F

110. Which of the following connector types are associated with fiber-optic cables? (Choose all that apply.)
   A. RJ11
   B. ST
   C. F
   D. LC
   E. MT-RJ

111. Which of the following types of cable, when installed, sometimes employed a device called a vampire tap?
   A. Unshielded twisted pair
   B. Shielded twisted pair
   C. Multimode fiber optic
   D. Single-mode fiber optic
   E. Coaxial

112. In an internal UTP cable installation, each horizontal cable run connects a wall plate in the work area to a centralized cabling nexus in a telecommunications room. Which of the following is the correct term for this cabling nexus?

    A. Telepole

    B. Demarc

    C. Backbone

    D. Patch panel

    E. Fiber distribution panel

113. Which of the following statements about single-mode and multimode fiber-optic cables are true?

    A. Single-mode cables can span longer distances than multimode cables.

    B. Single-mode cables are more resistant to electromagnetic interference than multimode cables.

    C. Single-mode cables are more difficult to install than multimode cables.

    D. Single-mode cables have a much larger core diameter than multimode cables.

114. Which of the following components are typically used only for telephone cable installations, and not for data networking? (Choose all that apply.)

    A. 66 blocks

    B. 110 blocks

    C. 25 pair UTP cables

    D. 100 pair UTP cables

115. Which of the following statements about single-mode fiber-optic cable are true? (Choose all that apply.)

    A. Single-mode cables use an LED light source, whereas multimode cables use a laser.

    B. Single-mode cables can span longer distances than multimode cables.

    C. Single-mode cables have a smaller core filament than multimode cables.

    D. Single-mode cables have a smaller bend radius than multimode, making them easier to install.

    E. Single-mode fiber-optic cables require a ground, whereas multimode cables do not.

116. Which of the following tools do cable installers use to connect bulk cable runs to wall plates and patch panels?

    A. A crimper

    B. A splicer

    C. A pigtail

    D. A punchdown block tool

117. Ralph has been hired by a client to install cabling to connect two existing networks. The two networks are in different buildings approximately 1000 feet apart. The cable type must support Gigabit Ethernet data rates of 1000 megabits per second (Mbps) and provide a high level of resistance to electromagnetic interference (EMI). Your client wants the most economical cabling solution that meets their needs. Which of the following cable types best meets the needs of this client?

   A. Multimode fiber-optic cable

   B. Shielded Twisted Pair (STP) cable

   C. Unshielded Twisted Pair (UTP) cable

   D. Thin coaxial cable

   E. Single-mode fiber-optic cable

118. Which of the following are connector types used with coaxial cables? (Choose all that apply.)

   A. BNC

   B. F-type

   C. N-type

   D. ST

   E. RJ-11

119. Alice has been hired by a corporation to design the cabling for their network. The corporation just moved into two different floors of an older building: a retail space on the ground floor and an office space on the 43rd floor. The building has existing Category 5 (CAT5) Unshielded Twisted Pair (UTP) cable. Alice's client wants two separate Local Area Networks (LANs), one on each of the two floors, with a backbone network connecting them. They want a 1 gigabit-per-second (Gbps) data rate for each LAN but plan on migrating to 10 Gbps in the future. The two networks are approximately 200 meters apart. Which of the following solutions best meets the client's needs?

   A. Install Category 6 (CAT6) or Category 6a (CAT6a) UTP cable for the LANs. These cables run at 1 Gbps and provide a migration path to 10 Gbps. Use twisted pair cable for the backbone network.

   B. Use the existing CAT5 cabling for the LANs, since CAT5 runs at 1 Gbps. Use thick coaxial cable for the backbone network.

   C. Install CAT6 or CAT6a UTP cable for the LANs. These cables run at 1 Gbps and provide a migration path to 10 Gbps. Use multimode fiber-optic cable for the backbone network.

   D. Install CAT6 or CAT6a UTP cable for the LANs. These cables run at 1 Gbps and provide a migration path to 10 Gbps. Use the existing CAT5 cable for the backbone network.

120. A maintenance worker, while replacing a light fixture in an office building, accidentally severs a network cable in the drop ceiling. The tenants use a variety of Local Area Network (LAN) technologies throughout the structure, but on that particular floor, there are three separate LANs: a 10-node Thin Ethernet LAN using coaxial cable in a bus topology, a 25-node Gigabit Ethernet LAN using twisted pair cable in a star topology, and a 5-node Fiber Distributed Data Interface (FDDI) LAN using multimode fiber-optic cable in a double ring topology. Without knowing which of the LANs the severed cable belongs to, what is the maximum number of computers that could be directly affected by the cable break?

A. 0

B. 1

C. 5

D. 10

E. 25

F. 40

121. In the punchdown process for Unshielded Twisted Pair (UTP) cable, which of the following is the last step that you perform when connecting bulk cables to jacks in wall plates and patch panels?

A. Cut off the excess wire that protrudes past the contacts.

B. Press the bare wire down between the two metal contacts that hold it in place.

C. Strip some of the insulating sheath off the cable end to expose the wires.

D. Insert the wires into the appropriate contacts in the jack.

E. Strip a small amount of insulation off each wire.

F. Separate the twisted wire pairs at the ends.

122. Which of the following cable connector types is not used with fiber-optic cable?

A. Straight Tip (ST)

B. Subscriber Connector (SC)

C. Mechanical Transfer–Registered Jack (MT-RJ)

D. F-type

E. Fiber Local Connector (LC)

123. Which of the following twisted pair cable types can you use to construct a 10GBase-T network with 100-meter segments? (Choose all that apply.)

A. CAT5

B. CAT5e

    C. CAT6

    D. CAT6a

    E. CAT7

    F. CAT8

124. Which of the following cable connector types have been rendered nearly obsolete by Universal Serial Bus (USB) connections? (Choose all that apply.)

    A. BNC

    B. RJ-11

    C. DB-9

    D. DB-25

125. Which of the following twisted pair cable types is rated for both a 10-megabit-per-second (Mbps) data rate (using two pairs) and a 100 Mbps data rate (using four pairs)?

    A. Category 3 (CAT3)

    B. Category 5 (CAT5)

    C. Category 5e (CAT5e)

    D. Category 6 (CAT6)

126. Ed has been hired to install network cabling for a small private company with 15 employees who need to share files and printers. All of the employees are physically located within the same building in two separate office spaces directly adjacent to each other, sharing a common wall and door for access. Both offices have drop ceilings. The client wants a simple Gigabit Ethernet installation that is easy to troubleshoot. In addition, Ed's client wants to keep installation costs to a minimum. Which of the following combinations of topology, cable type, and installation method would best meet the needs of Ed's client?

    A. Star topology, fiber-optic cabling, and internal installation

    B. Bus topology, coaxial cabling, and external installation

    C. Bus topology, twisted pair cabling, and internal installation

    D. Star topology, coaxial cabling, and external installation

    E. Star topology, twisted pair cabling, and external installation

127. Which of the following cable types are typically used in newly constructed Local Area Network (LAN) installations? (Choose all that apply.)

    A. Single-mode fiber optic

    B. Multimode fiber optic

    C. Coaxial

    D. Unshielded twisted pair

128. Which of the following statements are true about coaxial cable? (Choose all that apply.)

    A. Coaxial cable has three conductors within the same sheath.

    B. Coaxial cable has two conductors within the same sheath.

    C. Coaxial cable has a copper core that carries light pulse signals.

    D. Coaxial cable has a copper core that carries electrical signals.

    E. Coaxial cable has an insulating outer sheath made of braided strands.

    F. Coaxial cable has an insulating sheath made of either PVC or Teflon.

129. Which of the following twisted pair cable types are rated for 1000 megabit-per-second (Mbps) Gigabit Ethernet using two wire pairs? (Choose all that apply.)

    A. Category 3 (CAT3)

    B. Category 5 (CAT5)

    C. Category 5e (CAT5e)

    D. Category 6 (CAT6)

    E. Category 6a (CAT6a)

    F. None of the above

130. Which of the following twisted pair cable types support both 10-megabit-per-second (Mbps) and 100 Mbps data rates, using only two pairs? (Choose all that apply.)

    A. Category 3 (CAT3)

    B. Category 5 (CAT5)

    C. Category 5e (CAT5e)

    D. Category 6 (CAT6)

131. Which of the following statements about fiber-optic cabling are true? (Choose all that apply.)

    A. There are two main fiber-optic cable types: single-mode and multimode.

    B. Fiber-optic cable is typically used to span long distances.

    C. Fiber-optic cables use IBM Data Connector (IDC) connectors.

    D. Fiber-optic cables often use Straight Tip (ST) and Subscriber Connector (SC) connectors.

    E. Single-mode fiber-optic cable uses a laser light source and a glass core.

    F. Multimode fiber-optic cable uses a Light-Emitting Diode (LED) light source.

132. Which of the following are characteristics of an internal cable installation? (Choose all that apply.)

    A. An internal cable installation uses bulk spools of cabling with no connectors attached for most cable runs.

    B. An internal cable installation uses only prefabricated cables with connectors attached for all cable runs.

C. An internal cable installation uses solid wire conductors for all cable runs, regardless of distance.

D. An internal cable installation uses stranded wire conductors for short cable runs and solid core for longer cable runs.

E. In an internal cable installation, cables are typically not run through walls or ceilings.

F. In an internal cable installation, cables are typically run through walls or ceilings.

133. Which of the following Ethernet specifications calls for CAT8 UTP cable exclusively?

    A. 10GBase-T

    B. 40GBase-T

    C. 100Base-TX

    D. 1000Base-SX

134. Ralph has been hired to connect three Local Area Networks (LANs) together with redundant paths that form a fault-tolerant backbone. The LANs reside on different floors in the same building and are approximately 600 meters apart. Each LAN is currently configured in a star topology using twisted pair cabling. Each LAN includes wall plates and rack-mounted patch panels and switches. Building and fire codes allow cables to run through existing risers, ceilings, and walls, but a 50,000-watt radio station occupies one of the floors between the LANs. Which topology, cable type, and installation method are best suited for this network?

    A. Star topology, fiber-optic cabling, and internal installation

    B. Star topology, coaxial cabling, and external installation

    C. Mesh topology, fiber-optic cabling, and external installation

    D. Bus topology, twisted pair cabling, and internal installation

    E. Mesh topology, fiber-optic cabling, and internal installation

    F. Star topology, twisted pair cabling, and external installation

135. Alice is a network consultant who has been contracted to evaluate a network design created many years ago, to determine if the design is still viable. The network will support 20 workstations, scattered throughout the building, to run an inventory database application. The two most distant computers are 150 meters apart. The primary goal for the network design is to connect all 20 workstations to a single LAN running at 10 megabits per second (Mbps). The two secondary goals are to provide sufficient fault tolerance for a single cable break to occur without affecting the entire network and to provide resistance to the electromagnetic interference (EMI) generated by machinery in the building. The earlier design calls for a Thin Ethernet LAN with all of the computers connected to a single coaxial cable segment. Which of the following statements about the proposal is true?

    A. The solution achieves neither the primary goal nor either of the secondary goals.

    B. The solution achieves the primary goal but neither of the secondary goals.

    C. The solution achieves the primary goal and one of the secondary goals.

    D. The solution achieves the primary goal and both of the secondary goals.

136. Ed is a network consultant who has been contracted to design the network for a new manufacturing plant. The plant consists of two buildings 150 meters apart: an office with 20 computers and a manufacturing facility that has 30 computers. The two most distant computers at the site are 225 meters apart. Ed's design calls for a Gigabit Ethernet network using fiber-optic cable. On receiving the proposal, the client asks Ed to justify the additional labor and expense of installing fiber-optic cable instead of Unshielded Twisted Pair (UTP). Which of the following is not a valid reason for choosing fiber optic over UTP for this project?

   A. The 225-meter distance between the two most distant computers exceeds Ethernet's maximum cable segment length for UTP.

   B. Only fiber-optic cable can keep the two buildings electrically isolated.

   C. Fiber-optic cable is completely resistant to any electromagnetic interference generated by the equipment in the manufacturing plant.

   D. Fiber-optic cable provides a greater degree of tolerance to cable breaks than UTP.

137. In the 100Base-TX specification, which of the following are the functions of the Fast Link Pulse (FLP) signals exchanged by switches and network interface adapters? (Choose all that apply.)

   A. The FLP signals verify the integrity of the connection (or link) between the devices.

   B. The FLP signals enable the devices to negotiate the speed of the link between them.

   C. The FLP signals indicate when a collision has occurred.

   D. The devices use FLP signals to detect bad frames.

138. Which of the following 10 Gigabit Ethernet specifications calls for the use of copper cable?

   A. 10GBase-LR

   B. 10GBase-CX4

   C. 10GBase-ER

   D. 10GBase-LX4

   E. 10GBase-SR

139. Alice is a network consultant who has been contracted to upgrade an existing Ethernet network to Gigabit Ethernet. The network consists of 20 workstations with integrated 10Base-T/100Base-TX/1000Base-T network interface adapters. The network cabling is Category 5 (CAT5) Unshielded Twisted Pair (UTP), installed when the building was constructed. All of the workstations are connected to a single 100Base-TX switch. Which of the following options would Alice find to be a valid upgrade path to Gigabit Ethernet?

   A. Replace the CAT5 cable with at least Category 5e (CAT5e) or Category 6 (CAT6), and leave the existing network interface adapters and switch in place.

   B. Install a 1000Base-T network interface card in each computer, and leave the existing cables and switch in place.

   C. Replace the CAT5 cable with at least CAT5e or CAT6, and replace the 100Base-T switch with a 1000Base-T switch.

   D. Replace the 100Base-TX switch with a 1000Base-T switch, and leave the existing cables and network interface adapters in place.

140. Ralph is a network consultant with a client who wants him to design the Local Area Network (LAN) for his company's new branch office. The site consists of a building with Unshielded Twisted Pair (UTP) cable already installed, which the client considered a major selling point when selecting the property. He wants Ralph to install the fastest possible LAN using the existing cable. After examining the site, Ralph notes that the cable is Category 5 (CAT5), installed using a star topology, and that the individual cable runs are all less than 100 meters long. Which of the following Ethernet physical layer specifications can Ralph use for the new network to provide the fastest transmission speeds without replacing the cable?

    A. 10GBase-T

    B. 100Base-TX

    C. 1000Base-T

    D. 1000Base-LX

    E. 1000Base-SX

141. Which Institute of Electrical and Electronics Engineers (IEEE) standards for Ethernet support 10-megabit-per-second (Mbps) communications, and what are the correct segment limitations for each standard? (Choose all that apply.)

    A. 10Base2; segment maximum is 100 meters

    B. 10Base2; segment maximum is 185 meters

    C. 10Base5; segment maximum is 500 meters

    D. 100Base5; segment maximum is 500 meters

    E. 10Base-T; segment maximum is 100 meters

    F. 10Base-T segment maximum is 328 meters

142. Which of the following are Ethernet cable types that must be configured in a bus topology? (Choose all that apply.)

    A. RG-8

    B. RG-10

    C. RG-14

    D. RG-58

143. Ed has been hired by a company to upgrade its network infrastructure. The current network is 10 Mbps Ethernet running on Category 5 (CAT5) twisted pair cable. There are 100 computers on the network, all of which have 10/100/1000 multispeed network interface adapters. The computers are all connected to hubs. Users are complaining that the network is too slow, and connections are sometimes dropped. Management wants to upgrade to the fastest Ethernet standard possible, using the existing cabling, and still keep costs to a minimum. Which of the following implementations should Ed recommend to the client?

    A. Upgrade to 100Base-TX and keep the existing hubs.

    B. Upgrade to 1000Base-T and keep the existing hubs.

    C. Upgrade to 100Base-FX and replace all of the hubs with switches.

    D. Upgrade to 1000Base-T and replace all of the hubs with switches.

    E. Upgrade to 100Base-SX and replace all of the hubs with switches.

144. Ralph has been asked to create some new patch cables that will be used to connect patch panel ports to the network switches. He has been told to use the T568B pinout standard for all of the cable connectors. Ralph gathers the materials and the tools needed to complete the task, but he is not sure about the T568B pinout. Which of the following pinouts must Ralph use when creating the patch cables?

    A. White/orange, orange, white/green, blue, white/blue, green, white/brown, brown

    B. White/green, green, white/orange, blue, white/blue, orange, white/brown, brown

    C. White/orange, orange, white/green, green, white/blue, blue, white/brown, brown

    D. White/brown, white/green, white/orange, blue, white/blue, orange, green, brown

145. It is Ralph's first day working for a consultancy that does network cable installations. His new boss hands him a spool of Category 6 cable, a large plier-like device, and a bag of little clear plastic components and tells him to "get started on fives and tens." What is Ralph expected to do?

    A. Pull cable runs

    B. Create patch cables

    C. Attach keystone connectors

    D. Install a patch panel

146. Wavelength division multiplexing is a fiber-optic technique for carrying multiple signals on a single network medium. There are several types of this technique, including Coarse Wavelength Division Multiplexing (CWDM), Dense Wavelength Division Multiplexing (DWDM), and Bidirectional Wavelength Division Multiplexing (BWDM, or just WDM). Which of the following is not one of the ways in which these types of multiplexing differ?

    A. They use different wavelength spacings.

    B. They carry different numbers of channels on a single medium.

    C. They provide different amounts of signal amplification.

    D. None of the above.

147. Which of the following services enables computers on a private IPv4 network to access the Internet using a registered IP address?

    A. DHCP

    B. NAT

    C. DNS

    D. NTP

148. Which of the following best defines the concept of the dual stack?

   A.   A computer with two network interface adapters

   B.   A computer with two installed operating systems

   C.   A computer with two sets of networking protocols

   D.   A computer with connections to two different network segments

149. Network Address Translation (NAT) operates at which layer of the Open Systems Interconnection (OSI) model?

   A.   Data link

   B.   Network

   C.   Transport

   D.   Application

150. Which of the following is the most accurate description of the subnetting process on an IPv4 network?

   A.   You extend the IP address by adding bits for a subnet identifier.

   B.   You borrow bits from the network identifier to create a subnet identifier.

   C.   You borrow bits from the host identifier to create a subnet identifier.

   D.   You create a subnet identifier by borrowing half of the bits from the network identifier and half from the host identifier.

151. Which of the following IPv4 addresses are you unable to assign to a network host? (Choose all that apply.)

   A.   1.1.1.1

   B.   229.6.87.3

   C.   103.256.77.4

   D.   9.34.0.1

152. How many bits are allocated to the host identifier in an IPv4 address on the 10.72.0.0/17 network?

   A.   8

   B.   15

   C.   16

   D.   17

153. Which of the following are *not* valid IPv4 addresses in the private address space defined by RFC 1918? (Choose all that apply.)

   A.   10.16.225.1

   B.   172:33:19:7

   C.   192.168.254.77

    D. 10.255.255.255

    E. 172.15.2.9

154. Alice has been instructed to create an IPv4 network with 8 subnets and 30 hosts per subnet. She has been assigned a Class C network address. Which of the following subnet masks will she have to use?

    A. 255.255.255.128

    B. 255.255.255.192

    C. 255.255.255.224

    D. 255.255.255.240

    E. 255.255.255.248

    F. 255.255.255.252

155. Which of the following is the default subnet mask for an IPv4 Class A network?

    A. 255.0.0.0

    B. 255.255.0.0

    C. 255.255.255.0

    D. 255.255.255.255

156. Which of the following is the range of IPv4 addresses that Automatic Private IP Addressing (APIPA) assigns to DHCP clients that cannot access a DHCP server?

    A. 10.0.0.0 to 10.0.255.255

    B. 169.254.0.0 to 169.254.255.255

    C. 192.168.0.0 to 192.168.0.255

    D. 224.0.0.0 to 224.0.255.255

157. In which IPv4 class is the address 127.0.0.1 found?

    A. Class A

    B. Class B

    C. Class C

    D. None of the above

158. Which of the following is a valid IPv6 address?

    A. fe00::b491:cf79:p493:23ff

    B. 2001:0:49e6:39ff:8cf5:6812:ef56

    C. fe00::c955:c944:acdd:3fcb

    D. 2001:0:44ef68:23eb:99fe:72bec6:ea5f

159. To which class does the following IPv4 address belong: 190.126.14.251?

    A. Class A

    B. Class B

    C. Class C

    D. Class D

160. Classless Inter-Domain Routing (CIDR) is a standard for IPv4 addressing that includes the ability to create subnets using any number of IP address bits, rather than using 8-bit blocks. Which of the following terms describes this ability?

    A. VLSM

    B. APIPA

    C. VLAN

    D. EUI-64

161. Ralph has been instructed to use the network address 10.12.0.0/14 for the new network he is installing. What subnet mask value should he use when configuring his computers?

    A. 255.248.0.0

    B. 255.252.0.0

    C. 255.254.0.0

    D. 255.255.248.0

    E. 255.255.252.0

    F. 255.255.254.0

162. Ed has been hired to design a company's network. The company has an assigned Class C network address of 192.168.30.0. Ed's client wants the network to be configured with 10 subnets, each with 14 hosts. Is this configuration possible with the given address, and if so, how many subnets and hosts can Ed create on the network?

    A. Yes, this will work. By using 4 subnet bits, it is possible for Ed to create up to 16 subnets. He can then use the remaining 4 host bits to create 14 hosts on each subnet.

    B. No, this will not work. A Class C address cannot be subnetted to create 8 subnets.

    C. No, this will not work. Although there are sufficient bits available to create 10 subnets, there are not enough bits left over for Ed to create 14 hosts per subnet.

    D. Yes, this will work. Ed can create 10 subnets with 14 hosts per subnet. By using 3 subnet bits, he can create 10 subnets, which leaves 5 bits to create up to 30 hosts per subnet.

163. What is the greatest number of subnets you can create with a Class A IPv4 address if you use a 14-bit subnet identifier?

    A. 256

    B. 1,022

    C. 1,024

D. 16,382

E. 16,384

164. Alice has been asked to design her company's Internet Protocol (IPv4) addressing scheme. The company has been assigned a Class C network address of 192.168.30.0. Alice's director wants 4 subnets with 28 hosts per subnet. How many bits are required for subnets? How many bits are required for hosts? What will the new subnet mask be for this network?

A. 3 subnet bits, 5 host bits, and subnet mask 255.255.255.240

B. 4 subnet bits, 3 host bits, and subnet mask 255.255.255.248

C. 3 subnet bits, 5 host bits, and subnet mask 255.255.255.224

D. 5 subnet bits, 3 host bits, and subnet mask 255.255.255.192

165. A network interface adapter in a workstation has a hexadecimal MAC address of 001F9EFC7AD0. Which of the following would be the adapter's IPv6 link local address based on its EUI-64 value?

A. FE80::001F:9EFF:FEFC:7AD0

B. FE80::FFFE:021F:9EFC:7AD0

C. FE80::FF00:1F9E:FC7A:D0FE

D. FE80::021F:9EFF:FEFC:7AD0

166. The default mask for a IPv4 Class B network is 255.255.0.0. How many subnet bits do you need to create 600 subnets with 55 hosts per subnet, and what is the new subnet mask for the network?

A. 10 subnet bits with a subnet mask of 255.255.255.192

B. 9 subnet bits with a subnet mask of 255.255.255.128

C. 10 subnet bits with a subnet mask of 255.255.224.0

D. 11 subnet bits with a subnet mask of 255.255.255.192

167. What is the greatest number of host addresses you can create on a single subnet of a network with the following address: 172.16.0.0/20?

A. 142

B. 144

C. 4,094

D. 4,096

168. Ralph has an IPv4 Class B network with a subnet mask of 255.255.248.0. How many subnets can he create, and how many hosts can he create per subnet?

A. 64 subnets and 2046 hosts

B. 32 subnets and 2046 hosts

C. 30 subnets and 1022 hosts

D. 62 subnets and 1022 hosts

169. Convert the binary mask 11111111.11111111.11100000.00000000 into its equivalent decimal value. What is the decimal representation of this mask?

   A. 255.255.224.0

   B. 255.255.240.0

   C. 255.255.248.0

   D. 255.255.252.0

170. If you have an IPv4 network address of 192.168.1.32/27, what is the valid range of host addresses you can use for your workstations?

   A. 192.168.1.33 through 192.168.1.63

   B. 192.168.1.33 through 192.168.1.62

   C. 192.168.1.34 through 192.168.1.62

   D. 192.168.1.34 through 192.168.1.63

171. Alice has been assigned the IPv4 network address 172.21.0.0/22 for the creation of a new department network in her company. How many host addresses does she have available to her?

   A. 510

   B. 512

   C. 1022

   D. 1024

172. Automatic Private IP Addressing (APIPA) assigns IPv4 addresses from which of the following classes to Dynamic Host Configuration Protocol (DHCP) clients that cannot contact a DHCP server?

   A. Class A

   B. Class B

   C. Class C

   D. Class D

173. Which of the following Internet Protocol (IPv4) address classes identifies multicast addresses?

   A. Class A

   B. Class B

   C. Class C

   D. Class D

   E. Class E

174. Which of the following is an address that you can assign to a host on a private IPv4 network?

   A. 192.167.9.46

   B. 172.16.255.255

C. 10.1.0.253

D. 225.87.34.1

175. Which of the following is the correct subnet mask for an IPv4 network with the address 172.16.0.0/20?

A. 255.255.224.0

B. 255.255.240.0

C. 255.255.248.0

D. 255.255.255.224

E. 255.255.255.240

176. Ed has been assigned the IPv4 network address 192.168.2.32/28 for the computers in his department. Which of the following ranges of addresses can Ed use to configure the TCP/IP clients on his computers?

A. 192.168.2.32 to 192.168.2.55

B. 192.168.2.33 to 192.168.2.46

C. 192.168.2.33 to 192.168.2.40

D. 192.168.2.1 to 192.168.2.254

177. Which of the following IPv4 addresses is available for use on a network device?

A. 1.0.0.1

B. 127.98.127.0

C. 234.9.76.32

D. 240.65.8.124

178. Which of the following IPv6 address types is the functional equivalent of an IPv4 APIPA address?

A. Link local

B. Global unicast

C. Site local

D. Anycast

179. When two workstations access the Internet using the same Port Address Translation (PAT) router, which of the following does the router assign to each workstation? (Choose all that apply.)

A. A unique port number

B. A common public IPv4 address

C. A common port number

D. A unique public IPv4 address

180. Which of the following is the IPv6 equivalent of Automatic Private IP Addressing (APIPA)?

A. EUI-64

B. SLAAC

    C. APIPAv6

    D. DHCPv6

181. Which of the following are mechanisms by which IPv6 traffic can be transmitted on an IPv4 network through the use of tunneling? (Choose all that apply.)

    A. Teredo

    B. IPsec

    C. ICMPv6

    D. 6to4

182. Which of the following best describes why IPv6 hosts exchange ICMPv6 Router Solicitation and Router Advertisement messages with routers?

    A. To obtain the prefix needed to generate a link-local address

    B. To learn the IPv6 address of the nearest router

    C. To perform address conflict detection for its link-local address

    D. To encapsulate IPv4 packets and transmit them over the router

183. Which of the following are examples of Virtual IP (VIP) addresses? (Select all that apply.)

    A. An IP address assigned to a host workstation by a DHCP server

    B. A public IP address substituted for a host's own private IP address by a NAT router

    C. An IP address assigned to a host workstation by APIPA

    D. An IP address assigned to a virtual NIC

184. Which of the following is the best definition of a subinterface?

    A. A logical network interface created from a physical network interface

    B. One of the ports on a physical network interface adapter with multiple ports

    C. A physical network interface connected to a subnet

    D. One of the IP addresses associated with a network interface that has multiple IP addresses

185. Which of the following pairs of well-known ports are the default values you would use to configure a POP3 email client?

    A. 110 and 25

    B. 143 and 25

    C. 110 and 143

    D. 80 and 110

    E. 25 and 80

186. Which of the following server applications use two well-known port numbers during a typical transaction?

    A. NTP

    B. SNMP

    C. HTTP

    D. FTP

187. Which of the following protocols does the Ping utility use to exchange messages with another system?

   A. UDP

   B. TCP

   C. ICMP

   D. IGMP

188. Which of the following components does the port number in a transport layer protocol header identify?

   A. A transport layer protocol

   B. An application

   C. A gateway

   D. A proxy server

189. Which of the following organizations is responsible for assigning the well-known port numbers used in transport layer protocol headers?

   A. Institute for Electronic and Electrical Engineers (IEEE)

   B. Internet Assigned Numbers Authority (IANA)

   C. Internet Engineering Task Force (IETF)

   D. International Organization for Standardization (ISO)

190. Which of the following is the default well-known port number for the Hypertext Transfer Protocol (HTTP) used for web client/server communications?

   A. 22

   B. 20

   C. 80

   D. 443

191. The secured version of the Hypertext Transfer Protocol (HTTPS) uses a different well-known port from the unsecured version. Which of the following ports is used by HTTPS by default?

   A. 25

   B. 80

   C. 110

   D. 443

192. What field in the Transmission Control Protocol (TCP) Option subheader specifies the size of the largest segment a system can receive?

   A. MSS

   B. Window

   C. MMS

   D. WinMS

193. What is the term for the combination of an IPv4 address and a port number, as in the following example: 192.168.1.3:23?

A. Socket

B. OUI

C. Well-known port

D. Network address

E. Domain

194. Which of the following protocols generate messages that are carried directly within Internet Protocol (IPv4) datagrams, with no intervening transport layer protocol? (Choose all that apply.)

A. ICMP

B. IGMP

C. SMTP

D. SNMP

195. Which of the following protocols is used to exchange directory service information?

A. RDP

B. LDAP

C. SNMP

D. SMB

196. Ralph is configuring a new email client on a workstation to use the Simple Mail Transfer Protocol (SMTP) and Post Office Protocol (POP3) email protocols. He wants both protocols to use encryption when communicating with the email server. Which of the following port numbers should Ralph use to secure the SMTP connection with Transport Layer Security (TLS) and the POP3 connection with Secure Sockets Layer (SSL) encryption? (Choose all that apply.)

A. 110

B. 25

C. 587

D. 993

E. 995

197. Which of the following is not a port number used for Structured Query Language (SQL) communications?

A. 1433

B. 1521

C. 3306

D. 3389

198. Which of the following port numbers is assigned to a Unix logging services program?

    A. 389

    B. 514

    C. 636

    D. 993

199. Which of the following is the primary application layer protocol used by web browsers to communicate with web servers?

    A. HTTP

    B. HTML

    C. SMTP

    D. FTP

200. Which of the following protocols appears on the network as a service that client computers use to resolve names into IP addresses?

    A. DHCP

    B. BOOTP

    C. DNS

    D. SNMP

201. Which of the following protocols use(s) the term *datagram* to describe the data transfer unit it creates? (Choose all that apply.)

    A. Ethernet

    B. IP

    C. TCP

    D. UDP

202. What is the native file sharing protocol used on all Microsoft Windows operating systems?

    A. Hypertext Transfer Protocol (HTTP)

    B. Network File System (NFS)

    C. File Transfer Protocol (FTP)

    D. Server Message Block (SMB)

    E. Lightweight Directory Access Protocol (LDAP)

203. When analyzing captured TCP/IP packets, which of the following control bits must you look for in the Transmission Control Protocol (TCP) header to determine whether the receiving host has successfully received the sending host's data?

    A. ACK

    B. FIN

C. PSH

D. SYN

E. URG

204. Which of the following terms describes the Transmission Control Protocol (TCP) exchange that establishes a connection prior to the transmission of any data?

A. Synchronization

B. Initialization exchange

C. Connection establishment

D. Three-way handshake

205. Alice has been instructed to install 100 Windows workstations, and she is working on automating the process by configuring the workstations to use PXE boots. Each workstation therefore must obtain an IP address from a DHCP server and download a boot image file from a TFTP server. Which of the following well-known ports must Alice open on the firewall separating the workstations from the servers? (Choose all that apply.)

A. 65

B. 66

C. 67

D. 68

E. 69

206. Which of the following explanations best describes the function of a Transmission Control Protocol (TCP) or User Datagram Protocol (UDP) port number?

A. The port number indicates to the receiver that the sender can activate a specific port only.

B. The port number is used by both the sender and the receiver to identify the application that generated the information in the datagram.

C. The port number is used only by the receiver, to indicate the application process running on the sender.

D. The port number is used by both the sender and the receiver to negotiate a well-known server port for the communicating processes.

207. What is the valid range of numbers for the ephemeral client ports used by the Transmission Control Protocol (TCP) and User Datagram Protocol (UDP)?

A. 1023 through 65534

B. 1 through 1024

C. 49152 through 65535

D. 1024 to 49151

208. Which of the following statements about the User Datagram Protocol (UDP) are true? (Choose all that apply.)

    A. UDP does not use packet sequencing and acknowledgments.

    B. UDP uses packet sequencing and acknowledgments.

    C. UDP is a connection-oriented protocol.

    D. UDP is a connectionless protocol.

    E. UDP has an 8-byte header.

    F. UDP has a 20-byte header.

209. Which of the following port values are used by the File Transfer Protocol (FTP)? (Choose all that apply.)

    A. 21

    B. 23

    C. 20

    D. 53

    E. 69

210. Which of the following protocols provides connectionless delivery service at the transport layer of the Open Systems Interconnection (OSI) model?

    A. TCP

    B. HTTP

    C. UDP

    D. ARP

211. What is the valid range of numbers for the well-known Transmission Control Protocol (TCP) and User Datagram Protocol (UDP) ports used by servers?

    A. 1024 through 49151

    B. 1 through 49151

    C. 49152 through 65534

    D. 1 through 1023

212. Ralph is a network administrator who has just installed a new open-source email server for the users at his company. The server is configured to send and receive Internet email and create a mailbox for each user that will permanently store the user's mail on the server. Ralph next uses a protocol analyzer to examine the network traffic resulting from the new server installation. Which of the following new protocols should Ralph expect to see in his network traffic analysis? (Choose all that apply.)

    A. SNMP

    B. SMTP

    C. POP3

D. IMAP

E. RIP

213. Which of the following values could a web client use as an ephemeral port number when communicating with a web server?

A. 1

B. 23

C. 80

D. 1024

E. 1999

F. 50134

214. Which of the following protocols provides connection-oriented service with guaranteed delivery at the transport layer of the OSI model?

A. TCP

B. HTTP

C. UDP

D. IP

215. Which of the following protocols is limited to use on the local subnet only?

A. Address Resolution Protocol (ARP)

B. Dynamic Host Configuration Protocol (DHCP)

C. Domain Name System (DNS)

D. Simple Mail Transfer Protocol (SMTP)

216. Which of the following prefixes must you use in the URL you type into a web browser when the website you want to access has been secured with Transport Layer Security (TLS)?

A. TLS://

B. HTTPS://

C. HTTP://

D. HTLS://

217. What is the difference when you specify the HTTPS:// prefix in a Uniform Resource Locator (URL) instead of HTTP://? (Choose all that apply.)

A. The connection between the web browser and the server is encrypted.

B. The browser uses a different port number to connect to the server.

C. The connection uses SSL or TLS instead of HTTP.

D. The browser uses a different IP address to connect to the server.

218. You are a consultant installing a web server application for a client called Adatum. The domain name Adatum.com has been registered in the DNS, and the server has one public IP address, so the new website will be accessible to users on the Internet. You want to be able to access the web server application's administrative site from your remote office, so you configure that site to be encrypted and to use the port number 12354 instead of the default. Which of the following URLs will you have to use to access the administrative website?

    A. `http://www.adatum.com`

    B. `http://www.adatum.com:12354`

    C. `https://www.adatum.com:80`

    D. `https://www.adatum.com:12354`

219. Which of the following protocols does IPsec use to digitally encrypt packets before transmitting them over the network?

    A. ESP

    B. SSL

    C. AH

    D. MSCHAP

220. Which of the following are the protocols that IPsec uses to secure network traffic? (Choose all that apply.)

    A. SSH

    B. AH

    C. ESP

    D. SSL

221. What is the primary shortcoming of the File Transfer Protocol (FTP) that is addressed by FTPS and SFTP?

    A. Lack of security

    B. Slow file transfers

    C. File size limitations

    D. Lack of authentication

222. Which of the following File Transfer Protocol (FTP) variants transmit authentication passwords over the network in clear text?

    A. FTP

    B. FTPS

    C. SFTP

    D. TFTP

223. Which of the following File Transfer Protocol (FTP) variants is typically used to download boot image files during Preboot Execution Environment (PXE) startup sequences?

A. FTP

B. FTPS

C. SFTP

D. TFTP

224. Which of the following protocols does IPsec use to digitally sign packets before transmitting them over the network?

A. ESP

B. SSL

C. AH

D. MSCHAP

225. Which of the following security protocols used to protect traffic exchanged by web browsers and servers was created first?

A. SSL

B. TLS

C. SSH

D. DTLS

226. Which of the following security protocols for web servers or browsers was deprecated in 2015 in favor of Transport Layer Security (TLS) and Datagram Transport Layer Security (DTLS)?

A. SSH

B. SSL

C. RDP

D. IPsec

227. In which of the following DNS transactions does the querying system generate a recursive query? (Choose all that apply.)

A. A DNS client sends the server name www.adatum.com from a URL to its designated DNS server for resolution.

B. A client's DNS server sends a request to a root domain server to find the authoritative server for the com top-level domain.

C. A client's DNS server sends a request to the com top-level domain server to find the authoritative server for the adatum.com domain.

D. A client's DNS server, which has been configured to function as a forwarder, sends the server name www.adatum.com from a URL to its ISP's DNS server for resolution.

E. A client's DNS server sends a request to the adatum.com domain server to find the IP address associated with the server name www.

228. Which of the following devices would you most likely configure to function as a Dynamic Host Configuration Protocol (DHCP) server?

    A. A wireless router

    B. An unmanaged switch

    C. A hub

    D. A bridge

229. Which of the following protocols are responsible for assigning IP addresses to hosts? (Choose all that apply.)

    A. Dynamic Host Configuration Protocol (DHCP)

    B. Address Resolution Protocol (ARP)

    C. Domain Name System (DNS)

    D. File Transfer Protocol (FTP)

    E. Bootstrap Protocol (BOOTP)

230. Which of the following Domain Name System (DNS) resource records is used only for reverse name resolution?

    A. MX

    B. AAAA

    C. CNAME

    D. PTR

231. Which of the following features is supported by DHCP, but not by BOOTP and RARP?

    A. Dynamic address allocation

    B. Relay agents

    C. Manual address allocation

    D. Automatic address allocation

232. Which of the following message types are exchanged by Dynamic Host Configuration Protocol (DHCP) clients and servers during a successful IP address allocation transaction? (Choose all that apply.)

    A. DHCPDISCOVER

    B. DHCPOFFER

    C. DHCPINFORM

    D. DHCPACK

    E. DHCPREQUEST

    F. DHCPNAK

    G. DHCPRENEW

    H. DHCPRELEASE

233. Which of the following message types are exchanged by Dynamic Host Configuration Protocol (DHCP) clients and servers during a successful IP address lease renewal transaction? (Choose all that apply.)

    A. DHCPDISCOVER

    B. DHCPOFFER

    C. DHCPINFORM

    D. DHCPACK

    E. DHCPREQUEST

    F. DHCPNAK

    G. DHCPRENEW

    H. DHCPRELEASE

234. Which of the following is not a protocol used to allocate IP address assignments to clients on a network?

    A. ARP

    B. RARP

    C. BOOTP

    D. DHCP

235. Which of the following best describes what happens when a DNS server receives an iterative name resolution query?

    A. The DNS server responds immediately to the query with the best information it has in its resource records or in its cache, or failing that, with an error message stating that it could not resolve the requested name.

    B. The DNS server attempts to resolve the requested name by checking its own resource records and cache, or failing that, by issuing its own iterative queries to other DNS servers.

    C. The DNS server attempts to resolve the requested name by checking its own resource records and cache, or failing that, by forwarding the name resolution request to another DNS server in a recursive query.

    D. The DNS server responds immediately if it is the authoritative server for the domain in which the requested name is located. Otherwise, it returns an error message stating that it could not resolve the requested name.

236. What is the term used to refer to the DNS client mechanism that generates name resolution queries and sends them to DNS servers?

    A. Requestor

    B. Forwarder

    C. Authority

    D. Resolver

237. Which of the following TCP/IP parameters, configured on an end system, specifies the IP address of a device that performs domain name resolution services?

A. WINS Server Addresses

B. Default Gateway

C. DNS Server Addresses

D. Subnet Gateway

238. Which IP address allocation method is not supported by Dynamic Host Configuration Protocol (DHCP)?

A. Manual

B. Dynamic

C. Stable

D. Automatic

239. On a Dynamic Host Configuration Protocol (DHCP) server, what is the name of the element you create to specify which IP addresses the server should assign to clients?

A. Range

B. Scope

C. Pool

D. Subnet

240. Why is it necessary to use a relay agent to enable a Dynamic Host Configuration Protocol (DHCP) server to assign IP addresses to clients on other networks? (Choose all that apply.)

A. Because DHCP requires a separate license for each subnet.

B. Because clients cannot initiate an address assignment by contacting DHCP servers on other networks directly.

C. Because DHCP must use the Transmission Control Protocol (TCP) to communicate with clients.

D. Because the DHCP address assignment process relies on broadcast transmissions.

241. Which of the following Domain Name System (DNS) resource records is used to resolve a hostname into an IPv6 address?

A. MX

B. PTR

C. AAAA

D. CNAME

242. Ralph has configured a server called NE6 to function as a web server. He does not want to change the server's existing name, but he wants it to also be accessible to clients using the name www. What Domain Name System (DNS) modification can Ralph make to accomplish this?

A. Create an additional A resource record.

B. Create a new CNAME resource record.

C. Modify the existing A resource record.

D. Create a new PTR resource record.

243. Which of the following options should you configure on a Dynamic Host Configuration Protocol (DHCP) server to supply clients with a default gateway address?

A. Router

B. Time Server

C. Name Server

D. LPR Server

244. Dynamic Host Configuration Protocol (DHCP) clients rely on which of the following types of transmissions to locate and initiate contact with DHCP servers on the local network?

A. Unicast

B. Broadcast

C. Multicast

D. Anycast

245. Which of the following Domain Name System (DNS) resource record types specifies the IP addresses of the authoritative DNS servers for a particular zone?

A. NS

B. PTR

C. MX

D. SRV

E. SOA

F. TXT

246. Which of the following must you create on a DHCP server if you want it to always assign the same IP address to a particular computer?

A. Exclusion

B. Scope

C. Reservation

D. Relay

247. Which of the following DHCP address allocation methods enables the server to reclaim IP addresses when they are no longer in use by clients?

A. Automatic

B. Dynamic

C. Manual

D. Static

248. Which of the following technologies enables the IP addresses assigned to clients by a Dynamic Host Configuration Protocol (DHCP) server to be automatically added to the DNS namespace?

   A. Reverse name resolution

   B. Dynamic DNS

   C. Automatic allocation

   D. HOSTS

249. Which of the following is a tool that integrates DHCP and DNS so that each is aware of the changes made by the other?

   A. HOSTS

   B. DHCPv6

   C. IPAM

   D. APIPA

250. Which of the following is the term used to describe the logical distance of a Network Time Protocol (NTP) server from the time source to which it is synchronized?

   A. Layer

   B. Path

   C. Iteration

   D. Stratum

251. Which of the following protocols is used to synchronize computer clocks to a time signal provided by a server?

   A. TFTP

   B. HTTP

   C. SMTP

   D. NTP

252. Which of the words in the fully qualified domain name (FQDN) www.paris .mydomain.org represents the topmost layer in the DNS namespace hierarchy?

   A. www

   B. paris

   C. mydomain

   D. org

253. Which of the following Dynamic Host Configuration Protocol (DHCP) options prevents the client from transmitting IP datagrams that circulate endlessly around the network?

   A. Interface MTU

   B. Default IP TTL

   C. ARP cache timeout

   D. TCP keepalive interval

254. In designing a network for a client, Ed has decided to use both internal and external DNS servers. Which of the following resources should Ed register with the external DNS server? (Choose all that apply.)

  A. Company database servers

  B. Internet web servers

  C. Incoming email servers

  D. Domain controllers

255. Ralph is concerned that the IP address scope of available leases on his DHCP server is nearly exhausted. What happens to DHCP clients when there are no IP addresses left in the scope for assignment?

  A. Clients are assigned a 0.0.0.0 address.

  B. Clients self-assign APIPA addresses.

  C. Client DHCP requests are forwarded to another DHCP server.

  D. Clients are forced to share IP addresses.

256. Alice is the administrator of a subnet for which she has been allotted 100 IP addresses. She has installed a DHCP server with a scope containing all 100 available addresses for lease. There are currently 99 clients configured to use the DHCP server, many of which are mobile devices, and Alice fears that systems frequently leaving and rejoining the network might cause the scope of available leases to be exhausted. Which of the following adjustments can help to prevent this from happening?

  A. Increase the lease time for the scope.

  B. Decrease the lease time for the scope.

  C. Install a second DHCP server.

  D. Create a second scope for the subnet.

257. DHCP clients use broadcast messages to contact a DHCP server on the local subnet. Which of the following are mechanisms by which DHCP broadcast messages can be forwarded to a DHCP server on another subnet when there is none on the local subnet? (Choose all that apply.)

  A. DHCP relay

  B. UDP forwarding

  C. Zone transfer

  D. IP helper

258. Which of the following mechanisms enables administrators to maintain current DNS database information on multiple name servers, for fault tolerance and load balancing purposes?

  A. Multi-master replication

  B. UDP forwarding

  C. Iterative query

  D. Zone transfer

259. Which of the following Storage Area Network (SAN) protocols are capable of sharing a network medium with standard Local Area Network (LAN) traffic? (Choose all that apply.)

    A. iSCSI

    B. Fibre Channel

    C. FCoE

    D. InfiniBand

260. Which of the following protocols is not used for Storage Area Networks (SANs)?

    A. iSCSI

    B. FCoE

    C. VoIP

    D. Fibre Channel

261. Which of the following technologies do iSCSI initiators use to locate iSCSI targets on the network?

    A. Active Directory

    B. ICMP

    C. DNS

    D. iWINS

    E. iSNS

262. What is the highest possible data transfer rate on a Storage Area Network (SAN) using Fibre Channel?

    A. 8 Gbps

    B. 16 Gbps

    C. 32 Gbps

    D. 128 Gbps

    E. 256 Gbps

263. In its primary functionality, a network attached storage (NAS) device is most closely associated with which of the following devices?

    A. Failover cluster

    B. File server

    C. JBOD

    D. RAID

264. Which of the following statements about the differences between Network Attached Storage (NAS) and Storage Area Networks (SANs) are true? (Choose all that apply.)

    A. NAS provides file-level storage access, whereas SAN provides block-level storage access.

    B. NAS devices typically contain integrated iSCSI targets.

C. SAN devices have an operating system, whereas NAS devices do not.

D. NAS devices typically provide a filesystem, whereas SAN devices do not.

265. Which of the following statements specify advantages of FCoE over the original Fibre Channel standard? (Choose all that apply.)

A. FCoE is less expensive to implement than Fibre Channel.

B. FCoE can share a network with standard IP traffic, whereas Fibre Channel cannot.

C. FCoE is routable over IP networks, whereas Fibre Channel is not.

D. FCoE uses standard Ethernet networking hardware.

266. Which of the following are application layer protocols that Network Attached Storage (NAS) devices can use to serve shared files to clients on the network? (Choose all that apply.)

A. CIFS

B. NFS

C. RDMA

D. HTTP

267. Which of the following is not one of the advantages of iSCSI over Fibre Channel? (Choose all that apply.)

A. iSCSI is routable, whereas Fibre Channel is not.

B. iSCSI is less expensive to implement than Fibre Channel.

C. iSCSI includes its own internal flow control mechanism, whereas Fibre Channel does not.

D. iSCSI can share the same network as standard local area network traffic, whereas Fibre Channel cannot.

268. Which of the following Storage Area Network (SAN) technologies is primarily used by supercomputers as a high-speed, low-latency connection between Central Processing Units (CPUs) and storage systems?

A. InfiniBand

B. Fibre Channel

C. iSCSI

D. FCoE

269. Which of the following is the term for the client that accesses an iSCSI device on a storage area network?

A. Initiator

B. Target

C. Controller

D. Adapter

270. Which of the following protocols are included in an iSCSI packet? (Choose all that apply.)

    A. Ethernet

    B. IP

    C. TCP

    D. UDP

    E. None of the above

271. Which of the following protocols are included in a Fibre Channel packet?

    A. Ethernet

    B. IP

    C. TCP

    D. UDP

    E. None of the above

272. Which of the following protocol standards defines a layered implementation that does not correspond to the layers of the Open Systems Interconnection (OSI) model?

    A. iSCSI

    B. Fibre Channel

    C. PPP

    D. RDMA

273. Which of the following protocols are included in an FCoE packet?

    A. Ethernet

    B. IP

    C. TCP

    D. UDP

    E. None of the above

274. Which of the following protocols uses jumbo frames to increase performance levels on storage area networks?

    A. Ethernet

    B. IP

    C. Fibre Channel

    D. iSCSI

275. Which of the following is not the name of one of the layers in the three-tier datacenter architecture?

    A. Core

    B. Intermediate

    C. Distribution

    D. Access

276. Which of the following is not a reason why the leaf and spine datacenter topology is superior to the standard three-tier topology?

    A. The leaf and spine arrangement uses a full mesh switching topology.

    B. In a leaf and spine topology, all data flows require the same number of hops.

    C. The leaf and spine topology is less expensive to implement than the three-tier topology.

    D. The leaf and spine topology uses software-defined networking to direct traffic, rather than blocking ports using the spanning tree protocol.

277. Which of the following best describes the difference between east-west and north-south traffic in a datacenter?

    A. East-west describes traffic between devices at the same layer of the OSI model, while north-south describes traffic between OSI model layers.

    B. East-west is switch-to-switch traffic, while north-south is switch-to-router traffic.

    C. East-west traffic stays within the datacenter, while north-south traffic does not.

    D. East-west is backbone traffic among switches and routers, while north-south is traffic to end systems, such as servers.

278. Top-of-rack switches most commonly form which layer of the datacenter topology?

    A. Leaf

    B. Backbone

    C. Spine

    D. Core

279. Which of the following layers in a Software-Defined Network (SDN) architecture consists of hardware devices?

    A. Application

    B. Control

    C. Infrastructure

    D. Core

280. In a Software Defined Network (SDN), as defined in the RFC 7426 specification, a plane is a set of resources related to a particular function. Which of the following is not one of the five planes defined in the SDN architecture?

    A. Forwarding

    B. Operational

    C. Control

    D. Management

    E. Infrastructure

    F. Application

281. Ralph is designing the datacenter for his company's new branch office. He is considering various options, including building a new datacenter at the branch office facility, using a colocated datacenter, and creating a virtual datacenter using a public cloud provider. Which of the following statements about the differences between these options are true? (Choose all that apply.)

   A. A colocated datacenter would be less expensive to implement than a branch office or public cloud datacenter.

   B. In a branch office or colocated datacenter, Ralph's company would own the hardware.

   C. In all three datacenter options, the administrators in Ralph's company would be responsible for setting up and managing the hardware.

   D. In a branch office or colocated datacenter, Ralph's company would be responsible for all utility costs, including heating, cooling, and power.

   E. A public cloud datacenter would have greater physical security than the other two options.

   F. A public cloud datacenter is easier to expand than a colocated or branch office datacenter

282. Which of the following cloud service models enables you to perform a new installation of an operating system of your choice?

   A. IaaS

   B. PaaS

   C. SaaS

   D. DaaS

   E. All of the above

283. When you contract with a provider to obtain email services for your company using their servers in the public cloud, which of the following service models are you using?

   A. IaaS

   B. PaaS

   C. SaaS

   D. DaaS

   E. None of the above

284. Which of the following cloud service models provides the consumer with the most control over the cloud resources?

   A. IaaS

   B. PaaS

   C. SaaS

   D. DaaS

   E. IaaS, PaaS, SaaS, and DaaS all provide the same degree of control.

285. Alice has just created a new Windows Server 2016 virtual machine using remote controls provided by a cloud service provider on the Internet. Which of the following cloud architectures is she using? (Choose all that apply.)

   A. IaaS

   B. PaaS

   C. SaaS

   D. Public cloud

   E. Private cloud

   F. Hybrid cloud

   G. Community cloud

286. In which of the following cloud models can a single organization function as both the provider and the consumer of all cloud services?

   A. Public cloud

   B. Private cloud

   C. Hybrid cloud

   D. Ad hoc cloud

287. Ed is the overnight manager of his company's datacenter, and he is responsible for both private and public resources in the company's hybrid cloud. Due to a new TV commercial shown that night, the company's website experiences a massive upsurge in traffic. The web server farm on the private cloud is being overwhelmed, so Ed configures some virtual machines in the public cloud to take up the slack. Which of the following is a common term for what Ed has done?

   A. Cloud busting

   B. Cloud bursting

   C. Cloud splitting

   D. Cloud migrating

288. Microsoft's Outlook.com email service is an example of which of the following cloud service models?

   A. IaaS

   B. PaaS

   C. SaaS

   D. DaaS

   E. None of the above

289. Which of the following statements about cloud delivery models is true?

   A. A public cloud is inherently insecure because anyone can access it.

   B. A private cloud consists of hardware that is all located in a single datacenter.

    C. A hybrid cloud enables administrators to migrate services between public and private resources.

    D. Public, private, and hybrid clouds all utilize the same hardware resources.

290. Ed has just created a new Windows application for his company, and he wants to deploy it in the public cloud. He is looking for a provider that will furnish his company with a fully installed and configured Windows server on which he can install and run his application. Which of the following service models is he seeking to use?

    A. IaaS

    B. PaaS

    C. SaaS

    D. DaaS

    E. None of the above

291. Which of the following are valid advantages or disadvantages of multitenancy in a public cloud datacenter? (Choose all that apply.)

    A. Multitenancy presents a potential security risk because other tenants are utilizing the same hardware.

    B. Multitenancy reduces the cost of utilities and other overhead.

    C. Multitenancy introduces the possibility of competition for bandwidth with other tenants.

    D. Multitenancy separates tenants by assigning each one its own virtual machine.

292. Which of the following is not one of the advantages of Infrastructure as Code (IaC) deployment for cloud-based virtual machines?

    A. IaC provides rapid deployment of virtual machine configurations.

    B. IaC provides consistency in virtual machine configurations.

    C. IaC provides cost savings by automating the virtual machine configuration process.

    D. IaC provides increased security by encrypting the virtual machine configuration

    E. IaC provides elasticity and scalability by simplifying the virtual machine deployment process.

293. Ralph is designing a hybrid deployment for a corporate client that will require a connection between the client's private network and a public cloud provider. The client is concerned about this connection becoming a speed bottleneck at times of heavy user traffic. Which of the following options can Ralph offer the client that will best address this potential problem?

    A. Use a different ISP for the cloud connection.

    B. Use a VPN for the cloud connection.

    C. Use a cloud direct connection for the hybrid link.

    D. Use a leased line connection to the ISP

Chapter

2

Network Implementations

THE COMPTIA NETWORK+ EXAM N10-008 TOPICS COVERED IN THIS CHAPTER INCLUDE THE FOLLOWING:

✓ **2.1 Compare and contrast various devices, their features, and their appropriate placement on the network.**

- Networking devices
    - Layer 2 switch
    - Layer 3 capable switch
    - Router
    - Hub
    - Access point
    - Bridge
    - Wireless LAN controller
    - Load balancer
    - Proxy server
    - Cable modem
    - DSL modem
    - Repeater
    - Voice gateway
    - Media converter
    - Intrusion prevention system (IPS)/intrusion detection system (IDS) device
    - Firewall
    - VPN headend

- Networked devices
    - Voice over Internet Protocol (VoIP) phone
    - Printer
    - Physical access control devices
    - Cameras
    - Heating, ventilation, and air conditioning (HVAC) sensors
    - Internet of Things (IoT)
        - Refrigerator
        - Smart speakers
        - Smart thermostats
        - Smart doorbells
    - Industrial control systems/supervisory control and data acquisition (SCADA)

✓ **2.2 Compare and contrast routing technologies and bandwidth management concepts.**

- Routing
    - Dynamic routing
        - Protocols [Routing Information Protocol (RIP), Open Shortest Path First (OSPF), Enhanced
        - Interior Gateway Routing Protocol (EIGRP), Border Gateway
        - Protocol (BGP)]
        - Link state vs. distance vector vs. hybrid
        - Static routing
        - Default route
        - Administrative distance
        - Exterior vs. interior
        - Time to live
- Bandwidth management
    - Traffic shaping
    - Quality of service (QoS)

✓ **2.3 Given a scenario, configure and deploy common Ethernet switching features.**

- Data virtual local area network (VLAN)
- Voice VLAN
- Port configurations
    - Port tagging/802.1Q
    - Port aggregation
        - Link Aggregation Control Protocol (LACP)
    - Duplex
    - Speed
    - Flow control
    - Port mirroring
    - Port security
    - Jumbo frames
    - Auto-medium-dependent interface cross-over (MDI-X)
- Media access control (MAC) address tables
- Power over Ethernet (PoE)/Power over Ethernet plus (PoE+)
- Spanning Tree Protocol
- Carrier-sense multiple access with collision detection (CSMA/CD)
- Address Resolution Protocol (ARP)
- Neighbor Discovery Protocol

✓ **2.4 Given a scenario, install and configure the appropriate wireless standards and technologies.**

- 802.11 standards
    - a
    - b
    - g
    - n (WiFi 4)
    - ac (WiFi 5)
    - ax (WiFi 6)

- Frequencies and range
  - 2.4GHz
  - 5GHz
- Channels
  - Regulatory impacts
- Channel bonding
- Service set identifier (SSID)
  - Basic service set
  - Extended service set
  - Independent basic service set (Ad-hoc)
  - Roaming
- Antenna types
  - Omni
  - Directional
- Encryption standards
  - WiFi Protected Access (WPA)/ WPA2 Personal [Advanced Encryption Standard (AES)/Temporal Key Integrity Protocol (TKIP)]
  - WPA/WPA2 Enterprise (AES/TKIP)
- Cellular technologies
  - Code-division multiple access (CDMA)
  - Global System for Mobile Communications (GSM)
  - Long-Term Evolution (LTE)
  - 3G, 4G, 5G
- Multiple input, multiple output (MIMO) and multi-user MIMO (MU-MIMO)

1. Which of the following technologies associated with the Internet of Things (IoT) is often used to identify pets using embedded chips?

   A. Z-wave

   B. Bluetooth

   C. NFC

   D. RFID

2. Which of the following is typically *not* an example of the Internet of Things (IoT)?

   A. A key fob that unlocks your car

   B. A smartphone home automation app

   C. A remotely monitored cardiac pacemaker

   D. A seismic early warning system

3. A Wireless Access Point (WAP) enables computers equipped with wireless network interface adapters to function in which of the following topologies?

   A. Star

   B. Ad hoc

   C. Bus

   D. Infrastructure

4. Ralph has been hired by a company to redesign its Local Area Network (LAN). Right now, it has a single 100 Mbps Ethernet LAN with 40 users and 2 shared servers, all connected through 3 hubs. The users on the network must be able to share files with one another and also access the shared servers. The users are complaining that the network is too slow. Management states that cost is a factor that must be considered. Which of the following upgrade scenarios should Ralph recommend in this situation?

   A. Split the network into smaller segments with dedicated hubs as opposed to shared hubs.

   B. Split the network into two routed LANs with 20 users each.

   C. Replace the hubs with switches to define separate collision domains and filter unnecessary traffic from each segment.

   D. Replace the hubs with a layer 3 switch and define two Virtual LANs (VLANs) with 20 users each.

5. Which of the following devices can split a single network into two collision domains while maintaining a single broadcast domain?

   A. Hub

   B. Bridge

   C. Switch

   D. Router

   E. Repeater

6. Which two of the following functions is the multifunction device on a home or small office network known as a broadband router least likely to provide? (Choose two.)
    A. Wireless Access Point (WAP)
    B. Switch
    C. Proxy server
    D. DHCP server
    E. VPN headend

7. Which of the following devices run exclusively at the physical layer of the Open Systems Interconnection (OSI) model? (Choose all that apply.)
    A. Routers
    B. Hubs
    C. Repeaters
    D. Switches

8. Which of the following is the true definition of the term *modem*?
    A. A device that connects a computer to the Public Switched Telephone Network (PSTN)
    B. A device that connects a Local Area Network (LAN) to the Internet
    C. A device that converts analog signals to digital signals and back again
    D. A device that connects a Local Area Network (LAN) to a Wide Area Network (WAN)

9. Which of the following devices is used to physically connect computers in the same Virtual Local Area Network (VLAN)?
    A. A bridge
    B. A hub
    C. A switch
    D. A router

10. Which of the following best describes the function of a firewall?
    A. A device located between two networks that enables administrators to restrict incoming and outgoing traffic
    B. A device that connects two networks together, forwarding traffic between them as needed
    C. A device that enables Internet network clients with private IP addresses to access the Internet
    D. A device that caches Internet data for subsequent use by internal network clients

11. Which of the following terms is used to describe the method by which a firewall examines the port numbers in transport layer protocol headers?
    A. IP address filtering
    B. Service-dependent filtering
    C. Deep Packet Inspection (DPI)
    D. Next-Generation Firewall (NGFW)

12. Which of the following devices can also be described as a multiport repeater?

  A. Hub

  B. Bridge

  C. Switch

  D. Router

13. Which of the following bridging types has never been used on Ethernet Local Area Networks (LANs)?

  A. Store and forward

  B. Transparent

  C. Source route

  D. Multiport

14. Which of the following physical network devices can conceivably be implemented as software in a computer's operating system? (Choose all that apply.)

  A. Hub

  B. Switch

  C. Router

  D. Firewall

15. Which of the following criteria does a firewall capable of service-dependent filtering use to block traffic?

  A. Hardware addresses

  B. Protocol identifiers

  C. IP addresses

  D. Port numbers

16. Ralph is a freelance network consultant installing a three-node small business network. The computers are all in the same room and use wired Ethernet to connect to the switched ports of a multifunction device. The device also functions as a Network Address Translation (NAT) router for a cable modem connection to the Internet. NAT provides a measure of security, but Ralph wants to be sure that the network is protected from unauthorized Internet traffic and attacks against open ports. Which of the following solutions would enable Ralph to accomplish this goal with the minimum cost to the client?

  A. Install a hardware firewall between the multifunction device and the cable modem.

  B. Install an Intrusion Prevention System (IPS) between the multifunction device and the cable modem.

  C. Install a personal firewall on each of the computers.

  D. Connect an Intrusion Detection System (IDS) to one of the switched ports in the multifunction device.

  E. Use a port scanner to monitor the traffic entering the open ports on the computers.

17. Which of the following statements about hubs and switches are true? (Choose all that apply.)

   A. Hubs operate at the physical layer, whereas switches operate at the network layer.

   B. All of the devices connected to a hub are part of a single collision domain, whereas each device connected to a switch has its own collision domain.

   C. There are switches available with network layer functionality, but there are no hubs with that capability.

   D. Switches create a separate broadcast domain for each connected device, whereas hubs create a single broadcast domain for all of the connected devices.

18. Which of the following problems is the Spanning Tree Protocol (STP) intended to prevent? (Choose all that apply.)

   A. Broadcast storms

   B. Late collisions

   C. Bridging loops

   D. Crosstalk

19. Which of the following devices perform essentially the same function? (Choose two.)

   A. Hubs

   B. Bridges

   C. Switches

   D. Routers

20. Which of the following is not one of the five functional levels associated with a distributed control system such as Supervisory Control and Data Acquisition (SCADA) systems?

   A. Field level

   B. Remote access

   C. Direct control

   D. Plant supervisory

   E. Production control

   F. Production scheduling

21. Which of the following switch types immediately forwards frames after looking at only the destination address?

   A. Cut-through

   B. Source route

   C. Store-and-forward

   D. Destination

22. Which of the following does a switch use to forward incoming packets out through the correct ports?

   A. IP addresses

   B. MAC addresses

   C. DNS names

   D. MTU values

23. Which of the following statements about the Spanning Tree Protocol (STP) is not true?
    A. STP operates at the data link layer of the OSI model.
    B. STP is implemented in switches.
    C. STP prevents traffic from circulating endlessly around a network.
    D. STP compiles a database containing the IP addresses of connected devices.

24. Small Office Home Office (SOHO) networks typically use a multifunction connectivity device that can perform all but which one of the following functions?
    A. DHCP
    B. DNS
    C. Switch
    D. Router
    E. Hub
    F. NAT router
    G. Access Point (AP)

25. Which of the following is the correct term for the process by which the Spanning Tree Protocol (STP) on a switch evaluates the paths through the network and places each port in the forwarding or blocking state?
    A. Assimilation
    B. Convergence
    C. Tree-building
    D. Listening

26. A multilayer switch typically functions at which layers of the OSI reference model? (Choose two.)
    A. Data link
    B. Network
    C. Transport
    D. Application

27. Which of the following is something that only a firewall capable of stateful packet inspection can do?
    A. Filter traffic-based port numbers
    B. Block traffic destined for specific IP addresses
    C. Scan transport layer header fields for evidence of SYN floods
    D. Block all TCP traffic from entering a network

28. In local area networking, which of the following is not a type of bridge?
    A. Store and forward
    B. Routing
    C. Transparent
    D. Multiport

29. Which of the following are methods typically used by Intrusion Detection Systems (IDSs) to analyze incoming network traffic? (Choose all that apply.)

    A. Anomaly-based detection

    B. Behavior-based detection

    C. Signature-based detection

    D. Statistic-based detection

30. Virtual Local Area Networks (VLANs) create the administrative boundaries on a switched network that are otherwise provided by which of the following devices?

    A. Hubs

    B. Routers

    C. Firewalls

    D. Bridges

31. Which of the following devices can you use to connect two multimode fiber-optic Ethernet networks in different buildings 2000 meters apart using a single-mode fiber-optic cable segment running at the same speed, while maintaining a single collision domain?

    A. Bridge

    B. Switch

    C. Router

    D. Media converter

32. Which of the following is another term for a multiport bridge?

    A. Router

    B. Switch

    C. Hub

    D. Gateway

33. Which of the following devices enables two computers to communicate when they are using different protocols at each layer of the Open Systems Interconnection (OSI) reference model?

    A. A router

    B. A switch

    C. A hub

    D. A gateway

34. Review the following figure. How many collision domains and broadcast domains exist in the network diagram?

A. There are three collision domains and three broadcast domains.

B. There is one collision domain and three broadcast domains.

C. There is one broadcast domain and three collision domains.

D. There are no collision domains and only one broadcast domain.

E. There are nine collision domains and three broadcast domains.

35. Which of the following statements about switches and routers are true? (Choose all that apply.)

A. Routers operate at the network layer, whereas switches operate at the data link layer.

B. All of the devices connected to a switch are part of a single broadcast domain, whereas the networks connected to a router form separate broadcast domains.

C. Routers can communicate with each other and share information, but switches cannot.

D. Switches forward packets based on their hardware addresses, whereas routers forward packets based on their IP addresses.

36. Ralph is installing an Ethernet Local Area Network (LAN) for a small business with two offices on opposite sides of a courtyard. Ralph plans to run a multimode fiber-optic cable across the courtyard, but the budget is limited, and he cannot use fiber for the whole network. Therefore, he installs Unshielded Twisted Pair (UTP) cable in the two offices, which have 10 and 12 workstations, respectively. Which of the following devices should Ralph use to join the two UTP installations together into one LAN using the fiber-optic run across the courtyard, while keeping the cost to a minimum?

A. Media converters

B. Hubs

C. Switches

D. Routers

37. Five computers are connected to the same switch, but only four are able to communicate with each other. Assuming that all of the hardware is functioning properly, which of the following could be a reason for the fifth computer's communication problem?

A. The switch has the fifth computer connected to a Virtual Local Area Network (VLAN) that's different from that of the other four.

B. The network is experiencing a switching loop.

C. The fifth computer is experiencing an MTU black hole, whereas the other four computers are not.

D. There is a virtual router between the fifth computer and the other four.

38. Which of the following types of systems are frequently used to collect information from Intrusion Detection Systems (IDSs)?

A. SIEM

B. NGFW

C. RADIUS

D. VoIP

39. Which of the following network devices are "dumb"—that is, purely electrical devices with no electronic intelligence?

A. Hubs

B. Switches

C. Routers

D. Bridges

40. Which of the following explains why splitting a large, switched Ethernet LAN into two LANs by adding a router can help to alleviate traffic congestion and improve performance? (Choose all that apply.)

A. Adding a router reduces the amount of broadcast traffic on each of the two LANs.

B. Adding a router reduces the amount of unicast traffic on each of the two LANs.

C. Adding a router diverts traffic to an alternate path through the network.

D. Adding a router prevents computers on one LAN from communicating with computers on another LAN.

41. A small business office currently has a 100Base-TX Ethernet network with a single 8-port hub. All of the hub ports are populated, and the business owner wants to expand the network further. However, the hub does not have an uplink port. The owner has purchased a new hub, also with eight ports, which does have an uplink port, but he does not know how to connect them together. What must the owner do to install the new hub on the network?

A. Use a standard patch cable to connect a standard port on the existing hub to a standard port on the new hub.

B. Use a standard patch cable to connect a standard port on the existing hub to the uplink port on the new hub.

C. Purchase a crossover cable and use it to connect a standard port on the existing hub to the uplink port on the new hub.

D. Purchase a second new hub with an uplink port to replace the old one and use a standard patch cable to connect the two uplink ports together.

42. Which of the following tasks can you perform to split a large, switched Local Area Network (LAN) into multiple broadcast domains? (Choose all that apply.)

    A. Replace one or more switches with hubs.

    B. Install a firewall to filter broadcast traffic.

    C. Enable the Spanning Tree Protocol (STP) on the switches.

    D. Create Virtual Local Area Networks (VLANs) in the switches.

    E. Install routers on the network.

43. Which of the following statements about bridges and switches is true?

    A. Bridges and switches are network layer devices that use logical addressing to forward frames.

    B. Bridges and switches are data link layer devices that use Media Access Control (MAC) addresses to forward frames.

    C. Bridges and switches build their internal tables based on destination addresses and forward packets based on source addresses.

    D. Bridges and switches must support the network layer protocol implemented on the Local Area Network (LAN).

    E. Each port on a bridge or switch defines a separate broadcast domain.

44. Which of the following is a correct term describing the function of a switch?

    A. Layer 2 router

    B. Ethernet hub

    C. Multiport bridge

    D. Layer 3 repeater

45. Which of the following are available as Internet of Things (IoT) devices?

    A. Refrigerators

    B. Doorbells

    C. Thermostats

    D. Speakers

    E. All of the above

46. Which of the following is the primary reason why replacing hubs with switches on an Ethernet Local Area Network (LAN) improves its performance?

    A. Switches forward packets faster than hubs.

    B. Switches do not forward broadcast transmissions.

    C. Switches reduce the number of collisions on the network.

    D. Switches read the IP addresses of packets, not the hardware addresses.

47. Which of the following is a correct definition of a collision domain?

    A. A group of Local Area Networks (LANs), connected by routers, that enables any node to transmit to any other node

    B. A group of computers connected so that a broadcast transmission by any one device reaches all of the other devices

    C. A group of devices connected by cable segments that are longer than the maximum length stated in the physical layer specification

    D. A group of devices connected so that when two devices transmit at exactly the same time, a data collision occurs

48. Which of the following terms are used to describe the device used to place calls on a Voice over Internet Protocol (VoIP) installation? (Choose all that apply.)

    A. Terminal

    B. Gateway

    C. Endpoint

    D. PBX

49. Which of the following statements about hubs is not true?

    A. Hubs are data link layer devices that connect network devices in a star or ring topology.

    B. Hubs amplify and repeat signals received through one port out all other ports regardless of the destination.

    C. Hubs are physical layer devices that connect network devices in a star topology.

    D. Hubs provide internal crossover circuits and use uplink ports to form a hierarchical star.

50. Which of the following statements about routers are true? (Choose all that apply.)

    A. Routers are network layer devices that use IP addresses to forward frames.

    B. Routers are data link layer devices that use Media Access Control (MAC) addresses to forward frames.

    C. Routers build their internal tables based on destination MAC addresses and forward frames based on source MAC addresses.

    D. Routers must support the network layer protocol implemented on the Local Area Network (LAN).

    E. Each port on a router defines a separate broadcast domain.

51. Which of the following hub types are supported by the 100Base-TX physical layer specification? (Choose all that apply.)

    A. Class I

    B. Class II

    C. Class III

    D. Class IV

52. Which of the following statements about routers is not true?

    A. Routers can connect two or more networks with dissimilar data link layer protocols and media.

    B. Routers can connect two or more networks with the same data link layer protocols and media.

    C. Routers store and maintain route information in a local text file.

    D. Servers with multiple network interfaces can be configured to function as software routers.

    E. Routers can learn and populate their routing tables through static and dynamic routing.

53. The network administrator for a small business is installing a computer to function as a firewall protecting their internetwork from Internet intrusion. At which of the following locations should the administrator install the firewall system?

    A. Anywhere on the private internetwork, as long as the Internet is accessible

    B. Between the Internet access router and the Internet Service Provider's (ISP's) network

    C. At the ISP's network site

    D. Between the Internet access router and the rest of the private internetwork

54. What must you do to configure a firewall to admit File Transfer Protocol (FTP) traffic to the internal network using its default port settings? (Choose all that apply.)

    A. Open port 20

    B. Open port 21

    C. Open port 22

    D. Open port 23

    E. Open port 24

55. Proxy servers operate at which layer of the OSI reference model?

    A. Data link

    B. Network

    C. Transport

    D. Application

56. Which of the following is a feature that is not found in a traditional firewall product, but which might be found in a Next-Generation Firewall (NGFW)?

    A. Stateful packet inspection

    B. Deep Packet Inspection (DPI)

    C. Network Address Translation (NAT)

    D. Virtual Private Network (VPN) support

57. Which of the following statements about content filtering in firewalls is true?

   A. Content filters examine the source IP addresses of packets to locate potential threats.

   B. Content filters enable switches to direct packets out through the correct port.

   C. Content filters examine the data carried within packets for potentially objectionable materials.

   D. Content filters use frequently updated signatures to locate packets containing malware.

58. Which of the following is not one of the criteria typically used by load balancers to direct incoming traffic to one of a group of servers?

   A. Which server has the lightest load

   B. Which server has the fastest response time

   C. Which server is next in an even rotation

   D. Which server has the fastest processor

59. Which of the following devices enables you to use a standard analog telephone to place calls using the Internet instead of the Public Switched Telephone Network (PSTN)?

   A. Proxy server

   B. VPN headend

   C. VoIP gateway

   D. UTM appliance

60. Which of the following devices enable users on private networks to access the Internet by substituting a registered IP address for their private addresses? (Choose all that apply.)

   A. NAT router

   B. RADIUS server

   C. Proxy server

   D. UTM appliance

61. HVAC systems can use the Internet of Things (IoT) to monitor which of the following? (Choose all that apply.)

   A. Temperature

   B. Pressure

   C. Humidity

   D. Printers

   E. Occupancy

   F. Cameras

   G. Door locks

62. A VPN headend is an advanced type of which of the following devices?

   A. Switch

   B. Router

   C. Gateway

   D. Bridge

63. Which of the following technologies is typically associated with virtual PBX services?

    A. Quality of Service (QoS)

    B. Voice over IP

    C. CARP

    D. Round-robin DNS

64. Ralph, the administrator of a 500-node private internetwork, is devising a plan to connect the network to the Internet. The primary objective of the project is to provide all of the network users with access to web and email services while keeping the client computers safe from unauthorized users on the Internet. The secondary objectives of the project are to avoid having to manually configure IP addresses on each one of the client computers individually and to provide a means of monitoring and regulating the users' access to the Internet. Ralph submits a proposal calling for the use of private IP addresses on the client computers and a series of proxy servers with public, registered IP addresses, connected to the Internet using multiple T-1 lines. Which of the following statements about Ralph's proposed Internet access solution is true?

    A. The proposal fails to satisfy both the primary and secondary objectives.

    B. The proposal satisfies the primary objective but neither of the secondary objectives.

    C. The proposal satisfies the primary objective and one of the secondary objectives.

    D. The proposal satisfies the primary objective and both of the secondary objectives.

65. Which of the following protocols can be used by wireless controllers to communicate with the Access Points (APs) on a Wireless Local Area Network (WLAN)? Choose all that apply.

    A. CAPWAP

    B. LWAPP

    C. LDAP

    D. PPTP

66. Which of the following devices enables administrators of enterprise wireless networks to manage multiple Access Points (APs) from a central location?

    A. Hypervisor

    B. Wireless controller

    C. Wireless endpoint

    D. Demarcation point

67. Which of the following devices can administrators use to create multiple Virtual Local Area Networks (VLANs) and forward traffic between them?

    A. Multilayer switch

    B. Virtual router

    C. Load balancer

    D. Broadband router

68. Which of the following is not a mechanism for distributing incoming network traffic among multiple servers?

A. Load balancer

B. Round-robin DNS

C. NLB cluster

D. VPN headend

69. A load balancer is a type of which of the following devices?

A. Switch

B. Router

C. Gateway

D. Firewall

70. Which of the following devices expands on the capabilities of the traditional firewall by adding features like Deep Packet Inspection (DPI) and an Intrusion Prevention System (IPS)?

A. RADIUS server

B. CSU/DSU

C. NGFW

D. Proxy server

71. Which of the following is a device that switches calls between endpoints on the local IP network and provides access to external Internet lines?

A. VoIP PBX

B. VoIP gateway

C. VoIP endpoint

D. Multilayer switch

72. Which of the following statements about Internet access through a proxy server accounts for the security against outside intrusion that a proxy provides?

A. The proxy server uses a public IP address, and the client computers use private addresses.

B. The proxy server uses a private IP address, and the client computers use public addresses.

C. Both the proxy server and the client computers use private IP addresses.

D. Both the proxy server and the client computers use public IP addresses.

73. Which of the following statements about proxy servers and NAT servers are true? (Choose all that apply.)

A. NAT servers and proxy servers can both provide Internet access to clients running any application.

B. NAT servers and proxy servers both use public IP addresses.

C. NAT servers and proxy servers both access Internet servers and relay the responses to network clients.

D. Both NAT servers and proxy servers cache web data for later use.

74. A multilayer switch can operate at which layers of the Open Systems Interconnection (OSI) model? (Choose all that apply.)

 A. Physical

 B. Data link

 C. Network

 D. Transport

 E. Session

 F. Presentation

 G. Application

75. Which of the following devices can an administrator use to monitor a network for abnormal or malicious traffic?

 A. IDS

 B. UPS

 C. RADIUS

 D. DoS

 E. RAS

76. Which of the following is not a function that is typically provided by a unified threat management (UTM) appliance?

 A. Virtual private networking

 B. Network firewall

 C. Packet forwarding

 D. Antivirus protection

77. Which of the following features enables an Intrusion Detection System (IDS) to monitor all of the traffic on a switched network?

 A. Stateful packet inspection

 B. Port mirroring

 C. Trunking

 D. Service-dependent filtering

78. Which of the following network devices does not employ Access Control Lists (ACLs) to restrict access?

 A. Routers

 B. Hubs

 C. Switches

 D. Wireless Access Points (WAPs)

79. Which of the following TCP/IP parameters, configured on an end system, specifies the Internet Protocol (IP) address of a router on the local network that provides access to other networks?

A. WINS Server Addresses

B. Default Gateway

C. DNS Server Addresses

D. Subnet Gateway

80. Which of the following routing protocols uses the packet format shown in the figure?

```
1 2 3 4 5 6 7 8 1 2 3 4 5 6 7 8 1 2 3 4 5 6 7 8 1 2 3 4 5 6 7 8
```

Command	Version	Unused
Address Family Identifier		Unused
IP Address		
Unused		
Unused		
Metric		

A. RIPv1

B. RIPv2

C. OSPF

D. EIGRP

E. BGP

81. Which of the following statements about the Enhanced Interior Gateway Routing Protocol (EIGRP) is not true?

A. EIGRP does not support classless IPv4 addresses.

B. EIGRP is a hybrid routing protocol.

C. EIGRP can only transmit incremental routing table updates.

D. EIGRP shares routes within an autonomous system.

82. Which of the following are techniques used in traffic shaping to prevent networks from being overwhelmed by data transmissions? (Choose all that apply.)

A. Bandwidth throttling

B. Rate limiting

C. Broadcast storming

D. Network Address Translation (NAT)

83. Which of the following terms refers to methods by which network traffic is prioritized to prevent applications from suffering faults due to network congestion?

    A. Port forwarding

    B. Dynamic routing

    C. VLANs

    D. QoS

84. Which of the following statements about Routing Information Protocol version 1 (RIPv1) is true? (Choose all that apply.)

    A. RIPv1 broadcasts the entire contents of the routing table every 30 seconds.

    B. RIPv1 advertises the subnet mask along with the destination network.

    C. RIPv1 broadcasts only the elements in the routing table that have changed every 60 seconds.

    D. RIPv1 does not include the subnet mask in its network advertisements.

85. Which of the following mechanisms for prioritizing network traffic uses a 6-bit classification identifier in the Internet Protocol (IP) header?

    A. Diffserv

    B. CoS

    C. Traffic shaping

    D. QoS

    E. Administrative distance

86. Which of the following statements about static routing are true? (Choose all that apply.)

    A. Static routes are manually configured routes that administrators must add, modify, or delete when a change in the network occurs.

    B. Static routes are automatically added to the routing table by routing protocols when a new network path becomes available.

    C. Static routes adapt to changes in the network infrastructure automatically.

    D. Static routes are a recommended solution for large internetworks with redundant paths to each destination network.

    E. Static routes are a recommended solution for small internetworks with a single path to each destination network.

87. Which of the following TCP/IP routing protocols does not include the subnet mask within its route update messages, preventing it from supporting subnetting?

    A. Routing Information Protocol, version 1 (RIPv1)

    B. Routing Information Protocol, version 2 (RIPv2)

    C. Border Gateway Protocol (BGP)

    D. Open Shortest Path First (OSPF)

88. Which of the following terms refers to a routing protocol that does *not* rely on hop counts to measure the efficiency of routes?

   A. Interior gateway protocol

   B. Edge gateway protocol

   C. Distance vector protocol

   D. Link state protocol

89. What is the maximum number of routes that can be included in a single RIP broadcast packet?

   A. 20

   B. 25

   C. 32

   D. Unlimited

90. Which of the following routing protocols can you use on a TCP/IP internetwork with segments running at different speeds, making hop counts an inaccurate measure of route efficiency? (Choose all that apply.)

   A. Enhanced Interior Gateway Routing Protocol (EIGRP)

   B. Routing Information Protocol (RIP)

   C. Open Shortest Path First (OSPF)

   D. Border Gateway Protocol (BGP)

91. Which of the following statements about the Open Shortest Path First (OSPF) routing protocol are true? (Choose all that apply.)

   A. OSPF is an interior gateway protocol.

   B. OSPF is a link state routing protocol.

   C. OSPF does not support Classless Inter-Domain Routing (CIDR).

   D. OSPF shares routes within an autonomous system.

92. What is the term for the process by which dynamic routing protocols update other routers with routing table information?

   A. Convergence

   B. Distance vectoring

   C. Redistribution

   D. Dissemination

93. Which of the following TCP/IP routing protocols measures the efficiency of routes by the number of hops between the source and the destination?

   A. Routing Internet Protocol (RIP)

   B. Open Shortest Path First (OSPF)

   C. Border Gateway Protocol (BGP)

   D. Intermediate System to Intermediate System (IS-IS)

94. Which of the following types of routing protocols route datagrams between autonomous systems?

  A. EGP

  B. RIP

  C. IGP

  D. OSPF

95. Which of the following prevents packets on a TCP/IP internetwork from being transmitted endlessly from router to router?

  A. Open Shortest Path First (OSPF)

  B. Maximum Transmission Unit (MTU)

  C. Administrative distance

  D. Time to Live (TTL)

96. Which of the following command-line tools can you use to create and modify static routes on a Unix or Linux system? (Choose all that apply.)

  A. `route`

  B. `ifconfig`

  C. `traceroute`

  D. `ip`

97. Routers that use the Open Shortest Path First (OSPF) routing protocol calculate the relative costs of routes through the network by exchanging which of the following specifications for each interface with other routers?

  A. Transmission speed

  B. Data link layer protocol

  C. Network medium

  D. IP address

98. Which of the following statements about the Border Gateway Protocol (BGP) is not true?

  A. BGP is an exterior gateway protocol.

  B. BGP is a link state routing protocol.

  C. BGP supports Classless Inter-Domain Routing (CIDR).

  D. BGP shares routes among autonomous systems.

99. In an IPv4 routing table, what is the network destination address for the host system's default route?

  A. 0.0.0.0

  B. 127.0.0.0

  C. 127.255.255.255

  D. 255.255.255.255

100. Which of the following routing protocols uses the packet format shown in the figure?

```
1 2 3 4 5 6 7 8 1 2 3 4 5 6 7 8 1 2 3 4 5 6 7 8 1 2 3 4 5 6 7 8
```

Address Family Identifier	Route Tag
IP Address	
Subnet Mask	
Next Hop	
Metric	

A. RIPv1

B. RIPv2

C. OSPF

D. EIGRP

E. BGP

101. Which of the following routing protocols has both interior and exterior designations, based on whether it is used for routing within an autonomous system or on the Internet?

A. RIP

B. OSPF

C. EIGRP

D. BGP

102. Which of the following network layer protocols includes a Time to Live (TTL) field? (Choose all that apply.)

A. IPv4

B. IPv6

C. ICMP

D. IGMP

103. Which of the following is not a method of traffic shaping?

A. Rate limiting

B. WAN optimization

C. Bandwidth throttling

D. Self-limiting

104. An enterprise network has been designed with individual departmental switches because, in most cases, the devices in a specific department exchange network traffic with other devices in the same department. Each of the departmental switches is also connected to a host switch, which enables devices to communicate with other departments. Which of the following terms describes this switching architecture?

    A. Distributed switching

    B. Port forwarding

    C. Traffic shaping

    D. Neighbor discovery

    E. Flow control

105. Review the following figure. Note that each store-and-forward switch has three connected node ports and one port for switch-to-switch connections. All node ports and links are configured for half-duplex communication. The switch-to-switch links are configured for full-duplex communication. Which of the following statements about the switched network is true?

    A. There are nine collision domains, one for each half-duplex connection.

    B. There are 12 collision domains, one for each switch connection.

    C. There are three collision domains, one for each switch-to-switch connection.

    D. There is one collision domain for this network.

106. Which of the following could be a valid MAC address for a network interface adapter?

A. 10.124.25.43

B. FF:FF:FF:FF:FF:FF

C. 00:1A:6B:31:9A:4E

D. 03:AE:16:3H:5B:11

E. fe80::89a5:9e4d:a9d0:9ed7

107. Which of the following protocols prevents network switching loops from occurring by shutting down redundant links until they are needed?

A. RIP

B. STP

C. VLAN

D. NAT

E. ARP

108. Which of the following cable types can be used to connect an MDI port on a workstation to an Auto-MDI-X port on an Ethernet switch? (Choose all that apply.)

A. A crossover twisted pair cable

B. A straight-through twisted pair cable

C. A coaxial cable

D. A single-mode fiber optic cable

E. A multimode fiber optic cable

109. Which of the following is a network layer protocol that uses ICMPv6 messages to locate routers, DNS servers, and other nodes on an IPv6 network?

A. BGP

B. NDP

C. OSPF

D. PoE

110. Which of the following is a protocol that identifies VLANs by inserting a 32-bit field in the Ethernet frame?

A. IEEE 802.1P

B. IEEE 802.1Q

C. IEEE 802.1X

D. IEEE 802.1AB

E. IEEE 802.1AX

111. Each of the following Carrier-Sense Multiple Access with Collision Detection (CSMA/CD) events occurs on an Ethernet network when two stations transmit simultaneously, although not in the order listed. Which of the following events occurs immediately after the collision?

   A. The two stations observe a random backoff interval.
   B. The two stations transmit a jam signal.
   C. The two stations stop transmitting.
   D. The two stations listen to see if the channel is idle.
   E. The two stations begin retransmitting their frames.

112. For the Carrier-Sense Multiple Access with Collision Detection (CSMA/CD) mechanism to function properly on an Ethernet network, host systems must be able to detect when a collision occurs, so they can react to it. Which of the following cabling errors can prevent the collision detection process from functioning properly?

   A. Excessively long cable segments
   B. Incorrect wiring pinouts
   C. Too many systems on a single network
   D. An excessive number of collisions

113. When a packet collision between two systems occurs on an Ethernet network, Carrier-Sense Multiple Access with Collision Detection (CSMA/CD) causes the two systems to stop transmitting and generate a jam signal. After sending the jam signal, why do the two systems wait for a randomized backoff interval before retransmitting their packets?

   A. They need time to reassemble the packets.
   B. To prevent another collision from occurring.
   C. They need to rebuffer the packet.
   D. To recalculate the packets' checksum values.

114. Which of the following devices is used to physically connect computers in the same VLAN?

   A. A bridge
   B. A hub
   C. A switch
   D. A router

115. Which of the following statements is true about an Ethernet network that uses CSMA/CD?

   A. Collisions are a normal occurrence.
   B. Collisions never occur unless there is a network fault.
   C. Collisions cause data to be irretrievably lost.
   D. Collisions are the result of duplicate IP addresses.

116. Which of the following is an abnormal occurrence on an Ethernet network?

   A. Packet retransmissions

   B. Collision detection

   C. Jam signals

   D. Late collisions

117. VLANs create the administrative boundaries on a switched network that are otherwise provided by which of the following devices?

   A. Hubs

   B. Routers

   C. Domains

   D. Bridges

118. Which of the following statements about VLANs are true? (Choose all that apply.)

   A. All of the devices in a particular VLAN must be physically connected to the same switch.

   B. A VLAN creates a limited broadcast domain on a switched network.

   C. You must have VLANs on a switched network for communication between computers on different cable segments to occur.

   D. A router is required for communication between VLANs.

119. Which of the following elements can be used to identify the devices in a particular VLAN? (Choose all that apply.)

   A. Hardware addresses

   B. IP addresses

   C. DNS names

   D. Switch port numbers

120. Alice has a network that consists of three Virtual LANs (VLANs) defined on all of the network's switches. VLAN 10 is the Sales VLAN, VLAN 20 is the Marketing VLAN, and VLAN 30 is the Accounting VLAN. Users are reporting that they cannot communicate with anyone outside of their own VLANs. What is the problem, and what must Alice do?

   A. The problem is a faulty VLAN configuration on one of the switches. Alice needs to re-create the VLANs and configure each VLAN for routing.

   B. One of the VLANs is configured to filter all other VLAN traffic for security purposes. Alice needs to change the filter on this VLAN.

   C. VLANs are limited to data link layer communication only. To allow communication between VLANs, Alice must add a router or a layer 3 switch to the network and configure it to route traffic between the VLANs.

   D. The VLANs are using different data link layer protocols. VLANs must use the same data link layer protocol in order to communicate.

121. The jumbo frame capability is associated with which layer of the Open Systems Interconnection (OSI) model?

  A. Application

  B. Transport

  C. Network

  D. Data link

122. Which of the following technologies would you be less likely to find on the average home or small office network? (Choose all that apply.)

  A. NAT

  B. DHCP

  C. 10GBase-T

  D. VLAN

123. Which of the following modifications occur when you configure the native Virtual Local Area Network (VLAN) on your network switches to use 802.1q tagging? (Choose all that apply.)

  A. Double-tagged packets are prevented.

  B. BPDU guards are applied.

  C. Root guards are applied.

  D. Trunk traffic is routed, not switched.

124. Which of the following protocols is responsible for inserting the tags into frames that enable switches to forward them to the appropriate Virtual Local Area Network (VLAN)?

  A. IEEE 802.3x

  B. IEEE 802.1X

  C. IEEE 802.1q

  D. IEEE 802.11ac

125. Which of the following best explains how tagging the native Virtual Local Area Network (VLAN) traffic can improve in-band switch management security?

  A. By renaming the default VLAN

  B. By preventing double-tagged packets

  C. By encrypting in-band management traffic

  D. By moving in-band management traffic off the native VLAN

126. A switch with auto-medium-dependent interface crossover (MDI-X) ports eliminates the need for which of the following?

  A. 8P8C connectors

  B. Switch-to-switch connections

  C. Straight-through cables

  D. Crossover cables

127. Which of the following cable types is needed to connect an MDI port on a workstation to an MDI-X port on an Ethernet switch?

   A. A crossover twisted pair cable

   B. A straight-through twisted pair cable

   C. A coaxial cable

   D. A single-mode fiber optic cable

   E. A multimode fiber optic cable

128. Port security on an Ethernet switch is implemented through the use of which of the following methods?

   A. Blacklisted MAC addresses

   B. Whitelisted MAC addresses

   C. Port-by-port MAC address filtering

   D. Spoofed MAC addresses

129. Which of the following best explains why networks using Voice over IP (VoIP) often have separate voice and data Virtual Local Area Networks (VLANs)?

   A. To prevent voice and data packet conflicts

   B. To encrypt voice traffic

   C. To encrypt data traffic

   D. To prioritize voice traffic

130. Which of the following protocols uses a form of flow control called the sliding window technique?

   A. UDP

   B. HTTP

   C. TCP

   D. DNS

131. Which of the following Power over Ethernet (PoE) specifications supplies power to devices using the spare wire pair on a 10Base-T or 100Base-TX twisted pair network?

   A. Alternative A

   B. Alternative B

   C. 4PPoE

   D. All of the above

132. Which of the following best describes the process of whitelisting on a wireless network?

   A. Using an Access Control List (ACL) to specify the IP addresses that are permitted to access a wireless network

   B. Using port protection to specify the well-known port numbers of applications that users are permitted to run over a wireless network

   C. Using MAC filtering to create a list of devices that are permitted to access a wireless network

   D. Using an AAA server to create a list of users that are permitted to access a wireless network

133. Which of the following features helps to protect network switches from attacks related to the Spanning Tree Protocol (STP)? (Choose all that apply.)

   A. BPDU guard

   B. Root guard

   C. DHCP snooping

   D. Geofencing

134. Which of the following IEEE standards calls for the use of the Carrier-Sense Multiple Access with Collision Avoidance (CSMA/CA) Media Access Control (MAC) mechanism?

   A. 802.11ac

   B. 802.1X

   C. 802.3

   D. All of the above

135. Which of the following topologies enables wireless devices to access resources on a wired network?

   A. Ad hoc

   B. Star

   C. Infrastructure

   D. Bus

136. Which of the following components are required for two computers to communicate using an IEEE 802.11 wireless LAN in an ad hoc topology?

   A. A router connected to the Internet

   B. A Wireless Access Point (WAP)

   C. An external antenna

   D. None of the above

137. Which of the following wireless networking technologies will never experience interference from a 2.4 GHz wireless telephone? (Choose all that apply.)

   A. IEEE 802.11a

   B. IEEE 802.11b

   C. IEEE 802.11g

   D. IEEE 802.11n

   E.   IEEE 802.11ac

   F.   IEEE 802.11ax

138.   Which of the following wireless networking standards is capable of supporting speeds of 54 Mbps and is also backward compatible with IEEE 802.11b?

   A.   IEEE 802.11a

   B.   IEEE 802.11g

   C.   IEEE 802.11n

   D.   Bluetooth

   E.   IEEE 802.11

139.   Which of the following wireless LAN standards include the ability to use Multiple Input, Multiple Output (MIMO) antennae? (Choose all that apply.)

   A.   IEEE 802.11a

   B.   IEEE 802.11b/g

   C.   IEEE 802.11n

   D.   IEEE 802.11ac

   E.   IEEE 802.11ax

140.   Which of the following is a cellular communication technology that is virtually obsolete in the United States?

   A.   GSM

   B.   CDMA

   C.   TDMA

   D.   LTE

141.   Which of the following IEEE wireless LAN standards uses the Direct Sequence Spread Spectrum (DSSS) signal modulation technique?

   A.   802.11a

   B.   802.11b

   C.   802.11g

   D.   802.11n

   E.   802.11ac

142.   When designing a wireless LAN installation, which of the following are valid reasons to install a unidirectional antenna in an Access Point (AP), rather than an omnidirectional one? (Choose all that apply.)

   A.   The AP will be located against an outside wall.

   B.   There are many interior walls between the AP and the most distant workstation.

C. A unidirectional antenna can be focused to a specific signal pattern width.

D. All of the above

143. How do wireless networking devices conforming to the IEEE 802.11n and 802.11ac standards achieve transmission speeds greater than 72.2 Mbps?

A. By using direct sequence spread spectrum (DSSS) modulation

B. By using multiple antennae to transmit several data streams simultaneously

C. By using frequencies in the 5 GHz band

D. By sacrificing transmission range for speed

144. Which of the following are possible reasons why the 5 GHz frequency tends to perform better than the 2.4 GHz frequency on a wireless LAN? (Choose all that apply.)

A. The 5 GHz frequency has more channels than the 2.4 GHz frequency.

B. The 5 GHz frequency supports longer ranges than the 2.4 GHz frequency.

C. The 5 GHz frequency conflicts with fewer common household devices than the 2.4 GHz frequency.

D. The 5 GHz frequency transmits at faster speeds than the 2.4 GHz frequency.

145. Alice is attempting to deploy an IEEE 802.11b/g wireless LAN on the fifth floor of a 10-story office building that is surrounded on all sides by other office buildings, all of which seem to be running many wireless LANs. Scanning the 2.4 GHz band, she sees literally dozens of networks, spread across all of the available channels. As a result, her wireless devices have trouble connecting to their Access Point (AP), and when they do, they achieve only low speeds. Which of the following tasks should Alice perform to enable the wireless clients to connect to the network more reliably? (Choose two.)

A. Upgrade all of the wireless network devices to IEEE 802.11n.

B. Configure all of the network devices to use WPA2 encryption with AES.

C. Configure the wireless devices to use the 5 GHz band.

D. Configure the AP to suppress SSID broadcasts.

E. Upgrade all of the network devices to the latest firmware.

146. Which of the following is the fastest speed achievable by a wireless LAN using the currently ratified IEEE 802.11 standards?

A. 54 Mbps

B. 600 Mbps

C. 1.3 Gbps

D. 2.6 Gbps

147. What is the term for the technology implemented in the IEEE 802.11ac standard that enables a wireless device to transmit multiple frames to multiple clients simultaneously?

    A. MIMO

    B. Channel bonding

    C. CSMA/CA

    D. MU-MIMO

148. On an IEEE 802.11b/g/n wireless network running at 2.4 GHz with multiple Access Points (APs), the traditional best practice is to use channels 1, 6, and 11, with no two adjacent APs configured to use the same channel. Which of the following is the real reason why this is a good plan?

    A. Channels 1, 6, and 11 are the only channels with frequencies that do not overlap.

    B. Channels 1, 6, and 11 have more bandwidth than the other channels.

    C. Channels 1, 6, and 11 have greater ranges than the other channels.

    D. Channels 1, 6, and 11 are the default settings on most wireless devices.

149. Ralph is planning a wireless LAN installation for a warehouse with two offices at either end of the building, approximately 300 feet apart. If he installs a single Access Point (AP) in the center of the warehouse, equidistant from the two offices, which of the following standards should he look for when purchasing hardware so that workstations in both offices will be able to connect to the network at the best possible speed?

    A. IEEE 802.11a

    B. IEEE 802.11g

    C. IEEE 802.11n

    D. IEEE 802.11ac

150. Which of the following terms defines a wireless LAN transmission technique in which devices use multiple antennae to increase transmission speeds?

    A. MIMO

    B. TDMA

    C. PAN

    D. Ant+

151. What is the maximum channel width possible using wireless networking equipment based on the ratified IEEE 802.11 regulatory standards?

    A. 20 MHz

    B. 40 MHz

    C. 80 MHz

    D. 160 MHz

152. Which of the following wireless networking standards are capable of using only the 5 GHz frequency? (Choose all that apply.)

   A. IEEE 802.11a

   B. IEEE 802.11b

   C. IEEE 802.11g

   D. IEEE 802.11n

   E. IEEE 802.11ac

153. Which of the following IEEE wireless LAN standards provides the greatest possible throughput?

   A. 802.11a

   B. 802.11ac

   C. 802.11b

   D. 802.11g

   E. 802.11n

154. Which of the following IEEE 802.11 wireless LAN standards are capable of supporting both the 2.4 GHz and 5 GHz frequencies?

   A. 802.11a

   B. 802.11b

   C. 802.11g

   D. 802.11n

   E. 802.11ac

155. What is the maximum number of transmit and receive antennae supported by the currently ratified IEEE 802.11 wireless LAN standards?

   A. 2

   B. 4

   C. 8

   D. 16

156. Which of the following is the term for the network name that you use to connect a client device to an Access Point (AP) on a wireless LAN?

   A. BSS

   B. ESS

   C. SSID

   D. BSSID

157. Which of the following IEEE wireless LAN standards define devices with a maximum aggregate channel width of 20 MHz? (Choose all that apply.)

  A. 802.11a

  B. 802.11g

  C. 802.11n

  D. 802.11ac

158. At which layer of the Open Systems Interconnection (OSI) model do wireless range extenders operate?

  A. Physical

  B. Data link

  C. Network

  D. Transport

  E. Session

  F. Presentation

  G. Application

159. Which of the following wireless security protocols provides the greatest degree of network device hardening?

  A. WEP

  B. WPA

  C. WPA2

  D. EAP

160. Which of the following encryption protocols was introduced in the WiFi Protected Access (WPA) wireless security standard?

  A. CCMP-AES

  B. TKIP-RC4

  C. EAP-TLS

  D. TACACS+

161. TKIP-RC4 is an encryption protocol used with which of the following wireless network security standards?

  A. WEP

  B. WPA

  C. WPA2

  D. EAP

162. Which of the following protocols provides wireless networks with the strongest encryption?

    A. AES

    B. TKIP

    C. EAP

    D. 802.1X

163. When the WiFi Protected Access (WPA) wireless security protocol was released to replace Wired Equivalent Privacy (WEP), it included the Temporal Key Integrity Protocol (TKIP) for encryption. Which of the following is not one of the improvements that WPA and TKIP provide over WEP?

    A. TKIP enlarges the WEP encryption key.

    B. TKIP modifies the encryption key for every packet.

    C. WPA does not require a hardware upgrade for WEP devices.

    D. TKIP eliminates the use of Pre-Shared Keys (PSKs).

164. To connect a wireless client to a Wireless Access Point (WAP) using the WiFi Protected Access II (WPA2) security protocol with a Pre-Shared Key (PSK), which of the following must you supply on both devices?

    A. Base key

    B. Passphrase

    C. Serial number

    D. MAC address

165. Upgrading a wireless network from the Wired Equivalent Privacy (WEP) security protocol to WiFi Protected Access (WPA) enables it to use the Temporal Key Integrity Protocol (TKIP) for encryption, which generates a unique key for each packet. Which of the following types of attacks does this capability prevent?

    A. Denial-of-Service (DoS) attacks

    B. Brute-force attacks

    C. Replay attacks

    D. Deauthentication attacks

166. Which of the following wireless security protocols uses CCMP-AES for encryption?

    A. WEP

    B. WPA

    C. WPA2

    D. TKIP

167. Which of the following was the first wireless LAN security protocol to come into common usage?

A. WEP

B. WPA

C. WPA2

D. TKIP

168. Which of the following did the second version of the WiFi Protected Access (WPA) protocol add to the standard?

A. CCMP-AES

B. MIMO

C. WEP

D. TKIP

169. You are setting up a wireless LAN in a friend's home, using devices that conform to the IEEE 802.11g standard. You have installed and successfully tested the devices on an open network, and now you are ready to add security. Which of the following protocols should you choose to provide maximum security for the wireless network?

A. WEP

B. WPA2

C. IPsec

D. TLS

E. L2TP

170. CCMP-AES is an encryption protocol used with which of the following wireless network security standards?

A. WEP

B. WPA

C. WPA2

D. EAP

171. Which of the following encryption protocols was introduced in the WiFi Protected Access II (WPA2) wireless security standard?

A. CCMP-AES

B. TKIP-RC4

C. EAP-TLS

D. TACACS+

172. Which of the following wireless security protocols can enable network users to authenticate using smartcards?

   A. WEP

   B. WPA2

   C. EAP

   D. AES

173. Which of the following forms of the WiFi Protected Access (WPA) and WPA2 protocols require a RADIUS server? (Choose all that apply.)

   A. WPA-Personal

   B. WPA-PSK

   C. WPA-Enterprise

   D. WPA-802.1X

174. Which of the following forms of the WiFi Protected Access (WPA) and WPA2 protocols call for the use of a Pre-Shared Key (PSK)?

   A. WPA-Personal

   B. WPA-Enterprise

   C. WPA-EAP

   D. WPA-802.1X

175. Which of the following stream ciphers does the Temporal Key Integrity Protocol (TKIP) use for encryption on a wireless network?

   A. RC4

   B. AES

   C. CCMP

   D. SHA

176. Which of the following wireless security protocols uses CCMP for encryption?

   A. WEP

   B. WPA

   C. WPA2

   D. 802.1X

177. CCMP is based on which of the following encryption standards?

   A. TKIP

   B. RC4

   C. AES

   D. 802.1X

178. You have installed a new Wireless Access Point (WAP) on your network and configured it to use an SSID that is not broadcasted and WPA2 for security. Which of the following describes what you must do to configure your wireless clients?

    A. Select the SSID from a list and allow the client to automatically detect the security protocol.

    B. Select the SSID from a list and then select WPA2 from the security protocol options provided.

    C. Type the SSID manually and allow the client to automatically detect the security protocol.

    D. Type the SSID manually and then select WPA2 from the security protocol options provided.

179. Which of the following wireless LAN security protocols was rendered obsolete after it was found to be extremely easy to penetrate?

    A. WEP

    B. WPA

    C. WPA2

    D. EAP

180. Which of the following protocols does the WiFi Protected Access (WPA) security protocol use for encryption?

    A. AES

    B. TKIP

    C. MD5

    D. SHA

181. Which of the following wireless network security protocols provides open and shared key authentication options?

    A. WPA

    B. WEP

    C. WPA2

    D. EAP

182. Which of the following wireless security protocols uses TKIP for encryption?

    A. WEP

    B. WPA

    C. WPA2

    D. AES

183. Which of the following is not a factor that weakens the security of the Wired Equivalent Privacy (WEP) protocol used on early IEEE 802.11 wireless LANs?

    A. 40-bit encryption keys

    B. 24-bit initialization vectors

    C. Static shared secrets

    D. Open System Authentication

184. Which of the following encryption ciphers was replaced by CCMP-AES when the WPA2 wireless security protocol was introduced?

    A. EAP

    B. WEP

    C. TKIP

    D. CCMP

185. Which of the following wireless security protocols was substantially weakened by its initialization vector?

    A. WPA

    B. WEP

    C. WPA2

    D. PEAP

186. Ralph is installing a wireless LAN that includes three Access Points (APs) to provide coverage for a large building. Which of the following must Ralph do to ensure that users are able to roam without interruption from one AP to another using their portable devices? (Choose all that apply.)

    A. Configure each AP with the same IP address.

    B. Configure each AP with the same security passphrase.

    C. Configure each AP to use the same security protocol.

    D. Configure each AP with the same SSID.

187. Which of the following is the maximum theoretical download speed for a 5G cellular network?

    A. 42 megabits per second

    B. 150 megabits per second

    C. 1 gigabit per second

    D. 10 gigabits per second

    E. 100 gigabits per second

188. Which of the following statements about 5G cellular networks are true? (Choose all that apply.)

    A. 5G networks can operate on three frequency bands.

    B. 5G networks with the highest speeds also have a more limited range.

    C. 4G devices can connect to 5G networks at reduced speeds.

    D. On a 5G network, the lower frequency bands provide the highest speeds.

189. Which of the following IEEE standards describes an implementation of port-based access control for wireless networks?

    A. 802.11ac

    B. 802.11n

    C. 802.1X

    D. 802.3x

190. Unauthorized users are connecting to your Wireless Access Point (WAP) and gaining access to the network. Which of the following are steps you can take to prevent this from happening? (Choose all that apply.)

    A. Disable SSID broadcasting.

    B. Use Kerberos for authentication.

    C. Place the Access Point (AP) in a DMZ.

    D. Implement MAC address filtering.

191. On a Wireless Access Point (WAP) that uses an Access Control List (ACL) to specify which devices are permitted to connect to the network, which of the following is used to identify the authorized devices?

    A. Usernames

    B. IP addresses

    C. Device names

    D. MAC addresses

192. On a network carrying both voice and data traffic, separate Virtual Local Area Networks (VLANs) enable the voice traffic to be assigned a higher priority than the data traffic. Which of the following are methods for identifying the packets carrying voice traffic, so the switches can assign them to the voice VLAN? (Choose all that apply.)

    A. MAC addresses

    B. VLAN tags

    C. IP addresses

    D. DNS names

Network Operations

THE COMPTIA NETWORK+ EXAM N10-008 TOPICS COVERED IN THIS CHAPTER INCLUDE THE FOLLOWING:

✓ **3.1 Given a scenario, use the appropriate statistics and sensors to ensure network availability.**

- Performance metrics/sensors
    - Device/chassis
        - Temperature
        - Central processing unit (CPU) usage
        - Memory
    - Network metrics
        - Bandwidth
        - Latency
        - Jitter
- SNMP
    - Traps
    - Object identifiers (OIDs)
    - Management information bases (MIBs)
- Network device logs
    - Log reviews
        - Traffic logs
        - Audit logs
        - Syslog
    - Logging levels/severity levels
- Interface statistics/status
    - Link state (up/down)
    - Speed/duplex

- Send/receive traffic
- Cyclic redundancy checks (CRCs)
- Protocol packet and byte counts
- Interface errors or alerts
  - CRC errors
  - Giants
  - Runts
  - Encapsulation errors
- Environmental factors and sensors
  - Temperature
  - Humidity
  - Electrical
  - Flooding
- Baselines
- NetFlow data
- Uptime/downtime

✓ 3.2 Explain the purpose of organizational documents and policies.

- Plans and procedures
  - Change management
  - Incident response plan
  - Disaster recovery plan
  - Business continuity plan
  - System life cycle
  - Standard operating procedures
- Hardening and security policies
  - Password policy
  - Acceptable use policy
  - Bring your own device (BYOD) policy

- Remote access policy
- Onboarding and offboarding policy
- Security policy
- Data loss prevention
- Common documentation
  - Physical network diagram
    - Floor plan
    - Rack diagram
    - Intermediate distribution frame (IDF)/main distribution frame (MDF) documentation
  - Logical network diagram
  - Wiring diagram
  - Site survey report
  - Audit and assessment report
  - Baseline configurations
- Common agreements
  - Non-disclosure agreement (NDA)
  - Service-level agreement (SLA)
  - Memorandum of understanding (MOU)

✓ **3.3 Explain high availability and disaster recovery concepts and summarize which is the best solution.**

- Load balancing
- Multipathing
- Network interface card (NIC) teaming
- Redundant hardware/clusters
  - Switches
  - Routers
  - Firewalls
- Facilities and infrastructure support
  - Uninterruptible power supply (UPS)
  - Power distribution units (PDUs)

- Generator
- HVAC
- Fire suppression
- Redundancy and high availability (HA) concepts
  - Cold site
  - Warm site
  - Hot site
  - Cloud site
  - Active-active vs. active-passive
    - Multiple Internet service providers (ISPs)/ diverse paths
    - Virtual Router Redundancy Protocol (VRRP)/ First Hop Redundancy Protocol (FHRP)
  - Mean time to repair (MTTR)
  - Mean time between failure (MTBF)
  - Recovery time objective (RTO)
  - Recovery point objective (RPO)
- Network device backup/restore
  - State
  - Configuration

1. After starting work as the network administrator of Wingtip Toys, you discover that all of the switches in the company's datacenter have support for remote management, with built-in Simple Network Management Protocol (SNMP) agents in each port. Which of the following tasks must you perform to be able to gather information from the agents on those switches and display it on a central console? (Choose all that apply.)

   A. Install the network management software on a network computer.

   B. Install a Management Information Base (MIB) on each of the switches.

   C. Install an agent on the console computer.

   D. Install an MIB on the console computer.

   E. Purchase a network management product.

2. Which versions of the Simple Network Management Protocol (SNMP) do not include any security protection other than a cleartext community string? (Choose all that apply.)

   A. SNMPv1

   B. SNMPv2

   C. SNMPv2c

   D. SNMPv3

3. Which of the following statements about the Simple Network Management Protocol (SNMP) are not true? (Choose all that apply.)

   A. To effectively monitor a network using SNMP, you must be sure that all of the equipment you purchase when designing and building your network supports the protocol.

   B. SNMP is not only the name of a protocol, it is also the name of a network management product.

   C. SNMPv1 and SNMPv2 rely on a community string as their only means of security.

   D. Most of the network management products on the market today support SNMPv3.

4. What Windows utility is shown in the accompanying figure?

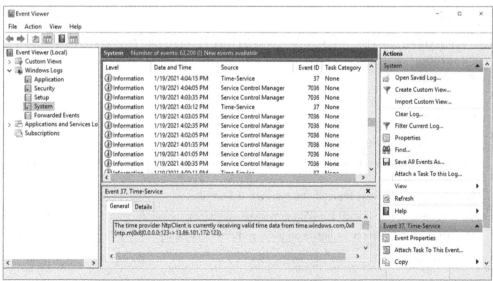

   A.   Network Monitor

   B.   System Monitor

   C.   Event Viewer

   D.   Log Viewer

5.   Which of the following was created to provide logging services for the Unix send-mail program?

   A.   Syslog

   B.   Netstat

   C.   SNMP

   D.   CARP

6.   You are the network administrator of your company's network. Your company wants to perform a baseline analysis of network-related traffic and statistics. They want to track broadcasts, Cyclical Redundancy Check (CRC) errors, and collisions for all traffic traversing a switched network. In addition, they want to provide historical and daily reports for management. They also want to keep track of software distribution and metering. What type of network software product best meets these needs?

   A.   SNMP management

   B.   Protocol analyzer

   C.   Performance Monitor

   D.   Network traffic monitor

7.   Which of the following technologies provides both real-time monitoring of security events and automated analysis of the event information gathered?

   A.   SIEM

   B.   SNMP

   C.   SEM

   D.   SIM

8.   SIEM products combine the capabilities of which of the following? (Choose all that apply.)

   A.   Syslog

   B.   SNMP

   C.   SEM

   D.   SIM

9.   Which of the following statements about web server logs is not true?

   A.   To analyze web server activity, you typically use an application that interprets the web server log files.

   B.   Web server logs are typically maintained as text files.

   C.   Web server logs record the IP addresses of all visiting users.

   D.   To interpret web server logs, you use a protocol analyzer.

10. Which of the following statements best describes a baseline?

    A. A baseline is an estimation of expected performance levels, based on manufacturers' specifications.

    B. A baseline is a record of performance levels captured under actual workload conditions.

    C. A baseline is a record of performance levels captured under simulated workload conditions.

    D. A baseline is a record of performance levels captured before the system is actually in use.

11. When monitoring performance metrics on one of your servers, you notice that the server is utilizing 100 percent of the network bandwidth available to it. What modification could you make to the server that will most likely address the problem?

    A. Add memory to the system.

    B. Install a second network adapter.

    C. Update the network adapter's firmware.

    D. Install a second processor.

12. Which of the following indicators is typically not included in an operating system's performance monitoring tool, such as the Windows Performance Monitor or the MacOS Activity Monitor?

    A. Temperature

    B. CPU/processor activity

    C. Memory consumption

    D. Network utilization

    E. Storage statistics

13. Which of the following syslog message severity levels indicates that a system is unusable?

    A. 0

    B. 1

    C. 2

    D. 3

    E. 4

14. Which of the following syslog message severity levels indicates a call for immediate action?

    A. 0

    B. 1

    C. 2

    D. 3

    E. 4

15. Which of the following syslog message severity levels indicates that the message is purely informational?

   A. 0

   B. 2

   C. 4

   D. 6

   E. 7

16. A Simple Network Management Protocol (SNMP) console can inform administrators when a managed device requires attention. For this to occur, the agent in the device first has to send a message to the console. What is the term used for a message sent by an SNMP agent to the central console?

   A. Ping

   B. Alert

   C. Notification

   D. Trap

17. Which of the following metrics would you typically not find displayed by an interface monitor?

   A. Error rate

   B. Bandwidth utilization

   C. Packet drops

   D. Rollbacks

18. Which of the following are reasons contributing to the number of packet drops displayed by an interface monitor? (Choose all that apply.)

   A. Resets

   B. Discards

   C. Errors

   D. Overflows

19. Which of the following is not a statistic that you would typically find in a server performance baseline?

   A. CPU utilization

   B. Disk transfer rate

   C. Network transmissions speed

   D. OS update history

   E. Memory utilization

20. Log management typically consists of which of the following tasks? (Choose all that apply.)

    A. Rollback

    B. Utilization

    C. Security

    D. Cycling

21. Which of the following Security Information and Event Management (SIEM) processes performs searches for specific criteria, during specific time frames, in logs located on different computers?

    A. Data aggregation

    B. Forensic analysis

    C. Correlation

    D. Retention

22. Which of the following terms best describes the Security Information and Event Management (SIEM) process of consolidating log information from multiple sources?

    A. Data aggregation

    B. Forensic analysis

    C. Correlation

    D. Retention

23. Which of the following terms best describes a connectivity problem on wired networks that is caused by individual packets that are delayed due to network congestion, different routing, or queuing problems?

    A. Latency

    B. Attenuation

    C. Jitter

    D. Bottleneck

24. Which of the following network interface occurrences are considered to be malfunctions on a full-duplex Ethernet network? (Choose all that apply.)

    A. Runts

    B. Giants

    C. Collisions

    D. Late collisions

25. Which of the following network applications are most likely to be obviously affected by the wired network connectivity problem known as jitter? (Choose all that apply.)

    A. Email

    B. VoIP

    C. Streaming video

    D. Instant messaging

26. Which of the following, originally created for the UNIX sendmail program, is now a standard for message logging that enables tools that generate, store, and analyze log information to work together?

A. Syslog

B. Netmon

C. Netstat

D. Top

27. Which of the following log types is the first place that a Windows administrator should look for information about a server's activities?

A. System log

B. Setup log

C. Application log

D. Security log

28. When a service fails to start on a Windows server, an entry is typically created in which of the following event logs?

A. Application

B. Security

C. Setup

D. System

29. Which of the following Windows applications would you most likely use to create a baseline of system or network performance?

A. Performance Monitor

B. Event Viewer

C. Syslog

D. Network Monitor

30. At what humidity level do electronic components become vulnerable to damage from electrostatic shock?

A. Below 30 percent

B. Below 50 percent

C. Above 70 percent

D. Above 90 percent

31. Which of the following event logs on a Windows server can record information about both successful and failed access attempts?

A. System

B. Application

C. Security

D. Setup

32. Which of the following is the database used by the Simple Network Management Protocol (SNMP) to store information gathered from agents distributed about the network?

    A. Trap

    B. Syslog

    C. MIB

    D. SIEM

33. Which of the following is the most likely cause of runt and giant frames on an Ethernet network interface?

    A. A network adapter malfunction

    B. Half-duplex communication

    C. Excessive cable length

    D. Electromagnetic interference

34. Which of the following is the most likely cause of Cyclic Redundancy Check (CRC) errors on an Ethernet network interface?

    A. Half-duplex communication

    B. A network adapter malfunction

    C. Electromagnetic interference

    D. Excessive cable length

35. Which of the following utilities can display the number of packets sent and received for a specific network interface on a Unix, Linux, MacOS or Windows computer?

    A. Top

    B. Ifconfig

    C. Netstat

    D. Nbtstat

36. Which of the following is a feature included in some routers that collects and analyzes network traffic data sent or received through a network interface?

    A. Netmon

    B. Netflow

    C. Netstat

    D. Nbtstat

37. Which of the following is not a type of error typically found in network interface statistics?

    A. Runt

    B. Encapsulation

    C. Giant

    D. CRC

    E. Jumbo

38. Which of the following is not an SNMP component?

   A. MIBs

   B. Traps

   C. OIDs

   D. CRCs

39. Ralph is designing the HVAC implementation for his company's new central datacenter, which will house all of the equipment for the corporate headquarters and the company's manufacturing facility. The datacenter must adhere to the Tier III standard defined by the Uptime Institute, which calls for at least 99.9 percent uptime. As part of the environmental infrastructure for the datacenter, Ralph plans to install sensors to monitor environmental factors that can affect computer equipment and generate alerts when conditions exceed accepted thresholds. Which of the following environmental factors is not one of those that Ralph should arrange to monitor to protect the equipment specific to a datacenter?

   A. Flood

   B. Humidity

   C. Radon

   D. Static electricity

   E. Temperature

40. Routers using link states and Dijkstra's algorithm to calculate the lowest cost route to a specific destination can conceivably be running which of the following interior gateway routing protocols? (Choose all that apply.)

   A. OSPF

   B. RIP

   C. EIGRP

   D. IS-IS

   E. BGP

41. Which of the following is the term usually applied to a representation of network devices, automatically compiled, and containing information such as IP addresses and connection speeds?

   A. Network map

   B. Network diagram

   C. Cable diagram

   D. Management information base

42. Which of the following types of network documentation is often overlaid on an architectural drawing or blueprint?

   A. Network map

   B. Network diagram

   C. Cable diagram

   D. Management information base

43. Which of the following is not one of the typical heights for devices mounted in IT equipment racks?

   A. 1 unit

   B. 2 units

   C. 3 units

   D. 4 units

44. The cable plant for your company network was installed several years ago by an outside contractor. Now, some of the paper labels have fallen off your patch panels, and you do not know which wall plate is connected to each port. Assuming that you are working on a properly maintained and documented network installation, which of the following is the easiest way to determine which port is connected to which wall plate?

   A. Consult the cable diagram provided by the cabling contractor at the time of the installation.

   B. Call the cable installation contractor and see if he or she can remember which ports go with which wall plates.

   C. Attach a tone generator to a patch panel port and then test each wall plate with a locator until you find the correct one. Repeat this for each port that needs labeling.

   D. Use a cable certifier to locate the patch panel port associated with each wall plate port.

45. Which of the following IT asset management documents published by the International Organization for Standardization (ISO) defines a standard for Software Identification Tags (SWIDs) containing inventory information about the software running on a computer or other device?

   A. ISO 19770-1

   B. ISO 19770-2

   C. ISO 19770-3

   D. ISO 19770-4

   E. ISO 19770-5

46. Which of the following are places where network wiring connections are found? (Choose all that apply.)

   A. MDF

   B. MTBF

   C. IDF

   D. RDP

47. A rack diagram is typically ruled vertically using which of the following measurements?

   A. Inches

   B. Centimeters

   C. Units

   D. Grids

48. In a standard Cisco network diagram, what component does the symbol in the figure represent?

   A. A switch

   B. A router

   C. A hub

   D. A gateway

49. Which of the following statements are true about the differences between a diagram of a patch panel installation organized physically and one that is organized logically? (Choose all that apply.)

   A. A physical diagram is organized according to the floors and rooms where the cable drops are located.

   B. A physical diagram is precisely scaled to represent the actual patch panel hardware.

   C. A logical diagram is organized according to the divisions within the company, such as departments and workgroups.

   D. A logical diagram uses an organization that represents company divisions but does not physically resemble the actual patch panels.

50. A diagram of a telecommunications room or Intermediate Distribution Frame (IDF) for an office building is typically based on which of the following?

   A. A hand-drawn sketch

   B. A series of photographs

   C. An architect's plan

   D. A 3D model

   E. A site survey report

51. The documentation for Main Distribution Frames (MDFs) and Intermediate Distribution Frames (IDFs) should incorporate details on which of the following elements? (Choose all that apply.)

   A. Power

   B. Environment

   C. Distances

   D. Costs

52. At what point in the installation process should patch panel ports and wall plates be labeled?

    A. When the patch panels and wall plates are installed

    B. When a length of cable is cut from the spool

    C. When the cables are attached to the connectors

    D. When the cable runs are tested, immediately after their installation

53. Which of the following is the term used to describe a wiring nexus that is typically the termination point for incoming telephone and Wide Area Network (WAN) services?

    A. MDF

    B. MTBF

    C. IDF

    D. RDP

    E. MOU

54. Your department is experiencing frequent delays as users wait for images to render using their outdated graphics software package. As a result, you are planning to submit a change request for a new software product at the monthly meeting of the company's change management team. Which of the following types of information are likely to be included in your request? (Choose all that apply.)

    A. The possibility of rolling back to the previous software, if necessary

    B. The procedure for installing and configuring the new software

    C. An estimate of the productivity increase realizable with the new software

    D. A list of software and hardware upgrades or modifications needed to run the new software

55. A rack diagram is typically ruled into vertical rack units, which are standard-sized divisions that hardware manufacturers use when manufacturing rack-mountable components. Which of the following is the standard vertical height of a single rack unit?

    A. 1.721 inches

    B. 1.75 inches

    C. 40 mm

    D. 3.5 inches

56. The change request for new graphics software that you submitted to your company's change management team has been approved. Now it is time to implement the change. Which of the following administrative tasks will most likely be the change management team's responsibility during the implementation process? (Choose all that apply.)

    A. Authorizing downtime

    B. Notifying users

    C. Designating a maintenance window

    D. Documenting all modifications made

57. Which of the following IT asset management documents published by the International Organization for Standardization (ISO) provides an overview of the ITAM concepts discussed in the ISO 19770 family of standards?

A. ISO 19770-1

B. ISO 19770-2

C. ISO 19770-3

D. ISO 19770-4

E. ISO 19770-5

58. A rack-mounted device that is four units tall will be approximately what height in inches?

A. 1.75

B. 3.5

C. 4

D. 7

59. Which of the following types of documentation should indicate the complete route of every internal cable run from wall plate to patch panel?

A. Physical network diagram

B. Asset management

C. Logical network diagram

D. Wiring schematic

60. Which of the following statements about physical network diagrams and logical network diagrams are true? (Choose all that apply.)

A. A physical network diagram is created automatically, and a logical network diagram is created manually.

B. A physical network diagram depicts hardware devices and the connections between them.

C. A logical network diagram contains all of the information you would need to rebuild your network from scratch.

D. A logical network diagram typically contains the IP addresses of network devices.

61. In a standard Cisco network diagram, what component does the symbol in the figure represent?

A. A switch

B. A router

C. A hub

D. A gateway

62. Which of the following is the term used to describe a wiring nexus—typically housed in a closet—where horizontal networks meet the backbone?

   A. MDF

   B. MTBF

   C. IDF

   D. SLA

   E. MOU

63. What is the width of a standard equipment rack in a datacenter?

   A. 12 inches

   B. 16 inches

   C. 19 inches

   D. 24 inches

64. In a standard Cisco network diagram, what component does the symbol in the figure represent?

   A. A switch

   B. A router

   C. A hub

   D. A gateway

65. The precise locations of devices in a datacenter are typically documented in which of the following documents?

   A. Rack diagram

   B. Network map

   C. Wiring schematic

   D. Logical diagram

   E. Business continuity plan

   F. Audit and assessment report

66. Which of the following statements about network maps is true?

   A. Network maps are typically drawn to scale.

   B. Network maps typically contain more information than network diagrams.

   C. Network maps must be read/write accessible to all personnel working on the network.

   D. Network maps diagram only the locations of cable runs and endpoints.

67. Which of the following types of documentation should contain the chemical composition of all cleaning compounds used in a datacenter?

A. ESD

B. MSDS

C. NDA

D. BYOD

E. SOP

68. After being hired for a job as an IT administrator, you have been assigned two user accounts, one of which is intended for general use and the other only for administrative tasks. You are also required to sign an agreement that outlines the restrictions for your account use. Specifically, you are not permitted to use the administrative account for anything other than administrative tasks, including browsing the Internet and accessing data for which you are not authorized. Which of the following is the best name for this type of agreement?

A. Remote access policies

B. Service level agreement

C. Acceptable use policy

D. Privileged user agreement

69. You are working for a company with numerous branch offices scattered around the country, and you are required to travel to these offices frequently. Each branch office has some means of accessing the network at the company headquarters. Some use frame relay, some use Virtual Private Networks (VPNs), and a few even use dial-in access. During one trip, you mention to a branch office manager that you intend to connect to the headquarters network that night from your hotel room. The manager warns you that this is against company policy, but you are not so sure. Where in the company documentation should you look to confirm this?

A. Remote access policies

B. Service level agreement

C. Acceptable use policy

D. Privileged user agreement

70. Which of the following is a document that a company's new hires might want to consult to determine whether they are permitted to install their own personal software on company computers?

A. SLA

B. AUP

C. NDA

D. BYOD

71. Many employees have been contacting the IT help desk asking how they can connect their personal smartphones and tablets to the company's wireless network. This has raised issues regarding network security and technical support. You have been asked to draft a policy for the in-house use of personal electronics that addresses these issues. Which of the following describes the document that you will be creating?

A. SLA

B. AUP

C. NDA

D. BYOD

72. You are going to work for a new company as a software developer, and Human Resources (HR) has notified you that you must sign a document guaranteeing that you will maintain confidentiality about the company's products and programming code in perpetuity. Which of the following documents contains this agreement?

A. SLA

B. AUP

C. NDA

D. MOU

E. BYOD

73. Which of the following are typical elements of a corporate password policy? (Choose all that apply.)

A. Minimum password length

B. Use of special characters

C. Unique passwords

D. Frequent password changes

74. Alice is implementing a new password policy that requires all users to change their passwords every seven days. What further modification can she make to the password policy to prevent users from thwarting the password change requirement?

A. Specify a minimum password length

B. Require the use of special characters

C. Require the creation of unique passwords

D. Specify a maximum password change interval

75. Which of the following are settings typically included in an account lockout policy? (Choose all that apply.)

A. Account lockout duration

B. Time allowed between attempts

C. Account lockout threshold

D. Reset account lockout threshold counter

76. How do account lockouts help to prevent intruders from cracking passwords?

 A. By forcing users to select passwords of a minimum length

 B. By preventing users from entering incorrect passwords more than a specified number of times

 C. By preventing users from reusing the same passwords

 D. By requiring an additional authentication method, such as a fingerprint

77. Which of the following data loss prevention terms is used to describe dangers pertaining to data that is being transmitted over a network? (Choose all that apply.)

 A. Data in use

 B. Data at rest

 C. Data in motion

 D. Data in transit

78. Which of the following data loss prevention terms is used to describe dangers pertaining to data while a user is loading it into an application?

 A. Data in use

 B. Data at rest

 C. Data in process

 D. Data in motion

79. Which of the following data loss prevention terms is used to describe potential dangers of data loss or data leakage to unauthorized parties while the data is stored without being used?

 A. Data in use

 B. Data at rest

 C. Data in motion

 D. Data on disk

80. Which of the following is not one of the standard terms used in data loss prevention?

 A. Data online

 B. Data at rest

 C. Data in motion

 D. Data in use

81. The terms *on-boarding* and *off-boarding* are typically associated with which of the following policies?

 A. Data loss prevention

 B. Incident response

 C. Inventory management

 D. Identity management

 E. Disaster recovery

 F. Business continuity

82. The term *off-boarding* refers to which of the following procedures?

   A. Removing a node from a cluster

   B. Disconnecting all cables from a switch

   C. Revoking a user's network privileges

   D. Retiring old workstations

83. Which of the following is most likely to be the last step in a change management procedure?

   A. Documentation

   B. Notification

   C. Approval

   D. Scheduling

84. Which of the following U.S. organizations are capable of imposing international export controls on software products? (Choose all that apply.)

   A. The company that created the software

   B. Department of State

   C. Department of Commerce

   D. Department of the Treasury

85. Which of the following is the primary result of an organization's security incident response policies?

   A. To know how to respond to a particular incident

   B. To prevent an incident from occurring again

   C. To identify the cause of an incident

   D. To document the procedures leading up to an incident

86. You are an IT director, and a fire has broken out in the lower floors of your company's office building. After the personnel are evacuated, the fire department asks you where they can find documentation about all chemicals and equipment used in the company's datacenter, which is threatened by the fire. You direct them to the correct filing cabinet in your office, which contains which of the following document types?

   A. ESD

   B. NDA

   C. BYOD

   D. MSDS

87. You have been asked to draft an Acceptable Use Policy (AUP) for new hires at your company to sign, which specifies what they can and cannot do when working with the company's computers and network. Which of the following is not one of the provisions typically found in this type of document?

   A. Privacy

   B. Ownership

   C. Illegal use

   D. Upgrades

88. You are starting a new job, and the company's Human Resources (HR) department has asked you to sign an Acceptable Use Policy (AUP) regarding computer and network use. The document includes a privacy clause. Which of the following are specifications you can expect to find in this clause? (Choose all that apply.)

   A. Any emails you send or receive can be monitored by the company at any time.

   B. All files and data that you store on company computers must be accessible to the company for scanning and monitoring.

   C. All work that you perform for the company becomes the sole property of the company, including copyrights and patents.

   D. All hardware, software, and any proprietary data stored on the company's computers remains the property of the company.

89. Which of the following tasks is not considered to be part of an IT department's incident response plan?

   A. Stopping an ongoing incident

   B. Containing the damage caused by an incident

   C. Repairing the damage caused by an incident

   D. Rebuilding an infrastructure destroyed by an incident

90. Which of the following are occurrences that are typically addressed by an IT department's incident response policies? (Choose all that apply.)

   A. Denial-of-Service (DoS) attack

   B. Hard disk failure

   C. Electrical fire

   D. Server outage

91. Which of the following terms would apply to the procedure of adding a user's personal smartphone to the network under a Bring Your Own Device (BYOD) policy?

   A. Out-of-band

   B. On-boarding

   C. In-band

   D. Off-boarding

92. Your company has been acquired by another firm and, as IT director, you will have to comply with the new firm's safety policies in your datacenter and other IT workspaces. One of the new requirements states that there must be a fail closed policy for the datacenter. Which of the following best describes what this policy dictates should occur in the event of an emergency?

   A. All computers that are logged on should automatically log off.

   B. All computers that are running should automatically shut down.

   C. All doors that are normally open should lock themselves.

   D. All doors that are normally locked should open themselves.

93. You are the first responder to an incident of computer crime at your company. The data-center's security has been penetrated, a server accessed, and sensitive company data stolen. The company's incident response plan lists the specific tasks that you are responsible for performing. Which of the following are likely to be among those tasks? (Choose all that apply.)

   A. Turn off the server.

   B. Secure the area.

   C. Document the scene.

   D. Collect evidence.

   E. Cooperate with the authorities.

94. Password policies frequently require users to specify complex passwords. Which of the following are characteristic of a complex password?

   A. Passwords that contain mixed upper- and lowercase letters, numbers, and symbols

   B. Passwords that exceed a specific length

   C. Passwords that do not duplicate a specific number of the user's previous passwords

   D. Passwords that do not duplicate the user's account name, birth date, or other personal information

95. Password policies that contain a history requirement typically have which of the following limitations?

   A. Users cannot reuse recent passwords.

   B. Users cannot create passwords containing names of relatives.

   C. Users cannot create passwords containing names of historical figures.

   D. Users cannot create passwords that duplicate those of any other users on the network.

96. Account lockout policies are designed to protect against which of the following types of attacks?

   A. Social engineering

   B. Spoofing

   C. Brute force

   D. Man in the middle

97. Which of the following types of password policies are designed to prevent brute-force attacks? (Choose all that apply.)

   A. Password length policies

   B. Account lockout policies

   C. Password history policies

   D. Complex password policies

98. Which of the following is not likely to be a procedural element of an IT asset disposal policy?

   A. Data deletion

   B. Recycling

   C. Data preservation

   D. Inventory

99. While negotiating a new contract with a service provider, you have reached a disagreement over the contracted reliability of the service. The provider is willing to guarantee that the service will be available 99 percent of the time, but you have been told to require 99.9 percent. When you finally reach an agreement, the negotiated language will be included in which of the following documents?

   A. SLA

   B. AUP

   C. NDA

   D. BYOD

100. Which of the following elements would you typically not expect to find in a Service Level Agreement (SLA) between an Internet Service Provider (ISP) and a subscriber?

   A. A definition of the services to be provided by the ISP

   B. A list of specifications for the equipment to be provided by the ISP

   C. The types and schedule for the technical support to be provided by the ISP

   D. The types of applications that the subscriber will use when accessing the ISP's services

101. You have just completed negotiating an annual contract with a provider to furnish your company with cloud services. As part of the contract, the provider has agreed to guarantee that the services will be available 99.9 percent of the time, around the clock, seven days per week. If the services are unavailable more than 0.1 percent of the time, your company is due a price adjustment. Which of the following terms describes this clause of the contract?

   A. SLA

   B. MTBF

   C. AUP

   D. MTTR

102. The technical support clause of a Service Level Agreement (SLA) will typically include which of the following elements? (Choose all that apply.)

   A. Whether the provider will provide on-site, telephone, or online support

   B. The time service for responses to support calls, which specifies how quickly the provider must respond to requests for support.

   C. The percentage of time that the service is guaranteed to be available

   D. The amount of support that will be provided and the costs for additional support

103. After switching from a standard public switched telephone network (PSTN) telephone system to a Voice over Internet Protocol (VoIP) system, users are complaining of service interruptions and problems hearing callers at certain times of the day. After examining a network traffic audit and assessment report, you determine that traffic levels on the Internet connection are substantially higher during the first and last hours of the day, the same times when most of the users experienced problems. Which of the following solutions can provide more reliable VoIP service during peak usage times?

   A. Implement traffic shaping

   B. Implement load balancing

   C. Upgrade the Local Area Network (LAN) from Fast Ethernet to Gigabit Ethernet

   D. Replace the router connecting the LAN to the Internet with a model that supports Simple Network Management Protocol (SNMP).

104. A server with dual power supplies must be running in which of the following modes for the system to be fault tolerant?

   A. Combined mode

   B. Redundant mode

   C. Individual mode

   D. Hot backup mode

105. Redundant power circuits can enable a server to continue running in spite of which of the following events?

   A. A citywide power outage

   B. A server power supply failure

   C. An uncorrected building circuit failure

   D. A failure of the server's Uninterruptable Power Supply (UPS)

106. Which of the following media types is Windows Server Backup unable to use to store backed-up data?

   A. Local hard disks

   B. Local optical disks

   C. Magnetic tape drives

   D. Remote shared folders

107. Which of the following Redundant Array of Independent Disks (RAID) levels provides fault tolerance by storing parity information on the disks, in addition to the data? (Choose all that apply.)

   A. RAID 0

   B. RAID 1

   C. RAID 5

   D. RAID 10

108. Installing an electrical generator for your datacenter is an example of which of the following fault tolerance concepts?

    A. Uninterruptible Power Supply (UPS)

    B. Power redundancy

    C. Dual power supplies

    D. Redundant circuits

109. Which of the following RAID levels uses disk striping with distributed parity?

    A. RAID 0

    B. RAID 1

    C. RAID 5

    D. RAID 10

110. Which of the following is not a fault tolerance mechanism?

    A. Port aggregation

    B. Clustering

    C. MTBF

    D. UPS

111. Which of the following is not a type of server load balancing mechanism?

    A. DNS round-robin

    B. Network Address Translation

    C. Content switching

    D. Multilayer switching

112. Which of the following mechanisms for load balancing web servers is able to read the incoming HTTP and HTTPS requests and perform advanced functions based on the information they contain?

    A. Content switches

    B. Multilayer switches

    C. Failover clustering

    D. DNS round-robin

113. Which of the following statements about the differences between online and standby Uninterruptible Power Supplies (UPSs) are correct? (Choose all that apply.)

    A. A standby UPS runs devices using battery power all the time.

    B. An online UPS provides no gap in the power supplied to the devices during a main power failure.

    C. An online UPS switches devices to battery power only during a main power failure.

    D. A standby UPS provides only enough power for an orderly shutdown of the devices.

114. Which of the following are valid reasons why online Uninterruptible Power Supplies (UPSs) are more expensive than standby UPSs?

  A. Online UPSs enable devices to run longer when a main power failure occurs.

  B. Online UPSs enable devices to run continuously when a main power failure occurs.

  C. Online UPSs are managed devices that can generate alerts.

  D. Online UPSs provide greater protection against power spikes and sags.

115. Which of the following are equivalent terms for the process of combining the bandwidth of two or more network adapters to increase the overall speed of the connection and provide fault tolerance? (Choose all that apply.)

  A. Bonding

  B. Link aggregation

  C. Clustering

  D. Port aggregation

  E. NIC teaming

116. A network load balancing cluster is made up of multiple computers that function as a single entity. Which of the following terms is used to describe an individual computer in a load balancing cluster?

  A. Node

  B. Host

  C. Server

  D. Box

117. Which of the following is an element of high availability systems that enables them to automatically detect problems and react to them?

  A. Backups

  B. Snapshots

  C. Failover

  D. Cold sites

118. Which of the following RAID levels does not provide fault tolerance?

  A. RAID 0

  B. RAID 1

  C. RAID 5

  D. RAID 10

119. Which of the following networking concepts frequently use virtual Internet Protocol (IP) addresses to provide high availability? (Choose all that apply.)

   A. Clustering

   B. Load balancing

   C. Network Address Translation (NAT)

   D. Network Interface Card (NIC) teaming

120. Which of the following disaster recovery mechanisms can be made operational in the least amount of time?

   A. A cold site

   B. A warm site

   C. A hot site

   D. All of the options are the same.

121. Which of the following datacenter disaster recovery mechanisms is the least expensive to implement?

   A. A cold site

   B. A warm site

   C. A hot site

   D. A cloud site

122. Which of the following terms defines how long it will take to restore a server from backups if a complete system failure occurs?

   A. RPO

   B. RTO

   C. BCP

   D. MIB

123. In a disaster recovery scenario, which of the following terms applies to devices that are not repairable?

   A. MTBF

   B. MTTF

   C. MTTR

   D. MDT

124. If you have a server with dual power supplies, both of which are connected to a single Uninterruptible Power Supply (UPS), with a building power circuit connected to a backup generator, which of the following failures can the server survive and keep running indefinitely? (Choose all that apply.)

   A. Failure of one server power supply

   B. Failure of the UPS

   C. Failure of the building power circuit

   D. Failure of the building backup generator

125. Which of the following is the primary function of an Uninterruptible Power Supply (UPS) during a two-hour building power failure.

    A. To keep servers running until building power is restored

    B. To keep servers running until they can be powered down safely

    C. To keep servers from being damaged by power spikes

    D. To keep servers running in the event of a computer power supply failure

126. If you have a server with dual power supplies, one of which is plugged into a single Uninterruptible Power Supply (UPS) and the other into a wall socket with a surge protector, and the building's power circuit is connected to a backup generator, which of the following failures can the server survive and keep running indefinitely? (Choose all that apply.)

    A. Failure of one server power supply

    B. Failure of the UPS

    C. Failure of the building power circuit

    D. Failure of the building backup generator

127. If you have a server with dual power supplies, each of which is connected to a separate Uninterruptible Power Supply (UPS), with each UPS connected to a separate building power circuit connected to a backup generator, which of the following failures can the server survive and keep running indefinitely? (Choose all that apply.)

    A. Failure of one server power supply

    B. Failure of one UPS

    C. Failure of one building power circuit

    D. Failure of the building backup generator

128. Which of the following is the criterion most commonly used to filter files for backup jobs?

    A. Filename

    B. File extension

    C. File attributes

    D. File size

129. Which of the following disaster recovery mechanisms is the least expensive to implement?

    A. A cold site

    B. A warm site

    C. A hot site

    D. All of the options cost the same.

130. Which of the following statements about port aggregation is not true?

    A. All of the aggregated ports use the same MAC address.

    B. Port aggregation can be a fault tolerance mechanism.

    C. Aggregating ports increases network throughput.

    D. Port aggregation provides load balancing

131. Which of the following can be provided by clustering servers?

    A. Fault tolerance

    B. Load balancing

    C. Failover

    D. All of the above

132. When you configure NIC teaming on a server with two network adapters in an active/ passive configuration, which of the following services is provided?

    A. Load balancing

    B. Fault tolerance

    C. Server clustering

    D. Traffic shaping

133. Which of the following is not a load balancing mechanism?

    A. NIC teaming

    B. Server clustering

    C. DNS round-robin

    D. RAID 1

134. Which of the following best describes the difference between cold, warm, and hot backup sites?

    A. Whether the backup site is owned, borrowed, or rented

    B. The age of the most recent backup stored at the site

    C. The cost of the hardware used at the site

    D. The time needed to get the site up and running

135. Which of the following specifications would you most want to examine when comparing hard disk models for your new Redundant Array of Independent Disks (RAID) array?

    A. MTBF

    B. SLA

    C. AUP

    D. MTTR

136. Which of the following RAID levels provides fault tolerance with the smallest amount of usable disk space? (Choose all that apply.)

    A. RAID 0

    B. RAID 1

    C. RAID 5

    D. RAID 10

137. Disk mirroring and disk duplexing are both fault tolerance mechanisms for hard disk data storage. Which of the following statements about disk mirroring and disk duplexing is true?

  A. Disk mirroring enables a server to survive the failure of a disk drive.

  B. Disk duplexing enables a server to survive the failure of a disk controller.

  C. Disk mirroring enables a server to survive a failure of a disk drive or a disk controller.

  D. Disk duplexing enables a server to survive a failure of a disk drive or a disk controller.

138. You are installing a new Windows server with two hard disk drives in it, and you want to use RAID to create a fault-tolerant storage system. Which of the following RAID levels can you configure the server to use?

  A. RAID 0

  B. RAID 1

  C. RAID 5

  D. RAID 10

139. Which of the following RAID levels provide fault tolerance without using parity data? (Choose all that apply.)

  A. RAID 0

  B. RAID 1

  C. RAID 5

  D. RAID 10

140. Which of the following backup job types does not reset the archive bits of the files it backs up?

  A. Full

  B. Incremental

  C. Differential

  D. Supplemental

141. What are the three elements in the Grandfather-Father-Son media rotation system for network backups?

  A. Hard disk drives, optical drives, and magnetic tape drives

  B. Incremental, differential, and full backup jobs

  C. Monthly, weekly, and daily backup jobs

  D. QIC, DAT, and DLT tape drives

142. Which of the following types of backup jobs are supported by the Windows Server Backup program? (Choose all that apply.)

  A. Incremental

  B. Differential

  C. Full

  D. Supplemental

143. Which of the following is a term for a read-only copy of a data set made at a specific moment in time?

   A. Snapshot

   B. Incremental

   C. Hot site

   D. Differential

144. Which of the following storage techniques prevents version skew from occurring during a system backup?

   A. Incrementals

   B. Differentials

   C. Iterations

   D. Snapshots

145. If you back up your network by performing a full backup every Wednesday at 6:00 p.m. and incremental backups in the evening of the other days of the week, how many jobs would be needed to completely restore a computer with a hard drive that failed on a Monday at noon?

   A. One

   B. Two

   C. Five

   D. Six

146. How does an autochanger increase the overall storage capacity of a backup solution?

   A. By compressing data before it is stored on the medium

   B. By automatically inserting media into and removing it from a drive

   C. By running a tape drive at half its normal speed

   D. By writing two tracks at once onto a magnetic tape

147. For a complete restore of a computer that failed at noon on Tuesday, how many jobs would be needed if you performed full backups to tape at 6:00 a.m. every Wednesday and Saturday and incremental backups to tape at 6:00 a.m. every other day?

   A. One

   B. Two

   C. Three

   D. Four

148. If you back up your network by performing a full backup every Wednesday at 6:00 p.m. and differential backups in the evening on the other six days of the week, how many jobs would be needed to completely restore a computer with a hard drive that failed on a Tuesday at noon?

   A. One

   B. Two

   C. Six

   D. Seven

149. Why does performing incremental backups to a hard drive, rather than a tape drive, make it possible to restore a server with a single job, rather than multiple jobs?

   A. Because hard drives hold more data than tape drives

   B. Because hard drives can transfer data faster than tape drives

   C. Because hard drives are random access devices and tape drives are not

   D. Because hard drives use a different block size than tape drives

150. Which of the following is not a fault tolerance mechanism?

   A. UPS

   B. RAID 1

   C. SNMP

   D. Clustering

151. Which of the following is the primary difference between the Power Distribution Units (PDUs) used in datacenters and the standard power strips used in offices and homes?

   A. More outlets

   B. Larger power input

   C. Larger power output

   D. All of the above

152. Which of the following statements about backing up a firewall's state and backing up its configuration are true? (Choose all that apply.)

   A. A backup of a firewall's state contains more data than a backup of its configuration.

   B. A backup of a firewall's configuration contains more data than a backup of its state.

   C. A backup of a firewall's state contains the exact same data as a backup of its configuration.

   D. A backup of a firewall's state includes its configuration.

   E. A backup of a firewall's configuration includes its state.

153. Which of the following is the most commonly recommended fire suppression system for a datacenter?

   A. Carbon Dioxide

   B. Water

   C. Foam

   D. HFC-125

154. Concurrent multipath routing (CMR) is a technique that provides which of the following benefits? (Choose all that apply.)

   A. Increased bandwidth

   B. Fault tolerance

   C. Data encapsulation

   D. Load balancing

155. A First Hop Redundancy Protocol (FHRP) is designed to dynamically alter which one of the following Internet Protocol (IP) configuration settings on a network host?

   A. IP address

   B. Subnet mask

   C. Default gateway

   D. DNS server address

156. Which of the following is not a First Hop Redundancy Protocol (FHRP)?

   A. CARP

   B. VRRP

   C. HSRP

   D. RARP

157. Ralph is designing a new network with the redundant switching arrangement shown in the accompanying figure. This redundancy enables every node on the network to communicate with any other node, even if one of the switches should fail. Which of the following is a potential drawback of this arrangement?

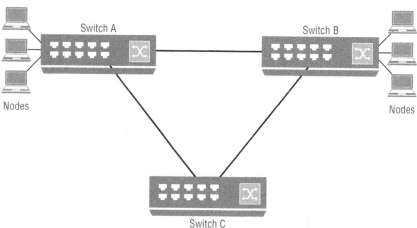

   A. Runt frames

   B. Late collisions

   C. Broadcast storms

   D. Corrupted switch lookup tables

158. Installing redundant firewalls in a parallel configuration, as shown in the accompanying graphic, provides which of the following benefits? (Choose all that apply.)

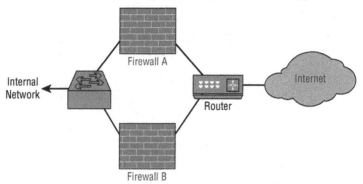

    A. Load balancing

    B. Fault tolerance

    C. Added security

    D. Enhanced performance

159. Redundant servers running in an active-active configuration provide which of the following advantages that the same servers in an active-passive configuration do not? (Choose all that apply.)

    A. Increased performance

    B. Fault tolerance

    C. Data encapsulation

    D. Load balancing

160. To build a network with redundant Internet connections that ensures full fault tolerance, it is necessary to use which of the following?

    A. Different ISPs

    B. Different WAN connections

    C. Different routers

    D. All of the above

Chapter

4

Network Security

THE COMPTIA NETWORK+ EXAM N10-008 TOPICS COVERED IN THIS CHAPTER INCLUDE THE FOLLOWING:

✓ **4.1 Explain common security concepts.**

- Confidentiality, integrity, availability (CIA)
- Threats
  - Internal
  - External
- Vulnerabilities
  - Common vulnerabilities and exposures (CVE)
  - Zero-day
- Exploits
- Least privilege
- Role-based access
- Zero Trust
- Defense in depth
  - Network segmentation enforcement
  - Screened subnet [previously known as demilitarized zone (DMZ)]
  - Separation of duties
  - Network access control
  - Honeypot
- Authentication methods
  - Multifactor
  - Terminal Access Controller Access-Control System Plus (TACACS+)
  - Single sign-on (SSO)

- Remote Authentication Dial-in User Service (RADIUS)
- LDAP
- Kerberos
- Local authentication
- 802.1X
- Extensible Authentication Protocol (EAP)

- Risk Management
  - Security risk assessments
    - Threat assessment
    - Vulnerability assessment
    - Penetration testing
    - Posture assessment
  - Business risk assessments
    - Process assessment
    - Vendor assessment

- Security information and event management (SIEM)

✓ 4.2 Compare and contrast common types of attacks.

- Technology-based
  - Denial-of-service (DoS)/distributed denial-of-service (DDoS)
    - Botnet/command and control
  - On-path attack (previously known as man-in-the-middle attack)
  - DNS poisoning
  - VLAN hopping
  - ARP spoofing
  - Rogue DHCP
  - Rogue access point (AP)
  - Evil twin
  - Ransomware

- Password attacks
  - Brute-force
  - Dictionary
- MAC spoofing
- IP spoofing
- Deauthentication
- Malware
- Human and environmental
  - Social engineering
    - Phishing
    - Tailgating
    - Piggybacking
    - Shoulder surfing

✓ **4.3 Given a scenario, apply network hardening techniques.**

- Best practices
  - Secure SNMP
  - Router Advertisement (RA) Guard
  - Port security
  - Dynamic ARP inspection
  - Control plane policing
  - Private VLANs
  - Disable unneeded switchports
  - Disable unneeded network services
  - Change default passwords
  - Password complexity/length
  - Enable DHCP snooping
  - Change default VLAN
  - Patch and firmware management

- Access control list
- Role-based access
- Firewall rules
  - Explicit deny
  - Implicit deny
- Wireless security
  - MAC filtering
  - Antenna placement
  - Power levels
  - Wireless client isolation
  - Guest network isolation
  - Preshared keys (PSKs)
  - EAP
  - Geofencing
  - Captive portal
- IoT access considerations

✓ **4.4 Compare and contrast remote access methods and security implications.**

- Site-to-site VPN
- Client-to-site VPN
  - Clientless VPN
  - Split tunnel vs. full tunnel
- Remote desktop connection
- Remote desktop gateway
- SSH
- Virtual network computing (VNC)
- Virtual desktop
- Authentication and authorization considerations
- In-band vs. out-of-band management

✓ **4.5 Explain the importance of physical security.**

- Detection methods
    - Camera
    - Motion detection
    - Asset tags
    - Tamper detection
- Prevention methods
    - Employee training
    - Access control hardware
        - Badge readers
        - Biometrics
    - Locking racks
    - Locking cabinets
    - Access control vestibule (previously known as a mantrap)
    - Smart lockers
- Asset disposal
    - Factory reset/wipe configuration
    - Sanitize devices for disposal

1. Which of the following are terms for an area of an enterprise network, separated by firewalls, which contains servers that must be accessible both from the Internet and from the internal network? (Choose all that apply.)

   A. Intranet

   B. DMZ

   C. EGP

   D. Stateless network

   E. Perimeter network

   F. Screened subnet

2. Which of the following authentication protocols do Windows networks use for Active Directory Domain Services (AD DS) authentication of internal clients?

   A. RADIUS

   B. WPA2

   C. Kerberos

   D. EAP-TLS

3. Which of the following are examples of multifactor authentication? (Choose all that apply.)

   A. A system that uses an external RADIUS server for authentication

   B. A system that requires two passwords for authentication

   C. A system that requires a smartcard and a PIN for authentication

   D. A system that requires a password and a retinal scan for authentication

4. Which of the following protocols can you use to authenticate Windows remote access users with smartcards?

   A. EAP

   B. MS-CHAPv2

   C. CHAP

   D. PAP

5. Which of the following statements best defines multifactor user authentication?

   A. Verification of a user's identity on all of a network's resources using a single sign-on

   B. Verification of a user's identity using two or more types of credentials

   C. Verification of a user's identity on two devices at once

   D. Verification of a user's membership in two or more security groups

6. Which of the following services are methods of tracking a user's activities on a network? (Choose all that apply.)

   A. Authentication

   B. Authorization

   C. Accounting

   D. Auditing

7. When a user supplies a password to log on to a server, which of the following actions is the user performing?

 A. Authentication

 B. Authorization

 C. Accounting

 D. Auditing

8. When a user swipes a finger across a fingerprint scanner to log on to a laptop computer, which of the following actions is the user performing?

 A. Authentication

 B. Authorization

 C. Accounting

 D. Auditing

9. Which of the following security protocols can authenticate users without transmitting their passwords over the network?

 A. Kerberos

 B. 802.1X

 C. TKIP

 D. LDAP

10. Which of the following statements about authentication auditing are not true?

 A. Auditing can disclose attempts to compromise passwords.

 B. Auditing can detect authentications that occur after hours.

 C. Auditing can identify the guess patterns used by password cracking software.

 D. Auditing can record unsuccessful as well as successful authentications.

11. When a user swipes a smartcard through a reader to log on to a laptop computer, which of the following actions is the user performing?

 A. Authentication

 B. Authorization

 C. Accounting

 D. Auditing

12. Combining elements like something you know, something you have, and something you are to provide access to a secured network resource is a definition of which of the following types of authentication?

 A. Multifactor

 B. Multisegment

 C. Multimetric

 D. Multifiltered

13. Which of the following terms describes a system that prevents computers from logging on to a network unless they have the latest updates and antimalware software installed?

A. NAC

B. LDAP

C. RADIUS

D. TKIP-RC4

14. Which of the following describes the primary difference between Single Sign-On (SSO) and same sign-on?

A. SSO enables users to access different resources with one set of credentials, whereas same sign-on requires users to have multiple credential sets.

B. SSO credentials consist of one username and one password, whereas same sign-on credentials consist of one username and multiple passwords.

C. SSO requires the user to supply credentials only once, whereas with same sign-on, the user must supply the credentials repeatedly.

D. SSO requires multifactor authentication, such as a password and a smartcard, whereas same sign-on requires only a password for authentication.

15. Which of the following is the best description of biometrics?

A. Something you know

B. Something you have

C. Something you are

D. Something you do

16. Which of the following authentication factors is an example of something you have?

A. A fingerprint

B. A smartcard

C. A password

D. A finger gesture

17. Which of the following statements best describes the primary scenario for the use of TACACS+?

A. TACACS+ was designed to provide authentication, authorization, and accounting services for wireless networks.

B. TACACS+ was designed to provide authentication, authorization, and accounting services for the Active Directory service.

C. TACACS+ was designed to provide authentication, authorization, and accounting services for remote dial-up users.

D. TACACS+ was designed to provide authentication, authorization, and accounting services for network routers and switches.

18. The new door lock on your company's datacenter door requires you to supply both a PIN and a thumbprint scan. Which of the following types of authentication factors does the lock use? (Choose all that apply.)

    A. Something you have

    B. Something you know

    C. Something you are

    D. Something you do

19. Your new smartphone enables you to configure the lock screen with a picture of your husband, on which you draw eyes, nose, and a mouth with your finger to unlock the phone. This is an example of which of the following authentication factors?

    A. Something you have

    B. Something you know

    C. Something you are

    D. Something you do

20. Which of the following authentication factors is an example of something you do?

    A. A fingerprint

    B. A smartcard

    C. A password

    D. A finger gesture

21. Which of the following authentication factors is an example of something you know?

    A. A fingerprint

    B. A smartcard

    C. A password

    D. A finger gesture

22. Which of the following authentication factors is an example of something you are?

    A. A fingerprint

    B. A smartcard

    C. A password

    D. A finger gesture

23. Which of the following is an implementation of Network Access Control (NAC)?

    A. RADIUS

    B. 802.1X

    C. LDAP

    D. TACACS+

24. Which of the following is not one of the roles involved in an 802.1X transaction?

    A. Supplicant

    B. Authentication server

    C. Authorizing agent

    D. Authenticator

25. In an 802.1X transaction, what is the function of the supplicant?

    A. The supplicant is the service that issues certificates to clients attempting to connect to the network.

    B. The supplicant is the service that verifies the credentials of the client attempting to access the network.

    C. The supplicant is the network device to which the client is attempting to connect.

    D. The supplicant is the client user or computer attempting to connect to the network.

26. In an 802.1X transaction, what is the function of the authenticator?

    A. The authenticator is the service that issues certificates to clients attempting to connect to the network.

    B. The authenticator is the service that verifies the credentials of the client attempting to access the network.

    C. The authenticator is the network device to which the client is attempting to connect.

    D. The authenticator is the client user or computer attempting to connect to the network.

27. An 802.1X transaction involves three roles: the supplicant, the authenticator, and the authentication server. Of the three, which role typically takes the form of a RADIUS implementation?

    A. The supplicant

    B. The authenticator

    C. The authentication server

    D. None of the above

28. Which of the following are standards that define combined Authentication, Authorization, and Accounting (AAA) services? (Choose all that apply.)

    A. 802.1X

    B. RADIUS

    C. TACACS+

    D. LDAP

29. Which of the following standards was originally designed to provide Authentication, Authorization, and Accounting (AAA) services for dial-up network connections?

   A. RADIUS

   B. TACACS+

   C. Kerberos

   D. LDAP

30. Which of the following statements about RADIUS and TACACS+ are correct?

   A. By default, RADIUS uses UDP, and TACACS+ uses TCP.

   B. By default, RADIUS uses TCP, and TACACS+ uses UDP.

   C. By default, both RADIUS and TACACS+ use TCP.

   D. By default, both RADIUS and TACACS+ use UDP.

31. Which of the following standards provides Authentication, Authorization, and Accounting (AAA) services for network routers and switches?

   A. RADIUS

   B. TACACS+

   C. Kerberos

   D. LDAP

32. Which of the following terms refers to the process of determining whether a user is a member of a group that provides access to a particular network resource?

   A. Authentication

   B. Accounting

   C. Authorization

   D. Access control

33. Which of the following terms refers to the process of confirming a user's identity by checking specific credentials?

   A. Authentication

   B. Accounting

   C. Authorization

   D. Access control

34. Which of the following terms refers to the process by which a system tracks a user's network activity?

   A. Authentication

   B. Accounting

   C. Authorization

   D. Access control

35. Which of the following statements are true about a public key infrastructure? (Choose all that apply.)

A. Data encrypted with a user's public key can be decrypted with the user's public key.

B. Data encrypted with a user's public key can be decrypted with the user's private key.

C. Data encrypted with a user's private key can be decrypted with the user's private key.

D. Data encrypted with a user's private key can be decrypted with the user's public key.

36. Which of the following technologies can maintain an account database that multiple remote access servers can employ to authenticate remote users?

A. RADIUS

B. IDS

C. NGFW

D. NAS

37. Which element of the Confidentiality-Integrity-Availability (CIA) triad prevents unauthorized modification of protected data?

A. Confidentiality

B. Integrity

C. Availability

D. None of the above

38. Which of the following is an example of local authentication?

A. A system that uses an external RADIUS server for authentication

B. A system that uses the Kerberos protocol for authentication

C. A system that authenticates users without network communication

D. A system that requires a password and a retinal scan for authentication

39. In some cases, network administrators create computers that function as enticing targets for attackers but that do not provide access to any legitimately sensitive services or information. Which of the following is the term used to describe this technique?

A. DMZ

B. Honeypot

C. Root guard

D. Spoofing

40. Honeypots and honeynets belong to which of the following categories of devices?

A. Mitigation techniques

B. Network attacks

C. Switch port protection types

D. Firewall filters

41. Which of the following best describes the process of penetration testing?

    A. Administrators create computers or networks that are alluring targets for intruders.

    B. Administrators attempt to access the network from outside using hacker tools.

    C. An organization hires an outside consultant to evaluate the security conditions on the network.

    D. An organization hires an outside consultant who attempts to compromise the network's security measures.

42. Which of the following types of servers are typically found in a screened subnet? (Choose all that apply.)

    A. Domain controllers

    B. DHCP servers

    C. Email servers

    D. Web servers

43. Which of the following statements best describes the difference between an exploit and a vulnerability?

    A. An exploit is a potential weakness in software, and a vulnerability is a potential weakness in hardware.

    B. A vulnerability is a potential weakness in a system, and an exploit is a hardware or software element that is designed to take advantage of a vulnerability.

    C. An exploit is a potential weakness in a system, and a vulnerability is a hardware or software element that is designed to take advantage of a vulnerability.

    D. A vulnerability is a potential weakness in software, and an exploit is a potential weakness in hardware.

44. Which of the following abbreviations describes a product that combines real-time monitoring of security events and automated analysis of the event information gathered?

    A. SIEM

    B. SNMP

    C. SEIM

    D. SEM/SIM

45. A technician in the IT department at your company was terminated today and had to be escorted from the building. Your supervisor has instructed you to disable all of the technician's accounts, change all network device passwords to which the technician had access, and have the datacenter doors rekeyed. Which of the following terms best describes your supervisor's concern in asking you to do these things?

    A. Social engineering

    B. Internal threats

    C. Logic bombs

    D. War driving

    E. External threats

46. Which of the following is the best description of a software product with a zero-day vulnerability?

A. A product with a vulnerability that has just been addressed by a newly-released fix

B. A product with a vulnerability that has been addressed by a fix, which nearly all users have applied

C. A vulnerability in a newly-released product for which no fix has yet been developed

D. A vulnerability in a product which no attackers have yet discovered or exploited

47. Ralph is evaluating software products for potential deployment on his company's network. Which of the following types of searches can Ralph use to identify security issues that have been discovered in specific products?

A. CIA

B. CVE

C. SKU

D. SIEM

48. Alice's company regularly hires a large number of operators for their phone center. The operators require access to a customer database and an order entry system. Because this is a high-turnover position, Alice has streamlined the on-boarding process by creating a security group with the appropriate permissions needed to access the necessary software. This way, she can simply add each new user to the group, rather than assigning the permissions individually. This is an example of which of the following security concepts?

A. Least privilege

B. Zero trust

C. Role-based access control

D. Defense in depth

49. When starting her new position as a network administrator, Alice was given two user accounts. One account is intended for standard user activities, and another has the additional permissions needed for Alice to perform administrative tasks. This is an example of which of the following security concepts?

A. Zero-day

B. Multifactor authentication

C. Least privilege

D. Defense in depth

50. Which of the following is a practice that a zero trust architecture is designed to protect against?

A. Zero-day vulnerabilities

B. External threats

C. Deauthentication

D. Lateral movement

51. Which of the following is not one of the mechanisms often used to implement a defense in depth strategy?

A. Screened subnets

B. Network segmentation enforcement

C. Honeypots

D. Access control vestibules

E. Social engineering

F. Separation of duties

52. As part of her company's new risk management initiative, Alice has been assigned the task of performing a threat assessment for the firm's data resources. For each potential threat she discovers, which of the following elements should Alice estimate? (Choose all that apply.)

A. Severity

B. Mitigation

C. Likelihood

D. Posture

53. Alice has been assigned the task of examining her department's order entry procedure, to determine whether it meets established cost, quality, and timeliness goals. Which of the following is the best term for this examination?

A. Vendor assessment

B. Process assessment

C. Business assessment

D. Risk assessment

54. A user calls the help desk, complaining that he cannot access any of the data on his computer. A message has also appeared on his screen stating that his data has been encrypted and that it will only be decrypted after he pays $768 in digital currency to an unknown address. Which of the following types of attack has the user experienced?

A. War driving

B. Ransomware

C. Denial-of-Service

D. ARP poisoning

55. Which of the following attack types typically involves modifying network packets while they are in transit? (Choose all that apply.)

A. Spoofing

B. Denial-of-Service

C. On-path

D. Logic bomb

56. Which of the following types of attack involves the modification of a legitimate software product?

    A. Social engineering

    B. War driving

    C. Logic bomb

    D. Evil twin

57. Which of the following steps can help to prevent war driving attacks from compromising your wireless network? (Choose all that apply.)

    A. Configure your access point to use a longer SSID.

    B. Configure your access point not to broadcast its SSID.

    C. Configure your clients and access point to use WPA2 security.

    D. Configure your clients and access point to use WEP security.

58. On the fence outside your home, you happen to notice a small sticker that has the Service Set Identifier (SSID) of your wireless network written on it, along with the name of the security protocol your network is using. To which of the following attacks have you been made a victim?

    A. War driving

    B. War chalking

    C. War tagging

    D. War signing

59. Which of the following is the name for an attack in which an intruder uses a Bluetooth connection to steal information from a wireless device, such as a smart phone?

    A. Bluedogging

    B. Bluesnarfing

    C. Bluesmurfing

    D. Bluejacking

60. Which of the following types of Denial-of-Service (DoS) attack does not involve flooding a server with traffic?

    A. Amplified

    B. Reflective

    C. Distributed

    D. Permanent

61. Which of the following statements best describes the difference between distributed and reflective Denial-of-Service (DoS) attacks?

A. A distributed DoS attack uses other computers to flood a target server with traffic, whereas a reflective DoS attack causes a server to flood itself with loopback messages.

B. A distributed DoS attack uses malware-infected computers to flood a target, whereas a reflective DoS attack takes advantage of other servers' native functions to make them flood a target.

C. A reflective DoS attack uses malware-infected computers to flood a target, whereas a distributed DoS attack takes advantage of other servers' native functions to make them flood a target.

D. A distributed DoS attack floods multiple target computers with traffic, whereas a reflective DoS attack only floods a single target.

62. Which of the following terms refers to a Denial-of-Service (DoS) attack that places more of a burden on the target server than just the flood of incoming traffic?

A. Amplified

B. Reflective

C. Distributed

D. Permanent

63. Which of the following types of attacks require no additional hardware or software components? (Choose all that apply.)

A. Brute-force

B. Social engineering

C. Denial-of-Service

D. Phishing

64. Which of the following attack types are specifically targeted at wireless network clients? (Choose all that apply.)

A. Logic bomb

B. Deauthentication

C. Evil twin

D. ARP poisoning

65. Which of the following is an effective method for preventing sensitive data from being compromised through social engineering?

A. Implement a program of user education and corporate policies.

B. Install an antivirus software product on all user workstations.

C. Install a firewall between the internal network and the Internet.

D. Use Internet Protocol Security (IPSec) to encrypt all network traffic.

66. Which of the following terms refer to Denial-of-Service (DoS) attacks that use other computers to flood a target server with traffic? (Choose all that apply.)

    A. Amplified

    B. Reflective

    C. Distributed

    D. Permanent

67. In which of the following ways is VLAN hopping a potential threat?

    A. VLAN hopping enables an attacker to scramble a switch's patch panel connections.

    B. VLAN hopping enables an attacker to rename the default VLAN on a switch.

    C. VLAN hopping enables an attacker to access different VLANs using 802.1q spoofing.

    D. VLAN hopping enables an attacker to change the native VLAN on a switch.

68. Which of the following tools are needed by an individual performing a war driving attack? (Choose all that apply.)

    A. A stolen credit card number

    B. A wireless-equipped computer or other device

    C. A screwdriver

    D. An automobile or other vehicle

    E. A telephone

69. Which of the following types of attacks can be used to enable an intruder to access a wireless network despite the protection provided by MAC filtering?

    A. Spoofing

    B. Brute-force

    C. DNS poisoning

    D. War driving

70. Which of the following terms refers to a type of Denial-of-Service (DoS) attack that uses multiple computers to bombard a target server with traffic?

    A. Amplified

    B. Reflective

    C. Distributed

    D. Permanent

71. Which of the following terms refers to a type of Denial-of-Service (DoS) attack that bombards a target server with traffic that requires a large amount of processing?

    A. Amplified

    B. Reflective

    C. Distributed

    D. Permanent

72. Which of the following types of attacks are rarely seen anymore because of changes in device design that were specifically designed to prevent them? (Choose all that apply.)

    A. VLAN hopping

    B. Logic bomb

    C. Phishing

    D. Smurf

73. Which of the following terms refers to a Denial-of-Service (DoS) attack in which an attacker breaks into a company's datacenter and smashes its servers with a sledgehammer?

    A. Amplified

    B. Reflective

    C. Distributed

    D. Permanent

74. Which of the following terms refers to a Denial-of-Service (DoS) attack that involves zombies?

    A. Amplified

    B. Reflective

    C. Distributed

    D. Permanent

75. Which of the following types of attacks can cause a user's attempts to connect to an Internet website to be diverted to an attacker's website instead?

    A. Evil twin

    B. ARP poisoning

    C. Spoofing

    D. DNS poisoning

76. Which of the following functions can be interfered with by a DNS poisoning attack?

    A. IP address resolution

    B. Name resolution

    C. Password protection

    D. Network switching

77. In testing the new application he has designed, Ralph has discovered that it contains a weakness that could enable an attacker to gain full administrative access. Which of the following is another term for this weakness?

    A. Exploit

    B. Mitigation

    C. Vulnerability

    D. Honeypot

78. A senior IT administrator at your company was terminated two weeks ago. Today, Friday, you arrived at the office and found that all of the hosts in the web server farm had had their data deleted. There are no unauthorized entries to the datacenter recorded, but you suspect the terminated administrator is responsible for deleting the data. Which of the following attack types might the administrator have directed at the web server farm?

    A. Social engineering

    B. ARP poisoning

    C. Evil twin

    D. Logic bomb

79. Which of the following attack types can be facilitated by ARP poisoning? (Choose all that apply.)

    A. Evil twin

    B. On-path

    C. Session hijacking

    D. Social engineering

80. Which of the following statements best describes a type of replay attack?

    A. An intruder reenters a resource previously compromised by another intruder.

    B. An intruder retransmits captured authentication packets to gain access to a secured resource.

    C. An intruder uses the same technique that provided access to other resources to penetrate a new resource.

    D. An intruder accesses a resource that was accidentally left unsecured by an authorized user.

81. Ed receives an email through his personal account, warning him that his checking account has been locked due to excessive activity. To confirm that the activity is fraudulent, the email instructs Ed to click the enclosed hyperlink, log on to his account, and review the list of charges. Ed clicks the link and is taken to a web page that appears to be that of his bank. He then supplies his username and password to log on. Which of the following types of attacks is Ed likely to be experiencing?

    A. Social engineering

    B. Phishing

    C. Logic bomb

    D. Spoofing

82. Which of the following attack types are specifically directed at wireless networks? (Choose all that apply.)

    A. Evil twin

    B. Phishing

    C. Deauthentication

    D. War driving

83. Which of the following are not considered to be Denial-of-Service (DoS) attacks? (Choose all that apply.)

    A. An intruder breaks into a company's datacenter and smashes their web servers with a sledgehammer.

    B. An attacker uses the `ping` command with the `-t` parameter to send a continuous stream of large Internet Control Message Protocol (ICMP) packets to a specific server.

    C. An attacker captures the packets transmitted to and from a domain controller to obtain encrypted passwords.

    D. An attacker connects a rogue access point to a company's wireless network, using their Service Set Identifier (SSID) in the hope of attracting their users.

84. In the hacker subculture, which of the following statements best describes a zombie?

    A. A computer that is remotely controllable because it has been infected by malware

    B. A computer that is no longer functioning because it is the target of a Denial-of-Service (DoS) attack

    C. A user that has fallen victim to a phishing attack

    D. A program that attackers use to penetrate passwords using brute-force attacks

85. Which of the following statements best describes a ransomware attack?

    A. A website is rendered inaccessible by a Denial-of-Service (DoS) attack until its owner agrees to pay a fee.

    B. A user's access to a specific resource, such as a bank's website, is blocked until the user pays a fee.

    C. A message appears on a user's screen, stating that system is locked and will only be released on payment of a fee.

    D. An application is supplied with limited usability until the user pays a license fee.

86. Which of the following types of attacks requires no computer equipment?

    A. Denial-of-Service

    B. Social engineering

    C. Brute-force

    D. Dictionary

    E. Phishing

87. Which of the following best describes a brute-force attack?

    A. An attacker breaking down the door of a datacenter

    B. An attacker cracking a password by trying thousands of guesses

    C. An attacker using zombie computers to flood a server with traffic

    D. An attacker deploying an unauthorized access point on a wireless network

88. An intruder has deployed a rogue access point on your company's wireless network and is using it to access traffic generated by users who have accidentally connected to it. Which of the following is the name for this type of attack?

   A. Evil twin

   B. War driving

   C. Social networking

   D. Spoofing

89. A person identifying herself as Trixie from IT telephones a user called Alice and tells her that there is a problem with her network user account that could cause all her data to be lost. To resolve the problem, Trixie says that she must log on using Alice's account and configure an important setting. All she needs to do this is Alice's account password. This call is, of course, an illicit attempt to learn Alice's password. Which of the following terms describes the type of attack that is currently occurring?

   A. On-path

   B. Spoofing

   C. Social engineering

   D. Evil twin

90. Regularly applying operating system updates and patches to network computers is an important mitigation procedure for which of the following security problems?

   A. Denial-of-Service attacks

   B. Malware

   C. Social engineering

   D. Port security

91. Which of the following is not a form of social engineering?

   A. Piggybacking

   B. Tailgating

   C. Shoulder surfing

   D. Evil twin

   E. Phishing

92. Which of the following standards defines a framework for the authentication process, but does not specify the actual authentication mechanism?

   A. WPA

   B. EAP

   C. TKIP

   D. TLS

93. EAP and 802.1X are components that help to provide which of the following areas of wireless network security?

    A. Authentication

    B. Authorization

    C. Encryption

    D. Accounting

94. Which of the following Extended Authentication Protocol (EAP) variants utilize tunneling to provide security for the authentication process? (Choose all that apply.)

    A. PEAP

    B. EAP-FAST

    C. EAP-TLS

    D. EAP-PSK

95. A wireless network is configured to allow clients to authenticate only when the signal strength of their connections exceeds a specified level. Which of the following terms best describes this configuration?

    A. Local authentication

    B. Port security

    C. Geofencing

    D. Motion detection

96. Which of the following best describes a wireless network that uses geofencing as a security mechanism?

    A. A wireless network that allows clients to authenticate only when the signal strength of their connections exceeds a specified level

    B. A wireless network that requires users to log on to a wired system before they can authenticate on a wireless device

    C. A wireless network that requires users to have an Active Directory account located within the local site

    D. A wireless network that requires users to type in the local Service Set Identifier (SSID) before they can authenticate

97. Which of the following elements associates a public and private key pair to the identity of a specific person or computer?

    A. Exploit

    B. Signature

    C. Certificate

    D. Resource record

98. In addition to EAP-TLS, which of the following are also Extensible Authentication Protocol (EAP) variants that use the Transport Layer Security (TLS) protocol? (Choose all that apply.)

A. PEAP

B. EAP-PWD

C. EAP-MD5

D. EAP-FAST

99. Which of the following can be described as wireless network hardening techniques? (Choose all that apply.)

A. Encryption

B. Authentication

C. MAC filtering

D. Social engineering

E. Antenna placement

100. Despite having imposed password policies on his network, compelling users to change their passwords frequently, create passwords of a specific length, and use complex passwords, Ralph has had several reports of account penetrations. The victims of the incidents had all apparently shared a "tip" suggesting that users cycle through the names of their children, nephews, nieces, and other relatives when forced to create new passwords, changing letters to numbers as needed. Which of the following actions can Ralph take to remedy the situation without creating a larger problem?

A. Distribute a list of common passwords that are insecure, such as those based on names, birth dates, etc.

B. Modify the password policies to force users to change passwords more frequently

C. Assign the users long passwords consisting of random-generated characters and change them often

D. Change the password history policy to a value greater than the number of children in any user's family

101. Which of the following devices are likely to have default credentials configured into them that attackers might know? (Choose all that apply.)

A. Wireless access points

B. Windows servers

C. Switches

D. Routers

102. One of the basic principles of network device hardening is to use secure protocols. Which of the following suggestions comply with this principle? (Choose all that apply.)

A. Use SSH instead of Telnet.

B. Use WEP instead of WPA2.

C. Use TKIP instead of AES.

D. Use HTTPS instead of HTTP.

103. On which of the following types of devices should you consider disabling unused ports as a security precaution? (Choose all that apply.)

    A. Hubs

    B. Servers

    C. Switches

    D. Wireless Access Points

104. For which of the following reasons is disabling the Service Set Identifier (SSID) broadcast of a wireless network to prevent unauthorized access a relatively weak method of device hardening?

    A. Attackers have ways of connecting to the network without the SSID.

    B. Attackers can capture packets transmitted over the network and read the SSID from them.

    C. Every access point's SSID is printed on a label on the back of the device.

    D. Attackers have software that can easily guess a network's SSID

105. Which of the following cannot be considered to be a server hardening policy?

    A. Disabling unnecessary services

    B. Disabling unused TCP and UDP ports

    C. Upgrading firmware

    D. Creating privileged user accounts

106. Which of the following are valid reasons not to disable unused switch ports? (Choose all that apply.)

    A. The datacenter is secured from unauthorized access.

    B. The unused ports are not patched in to wall jacks.

    C. The unused ports are left open to facilitate the on-boarding of new users.

    D. The switch is configured to use a MAC-based access control list.

107. Which of the following Windows password policies includes a provision to prevent users from specifying common passwords?

    A. Maximum password age

    B. Enforce password history

    C. Minimum password length

    D. Passwords must meet complexity requirements

108. Which of the following is not a method for hardening a Wireless Access Point (WAP)?

    A. Upgrading firmware

    B. Changing default credentials

    C. Generating new Pre-Shared Keys

    D. Deauthentication

109. Creating a policy instructing users to avoid passwords that use commonly shared information, such as birth dates and the names of children and pets, is an example of which of the following?

   A. Mitigation techniques

   B. Multifactor authentication

   C. Network hardening

   D. Access control

110. Which of the following are the default administrative user accounts found in Windows and Linux operating systems? (Choose all that apply.)

   A. Administrator

   B. root

   C. admin

   D. Control

111. Which of the following are network segmentation methods that can prevent intruders from gaining full access to a network? (Choose all that apply.)

   A. ACL

   B. VLAN

   C. NAC

   D. DMZ

112. Which of the following types of mitigation techniques is not applicable to servers?

   A. Role separation

   B. Applying ACLs

   C. File integrity monitoring

   D. DHCP snooping

113. Which of the following services are provided by Access Control Lists (ACLs)?

   A. Authentication

   B. Authorization

   C. Accounting

   D. Auditing

114. Which of the following terms describes the threat mitigation technique of deploying individual applications and services on virtual servers so that no more than one is endangered at any one time, rather than deploying multiple applications on a single server?

   A. Geofencing

   B. Network segmentation

   C. Role separation

   D. VLAN hopping

115. Role separation is a threat mitigation technique that is applied to which of the following types of network components?

   A. Switches

   B. Servers

   C. Routers

   D. Wireless Access Points (WAPs)

116. A server's firewall is configured using a default policy that does not allow any users remote access to the server unless an administrator creates a rule granting them access. Which of the following terms describes this default policy?

   A. Explicit allow

   B. Explicit deny

   C. Implicit allow

   D. Implicit deny

117. Dynamic ARP Inspection (DAI) is a feature in some network switches that prevents on-path (man-in-the-middle) attacks facilitated by Address Resolution Protocol (ARP) poisoning, the deliberate insertion of fraudulent information into the ARP cache. A switch with DAI inspects incoming ARP packets and rejects those that contain incorrect pairs of IP and Media Access Control (MAC) addresses. Which of the following is the means by which the switch compiles a table of the correct ARP information for comparison with the incoming packets?

   A. DHCP snooping

   B. Secure SNMP

   C. DNS name resolution

   D. NDP

118. Which of the following statements about DHCP snooping is not true?

   A. DHCP snooping detects rogue DHCP servers.

   B. DHCP snooping is implemented in network switches.

   C. DHCP snooping drops DHCP messages arriving over the incorrect port.

   D. DHCP snooping prevents DNS cache poisoning.

119. At which layer of the Open Systems Interconnection (OSI) reference model does Dynamic Host Configuration Protocol (DHCP) snooping operate?

   A. Data link

   B. Network

   C. Transport

   D. Application

120. Which of the following types of attacks on a network switch can a flood guard help to prevent?

   A. DNS poisoning

   B. War driving

   C. MAC flooding

   D. Evil twin

121. Which of the following protocols is a root guard designed to affect?

   A. EAP

   B. STP

   C. LDAP

   D. ARP

122. Which of the following mitigation techniques helps organizations maintain compliance to standards such as HIPAA and FISMA?

   A. File integrity monitoring

   B. Role separation

   C. Deauthentication

   D. Tamper detection

   E. Router Advertisement guard

123. Which of the following functions cannot be implemented using digital signatures?

   A. Integrity

   B. Nonrepudiation

   C. Segmentation

   D. Authentication

124. When Ralph digitally signs and encrypts a document with his private key, Alice can decrypt the document only by using Ralph's public key. As long as the private key is accepted to be secure, which of the following statements are true? (Choose all that apply.)

   A. Ralph cannot deny having created the document.

   B. No one has altered the document since Ralph sent it.

   C. No one but Ralph can have created the document.

   D. No one but Alice can decrypt and read the document.

125. When Alice encrypts a document with Ralph's public key, Ralph can decrypt the document only by using his private key. As long as the private key is accepted to be secure, which of the following statements are true? (Choose all that apply.)

   A. Alice cannot deny having created the document.

   B. No one has opened the document since Alice sent it.

   C. No one but Alice can have created the document.

   D. No one but Ralph can decrypt and read the document.

126. Which of the following types of patches is most typically applied to a hardware device?

 A. Firmware updates

 B. Driver updates

 C. Feature changes

 D. Vulnerability patches

127. Which of the following software releases is a fix designed to address one specific issue?

 A. A patch

 B. An update

 C. An upgrade

 D. A service pack

128. Unlike individual users, who usually have their operating system patches downloaded and installed automatically, corporate IT departments typically evaluate new patches before deploying them. Which of the following is not a common step in this evaluation process?

 A. Testing

 B. Researching

 C. Rolling back

 D. Backing up

129. Which of the following terms refers to the process of uninstalling a recently released patch to resume using the previous version?

 A. Backslide

 B. Downgrade

 C. Reset

 D. Rollback

130. How does Media Access Control (MAC) address filtering increase the security of a Wireless Local Area Network (WLAN)?

 A. By preventing access points from broadcasting their presence

 B. By allowing traffic sent to or from specific MAC addresses through the Internet firewall

 C. By substituting registered MAC addresses for unregistered ones in network packets

 D. By permitting only devices with specified MAC addresses to connect to an access point

 E. By isolating specific wireless clients from the rest of the network

131. Which of the following is the best description of geofencing?

 A. Something you have

 B. Something you know

 C. Something you do

 D. Somewhere you are

132. MAC filtering is an access control method used by which of the following types of hardware devices?

   A. Wireless Access Point

   B. RADIUS server

   C. Domain controller

   D. Smartcards

133. Which of the following technologies utilize Access Control Lists (ACLs) to limit access to network resources? (Choose all that apply.)

   A. NTFS

   B. LDAP

   C. WAP

   D. Kerberos

134. Alice is a consultant working in your office, who has been given the Secure Set Identifier (SSID) and the passphrase for the company's main wireless network, but she is unable to connect with her laptop. Which of the following security measures might be preventing her from connecting?

   A. MAC filtering

   B. Disabling SSID broadcast

   C. Geofencing

   D. Using WPA2

   E. Guest network isolation

135. On a wireless network, which of the following best describes an example of a captive portal?

   A. A switch port used to connect to other switches

   B. A web page with which a user must interact before being granted access to a wireless network

   C. A series of two doors through which people must pass before they can enter a secured space

   D. A web page stating that the user's computer has been locked and will only be unlocked after payment of a fee

136. A user attempting to connect to a WiFi hotspot in a coffee shop is taken to a web page that requires her to accept an End User License Agreement (EULA) before access to the network is granted. Which of the following is the term for such an arrangement?

   A. Captive portal

   B. Ransomware

   C. Port security

   D. Root guard

137. Which of the following is another term for a switching technique called port isolation?

A. Frame relay

B. Private VLAN

C. Site-to-site VPN

D. Screened subnet

138. The Internet of Things (IoT) encompasses a huge number of device types ranging from personal electronics to household appliances to medical equipment to industrial machinery. Many of these devices deal with sensitive information, and many perform critically important tasks. The field of IoT security is still in its infancy; there is no all-encompassing standard defining IoT protection protocols. IoT devices have vastly different security requirements and also vastly different functional capabilities, making it difficult to create a blanket protection mechanism for all of them. Which of the following are potentially viable methods for securing all IoT devices against attack? (Choose all that apply.)

A. Network segmentation

B. Network Access Control (NAC)

C. Security gateways

D. Firewalls

139. Which of the following statements about a switch's default VLAN are true? (Choose all that apply.)

A. Administrators must create a default VLAN when configuring a new switch.

B. The default VLAN on a switch cannot be deleted.

C. The default VLAN on most switches is designated as VLAN 0.

D. The default VLAN on a switch cannot be renamed.

140. Control plane policing (CPP or CoPP) is a feature on some routers and switches that limits the rate of traffic on the device's processor, to prevent Denial-of-Service (DoS) and reconnaissance attacks, using which of the following technologies?

A. IPSec

B. 802.1X

C. RA Guard

D. QoS

E. VLAN hopping

141. Which of the following technologies enables Virtual Private Network (VPN) clients to connect directly to each other, as well as to the VPN server at the home site?

A. VPN concentrator

B. DMVPN

C. SIP trunk

D. MPLS

E. Clientless VPN

142. Which of the following Virtual Private Network (VPN) protocols is generally considered to be obsolete?

A. IPSec

B. L2TP

C. PPTP

D. SSL/TLS

143. Which of the following Virtual Private Network (VPN) protocols does not provide encryption within the tunnel?

A. PPTP

B. IPSec

C. L2TP

D. SSL

144. Which of the following elements must be identical in both the client and server computers to establish a remote Wide Area Network (WAN) connection? (Choose all that apply.)

A. The WAN type

B. The data link layer protocol

C. The authentication method

D. The operating system

145. Which of the following is not a protocol that is typically used to secure communication between web servers and web browsers?

A. SSL

B. TLS

C. SSH

D. DTLS

146. Which of the following types of Virtual Private Network (VPN) connection is the best solution for allowing clients limited access to your corporate network?

A. Host-to-site

B. Site-to-site

C. Host-to-host

D. Extranet

147. Which of the following protocols is not used for remote control of computers?

A. RDP

B. TFTP

C. SSH

D. Telnet

148. Which of the following services is provided by the Remote Desktop Protocol (RDP)?

    A. Thin client computing

    B. Clientless virtual private networking

    C. Encrypted tunneling

    D. Unauthenticated file transfers

149. Which of the following types of Virtual Private Network (VPN) connection is the best solution for connecting a branch office to a corporate headquarters?

    A. Host-to-site

    B. Site-to-site

    C. Host-to-host

    D. Extranet

150. Ralph is a network administrator for a firm that is allowing employees to telecommute for the first time, and he is responsible for designing a remote access solution that will enable users to access network resources, such as company email and databases, securely. All of the remote users have been issued smartcards and will be connecting using Virtual Private Network (VPN) connections on company-supplied laptop computers running Windows 10 and equipped with card readers. The users will be logging on to the company network using their standard Active Directory Domain Services accounts, so it is important for Ralph to design a solution that provides the maximum protection for their passwords, both inside and outside the office. Which of the following authentication protocols should Ralph configure the remote access servers and the laptop computers to use?

    A. Password Authentication Protocol (PAP)

    B. Challenge Handshake Authentication Protocol (CHAP)

    C. Extensible Authentication Protocol (EAP)

    D. Microsoft Challenge Handshake Authentication Protocol (MSCHAPv2)

151. Which of the following remote access protocols provides users with full graphical control over a Windows computer? (Choose all that apply.)

    A. SSH

    B. RDP

    C. VNC

    D. Telnet

152. Ralph has come upon the term *virtual desktop*, and he is not exactly sure what it means. After performing some Internet searches, he finds multiple definitions. Which of the following is not one of the technologies that uses the term *virtual desktop*?

    A. A three-dimensional realization of a computer display created using a virtual reality hardware device

    B. A computer display with a virtual operating system desktop that is larger than can be displayed on a monitor

    C. A cloud-based Windows 10 deployment that enables users to access their desktops using any remote device

    D. A hardware device that projects a computer desktop on a screen, rather than displaying it on a monitor

153. Which of the following types of traffic are carried by the Remote Desktop Protocol (RDP)? (Choose all that apply.)

   A. Keystrokes

   B. Mouse movements

   C. Display information

   D. Application data

154. Which of the following types of traffic are transmitted by Virtual Network Computing (VNC)? (Choose all that apply.)

   A. Keystrokes

   B. Mouse movements

   C. Display information

   D. Application data

155. Which of the following types of traffic are carried by Telnet? (Choose all that apply.)

   A. Keystrokes

   B. Mouse movements

   C. Display information

   D. Application data

156. Which of the following describes the primary function of a Remote Desktop Gateway?

   A. Provides multiple users with Remote Desktop client access to one workstation

   B. Provides a single Remote Desktop client with simultaneous access to multiple workstations

   C. Enables remote users outside the network to access network workstations

   D. Enables remote users to access workstations without the need for a Remote Desktop client.

157. Which of the following statements about in-band management and out-of-band management are true? (Choose all that apply.)

   A. Out-of-band management tools do not provide access to the remote system's BIOS or UEFI firmware.

   B. Out-of-band management tools enable you to reinstall the operating system on a remote computer.

   C. Telnet, Secure Shell (SSH), and Virtual Network Computing (VNC) are in-band management tools.

   D. To perform out-of-band management on a device, it must have an IP address.

158. Which of the following statements best defines out-of-band management?

  A. Out-of-band management is a method for accessing network devices from a remote location.

  B. Out-of-band management is a method for accessing network devices using a direct cable connection.

  C. Out-of-band management is a method for accessing network devices using a connection to the system other than the production network to which the device is connected.

  D. Out-of-band management is a method for accessing network devices using any tool that operates over the production network to which the device is connected.

159. What four components are required for a computer to establish a remote Transmission Control Protocol/Internet Protocol (TCP/IP) connection?

  A. Common protocols

  B. Remote Access Service (RAS)

  C. A physical layer connection

  D. TCP/IP configuration

  E. Point-to-Point Tunneling Protocol (PPTP)

  F. Host and remote software

160. Which of the following statements explains why web browsing over a client-to-site Virtual Private Network (VPN) connection is usually so much slower than browsing locally?

  A. The browser application is running on the VPN server.

  B. The browser is using the remote network's Internet connection.

  C. The VPN tunnel restricts the amount of bandwidth available.

  D. VPN encryption is processor intensive.

161. In a site-to-site Virtual Private Network (VPN) connection, which of the following combinations of endpoint devices would most likely be involved?

  A. Two workstations

  B. A workstation and a server

  C. A workstation and a VPN concentrator

  D. Two VPN concentrators

162. In a client-to-site Virtual Private Network (VPN) connection, which of the following combinations of endpoint devices would most likely be involved?

  A. Two workstations

  B. A workstation and a server

  C. A workstation and a VPN concentrator

  D. Two VPN concentrators

163. Which of the following are the two most common types of Transport Layer Security/ Secure Sockets Layer (TLS/SSL) Virtual Private Network (VPN) connections? (Choose all that apply.)

    A. TLS/SSL client

    B. TLS/SSL portal

    C. TLS/SSL tunnel

    D. TLS/SSL gateway

164. In a host-to-host Virtual Private Network (VPN) connection, which of the following combinations of endpoint devices would most likely be involved?

    A. Two workstations

    B. A workstation and a server

    C. A workstation and a VPN concentrator

    D. Two VPN concentrators

165. Many managed switches and routers include a console port for administrative access, to which you can connect a laptop and run a terminal program to access the device's interface. Which of the following is the best term for this type of access to the device?

    A. Out-of-band

    B. In-band

    C. Client-to-site

    D. BYOD

166. Which of the following statements about running a site-to-site Virtual Private Network (VPN) connection to join two distant Local Area Networks (LANs) together, rather than using a Wide Area Network (WAN) connection, are generally true? (Choose all that apply.)

    A. The VPN is cheaper.

    B. The VPN is slower.

    C. The VPN is less secure.

    D. The VPN is harder to maintain.

167. Which of the following are examples of out-of-band device management? (Choose all that apply.)

    A. Logging on remotely from a network workstation

    B. Plugging a laptop into a console port

    C. Establishing a point-to-point modem connection

    D. Connecting dedicated ports on each device to a separate switch

168. Which of the following is not an advantage of the Virtual Network Computing (VNC) terminal emulation product over its competitors?

   A. VNC is free.

   B. VNC runs on many operating systems.

   C. VNC runs faster than the competition.

   D. VNC can run through a web browser.

169. Which of the following was the first Transmission Control Protocol/Internet Protocol (TCP/IP) terminal emulation program?

   A. Telnet

   B. SSH

   C. Windows Terminal Services

   D. Virtual Network Computing

170. Which of the following techniques do Virtual Private Networks (VPNs) use to secure the data that they transmit over the Internet? (Choose all that apply.)

   A. Tunneling

   B. Socketing

   C. Message integrity

   D. Authentication

171. Virtual Private Networks (VPNs) use tunneling, which is the process of encapsulating a data packet within another packet for transmission over a network connection, typically using the Internet. The system encrypts the entire encapsulated data packet for protection. Split tunneling is a variation of this method that provides which of the following advantages? (Choose all that apply.)

   A. Conservation of VPN bandwidth

   B. Access to local network devices while connected to the VPN

   C. Additional data integrity protection

   D. Faster data transmission through multiplexing

172. SSH was created to be an improvement on the Telnet terminal emulation program. In which of the following ways is it an improvement?

   A. SSH is faster than Telnet.

   B. SSH provides graphical terminal emulation.

   C. SSH encrypts passwords and data.

   D. SSH is less expensive than Telnet.

173. Remote Desktop Protocol (RDP) was created for use with which of the following terminal emulation programs?

    A. Windows Terminal Services

    B. Virtual Network Computing (VNC)

    C. Citrix WinFrame

    D. Telnet

174. Your company has two users who want to telecommute from home. They do not have any hardware or software configured or installed. They need to transfer files to the corporate network over a secure link. Your company has a Virtual Private Network (VPN) concentrator that uses Layer 2 Tunneling Protocol (L2TP) and Internet Protocol Security (IPSec). The users want to implement the fastest available service. Both of the users' homes are within 10,000 feet of a central office. Which of the following solutions address this scenario? (Choose all that apply.)

    A. Each user should install a modem and VPN client software, and configure it to dial through a local Internet Service Provider (ISP) to connect to the company server using L2TP and IPSec.

    B. Each user should establish a Digital Subscriber Line (DSL) connection by either ordering a new line or using the existing line. Each user then needs to install VPN client software and configure it to connect to the company server using L2TP and IPsec.

    C. Each user should establish a cable television (CATV) connection with a local broadband ISP. Each user then needs to install VPN client software and configure it to connect to the company server using L2TP and IPSec.

    D. Each user should install an Integrated Services Digital Network (ISDN) line in his or her house. Each user then needs to install VPN client software and configure it to dial through a local ISP to connect to the company server using L2TP and IPsec.

175. Which of the following is a PPP authentication protocol that enables users to authenticate using smartcards, badge readers, and fingerprint scanners, as well as usernames and passwords?

    A. PPTP

    B. PAP

    C. CHAP

    D. EAP

176. A laptop that is equipped with a fingerprint scanner that authenticates the user is using which of the following types of technology?

    A. Pattern recognition

    B. Hand geometry

    C. Biometrics

    D. Tamper detection

177. An IT department receives a shipment of 20 new computers, and Alice has been assigned the task of preparing them for deployment to end users. The first thing she does is affix a metal tag with a bar code on it to each computer. Which of the following terms best describes the function of this procedure?

   A. Asset tracking

   B. Tamper detection

   C. Device hardening

   D. Port security

178. Which of the following types of physical security is most likely to detect an insider threat?

   A. Smartcards

   B. Motion detection

   C. Video surveillance

   D. Biometrics

179. Which of the following physical security mechanisms can either "fail close" or "fail open"?

   A. Motion detectors

   B. Video cameras

   C. Honeypots

   D. Door locks

180. Smart lockers are storage devices that can provide users with access to supplies, deliveries, and other items using various security mechanisms. Which of the following are technologies that smart lockers can use to authenticate users and provide secure access to their contents?

   A. NFC

   B. RFID

   C. Bluetooth

   D. Biometrics

   E. PIN

   F. All of the above

181. Which of the following are common types of cameras used for video surveillance of secured network installations? (Choose all that apply.)

   A. IP

   B. LDAP

   C. CCTV

   D. NAC

182. Which of the following types of attack can best be prevented by implementing a program of employee education and training?

   A. Social engineering

   B. War driving

   C. Logic bomb

   D. Evil twin

183. Which of the following statements describes what it means when the automated lock on the door to a datacenter is configured to fail open?

   A. The door remains in its current state in the event of an emergency.

   B. The door locks in the event of an emergency.

   C. The door unlocks in the event of an emergency.

   D. The door continues to function using battery power in the event of an emergency.

184. A high security installation that requires entrants to submit to a retinal scan before the door unlocks is using which of the following types of technology?

   A. Pattern recognition

   B. Hand geometry

   C. Biometrics

   D. Tamper detection

185. Which of the following are means of preventing unauthorized individuals from entering a sensitive location, such as a datacenter? (Choose all that apply.)

   A. Biometric scans

   B. Identification badges

   C. Key fobs

   D. Motion detection

186. Which of the following security measures can monitor the specific activities of authorized individuals within sensitive areas?

   A. Video surveillance

   B. Identification badges

   C. Key fobs

   D. Motion detection

   E. Locking cabinets

187. Which of the following physical security devices can use passive RFIDs to enable an authorized user to enter a secured area? (Choose all that apply.)

   A. Key fob

   B. Keycard lock

   C. Proximity card

   D. Cypher lock

   E. Smart locker

188. Some key fobs used for authenticated entrance to a secured area have a keypad that requires the user to enter a PIN before the device is activated. Which of the following authentication factors is this device using? (Choose all that apply.)

A. Something you do

B. Something you have

C. Something you are

D. Something you know

189. Which of the following physical security devices can enable an authorized user to enter a secured area without any physical contact with the device? (Choose all that apply.)

A. Key fob

B. Keycard lock

C. Proximity card

D. Cypher lock

190. Video surveillance of sensitive areas, such as datacenters, can aid in the detection of which of the following types of attacks? (Choose all that apply.)

A. Social engineering

B. Evil twin

C. Brute-force

D. Insider threats

191. Which of the following statements is true when a biometric authentication procedure results in a false positive?

A. A user who should be authorized is denied access.

B. A user who should not be authorized is denied access.

C. A user who should be authorized is granted access.

D. A user who should not be authorized is granted access.

192. In the datacenter of a company involved with sensitive government data, all servers have crimped metal tags holding the cases closed. All of the hardware racks are locked in clear-fronted cabinets. All cable runs are installed in transparent conduits. These are all examples of which of the following physical security measures?

A. Tamper detection

B. Asset tracking

C. Geofencing

D. Port security

193. A secured government building that scans the faces of incoming people and compares them to a database of authorized entrants is using which of the following types of technology?

A. Pattern recognition

B. Hand geometry

C. Biometrics

D. Tamper detection

194. Which of the following is not a means of preventing physical security breaches to a network datacenter?

A. Badges

B. Locks

C. Key fobs

D. Tailgaters

195. Identification badges, key fobs, and access control vestibules all fall into which of the following categories of security devices?

A. Physical security

B. Data security

C. Asset tracking

D. Port security

196. Which of the following are not means of detecting intruders in a network datacenter? (Choose all that apply.)

A. Motion detection

B. Video surveillance

C. Biometrics

D. Smartcards

197. Which of the following statements describes what it means when the automated lock on the door to a datacenter is configured to fail closed?

A. The door remains in its current state in the event of an emergency.

B. The door locks in the event of an emergency.

C. The door unlocks in the event of an emergency.

D. The door continues to function using battery power in the event of an emergency.

198. After an incident in which your company's datacenter was penetrated by an intruder, the management has installed a double doorway at the entrance to the datacenter. The two doors have a small vestibule in between them, and one door must be closed before the other one can open. Which of the following terms describes this arrangement?

A. Server closet

B. Mantrap

C. Controlled entrance

D. Honeypot

199. Ralph's company has purchased new computers to replace some of the older workstations currently in use. Ralph has been assigned the task of preparing the old computers for disposal. They will be sold to a local secondhand dealer. For the dealer to accept the computers, they must have a functional operating system. Company policy also dictates that the computers be permanently wiped of all applications and data before disposal. Which of the following tasks will Ralph have to perform before the computers are sold? (Choose all that apply.)

    A. Reinstall the operating system

    B. Uninstall all applications

    C. Delete all data files

    D. Run a disk wipe utility

    E. Perform a factory reset

200. Which of the following is not one of the functions provided by TACACS+?

    A. Authentication

    B. Authorization

    C. Administration

    D. Accounting

Chapter 5

Network Troubleshooting

✓ **5.1 Explain the network troubleshooting methodology.**

- Identify the problem
    - Gather information
    - Question users
    - Identify symptoms
    - Determine if anything has changed
    - Duplicate the problem, if possible
    - Approach multiple problems individually
- Establish a theory of probable cause
    - Question the obvious
    - Consider multiple approaches
        - Top-to-bottom/bottom-to-top OSI model
        - Divide and conquer
- Test the theory to determine the cause
    - If the theory is confirmed, determine the next steps to resolve the problem
    - If the theory is not confirmed, reestablish a new theory or escalate
- Establish a plan of action to resolve the problem and identify potential effects
- Implement the solution or escalate as necessary
- Verify full system functionality and, if applicable, implement preventive measures
- Document findings, actions, outcomes, and lessons learned

✓ **5.2 Given a scenario, troubleshoot common cable connectivity issues and select the appropriate tools.**

- Specifications and limitations
  - Throughput
  - Speed
  - Distance
- Cable considerations
  - Shielded and unshielded
  - Plenum and riser-rated
- Cable application
  - Rollover cable/console cable
  - Crossover cable
  - Power over Ethernet
  - Common issues
  - Attenuation
  - Interference
  - Decibel (dB) loss
  - Incorrect pinout
  - Bad ports
  - Open/short
  - Light-emitting diode (LED) status indicators
  - Incorrect transceivers
  - Duplexing issues
  - Transmit and receive (TX/RX) reversed
  - Dirty optical cables
- Common tools
  - Cable crimper
  - Punchdown tool
  - Tone generator
  - Loopback adapter

- Optical time-domain reflectometer (OTDR)
- Multimeter
- Cable tester
- Wire map
- Tap
- Fusion splicers
- Spectrum analyzers
- Snips/cutters
- Cable stripper
- Fiber light meter

✓ **5.3 Given a scenario, use the appropriate network software tools and commands.**

- Software tools
  - WiFi analyzer
  - Protocol analyzer/packet capture
  - Bandwidth speed tester
  - Port scanner
  - iperf
  - NetFlow analyzers
  - Trivial File Transfer Protocol (TFTP) server
  - Terminal emulator
  - IP scanner
- Command line tool
  - ping
  - ipconfig/ifconfig/ip
  - nslookup/dig
  - traceroute/tracert
  - arp
  - netstat
  - hostname

- route
- telnet
- tcpdump
- nmap
- Basic network platform commands
  - show interface
  - show config
  - show route

✓ **5.4 Given a scenario, troubleshoot common wireless connectivity issues.**

- Specifications and limitations
  - Throughput
  - Speed
  - Distance
  - Received signal strength indication (RSSI) signal strength
  - Effective isotropic radiated power (EIRP)/ power settings
- Considerations
  - Antennas
    - Placement
    - Type
    - Polarization
  - Channel utilization
  - AP association time
  - Site survey
- Common issues
  - Interference
    - Channel overlap
  - Antenna cable attenuation/signal loss
  - RF attenuation/signal loss

- Wrong SSID
- Incorrect passphrase
- Encryption protocol mismatch
- Insufficient wireless coverage
- Captive portal issues
- Client disassociation issues

✓ **5.5 Given a scenario, troubleshoot general networking issues.**

- Considerations
  - Device configuration review
  - Routing tables
  - Interface status
  - VLAN assignment
  - Network performance baselines
- Common issues
  - Collisions
  - Broadcast storm
  - Duplicate MAC address
  - Duplicate IP address
  - Multicast flooding
  - Asymmetrical routing
  - Switching loops
  - Routing loops
  - Rogue DHCP server
  - DHCP scope exhaustion
  - IP setting issues
    - Incorrect gateway
    - Incorrect subnet mask
    - Incorrect IP address
    - Incorrect DNS

- Missing route
- Low optical link budget
- Certificate issues
- Hardware failure
- Host-based/network-based firewall settings
- Blocked services, ports, or addresses
- Incorrect VLAN
- DNS issues
- NTP issues
- BYOD challenges
- Licensed feature issues
- Network performance issues

1. Which of the following troubleshooting steps involves prioritizing trouble tickets based on the severity of the problem?

   A. Identify symptoms of the problem

   B. Establish a theory of probable cause

   C. Test the theory to determine cause

   D. Establish a plan of action to resolve the problem and identify potential effects

   E. Implement the solution or escalate as necessary

   F. Verify full system functionality and, if applicable, implement preventive measures

   G. Document findings, actions, and outcomes

2. Which of the following is considered a systemwide error?

   A. A problem with an order entry or customer service call center resource

   B. A problem with a router that affects only one Local Area Network (LAN)

   C. A fatal error that causes a single computer to fail

   D. A problem with an email server that affects all network users

3. Which of the following is a networkwide problem?

   A. A problem with an order entry or customer service call center resource

   B. A fatal error that causes a single computer to fail

   C. A problem with an application server that affects a single Local Area Network (LAN)

   D. A problem with a router that connects an entire network to the Internet

4. A user reports that she cannot connect to a server on her network. Ed wants to identify the scope of the problem, so he tries to reproduce the problem on the user's computer. The problem still remains. No other users are reporting this problem. What is the next logical step that Ed should perform to identify the affected area?

   A. Verify that the local router is forwarding traffic.

   B. Try performing the same task on another computer attached to the same segment.

   C. Verify that the server is configured properly.

   D. Verify that the switch the client is connected to is functioning.

5. Which of the following troubleshooting steps involves asking the user preliminary questions such as, "What were you doing when the problem occurred?"

   A. Identify the problem

   B. Establish a theory of probable cause

   C. Test the theory to determine cause

   D. Establish a plan of action to resolve the problem and identify potential effects

   E. Implement the solution or escalate as necessary

   F. Verify full system functionality and, if applicable, implement preventative measures

   G. Document findings, actions, and outcomes

6. When troubleshooting, you begin by taking steps to identify the problem. After you do this, which of the following steps should you perform next?

   A. Implement the solution

   B. Establish a plan of action

   C. Establish a theory of probable cause

   D. Verify full system functionality

7. In which troubleshooting step do you try to duplicate a network problem to logically and methodically eliminate elements that are not the source of the problem?

   A. Identify the problem.

   B. Establish a theory of probable cause.

   C. Test the theory to determine cause.

   D. Establish a plan of action to resolve the problem and identify potential effects.

   E. Implement the solution or escalate as necessary.

   F. Verify full system functionality and, if applicable, implement preventative measures.

   G. Document findings, actions, and outcomes.

8. Ralph is a first-tier technician working the help desk. After identifying a network problem submitted by multiple users, Ralph comes up with a theory specifying a possible source of the problem and sets about testing his theory. Unfortunately, testing indicates that Ralph's theory is wrong; the source he suspected is not the cause of the problem. Which of the following should not be the next step in Ralph's troubleshooting process?

   A. Reinterview the users to gather more information about the problem

   B. Escalate the problem to a second-tier technician

   C. Repeat the process of establishing a theory of probable cause

   D. Begin replacing components that might contribute to the problem

9. Ralph is a first-tier technician working the help desk. A user calls in, saying that when she turned her computer on that morning, nothing appeared on the screen. Which of the following should be Ralph's first question to the user?

   A. What is your computer's IP address?

   B. Have you applied the latest system updates?

   C. Are the computer and monitor plugged in to AC power?

   D. Has anyone else been using your computer?

10. You have a problem with a server or other network component that prevents many users from working. What type of problem is this?

   A. A networkwide problem

   B. A shared resource problem

   C. A systemwide problem

   D. A user application problem

11. A single Windows user suddenly cannot connect to any hosts on the network (local or remote). Alice interviews the user and finds out that he made some changes to his computer's Internet Protocol (IP) configuration properties. What should she do next?

   A. Run the `ipconfig` command to view the local configuration

   B. Check the Domain Name System (DNS) server to see if it is resolving IP hostnames

   C. Check the Windows Internet Name Service (WINS) server to see if it is resolving Network Basic Input/Output System (NetBIOS) names

   D. Verify that the router is functioning

12. Alice has a network with a Domain Name System (DNS) server, a proxy server, and an Internet router. A user is complaining that she suddenly cannot connect to hosts on her own Local Area Network (LAN) and other internal LANs, and she cannot access hosts on the Internet. What is the likeliest problem?

   A. The user's local configuration

   B. The proxy server

   C. The DNS server

   D. The router

13. Alice takes a call from a user who is unable to send email to a colleague in one of the company's branch offices. Alice begins by having the user try to send emails to different people at the branch office, to people in the local office, and to people on the Internet. She then checks the user's Internet Protocol (IP) configuration settings, the computer's Local Area Network (LAN) communication, and the cable connection to the network. Which of the following approaches is Alice using to troubleshoot the problem?

   A. OSI bottom-to-top

   B. Divide and conquer

   C. OSI top-to-bottom

   D. Question the obvious

14. Alice is working the help desk when a user calls and reports that she is unable to connect to the Internet. Which of the following steps is the one Alice is least likely to perform first when troubleshooting the problem?

   A. Check the configuration of the router connecting the LAN to the Internet

   B. Ask the user if she can access resources on the local network

   C. Check to see if anyone else is experiencing the same problem

   D. Check the user's job title to see if she is an important person in the company

15. In the standard troubleshooting methodology, which of the following steps appears last, but must actually be practiced throughout the troubleshooting process?

   A. Test the theory to determine cause

   B. Document findings, actions, and outcomes

   C. Verify full system functionality and, if applicable, implement preventive measures

   D. Implement the solution or escalate as necessary

E. Establish a plan of action to resolve the problem and identify potential effects

F. Establish a theory of probable cause

G. Identify the problem

16. In which troubleshooting step is a trouble ticket created?

A. Establish a theory of probable cause

B. Verify full system functionality and, if applicable, implement preventive measures

C. Implement the solution or escalate as necessary

D. Test the theory to determine cause

E. Identify the problem

F. Document findings, actions, and outcomes

G. Establish a plan of action to resolve the problem and identify potential effects

17. Which step of the troubleshooting model involves identifying whether hardware or software has been recently installed or reconfigured?

A. Identify symptoms

B. Establish a theory of probable cause

C. Establish a plan of action to resolve the problem and identify potential effects

D. Determine if anything has changed.

E. Test the theory to determine cause

F. Document findings, actions, and outcomes

18. Which step of the troubleshooting model involves replacing components until a faulty hardware device is identified?

A. Duplicate the problem

B. Gather information

C. Test the theory to determine the cause

D. Establish a plan of action to resolve the problem

E. Verify full system functionality

F. Document findings, actions, and outcomes

19. Which of the following are not general troubleshooting steps? (Choose all that apply.)

A. Identify the problem

B. Establish a theory of probable cause

C. Test the theory to determine cause

D. Verify that the client's Internet Protocol (IP) configuration is correct

E. Establish a plan of action to resolve the problem and identify potential effects

F. Verify that the router is forwarding.

G. Implement the solution or escalate as necessary

H. Verify full system functionality and, if applicable, implement preventive measures

I. Document findings, actions, and outcomes

20. Which of the following are reasons for documenting a network problem or incident? (Choose all that apply.)

    A. Documentation makes it easier to escalate calls to senior technicians.

    B. Documentation makes it easier to prioritize administrative tasks.

    C. Documentation makes it easier to prioritize each help call.

    D. Documentation makes it easier to escalate calls to first-tier technicians.

21. Which of the following statements about prioritizing help calls are true? (Choose all that apply.)

    A. Individual desktop problems take precedence over problems with shared resources.

    B. Problems with shared resources take precedence over individual desktop problems.

    C. Departmental problems take precedence over networkwide problems.

    D. Networkwide problems take precedence over departmental problems.

22. Which of the following statements about multitiered technical support organizations are true? (Choose all that apply.)

    A. Help calls are always escalated to second-tier technicians when they involve mission-critical network components such as routers.

    B. First-tier technicians generally handle desktop problems.

    C. Second-tier technicians are generally less experienced than first-tier technicians.

    D. First-tier technicians are generally less experienced than second-tier technicians.

23. Ed is a first-tier support technician. He receives the help calls listed here. His job is to prioritize them based on their severity. Which of the following should be the problem that receives the highest priority?

    A. A problem with an order entry or customer service call center resource that affects an entire department, with multiple Local Area Networks (LANs)

    B. A fatal error that causes a single computer to fail

    C. A problem with a mission-critical backbone router that affects an entire network

    D. A problem with an application server that affects a single LAN

24. Ed is a first-tier support technician. He receives the help calls listed here. His job is to prioritize them based on their severity. Which of the following should be the problem that receives the lowest priority?

    A. A problem with an order entry or customer service call center resource that affects an entire department, with multiple Local Area Networks (LANs)

    B. A fatal error that causes a single computer to fail

    C. A problem with a mission-critical backbone router that affects an entire network

    D. A problem with an application server that affects a single LAN

25. When you troubleshoot a network problem, it is possible to introduce another problem while attempting to fix the original one. In which step of the troubleshooting process should you be aware of the residual effects that changes might have on the network?

- **A.** Identify the problem
- **B.** Establish a theory of probable cause
- **C.** Test the theory to determine cause
- **D.** Establish a plan of action to resolve the problem
- **E.** Implement the solution or escalate as necessary
- **F.** Verify full system functionality
- **G.** Document findings, actions, and outcomes

26. In which troubleshooting step do you create a record of your activities and inform the user of what happened and why?

- **A.** Identify the problem
- **B.** Establish a theory of probable cause
- **C.** Test the theory to determine cause
- **D.** Establish a plan of action to resolve the problem and identify potential effects
- **E.** Implement the solution or escalate as necessary
- **F.** Verify full system functionality and, if applicable, implement preventive measures
- **G.** Document findings, actions, and outcomes

27. On Monday morning, Alice arrives at work to find multiple email and telephone messages from users who are unable to access the Accounting department's file server. Which of the following are the best questions to ask during the beginning stage of the troubleshooting process? (Choose two.)

- **A.** What has changed since the users were last able to access the server?
- **B.** Are there any software updates that Alice should apply to the server?
- **C.** Has the server suffered a hard disk failure?
- **D.** Which users are reporting a problem, and where are they located?

28. A user calls Alice at the help desk to report that her mouse has stopped working, she cannot access the Internet, and all of her email has disappeared from her inbox. Which of the following would be the best course of action for Alice to take?

- **A.** Create a separate trouble ticket for each problem
- **B.** Escalate the call to a senior technician
- **C.** Have the caller's computer replaced with a new one
- **D.** Send a technician to the user's site to address all of the problems

29. Alice receives a call in which a user reports that he is unable to send print jobs to the network-attached workgroup printer near his desk. Which of the following tasks should Alice perform first?

- **A.** Reinstall the printer driver on the user's workstation.
- **B.** Test network connectivity to the printer using the ping utility.
- **C.** Examine the switches to which the user's workstation and the printer are connected.
- **D.** Check to see if there are printer firmware upgrades available.

30. Which of the following types of Unshielded Twisted Pair (UTP) wiring faults cannot be detected by a wiremap tester?

   A. Split pairs

   B. Open circuits

   C. Short circuits

   D. Transposed wires

31. After connecting a tone generator to the green wire at one end of a twisted-pair cable run, Ralph proceeds to the other end of the cable and touches the locator to each of the eight pins in turn. The green wire and the green striped wire both produce a tone. What type of wiring fault has Ralph discovered?

   A. Split pair

   B. Far end crosstalk

   C. Transposed wires

   D. Short circuit

   E. Delay skew

32. Which of the following types of cables is used to connect a terminal to the console port of a router or switch?

   A. Rollover

   B. Straight through

   C. Crossover

   D. Plenum

   E. Shielded

   F. Tap

33. Which of the following types of patch cables is used to connect a computer to a wall plate?

   A. Straight through

   B. Crossover

   C. Rollover

   D. Plenum

34. What is the name for a device that determines the length of a cable by transmitting a signal at one end and measuring how long it takes for a reflection of the signal to return from the other end?

   A. Fox and hound tester

   B. Wiremap tester

   C. Time-domain reflectometer

   D. Voltage event recorder

   E. Butt set

   F. Spectrum analyzer

35. A routine test of a newly installed twisted-pair cable run with a wiremap tester indicates that there is a short circuit on one of the wires. Which of the following procedures might possibly correct the fault?

A. Use a different pinout on both ends of the cable

B. Replace the connectors at both ends of the cable run

C. Move the cable away from any potential sources of electromagnetic interference

D. Use a higher grade of Unshielded Twisted Pair (UTP) cable

36. Ralph is a new hire working on a network that uses Category 5 (Cat 5) Unshielded Twisted Pair (UTP) cable, which was installed several years ago. Over time, some of the paper labels that the original cable installers used to identify the wall plates and patch panel connectors have worn away or fallen off. As a result, Ralph has quite a few cable runs that he is unable to identify. After checking with his supervisor, Ralph discovers that the company has no cable testing equipment and is unwilling to hire a consultant just to identify cable runs. What is the most inexpensive tool Ralph can use to associate unlabeled wall plates with the correct patch panel ports?

A. A wiremap tester

B. A cable certifier

C. A tone generator and locator

D. A time-domain reflectometer (TDR)

37. Which of the following devices is an essential tool for technicians working on telephone cables but is not needed for data networking cable installations?

A. Tone generator and locator

B. Wiremap tester

C. Cable certifier

D. Butt set

38. Which of the following tools might you use when connecting internal twisted-pair cable runs to the keystone connectors that snap into wall plates? (Choose all that apply.)

A. A crimper

B. A punchdown tool

C. A pigtail splicer

D. A wire stripper

E. A fusion splicer

39. Which of the following tools can you use to test the optical loss in a fiber-optic cable?

A. An OLTS

B. A TDR

C. A tone generator and locator

D. A wiremap tester

40. Which of the following troubleshooting tools can test cabling for length, attenuation, near-end crosstalk (NEXT), equal level far-end crosstalk (ELFEXT), propagation delay, delay skew, and return loss?

    A. Wiremap tester

    B. Cable certifier

    C. Time-domain reflectometer (TDR)

    D. Optical loss test set (OLTS)

    E. Spectrum analyzer

41. Under which of the following conditions is a cable installer required to use plenum cable?

    A. When cables run close to sources of electromagnetic interference (EMI)

    B. When cables are running through building air flow spaces

    C. When data and voice traffic will be running over the same cable

    D. When cables are running through areas of low temperature

42. Which of the following troubleshooting tools is not used to test copper cabling installations?

    A. Wiremap tester

    B. Multimeter

    C. Tone generator and locator

    D. OTDR

43. Which of the following devices is not one of the tools generally used by a data networking cable installer?

    A. Tone generator and locator

    B. Wiremap tester

    C. Butt set

    D. Cable certifier

44. Ralph is a new hire for a consulting firm that frequently performs cable installations. He is trying to learn more about the tools needed to install internal cable runs. To that end, which of the following statements about cable crimpers has Ralph found to be true?

    A. Cable installers use a crimper to attach keystone connectors to lengths of bulk cable.

    B. Cable installers use a crimper to attach RJ45 connectors to lengths of bulk cable.

    C. You need to purchase a separate crimper for each type of cable to which you want to attach connectors.

    D. Making your own patch cables by applying connectors yourself is always more economical than buying prefabricated patch cables.

45. Which of the following statements about cable certifiers are true? (Choose all that apply.)

    A. A cable certifier eliminates the need for tools like tone generators and wiremap testers.

    B. Cable certifiers are the most inexpensive cable testing solution.

    C. Cable certifiers must be reconfigured whenever a new cable specification is standardized.

    D. Cable certifiers can only test copper-based cables.

46. Alice is the network administrator of her company's network. The company has just moved into a building that has existing Category 6 (Cat 6) Unshielded Twisted Pair (UTP) cabling. However, none of the cable connections have been labeled, and Alice is trying to identify and document where each cable run starts and ends. Which tools can Alice use for this purpose? (Choose all that apply.)

    A. A packet sniffer

    B. A loopback adapter

    C. A tone generator and locator

    D. A wiremap tester

47. Which of the following tools can you use to create your own twisted pair patch cables? (Choose all that apply.)

    A. Punchdown tool

    B. Crimper

    C. Pliers

    D. Wire stripper

48. Which of the following cable installation tools is likely to be the most expensive?

    A. A crimper

    B. A cable certifier

    C. A punchdown tool

    D. A wiremap tester

49. What is the function of the tool shown in the following figure?

Reprinted from *CompTIA Network+ Study Guide: Exam N10-006, Third Edition* by Todd Lammle (Wiley, 2015)

  A. By placing the tool at one end of a wire, it generates a tone that can be detected at the other end.

  B. To connect a bulk cable to a keystone connector, you use the tool to punch each wire down into the correct receptacle on the connector.

  C. By touching the end of the tool to a copper cable, you can detect and measure the electrical current flowing through it.

  D. By connecting the tool to the end of a fiber-optic cable, you can measure the length of the cable run.

50. What is the function of the tool shown in the following figure?

Reprinted from *CompTIA Network+ Study Guide: Exam N10-006, Third Edition* by Todd Lammle (Wiley, 2015)

  A. When you place the tool at one end of a wire, it generates a tone that can be detected at the other end.

  B. To connect a bulk cable to a keystone connector, you use the tool to punch each wire down into the correct receptacle on the connector.

  C. By touching the end of the tool to a copper cable, you can detect and measure the electrical current flowing through it.

  D. By connecting the tool to the end of a fiber-optic cable, you can measure the length of the cable run.

51. What is the function of the tool shown in the following figure?

Reprinted from *CompTIA Network+ Study Guide: Exam N10-006, Third Edition* by Todd Lammle (Wiley, 2015)

A. When you place the tool at one end of a wire, it generates a tone that can be detected at the other end.

B. To connect a bulk cable to a keystone connector, you use the tool to punch each wire down into the correct receptacle on the connector.

C. By touching the end of the tool to a copper cable, you can detect and measure the electrical current flowing through it.

D. By connecting the tool to the end of a fiber-optic cable, you can measure the length of the cable run.

52. What is the function of the tool shown in the following figure?

Reprinted from *CompTIA Network+ Study Guide: Exam N10-006, Third Edition* by Todd Lammle (Wiley, 2015)

A. When you place the tool at one end of a wire, it generates a tone that can be detected at the other end.

B. To attach a bulk cable end to an RJ45 connector, you use the tool to squeeze the connector closed, forcing the wire ends to contact the connector's pins.

C. By touching the end of the tool to a copper cable, you can detect and measure the electrical current flowing through it.

D. By connecting the clips to pins in a punchdown block, you can access telephone circuits in order to test them or place telephone calls.

53. What is the name of the tool shown in the following figure?

Reprinted from *CompTIA Network+ Study Guide: Exam N10-006, Third Edition* by Todd Lammle (Wiley, 2015)

A. Butt set

B. Crimper

C. Tone generator and locator

D. Punchdown tool

54. Ralph has to spend the day completing a twisted-pair cable installation in his office. Contractors have already pulled the cables through the walls and ceilings. Ralph only has to attach connectors to the ends of the cables, both internal cable runs and patch cables. Which of the following tools will Ralph need? (Choose all that apply.)

A. Telepole

B. Crimper

C. Punchdown tool

D. Pigtail splicer

55. Ralph is testing a twisted-pair cable run using a tone generator and locator. When he applies the tone generator to one particular wire at one end of the cable, he fails to detect a tone at the other end. Which of the following faults has Ralph discovered?

A. Open

B. Short

C. Split pair

D. Crosstalk

56. Ralph is testing a twisted-pair cable run using a tone generator and locator. When he applies the tone generator to a particular pin at one end of the cable, he detects a tone on two pins at the other end. Which of the following faults has Ralph discovered?

A. Open

B. Short

C. Split pair

D. Crosstalk

57. Ralph is using a tone generator and locator to test some newly installed twisted-pair cable runs on his network. Which of the following cable faults will he be unable to detect?

A. Open

B. Short

C. Split pair

D. Transposed pairs

58. Which of the following cable faults increases a twisted-pair cable's susceptibility to crosstalk?

A. Open

B. Short

C. Split pair

D. Transposed pairs

59. Alice has been told by a consultant that the newly installed twisted-pair cable runs on her network might have split pairs. Which of the following cable testing tools can she use to detect split pairs?

A. Tone generator and locator

B. Wiremap tester

C. Multimeter

D. Cable certifier

60. Ralph is testing some newly installed twisted-pair cable runs on his network using a wiremap tester, and he has found one run that appears to have a cable break. However, the connectors at both ends are correctly installed, so the break must be somewhere inside the cable itself, which is nearly 100 meters long. Which of the following tools can Ralph use to determine the location of the cable break? (Choose all that apply.)

A. Tone generator and locator

B. Multimeter

C. Time-domain reflectometer

D. Cable certifier

61. Alice's company has moved to a building that was prewired for twisted-pair Ethernet. However, since installing the company's Gigabit Ethernet equipment using the existing cable runs, performance has been poor. After performing some packet captures and analyzing the traffic samples, Alice discovers that there are a great many Ethernet frames being retransmitted. Next, she examines the cable runs in the drop ceilings. They do not appear to be overly long, and they do not appear to run near any major sources of electromagnetic interference. Which of the following could be the problem?

A. Some of the cable runs are using T568A pinouts and some are using T568B.

B. The cables only have two wire pairs connected, instead of four.

C. The existing cable is not rated for use with Gigabit Ethernet.

D. There are mismatched transceivers at the cable ends.

62. Ralph is working on a new twisted-pair network cable installation on which the individual cable runs were not properly labeled as they were pulled. Ralph now has to trace each of the cable ends in the office area to the correct cable end in the data center and label them correctly. Which of the following tools should Ralph use to locate the correct cable in a bundle of unlabeled cable ends?

A. Cable certifier

B. Tone generator and locator

C. OTDR

D. Multimeter

63. Ralph's company has engaged a firm of wiring contractors to install some new fiber-optic cable runs. Before the cables are connected to any devices, Ralph wants to confirm that they have been installed to proper specifications. He brings in a contractor from another firm to test the cable runs. To test each cable run, the contractor connects a light source to one end of the cable and a measuring device to the other end. Which of the following is the correct name for this testing device?

A. Optical power meter

B. OLTS

C. OTDR

D. Multimeter

64. Ed is experiencing poor network performance on some new twisted-pair cable runs. After ruling out all other causes, he tests the cables with a tone generator and locator and finds no faults. Finally, he examines the cable connectors more closely and finds that, while the pins at one end of the cable are correctly connected to their corresponding pins at the other end, in some cases there are two solid color wires twisted together in a pair. Which of the following types of faults has Ed discovered?

A. Open circuit

B. Short circuit

C. Split pairs

D. Transposed wires

65. Which of the following terms describes the progressive weakening of transmitted signals as they travel along a network medium?

  A. Absorption

  B. Latency

  C. Attenuation

  D. Crosstalk

66. After experiencing some problems with devices connected to the company's fiber-optic network, Alice brings in a contractor to test the fiber-optic cable runs. The contractor detects a significant amount of decibel (dB) loss in some of the cable runs, which could be the source of the problems. Which of the following are possible causes of the decibel loss? (Choose all that apply.)

  A. Electromagnetic interference

  B. Dirty optical cables

  C. Excessive cable length

  D. Signal crosstalk

67. Which of the following should a troubleshooter look for when a duplex mismatch is suspected on an Ethernet network? (Choose all that apply.)

  A. Collisions

  B. Runt frames

  C. CRC errors

  D. Failed ping tests

68. Ed is trying to troubleshoot a problem that has caused a wired network connection to fail completely. Which of the following wired network problems will cause a complete failure of a network connection? (Choose all that apply.)

  A. Bottleneck

  B. Speed mismatch

  C. Duplex mismatch

  D. TX/RX reversal

  E. Bad switch port

69. Ed is trying to troubleshoot a problem that has caused a wired network connection to slow down noticeably. Which of the following wired network problems will cause a drastic slowdown of a network connection, without causing it to fail completely? (Choose all that apply.)

  A. Bottleneck

  B. Speed mismatch

  C. Duplex mismatch

  D. TX/RX reversal

70. Ed has discovered that some of the twisted-pair cable runs on his newly installed Ethernet network are well over 100 meters long. Which of the following problems is his network likely to experience due to cable segments that are greater than the specified length?

A. Jitter

B. Attenuation

C. Crosstalk

D. EMI

71. Ed is trying to troubleshoot a problem with his wired network, and his research has led him to a list of possible network faults. The list is rather old, however, and Ed is wondering if some of the problems are relevant. Which of the following wired network problems no longer occur with modern Gigabit Ethernet switches and network adapters in their default configurations? (Choose all that apply.)

A. Bottleneck

B. Speed mismatch

C. Duplex mismatch)

D. Transmit and Receive (TX/RX reversal

72. Ed has discovered that some of the twisted-pair cables on his newly installed network are running right alongside fluorescent light fixtures in the drop ceiling. Which of the following problems is the network likely to experience due to the cables' proximity to the fixtures?

A. Jitter

B. Attenuation

C. Crosstalk

D. EMI

73. Which of the following indicators can you use to determine whether an adapter is connected to a functioning hub or switch?

A. Speed Light-Emitting Diode (LED)

B. Collision LED

C. Link pulse LED

D. Status LED

74. Ralph wants to use Power over Ethernet (PoE) to supply power to security cameras located throughout his company's datacenter. The Ethernet network is currently running at Gigabit Ethernet speed, but Ralph is planning to downgrade the camera connections to 100Base-TX, because that standard has two wire pairs free for the transmission of power. Which of the following statements about Ralph's plan is true?

A. Ralph's planning is correct; only 10Base-T and 100Base-TX support PoE.

B. Ralph's plan will not work because 100Base-TX is not compatible with PoE.

C. Ralph's plan will work, but it is not necessary to downgrade the connections to 100Base-TX.

D. Ralph's plan will not work, because PoE cannot supply enough power for the cameras.

75. Delays in the transmission of data packets over a network can result in temporary service interruptions, dropouts, or even data loss. Which of the following terms is used to describe these delays?

   A. Crosstalk

   B. Electromagnetic interference (EMI)

   C. Jitter

   D. Attenuation

76. Ralph's company has expanded to include an additional building on the far end of the corporate campus, approximately 4 kilometers away from the building housing the datacenter. A single-mode fiber-optic cable connection has been installed between the new building and the datacenter for a 1000Base-BX10 connection, but the cable is not yet connected to a transceiver at the datacenter end. Noticing that there is a 1000Base-SX transceiver module in the datacenter storeroom, Ralph is wondering if he could use this on the new cable run. Which of the following are reasons why this might not work? (Choose all that apply.)

   A. Transceiver mismatch

   B. Incorrect cable type

   C. Excessive cable length

   D. Wavelength mismatch

77. Alice has recently installed some new computers onto her Gigabit Ethernet network. To ensure the best possible network performance, she has configured the network adapters in the new computers to run at 1 Gbps speed and use full-duplex communication. Once the computers are in service, however, Alice begins getting reports of extremely poor network performance on those machines. She tries running some ping tests and does not see any problem. She calls in a consultant to perform a packet analysis, and the consultant detects large numbers of packet collisions, late collisions, Cyclic Redundancy Check (CRC) errors, and runt frames. Which of the following could conceivably be the problem?

   A. Duplex mismatch

   B. TX/RX reversal

   C. Incorrect cable type

   D. Damaged cables

78. Ralph is attempting to access a Domain Name System (DNS) server located on the other side of a router, but his attempt fails with an error stating that the destination port UDP 53 is unreachable. His first step in troubleshooting the problem is to try using the nslookup utility to access that specific DNS server. This too fails. Next, he uses the ping utility with the DNS server's Internet Protocol (IP) address. The ping test is successful, indicating that the server is up and running. Which of the following are possible causes of the problem? (Choose all that apply.)

   A. The router connecting the networks is not running DNS and will not forward this type of datagram.

   B. The DNS process on the remote server is not running.

   C. The TCP/IP host configuration on your computer is improperly configured.

   D. The TCP/IP host configuration on the DNS server computer is improperly configured.

   E. There is a firewall blocking the DNS server's UTP 53 port.

79. Which of the following application layer protocols includes a program that enables a user to log on to a network device and execute commands on the remote system using a command-line interface? (Choose all that apply.)

   A. Telnet

   B. File Transfer Protocol (FTP)

   C. Simple Network Management Protocol (SNMP)

   D. Domain Name System (DNS)

   E. Nslookup

80. Which of the following Windows tools uses Internet Control Message Protocol (ICMP) messages and manipulates IPv4 time-to-live values to illustrate the route packets take through an internetwork?

   A. `ping`

   B. `netstat`

   C. `route`

   D. `tracert`

   E. `nslookup`

   F. `hostname`

81. Users are having trouble connecting to Internet hosts. Alice suspects that there is a problem with the Domain Name System (DNS) server, and she wants to verify this. Which of the following steps can she take to determine whether the DNS server is resolving Internet hostnames?

   A. Issue the `ipconfig` command from a local workstation

   B. Try to connect to a host using the IP address instead of the hostname

   C. Ping the DNS server to see if it is functioning

   D. Use the `tracert` command to test the functionality of the DNS server

82. Which of the following utilities can you use to view resource record information on a particular Domain Name System (DNS) server? (Choose all that apply.)

   A. `netstat`

   B. `nslookup`

   C. `nbtstat`

   D. `arp`

   E. `dig`

83. Which of the following Windows command-line utilities produced the output shown here?

```
Interface: 192.168.2.24 --- 0x2
  internet Address      Physical Address     Type
  192.168.2.2           d4-ae-52-bf-c3-2d    dynamic
  192.168.2.20          00-26-c7-7e-00-e0    dynamic
```

```
192.168.2.22       00-90-a9-a2-43-8f    dynamic
192.168.2.27       1c-c1-de-ca-1f-12    dynamic
192.168.2.28       30-f7-72-38-e9-1d    dynamic
192.168.2.255      ff-ff-ff-ff-ff-ff    static
224.0.0.22         01-00-5e-00-00-16    static
224.0.0.251        01-00-5e-00-00-fb    static
224.0.0.252        01-00-5e-00-00-fc    static
224.0.0.253        01-00-5e-00-00-fd    static
239.255.255.250    01-00-5e-7f-ff-fa    static
255.255.255.255    ff-ff-ff-ff-ff-ff    static
```

A. ping

B. tracert

C. netstat

D. arp

E. hostname

84. Which of the following Windows command-line utilities produced the output shown here?

```
1    <1 ms    <1 ms    <1 ms RT-N86U [192.168.2.99]
2     3 ms     5 ms     4 ms 192.168.3.1
3    25 ms    30 ms    17 ms 10.172.1.1
4    20 ms    19 ms    29 ms gateway-BE1-EBlocal.eh.lpod.net [207.44.123.89]
5    26 ms    29 ms    29 ms gateway-be1-abn2abn2.ab.lpod.net [207.44.127.49]
6      *        *         * Request timed out.
7   111 ms   108 ms   109 ms be38.trmc0215-01.ars.mgmt.hox3.kkg [184.168.0.69]
8   108 ms   107 ms   108 ms be38.trmc0215-01.ars.mgmt.hox3.kkg [184.168.0.69]
9   106 ms   109 ms   108 ms ip-216-69-188-102.ip.srvr.net [216.69.188.102]
10  106 ms   108 ms    99 ms p3nlh153.shr.prod.phx3.srvr.net [97.74.144.153]
```

A. ping

B. tracert

C. netstat

D. arp

E. hostname

85. Which of the following Windows command-line utilities produced the output shown here?

```
Reply from 97.74.144.153: bytes=32 time=111ms TTL=53
Reply from 97.74.144.153: bytes=32 time=109ms TTL=53
Reply from 97.74.144.153: bytes=32 time=108ms TTL=53
Reply from 97.74.144.153: bytes=32 time=109ms TTL=53
Statistics for 97.74.144.153:
```

```
   Packets: Sent = 4, Received = 4, Lost = 0 (0% loss),
Approximate round trip times in milli-seconds:
   Minimum = 108ms, Maximum = 111ms, Average = 109ms
```

A. ping

B. tracert

C. netstat

D. arp

E. hostname

86. Which of the following Windows command-line utilities produced the output shown here?

```
Active Connections
  Proto Local Address          Foreign Address        State
  TCP   127.0.0.1:5327         CM412:49770            ESTABLISHED
  TCP   127.0.0.1:49770        CM412:5327             ESTABLISHED
  TCP   127.0.0.1:52114        CM412:52115            ESTABLISHED
  TCP   192.168.2.24:2869      RT-M96U:42173          ESTABLISHED
  TCP   192.168.2.24:2869      RT-M96U:44356          ESTABLISHED
  TCP   192.168.2.24:51386     autodiscover:https     ESTABLISHED
  TCP   192.168.2.24:51486     autodiscover:https     ESTABLISHED
  TCP   192.168.2.24:51535     108-174-11-1:https     ESTABLISHED
  TCP   192.168.2.24:51578     aki-cache:http         TIME_WAIT
  TCP   192.168.2.24:51579     ia3s43-in-f142:http    TIME_WAIT
  TCP   192.168.2.24:51591     208:https              TIME_WAIT
  TCP   192.168.2.24:51592     208:https              TIME_WAIT
  TCP   192.168.2.24:51593     198.8.20.212:https     TIME_WAIT
```

A. ping

B. tracert

C. netstat

D. arp

E. hostname

87. Which of the following command-line utilities is capable of performing the same basic function as traceroute or tracert?

A. ping

B. pathping

C. netstat

D. route

88. Which TCP/IP utility should you use to most easily identify a malfunctioning router on your network?

   A. ifconfig

   B. ping

   C. traceroute

   D. netstat

89. Which of the following protocols does the ping program never use to carry its messages?

   A. Ethernet

   B. ICMP

   C. IP

   D. UDP

   E. TCP

90. Which of the following commands displays the routing table on the local computer?

   A. arp -r

   B. netstat -r

   C. ifconfig -r

   D. telnet -r

91. Which of the following command lines will produce the output shown in the figure?

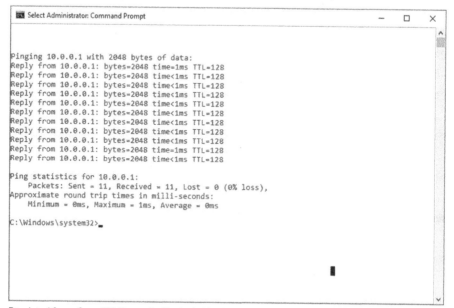

```
Select Administrator: Command Prompt                                          –   □   ✕

Pinging 10.0.0.1 with 2048 bytes of data:
Reply from 10.0.0.1: bytes=2048 time=1ms TTL=128
Reply from 10.0.0.1: bytes=2048 time<1ms TTL=128
Reply from 10.0.0.1: bytes=2048 time<1ms TTL=128
Reply from 10.0.0.1: bytes=2048 time<1ms TTL=128
Reply from 10.0.0.1: bytes=2048 time<1ms TTL=128
Reply from 10.0.0.1: bytes=2048 time<1ms TTL=128
Reply from 10.0.0.1: bytes=2048 time<1ms TTL=128
Reply from 10.0.0.1: bytes=2048 time<1ms TTL=128
Reply from 10.0.0.1: bytes=2048 time<1ms TTL=128
Reply from 10.0.0.1: bytes=2048 time=1ms TTL=128
Reply from 10.0.0.1: bytes=2048 time<1ms TTL=128

Ping statistics for 10.0.0.1:
    Packets: Sent = 11, Received = 11, Lost = 0 (0% loss),
Approximate round trip times in milli-seconds:
    Minimum = 0ms, Maximum = 1ms, Average = 0ms

C:\Windows\system32>_
```

Reprinted from *CompTIA Network+ Study Guide: Exam N10-006, Third Edition* by Todd Lammle (Wiley, 2015)

    A. `ping 10.0.0.1 -t`

    B. `ping 10.0.0.1 -n 2048`

    C. `ping 10.0.0.1 -l 2048 -n 11`

    D. `ping 10.0.0.1 -l 2048 -t`

    E. `ping 10.0.0.1 -n 2048 -t 11`

92. Which of the following commands enables you to view the Address Resolution Protocol (ARP) table stored in memory?

    A. `arp -c`

    B. `arp -d`

    C. `arp -a`

    D. `arp -s`

93. Which of the following command-line utilities enables you to generate Domain Name System (DNS) request messages?

    A. `ifconfig`

    B. `nslookup`

    C. `nbtstat`

    D. `netstat`

    E. `iperf`

94. Which of the following command-line utilities enables you to view the Internet Protocol (IP) configuration on a Unix or Linux host?

    A. `ifconfig`

    B. `nslookup`

    C. `ipconfig`

    D. `netstat`

    E. `iperf`

95. Which of the following parameters causes the ping tool to transmit messages continually until manually halted?

    A. `-n`

    B. `-t`

    C. `-i`

    D. `-a`

96. Which of the following Windows commands enables you to delete the entire ARP cache?

    A. `arp -c *`

    B. `arp -d *`

    C. `arp -a`

    D. `arp -s`

97. Ralph has been advised to check his Linux web servers for open ports that attackers might be able to use to penetrate the servers' security. Which of the following utilities can Ralph use to do this?

A. `tcpdump`

B. `dig`

C. `iptables`

D. `nmap`

E. `iperf`

98. While performing a protocol analysis, Alice notes that there are many Internet Control Message Protocol (ICMP) packets in her captured traffic samples. She attributes these to her frequent use of Transmission Control Protocol/Internet Protocol (TCP/IP) trouble-shooting tools. Which of the following utilities are used to test network layer characteristics of a host using ICMP messages? (Choose all that apply.)

A. `ipconfig`

B. `netstat`

C. `ping`

D. `tracert`

99. Which of the following parameters enables you to specify the Time to Live (TTL) value of the messages that `ping` transmits?

A. `-n`

B. `-t`

C. `-i`

D. `-a`

100. Ralph is the network administrator of his company's network. He has had three users call the help desk to report that they are having problems connecting to the local application server. Comparing their stories, Ralph suspects that their Transmission Control Protocol (TCP) connections are being dropped. The users are not having problems connecting to any other hosts on the network. To troubleshoot this problem, Ralph decides to use a protocol analyzer. He wants to store and view only the traffic relating to the hosts and server that are having problems. How can Ralph do this?

A. Configure a display filter

B. Configure a capture filter

C. Set a trap on the analyzer

D. Configure both a capture filter and a display filter

101. Ralph is the administrator of his company's network. All of the users on the network are reporting that they are having difficulty connecting to a particular application server that is located on a perimeter network, on the other side of a router. The users are not having trouble connecting to local hosts. Which of the following troubleshooting tools can Ralph use to verify the network layer functionality of the application server and the router? (Choose all that apply.)

- **A.** ping
- **B.** route
- **C.** arp
- **D.** traceroute

102. Which of the following troubleshooting tools enables you to copy all of the packets transmitted over a network to a buffer, interpret the protocols used in the packets, and display the output?

- **A.** Event Viewer
- **B.** Traffic monitor
- **C.** Protocol analyzer
- **D.** Management console

103. Which of the following is not a tool that runs only on Unix or Linux systems?

- **A.** tcpdump
- **B.** dig
- **C.** iptables
- **D.** ifconfig
- **E.** route

104. Which of the following Windows command-line utilities produced the output shown here?

```
Server: trv213.pljd.net
Address: 203.186.120.114
Non-authoritative answer:
Name: microsoft.com
Addresses: 104.43.195.251
          23.100.122.175
          23.96.52.53
          191.239.213.197
          104.40.211.35
```

- **A.** nslookup
- **B.** pathping
- **C.** netstat
- **D.** route

105. Which of the following parameters enables you to specify the number of messages the ping tool transmits?

 A. -n

 B. -t

 C. -i

 D. -a

106. Which of the following command-line utilities can run on Windows, Unix, or Linux systems? (Choose all that apply.)

 A. ping

 B. traceroute

 C. ifconfig

 D. iptables

 E. nslookup

107. Which of the following command-line utilities can only run on Unix and Linux systems?

 A. ping

 B. ipconfig

 C. tracert

 D. ifconfig

 E. netstat

108. Which of the following command-line utilities can only run on Windows systems?

 A. ping

 B. ipconfig

 C. traceroute

 D. ifconfig

 E. netstat

109. Ralph is working on his company's perimeter network, which has five web servers running Linux, a Cisco router, a CSU/DSU providing a leased line connection, and a Windows-based firewall. While trying to troubleshoot a network communications failure, Ralph types the following command on one of the systems: traceroute adatum.com. Which of the following systems might Ralph be working on? (Choose all that apply.)

 A. The Windows-based firewall

 B. The Cisco router

 C. The CSU/DSU console

 D. One of the Linux web servers

110. Which of the following `netstat` commands can tell you how many IPv6 packets have been received on a particular Windows workstation?

    A. `netstat -a`

    B. `netstat -s`

    C. `netstat -e`

    D. `netstat -r`

111. Which of the following commands can Ralph use to display the number of bytes that a Windows workstation has transmitted?

    A. `netstat`

    B. `tcpdump`

    C. `ipconfig`

    D. `iptables`

112. Ralph is working on his company's perimeter network, which has five web servers running Linux, a Cisco router, a CSU/DSU providing a leased line connection, and a Windows-based firewall. While trying to troubleshoot a network communications failure, Ralph types the following command on one of the systems: `ping 192.168.1.76`. Which of the following systems might Ralph be working on? (Choose all that apply.)

    A. The Windows-based firewall

    B. The Cisco router

    C. The CSU/DSU console

    D. One of the Linux web servers

113. Alice is troubleshooting a Windows server, and while doing so she runs the following command: `ping 127.0.0.1`. The command completes successfully. What has Alice proven by doing this?

    A. That the computer's network adapter is functioning properly

    B. That the computer's TCP/IP networking stack is loaded and functioning

    C. That the computer's IP address is correct for the network

    D. Nothing at all

114. Ed suspects that his workstation is experiencing Transmission Control Protocol/Internet Protocol (TCP/IP) communication problems. Which of the following commands can he use to confirm that the computer's TCP/IP stack is loaded and functioning? (Choose all that apply.)

    A. `ping loopback`

    B. `ping localhost`

    C. `ping 127.0.0.1`

    D. `ping 127.0.0.0`

115. Ralph is the administrator of his company's network. He has a Dynamic Host Configuration Protocol (DHCP) server configured to supply Internet Protocol (IP) addresses and configuration information to all of the Windows computers on the network. One of the Windows users reports that she cannot connect to the network. Which of the following commands can Ralph run on her computer to verify the status of the computer's IP settings and configuration parameters?

A. `ifconfig`

B. `ipconfig`

C. `msinfo32`

D. `tracert`

116. Which of the following are the three main categories of information that you can display by running the `netstat` command on a Windows computer?

A. Connection state

B. Active connections

C. Routing table

D. Interface statistics

117. Which of the following `route` commands displays the contents of a Windows computer's IPv6 routing table only?

A. `route print`

B. `route print -6`

C. `route list -6`

D. `route list`

118. Which of the following Windows command-line utilities produced the output shown here?

```
Interface Statistics

                        Received          Sent
Bytes                   663321544    1088192828
Unicast packets          29291610      10424979
Non-unicast packets        817568         58116
Discards                     1628             0
Errors                          0             0
Unknown protocols               0             0
```

A. `ping`

B. `tracert`

C. `netstat`

D. `arp`

119. Which of the following Linux commands generated the output shown in the figure?

```
Address                HWtype  HWaddress            Flags Mask       Iface
192.168.2.99           ether   50:46:5d:00:33:18    C                eth0
```

A. `arp -a`

B. `arp -e`

C. `arp -d`

D. `arp -s`

120. Which of the following Windows commands enables you to create a new entry in the Address Resolution Protocol (ARP) cache?

A. `arp -N`

B. `arp -d`

C. `arp -a`

D. `arp -s`

121. Which of the following Unix/Linux tools is a packet analyzer?

A. `iptables`

B. `nmap`

C. `tcpdump`

D. `pathping`

122. Which of the following tools can administrators use to monitor network bandwidth and traffic patterns?

A. Protocol analyzer

B. Bandwidth speed tester

C. NetFlow analyzer

D. IP scanner

123. Based on the output shown here, what is the average response time of the destination system?

```
 1    <1 ms    <1 ms     <1 ms RT-N86U [192.168.2.99]
 2     3 ms     5 ms      4 ms 192.168.3.1
 3    25 ms    30 ms     17 ms 10.172.1.1
 4    20 ms    19 ms     29 ms gateway-BE1-EBlocal.eh.lpod.net [207.44.123.89]
 5    26 ms    29 ms     29 ms gateway-be1-abn2abn2.ab.lpod.net [207.44.127.49]
 6     *        *          * Request timed out.
 7   111 ms   108 ms    109 ms be38.trmc0215-01.ars.mgmt.hox3.kkg [184.168.0.69]
 8   108 ms   107 ms    108 ms be38.trmc0215-01.ars.mgmt.hox3.kkg [184.168.0.69]
 9   106 ms   109 ms    108 ms ip-216-69-188-102.ip.srvr.net [216.69.188.102]
10   106 ms   108 ms     99 ms p3nlh153.shr.prod.phx3.srvr.net [97.74.144.153]
```

A. 109.5 ms

B. 104.33 ms

C. 106 ms

D. 99.66 ms

124. Which of the following Linux commands produced the output shown in the figure?

```
;; global options: +cmd
;; Got answer:
;; ->>HEADER<<- opcode: QUERY, status: NOERROR, id: 41835
;; flags: qr rd ra; QUERY: 1, ANSWER: 4, AUTHORITY: 0, ADDITIONAL: 1

;; OPT PSEUDOSECTION:
; EDNS: version: 0, flags:; udp: 4096
;; QUESTION SECTION:
;microsoft.com.                IN      NS

;; ANSWER SECTION:
microsoft.com.         65776   IN      NS      ns4.msft.net.
microsoft.com.         65776   IN      NS      ns1.msft.net.
microsoft.com.         65776   IN      NS      ns2.msft.net.
microsoft.com.         65776   IN      NS      ns3.msft.net.

;; Query time: 27 msec
;; SERVER: 204.186.110.114#53(204.186.110.114)
;; WHEN: Sat Nov 18 14:14:49 EST 2017
;; MSG SIZE  rcvd: 122
```

A. `netstat -ns microsoft.com`

B. `dig microsoft.com ns`

C. `nslookup microsoft.com`

D. `route -s microsoft.com`

125. Which of the following protocols does the `traceroute` utility on Unix and Linux systems use to test TCP/IP connectivity?

A. ICMP

B. HTTP

C. TCP

D. UDP

126. A user calls Alice at the help desk to report that he cannot access the Internet. He can access systems on the local network, however. Alice examines the routing table on the user's workstation. Which of the following statements explains why the user cannot access the Internet?

```
IPv4 Route Table
===========================================================================
Active Routes:
Network Destination   Netmask           Gateway    Interface      Metric
    127.0.0.0         255.0.0.0         On-link    127.0.0.1      331
    127.0.0.1         255.255.255.255   On-link    127.0.0.1      331
    127.255.255.255   255.255.255.255   On-link    127.0.0.1      331
    192.168.2.0       255.255.255.0     On-link    192.168.2.37   281
    192.168.2.37      255.255.255.255   On-link    192.168.2.37   281
```

```
192.168.2.255      255.255.255.255  On-link   192.168.2.37  281
224.0.0.0          240.0.0.0        On-link   127.0.0.1     331
224.0.0.0          240.0.0.0        On-link   192.168.2.37  281
255.255.255.255    255.255.255.255  On-link   127.0.0.1     331
255.255.255.255    255.255.255.255  On-link   192.168.2.37  281
=========================================================================
```
Persistent Routes:
 None

    A. The routing table contains a loopback address.

    B. The routing table does not specify a default gateway address.

    C. The routing table does not specify a DNS server address.

    D. The routing table contains two different routes to the 224.0.0.0 network.

127. Ed has configured his workstation to use Internet Protocol Security (IPSec) encryption for network communications. Which of the following tools can he use to verify that his network traffic is encrypted?

    A. Multimeter

    B. Packet sniffer

    C. Port scanner

    D. Protocol analyzer

    E. IP scanner

128. Which of the following statements describes the difference between a packet sniffer and a protocol analyzer?

    A. A packet sniffer captures network traffic, and a protocol analyzer examines packet contents.

    B. A protocol analyzer captures network traffic, and a packet sniffer examines packet contents.

    C. A packet sniffer only captures the local workstation's traffic, whereas a protocol analyzer can capture all the traffic on the network.

    D. There is no difference. Packet sniffers and protocol analyzers perform the same functions.

129. Ed has recently discovered a rogue Dynamic Host Configuration Protocol (DHCP) server on his network. After disabling the server, he now needs to terminate all of the rogue Internet Protocol (IP) address leases currently held by Windows DHCP clients on the network and have them request new leases from the authorized DHCP server. Which of the following commands must he use on each Windows client to do this? (Choose all that apply.)

    A. `ipconfig /dump`

    B. `ipconfig /renew`

    C. `ipconfig /lease`

    D. `ipconfig /discard`

    E. `ipconfig /release`

130. Ed is implementing a web server farm on his company's network and has created a screened subnet (or perimeter network) on which the web servers will be located. The screened subnet is using the network Internet Protocol (IP) address 192.168.99.0/24. He has also installed a router connecting the screened subnet to the internal network, which uses the 192.168.3.0/24 network address. The IP addresses of the router's interfaces are 192.168.3.100 and 192.168.99.1. Ed needs to access the web servers from his Windows workstation on the internal network, but right now, he cannot do so. Because he needs to have a different router specified as his default gateway, Ed decides to add a route for the screened subnet to his computer's routing table. Which of the following commands will create a routing table entry that enables Ed to access the screened subnet?

A. `route add 192.168.3.0 MASK 255.255.255.0 192.168.3.100`

B. `route add 192.168.99.1 MASK 255.255.255.0 192.168.3.0`

C. `route add 192.168.3.100 MASK 255.255.255.0 192.168.99.0`

D. `route add 192.168.99.0 MASK 255.255.255.0 192.168.3.100`

131. Alice has recently created a new screened subnet (or perimeter network) for the company's web server cluster, along with a router to connect it to the internal network. When she is finished, she sends Ralph an email instructing him to run the following command on his Windows workstation so that he can access the servers on the screened subnet. What function does the IP address 192.168.87.226 perform in this command?

`route add 192.168.46.0 MASK 255.255.255.0 192.168.87.226`

A. 192.168.87.226 is the address of Ralph's workstation.

B. 192.168.87.226 is the network address of the perimeter network.

C. 192.168.87.226 is the address of one of the router's interfaces.

D. 192.168.87.226 is the address of the web server cluster.

132. Which of the following processes scans multiple computers on a network for a particular open Transmission Control Protocol (TCP) or User Datagram Protocol (UDP) port?

A. Port scanning

B. War driving

C. Port sweeping

D. Bluejacking

133. Which of the following statements about protocol analyzers is not true?

A. To troubleshoot using a protocol analyzer, you must be familiar with the OSI model and the protocols that operate at each of its layers.

B. Protocol analyzers can be a network security risk.

C. Some network monitoring products are both analyzers and sniffers.

D. All Windows operating systems include a protocol analyzer.

134. Which of the following utilities can be classified as port scanners? (Choose all that apply.)

    A. Nmap

    B. Nessus

    C. Network Monitor

    D. Performance Monitor

135. Which Unix/Linux performance monitoring tool, with output shown in the figure, enables you to display information about processes that are currently running on a system?

```
 8:13am  up 2 min,  1 user,  load average: 0.16, 0.11, 0.04
30 processes: 29 sleeping, 1 running, 0 zombie, 0 stopped
CPU states:  0.0% user,  0.0% system,  0.0% nice, 100.0% idle
Mem:   255524K av,   33296K used,  222228K free,       0K shrd,    5516K buff
Swap:  530104K av,       0K used,  530104K free                   15852K cached

  PID USER      PRI  NI  SIZE  RSS SHARE STAT %CPU %MEM   TIME COMMAND
    1 root       9   0   544  544   472 S     0.0  0.2  0:04 init
    2 root       8   0     0    0     0 SW    0.0  0.0  0:00 keventd
    3 root       9   0     0    0     0 SW    0.0  0.0  0:00 kapm-idled
    4 root       9   0     0    0     0 SW    0.0  0.0  0:00 kswapd
    5 root       9   0     0    0     0 SW    0.0  0.0  0:00 kreclaimd
    6 root       9   0     0    0     0 SW    0.0  0.0  0:00 bdflush
    7 root       9   0     0    0     0 SW    0.0  0.0  0:00 kupdated
    8 root      -1 -20     0    0     0 SW<   0.0  0.0  0:00 mdrecoveryd
   78 root       9   0     0    0     0 SW    0.0  0.0  0:00 khubd
  289 root       2   0   528  528   448 S     0.0  0.2  0:00 vmware-guestd
  636 root       9   0   600  600   500 S     0.0  0.2  0:00 syslogd
  641 root       9   0  1100 1100   456 S     0.0  0.4  0:00 klogd
  655 rpc        9   0   596  596   504 S     0.0  0.2  0:00 portmap
  670 rpcuser    9   0   776  776   668 S     0.0  0.3  0:00 rpc.statd
  754 root       8   0   532  532   464 S     0.0  0.2  0:00 apmd
  803 root       8   0   648  648   544 S     0.0  0.2  0:00 automount
  815 daemon     9   0   584  584   508 S     0.0  0.2  0:00 atd
  865 root       8   0  1936 1936  1416 S     0.0  0.7  0:00 sendmail
```

    A. `monitor`

    B. `top`

    C. `netstat`

    D. `cpustat`

136. You have finished capturing traffic with a protocol analyzer. The analyzer reports that 2000 frames have been seen, but only 1500 frames have been accepted. What does this mean?

    A. 2000 frames have passed the display filter, but only 1500 meet the criteria for display.

    B. Only 1500 frames have passed the capture filter and are currently being held in the buffer.

    C. You lost 500 frames and need to start over—something is obviously wrong.

    D. 500 frames were damaged and never made it into the buffer.

137. When you run a port scanner on a server, which of the following is the result?

    A. A list of processes running on the system

    B. A list of open ports through which the system can be accessed

    C. A list of protocols used by the system for network communication

    D. A list of Internet Protocol (IP) addresses used on the network

138. A port scanner examines a system for network vulnerabilities at which layer of the Open Systems Interconnection (OSI) model?

  A. Application

  B. Transport

  C. Network

  D. Data Link

139. Which of the following best describes the primary function of a port scanner?

  A. A port scanner examines a computer' hardware and compiles a list of the physical ports in the system.

  B. A port scanner examines a computer for TCP and UDP endpoints that are accessible from the network.

  C. A port scanner examines a specified range of IP addresses on a network, to determine whether they are in use.

  D. A port scanner accepts a computer name as input and scans the network for the IP address associated with that name.

140. Programs such as File Transfer Protocol (FTP) and Telnet are widely criticized because they transmit all data as clear text, including usernames and passwords. Which of the following types of tools might unscrupulous individuals use to read those passwords?

  A. Packet sniffer

  B. Terminal emulator

  C. Packet analyzer

  D. Vulnerability scanner

  E. TFTP server

141. Which of the following best states the potential security threat inherent in running a protocol analyzer?

  A. A protocol analyzer can display the application data in packets captured from the network.

  B. A protocol analyzer can display the IP addresses of the systems on the network.

  C. A protocol analyzer can decrypt protected information in packets captured from the network.

  D. A protocol analyzer can detect open ports on network systems and launch attacks against them.

142. Which of the following is not a tool that provides vulnerability scanning capabilities?

  A. Nessus

  B. MAP Toolkit

  C. Nmap

  D. MBSA

143. Which of the following is a function typically classified as vulnerability scanning?

A. Network mapping

B. Remediation

C. Penetration testing

D. Port scanning

144. Alice is attempting to troubleshoot a communication problem between two hosts on the same network. She decides to use a protocol analyzer to capture traffic on the network. After finishing the capture, Alice notices that there are over 15,000 frames in the protocol analyzer's capture buffer. She is having a difficult time identifying the frames that relate to the problem because there are so many in the buffer. She wants to eliminate the extraneous frames from her view, enabling her to view only the frames transmitted by these two hosts. What does Alice have to do to accomplish this?

A. Configure a display filter

B. Configure a capture filter

C. Delete the extraneous frames from the buffer

D. Configure a capture and display filter

145. Ralph has purchased some old 802.11b wireless networking equipment at a garage sale, which he plans to use to build a home network. When he installs the network adapters in his computers and sets up the Access Point (AP), he finds that the connections between the devices are no faster than 11 Mbps. What can Ralph do to improve the performance of his network?

A. Nothing. The network is functioning at its top speed.

B. Change the channel used by the devices.

C. Move the computers closer to the AP.

D. Install a larger antenna on the AP

146. Ralph is setting up a wireless network using the 2.4 GHz band. Which of the following channels should he use to avoid channel overlap? (Choose all that apply.)

A. 1

B. 4

C. 6

D. 8

E. 11

147. Ralph is adding new workstations to his wireless network, which uses an Access Point (AP) that is configured to use WiFi Protected Access II (WPA2) encryption. However, after configuring the wireless network adapter on the first workstation, Ralph finds that it is not connecting to the network. The AP is listed on the Available Networks display, and there are no error messages or indications of a problem, just a failure to connect. Which of the following is most likely to be the problem?

A. Incorrect passphrase

B. Channel overlap

C. Incorrect SSID

D. Incorrect antenna placement

148. Ralph is adding new workstations to his wireless network, which uses an Access Point (AP) that is configured to use WiFi Protected Access II (WPA2) encryption. However, after installing the wireless network adapter on the first workstation, Ralph finds that he cannot see the Wireless Access Point (WAP) on the Available Networks display. Which of the following could be the problem? (Choose all that apply.)

A. Incorrect passphrase

B. Channel overlap

C. Incorrect SSID

D. Incorrect antenna polarization

E. Antenna cable attenuation

149. Ralph is the administrator of a small company's wireless network. He has recently discovered evidence that users outside of the company's office space have been accessing its wireless network. The office is located in a narrow space against the building's outside wall. Ralph is concerned that the network's Wireless Access Point (WAP) is extending coverage outside the building. Speaking with a consultant friend of his, Ralph is advised to install a different type of antenna on his Access Point (AP). Which of the following antenna types would most likely help Ralph to alleviate the problem?

A. Dipole

B. Yagi

C. Patch

D. Unidirectional

150. Trixie has recently moved to a new office in her company's building, down the hall from her old one. Since the move, she has only been able to access the wireless network with her laptop intermittently. She never had a problem in her previous location. Which of the following could possibly be the cause of her problem? (Choose all that apply.)

A. Trixie's new office is farther from the Access Point (AP) than her old one.

B. Her laptop is connecting to the wrong SSID.

C. The AP is using an omnidirectional antenna.

D. There are too many walls between Trixie's new office and the AP.

151. Alice is a new hire at Adatum Corp., and when she asks about wireless network access for her laptop, she is given a Service Set Identifier (SSID) and a WiFi Protected Access II (WPA2) passphrase. Later, in the lunchroom, when she tries to connect her laptop to the network, she cannot see the SSID she was given in the Available Networks list, although she can see other networks. What should Alice do next to try to resolve the problem?

A. Type in the WPA2 passphrase.

B. Type the SSID in manually.

C. Move closer to the Wireless Access Point (WAP).

D. Move away from the microwave in the lunchroom.

152. Alice is a new hire at Adatum Corp., and when she asks about wireless network access for her laptop, she is given a Service Set Identifier (SSID) and a passphrase. She is also told that she must add the SSID manually. Later, she types in the SSID she was given, and the computer prompts her to select a security type. Not knowing which option to choose, she selects 802.1x, because it sounds as though it should be the most secure. However, this option does not enable her to enter her passphrase, so she selects another option, WEP, and is able to type in the passphrase. However, her laptop says she "Can't connect to this network." Which of the following is the most likely cause of Alice's problem?

    A. Overcapacity

    B. Distance limitations

    C. Frequency mismatch

    D. Encryption protocol mismatch

153. Ralph purchases some 802.11a wireless network adapters for desktop computers at a yard sale, which he intends to use on his 802.11g home network. He installs one of the adapters in a computer and attempts to connect it to the network, but he cannot see his Service Set Identifier (SSID). He tries a different adapter, thinking the first one might be broken, but that one does not work either. What can Ralph do to resolve the problem and connect the computer to his network?

    A. Move the computer closer to the Access Point (AP).

    B. Configure the AP to use the 5 GHz frequency.

    C. Manually enter the SSID in the computer's client software.

    D. Nothing. 802.11a equipment cannot connect to an 802.11g network.

154. Ralph is responsible for a Wireless Local Area Network (WLAN) that consists of an 802.11n 2x2:2 Access Point (AP) and laptop computers with a variety of network adapters. Some of the laptops support 802.11n, most support 802.11g, and a few older models have 802.11a adapters. The WLAN is located in a large office building with many other wireless networks, and Ralph is having trouble finding a channel on the 2.4 GHz band that is not congested with traffic. Scanning the 5 GHz band, he finds relatively little traffic, so he reconfigures the AP to use a 5 GHz channel. The result is that some of the laptops are able to connect to the network, whereas others are not. What is the most likely reason for the connection failures, and what must Ralph do to enable all of the laptops to connect to the wireless network?

    A. The 5 GHz band does not support automatic channel selection. Ralph must configure each laptop to use the same channel as the AP for all the laptops to connect successfully.

    B. The 802.11g standard does not support communication using the 5 GHz band. Ralph must configure the AP to support 2.4 GHz for all the laptops to connect successfully.

    C. The 5 GHz band does not support Multiple Input, Multiple Output (MIMO) communications, so the 802.11n laptops are unable to connect to the network. Ralph must replace the AP with an 802.11g unit for all the laptops to connect successfully.

    D. The 802.11a standard does not support communication using the 5 GHz band. Ralph must replace the network adapters in those laptops with newer models for them to connect successfully.

155. Alice is the administrator of a wireless network that has client computers in a number of small offices, all located on the same floor of an office building built in the mid-twentieth century. The network has an IEEE 802.11g Access Point (AP) located at the approximate center of the floor. Workstations in most of the rooms connect to the network at 54 Mbps, but the computers in one particular room rarely connect at speeds above 11 Mbps. Which of the following might be the cause of the problem?

A. The computers in the problematic room are configured to use a different wireless encryption protocol than the AP.

B. The computers in the problematic room are experiencing an SSID mismatch.

C. The network adapters in the problematic computers support IEEE 802.11a, not 802.11g.

D. The RSSI of the problematic computers might be low, due to excessive distance from the AP.

156. Which of the following is not a potential solution for an IEEE 802.11g wireless computer that has intermittent problems connecting to an IEEE 802.11b/g Access Point (AP)?

A. Install a higher gain antenna on the AP

B. Replace the AP with a model that supports 802.11n

C. Move the computer closer to the AP

D. Change the channel used by the AP

157. Ed has installed a separate 802.11n wireless network for guest users working in his company's offices. The guest network is unsecured, and Ed has recently become aware that people outside the building are able to access it. It is not possible to move the Access Point (AP), and it must run at maximum power to reach the entire building. Which of the following is the most convenient way to prevent users outside the building from accessing the guest network while leaving it available to users inside the building?

A. Change the passphrase daily

B. Switch the network frequency

C. Disable SSID broadcasting

D. Implement MAC filtering

158. Alice is trying to provide users in a warehouse with wireless network connectivity for their tablets. The warehouse is a huge concrete structure with many internal cinderblock walls. Which of the following types of signal interference are inhibiting Alice's efforts?

A. Refraction

B. Reflection

C. Diffraction

D. Absorption

159. Ralph is having trouble providing satisfactory wireless network performance to some executive offices at the far end of the building. The wireless Access Point (AP) is based on the 802.11g standard. The offices have heavy doors and insulated walls for sound damping, and the occupants typically leave their doors closed during work hours. Which of the following actions can Ralph take to provide the users in these offices with better wireless network performance?

A. Install an additional AP nearer to the offices.

B. Modify the AP to use higher number channels.

C. Upgrade the AP to a model based on the 802.11n standard.

D. Configure the AP to disable SSID broadcasting.

160. Ralph is having trouble providing satisfactory wireless network performance to some executive offices at the far end of the building. The offices have heavy doors and insulated walls for sound dampening, and the occupants typically leave their doors closed during work hours. Which of the following types of radio signal interference is Ralph trying to overcome?

A. Reflection

B. Refraction

C. Diffraction

D. Absorption

161. Ralph is having trouble providing satisfactory wireless network performance to a row of glass-walled conference rooms at the far end of the building. The doors to the conference rooms are also made of glass and are always closed when meetings are in progress. Which of the following types of radio signal interference are likely to be the main issues that Ralph is trying to overcome? (Choose all that apply.)

A. Reflection

B. Refraction

C. Diffraction

D. Attenuation

162. Alice receives a call from a user who cannot connect to the company's 802.11g wireless network with a new laptop that has an 802.11ac network adapter. Other users working in the same area are able to connect to the network without difficulty. Which of the following are tasks that Alice can perform to resolve the problem? (Choose all that apply.)

A. Install an 802.11ac wireless Access Point (AP) on the network

B. Change the channel used by the Wireless Access Point (WAP)

C. Install an 802.11g wireless network adapter in the user's laptop

D. Move the user closer to the WAP

163. Several accounting consultants are working in Ed's office for the first time, and they are unable to connect to the 802.11g wireless network with their laptops. They are selecting the correct Service Set Identifier (SSID) from the Available Networks list, but they cannot connect, and there are no error messages of any kind. Which of the following tasks should Ed perform to try to resolve the problem?

   A. Check the network adapters in the laptops for channel overlap

   B. Change the frequency used by the Wireless Access Point (WAP) from 2.4 GHz to 5 GHz

   C. Examine the area where the consultants are working for possible sources of signal interference

   D. Make sure that the consultants' laptops are configured to use the correct wireless security protocol

164. Ed has installed a separate 802.11n wireless network for guest users working in his company's offices. The guest network uses no security protocol, and Ed has recently become aware that people outside the building are able to access it. Which of the following steps can Ed take to prevent users outside the building from accessing the guest network, while leaving it available to users inside the building? (Choose all that apply.)

   A. Move the Wireless Access Point (WAP) to the center of the building

   B. Lower the power level of the WAP

   C. Disable Service Set Identifier (SSID) broadcasting

   D. Implement Media Access Control (MAC) filtering

   E. Install a captive portal

165. Alice receives a call from a user who cannot connect to the company's 802.11n wireless network with a laptop that has an 802.11g network adapter. Other users working in the same area are able to connect to the network without difficulty. Which of the following steps should Alice take first to try to resolve the problem? (Choose all that apply.)

   A. Change the channel used by the Wireless Access Point (WAP)

   B. Check whether the user is connecting to the correct Service Set Identifier (SSID)

   C. Check whether the wireless adapter in the user's laptop is enabled

   D. Provide the user with an 802.11n wireless network adapter

166. Users on Ed's 802.11n wireless network are dropping their connections intermittently. Which of the following might help to resolve the problem?

   A. Restart the Wireless Access Point (WAP)

   B. Change the network's Service Set Identifier (SSID)

   C. Change the channel the devices are using

   D. Change the wireless security protocol

167. Several accounting consultants are working in Ed's office for the first time, and they are unable to connect to the 802.11n wireless network with their laptops. Which of the following tasks should Ed perform first to try to resolve the problem? (Choose all that apply.)

A. Check the network adapters in the laptops for channel overlap

B. Make sure that the consultants are attempting to connect to the correct SSID

C. Examine the area where the consultants are working for possible sources of signal interference

D. Make sure that the consultants' laptops are configured to use the correct wireless encryption protocol

168. Ralph is deploying an 802.11n wireless network for a client that calls for the best possible security without deploying additional servers. When setting up the Wireless Access Point (WAP), Ralph disables Service Set Identifier (SSID) broadcasts, selects WiFi Protected Access security with Pre-Shared Keys (WPA-PSKs), and configures Media Access Control (MAC) address filtering. Which of the following statements about the security of this arrangement is true?

A. The configuration is as secure as Ralph can make it with the specified equipment.

B. Ralph should not disable SSID broadcasts since this prevents users from connecting to the network.

C. Ralph should not use MAC address filtering, because it exposes MAC addresses to possible attacks.

D. Ralph should use WiFi Protected Access II (WPA2) instead of WPA, because it is more resistant to certain types of attacks.

169. Ralph is experiencing long Access Point (AP) association times and generally poor performance on his home 802.11n wireless network. Ralph lives in a large apartment complex, and when he runs a WiFi analyzer, he sees many other nearby networks using the often-recommended channels 1, 6, and 11 on the 2.4 GHz frequency. Using the 5 GHz frequency is not an option for Ralph's equipment. What should Ralph do to improve his network performance?

A. Configure his equipment to use channel 2

B. Configure his equipment to use channel 5

C. Configure his equipment to use channel 9

D. Configure his equipment to use channel 10

170. Which of the following is a power measurement of a specific transmitter and antenna combination, as used in a wireless access point?

A. RSSI

B. EIRP

C. SSID

D. MIMO

171. Ed is working the help desk at a local computer store, and he receives a call from a customer trying to set up a home network using Windows 10 and wired Ethernet equipment. The customer reports that, from her computer, she can see the two other computers in the house, but she cannot access the Internet. Ed asks her to run the `ipconfig /all` command and read the results to him. She says that her IP address is 172.16.41.2, her subnet mask is 255.255.255.0, and her default gateway is 172.16.43.1. Which of the following is most likely the cause of the customer's problem?

A. The customer's network cable is unplugged.

B. The customer has an incorrect subnet mask.

C. The customer has an incorrect default gateway address.

D. The computer's DNS record contains the wrong information.

E. The computer is inhibited by a switching loop.

172. Ralph has a wired home network with three Windows computers, a switch, and a cable modem/router that provides access to the Internet. All three computers are able to access the Internet, but none of them can access filesystem shares on the others. Which of the following is the most likely cause of the problem on the three network computers?

A. Incorrect IP addresses

B. Incorrect subnet mask

C. Incorrect default gateway address

D. Incorrect ACL settings

173. Alice has been asked to update an accounts receivable spreadsheet with information about the day's incoming payments, a task she has never performed before. After locating and opening the spreadsheet on the network server, she types in her new information, but when she attempts to save the changes, she receives an error message that directs her to save the file on her local drive instead of the network server. Which of the following is the probable cause of the problem?

A. Blocked Transmission Control Protocol/User Datagram Protocol (TCP/UDP) ports

B. Incorrect filesystem Access Control List (ACL) settings

C. Incorrect firewall settings

D. Untrusted Secure Sockets Layer (SSL) certificate

174. Which of the following Internet Protocol (IP) address assignments indicates that a computer has been unable to communicate with a Dynamic Host Configuration Protocol (DHCP) server?

A. 127.0.0.1

B. 255.255.255.0

C. 240.15.167.251

D. 169.254.199.22

175. A user reports to Ralph that he cannot access the Internet, although he is able to connect to computers on the local network. Ralph runs `ipconfig /all` on the user's workstation and examines the output. Which of the following is the most likely explanation for the user's problem, based on these `ipconfig` results?

```
Windows IP Configuration
    Host Name . . . . . . . . . . . . : Client12
    Primary Dns Suffix . . . . . . . :
    Node Type . . . . . . . . . . . . : Hybrid
    IP Routing Enabled. . . . . . . . : No
    WINS Proxy Enabled. . . . . . . . : No
Ethernet adapter Local Area Connection:
    Connection-specific DNS Suffix . :
    Description . . . . . . . . . . . : PCIe Family Controller
    Physical Address. . . . . . . . . : 60-EB-69-93-5E-E5
    DHCP Enabled. . . . . . . . . . . : No
    Autoconfiguration Enabled . . . . : Yes
    Link-local IPv6 Address . . . . . : fe80::c955:c944:acdd:3fcb%2
    IPv4 Address. . . . . . . . . . . : 192.168.4.24
    Subnet Mask . . . . . . . . . . . : 255.255.255.0
    Lease Obtained. . . . . . . . . . : Monday, October 23, 2017 6:23:47 PM
    Lease Expires . . . . . . . . . . : Saturday, November 18, 2017 9:49:24 PM
    Default Gateway . . . . . . . . . : 192.168.6.99
    DHCPv6 IAID . . . . . . . . . . . : 241232745
    DHCPv6 Client DUID. . . . . . . . : 00-01-00-01-18-10-22-0D-60-EB-69-93-5E-E5
    DNS Servers . . . . . . . . . . . : 202.86.10.114
    NetBIOS over Tcpip. . . . . . . . : Enabled
```

A. The Subnet Mask setting is incorrect.

B. The Default Gateway setting is incorrect.

C. The DNS Servers setting is located on another network.

D. DHCP is not enabled.

176. Ralph is troubleshooting a workstation that cannot access the network. The workstation is plugged into a wall plate that should provide it with access to a DHCP-equipped network using the 192.168.4.0/24 network address. No one else on that network is reporting a problem. Ralph checks that the patch cable is properly plugged into the workstation and the wall plate, which they are, and then runs `ipconfig /all` on the user's workstation and examines the output. Which of the following could be the explanation for the user's problem, based on these `ipconfig` results?

```
Windows IP Configuration
    Host Name . . . . . . . . . . . . : Client12
    Primary Dns Suffix . . . . . . . :
```

```
Node Type . . . . . . . . . . . . : Hybrid
IP Routing Enabled. . . . . . . . : No
WINS Proxy Enabled. . . . . . . . : No
Ethernet adapter Local Area Connection:
  Connection-specific DNS Suffix . :
  Description . . . . . . . . . . . : PCIe Family Controller
  Physical Address. . . . . . . . . : 60-EB-69-93-5E-E5
  DHCP Enabled. . . . . . . . . . . : Yes
  Autoconfiguration Enabled . . . . : Yes
  Link-local IPv6 Address . . . . . : fe80::c955:c944:acdd:3fcb%2
  IPv4 Address. . . . . . . . . . . : 169.254.203.42
  Subnet Mask . . . . . . . . . . . : 255.255.0.0
  Lease Obtained. . . . . . . . . . : Monday, October 23, 2017 6:23:47 PM
  Lease Expires . . . . . . . . . . : Saturday, November 18, 2017 9:49:24 PM
  Default Gateway . . . . . . . . . :
  DHCPv6 IAID . . . . . . . . . . . : 241232745
  DHCPv6 Client DUID. . . . . . . . : 00-01-00-01-18-10-22-0D-60-EB-69-93-5E-E5
  DNS Servers . . . . . . . . . . . : fec0:0:0:ffff::1%1
                                      fec0:0:0:ffff::2%1
                                      fec0:0:0:ffff::3%1
  NetBIOS over Tcpip. . . . . . . . : Enabled
```

A. The Subnet Mask is incorrect.

B. The Default Gateway address is missing.

C. The DHCPv4 scope is exhausted.

D. The DNS server addresses are incorrect.

177. Ralph is troubleshooting a workstation that cannot access the network. The workstation is plugged into a wall plate that should provide it with access to a DHCP-equipped network using the 192.168.32.0/20 network address. Ralph checks that the patch cable is properly plugged into the workstation and the wall plate, which they are, and then runs `ipconfig /all` on the user's workstation and examines the output. Which of the following could be the explanation for the user's problem, based on these `ipconfig` results?

```
Windows IP Configuration
  Host Name . . . . . . . . . . . . : Client12
  Primary Dns Suffix . . . . . . . :
  Node Type . . . . . . . . . . . . : Hybrid
  IP Routing Enabled. . . . . . . . : No
  WINS Proxy Enabled. . . . . . . . : No
Ethernet adapter Local Area Connection:
  Connection-specific DNS Suffix . :
```

```
Description . . . . . . . . . . . . : PCIe Family Controller
Physical Address. . . . . . . . . : 60-EB-69-93-5E-E5
DHCP Enabled. . . . . . . . . . . : No
Autoconfiguration Enabled . . . . : Yes
Link-local IPv6 Address . . . . . : fe80::c955:c944:acdd:3fcb%2
IPv4 Address. . . . . . . . . . . : 192.168.42.24
Subnet Mask . . . . . . . . . . . : 255.255.255.0
Lease Obtained. . . . . . . . . . : Monday, October 23, 2017 6:23:47 PM
Lease Expires . . . . . . . . . . : Saturday, November 18, 2017 9:49:24 PM
Default Gateway . . . . . . . . . : 192.168.42.99
DHCPv6 IAID . . . . . . . . . . . : 241232745
DHCPv6 Client DUID. . . . . . . . : 00-01-00-01-18-10-22-0D-60-EB-69-93-5E-E5
DNS Servers . . . . . . . . . . . : 202.86.10.114
NetBIOS over Tcpip. . . . . . . . : Enabled
```

A. The IPv4 Address setting is incorrect.

B. The Subnet Mask setting is incorrect.

C. The Default Gateway setting is incorrect.

D. The DNS Servers setting is located on another network.

178. Ralph is troubleshooting a workstation that cannot access the network. The workstation is plugged into a wall plate that should provide it with access to a DHCP-equipped network using the 192.168.4.0/24 network address. Ralph checks that the patch cable is properly plugged into the workstation and the wall plate, which they are, and then runs `ipconfig /all` on the user's workstation and examines the output. Which of the following could be the explanation for the user's problem, based on these `ipconfig` results?

```
Windows IP Configuration
   Host Name . . . . . . . . . . . . . . : Client12
   Primary Dns Suffix . . . . . . . . :
   Node Type . . . . . . . . . . . . . : Hybrid
   IP Routing Enabled. . . . . . . . : No
   WINS Proxy Enabled. . . . . . . . : No
Ethernet adapter Local Area Connection:
   Connection-specific DNS Suffix . :
   Description . . . . . . . . . . . : PCIe Family Controller
   Physical Address. . . . . . . . . : 60-EB-69-93-5E-E5
   DHCP Enabled. . . . . . . . . . . : Yes
   Autoconfiguration Enabled . . . . : Yes
   Link-local IPv6 Address . . . . . : fe80::c955:c944:acdd:3fcb%2
   IPv4 Address. . . . . . . . . . . : 10.124.16.8
   Subnet Mask . . . . . . . . . . . : 255.0.0.0
```

```
Lease Obtained. . . . . . . . . . . : Monday, October 23, 2017 6:23:47 PM
Lease Expires . . . . . . . . . . . : Saturday, November 18, 2017 9:49:24 PM
Default Gateway . . . . . . . . . . :
DHCPv6 IAID . . . . . . . . . . . . : 241232745
DHCPv6 Client DUID. . . . . . . . . : 00-01-00-01-18-10-22-0D-60-EB-69-93-5E-E5
DNS Servers . . . . . . . . . . . . : fec0:0:0:ffff::1%1
                        fec0:0:0:ffff::2%1
                        fec0:0:0:ffff::3%1
NetBIOS over Tcpip. . . . . . . . . : Enabled
```

A. The workstation could not connect to a DHCP server.

B. There is a rogue DHCP server on the network.

C. The workstation is not configured to use DHCP.

D. The IP address assigned by the DHCP server has expired.

179. Ralph is responsible for the network installation in a new building purchased by his company, and he has elected to have Category 6 (Cat 6) Unshielded Twisted Pair (UTP) cable installed. The company president has asked him if it is possible to run their Gigabit Ethernet network using two of the wire pairs in the cable, while using the other two pairs for telephone connections. Ralph is not sure, so he sets up a lab network using cables with only two pairs connected. When he plugs computers into the switch and turns them on, the Light-Emitting Diodes (LEDs) labeled 1000 light up, indicating that a Gigabit Ethernet connection has been established. Ralph gets excited at the thought of how much money he might save the company by using the same cable for both telephone and data. However, while the LED is lit, he cannot seem to connect to another system over his test network. Which of the following describes what he must do to correct the problem?

A. Ralph must manually configure the network adapters to use Gigabit Ethernet, rather than let them autonegotiate.

B. Ralph is using the wrong two wire pairs for the Gigabit Ethernet connection. He must rewire the connectors.

C. Ralph is using the wrong pinout standard on his lab network. He must use T568A.

D. Ralph must use all four wire pairs for a Gigabit Ethernet connection.

180. Ed is inspecting the cable runs recently installed for some new Gigabit Ethernet systems on his network. Looking at the patch panel connections, he notices that they are wired using the T568B pinout standard. However, when he examines the wall plate connections, he sees that they are wired using the T568A standard. What is the best way for Ed to resolve the problem?

A. Call the contractor and have all of the wall plate connectors rewired using the T568B standard.

B. Purchase crossover patch cables for all of the connections between the patch panel and the switches.

C. Configure the switches to not use a crossover circuit for all of the ports connected to the patch panel.

D. Do nothing. The cable runs will function properly as is.

181. Ralph has two computers that he long ago networked together by plugging one end of an Ethernet cable into each machine. He recently bought an old Ethernet hub at a garage sale and wants to use it to expand his network. The hub has four numbered ports and a fifth port marked with an X. Ralph plugs one computer into port 1 using his existing cable and buys a new cable to plug the other computer into port 4. The two computers cannot communicate, however. Which of the following solutions will not enable his computers to communicate?

    A. Move the port 4 cable to port 2

    B. Replace the old cable with a second new one

    C. Plug the computer with the old cable into the X port

    D. Plug the computer with the new cable into the X port

182. Ralph recently bought an old Ethernet hub and some twisted-pair cables at a garage sale and wants to use them to build a home network. He plugs two computers into the hub using the cables but finds that the computers are unable to communicate. Then he notices that one of the ports in the hub is labeled with an X. He tries plugging one of the computers into the X port, and now they can communicate. Which of the following statements is the most likely explanation for this behavior?

    A. The hub has a bad port.

    B. One of the cables is a crossover cable.

    C. Both of the cables are crossover cables.

    D. The X port provides extra strength to the signals.

183. Alice is a consultant who has been hired to move a client's old 20-node coaxial Ethernet network to a new location. She disassembles all of the network cabling and other components and packs them for shipping. At the new site, she sets up all of the computers, plugs a T-connector into each network adapter, and connects the cables, running them from one computer to the next to form the bus. When Alice is finished, she starts the computers and tests their network connectivity. She finds that 12 consecutive computers can communicate with each other, and the other 8 can communicate with each other, but the 12 cannot communicate with the 8. She makes sure that all of the connectors are securely tightened, especially the ones on the 12th computer, but the problem persists. Which of the following is the most likely cause of the difficulty?

    A. Alice has forgotten to terminate the computers at each end of the bus.

    B. One of the connectors on the 12th computer has a bent pin.

    C. Alice has forgotten to ground the network.

    D. The transmit and receive pins are reversed on the 12th computer.

184. Ed is troubleshooting some network performance problems. After exhausting many other possibilities, he is examining the twisted-pair cable runs in the office's drop ceiling. He finds that some cables have been damaged, apparently by electricians working in that space. In some cases, the cable sheath has been split along its length, and some of the insulation on the wires inside has been scraped off as well. Which of the following types of faults might be caused by this damage? (Choose all that apply.)

A. Open circuits

B. Short circuits

C. Split pairs

D. Transposed wires

185. Which of the following types of interference on a twisted-pair network are designed to be prevented by the twists in the wire pairs inside the cable?

A. Crosstalk

B. EMI

C. Attenuation

D. Latency

186. Ralph has been asked to create some new patch cables that will be used to connect patch panel ports to the network switches. He has been told that the patch panel connectors are all wired using the T568A pinout standard. Which of the following instructions should Ralph use when creating the patch cables?

A. Use T568A at both ends

B. Use T567B at both ends

C. Use T568A at one end and T568B at the other end

D. Use either standard, as long as both ends are the same

187. Ed has discovered that, on some of his newly installed twisted-pair cable runs, the installer has stripped away nearly a foot of the cable sheath at each end and has untwisted the wire pairs before attaching them to the connectors. Which of the following problems is the network more likely to experience due to the untwisted wires?

A. Jitter

B. Attenuation

C. Crosstalk

D. EMI

188. Ed is the administrator of his small company's network. A user calls the help desk and reports that she cannot connect to the network. She has never had any problems connecting before now, and she says that nothing on her computer has changed. Ed goes to the user's location to investigate and notices that the link pulse Light-Emitting Diode (LED) on the switch port for the user's computer is not lit. What should Ed do next to isolate and fix the problem? (Choose all that apply.)

A. Verify that the cable is securely connected to the switch

B. Verify that the patch cable is pinned and paired properly

C. Replace the existing patch cable with a straight-through cable that is known to be good

D. Replace the existing patch cable with a crossover cable that is known to be good

189. Ed is examining some twisted-pair cable runs that were recently installed in his office by an outside contractor. Looking at the connectors, he sees a variety of pinout combinations. Which of the following pinouts must Ed have rewired because they are incorrect? (Choose all that apply.)

A. White/orange, orange, white/green, blue, white/blue, green, white/brown, brown

B. White/green, green, white/orange, blue, white/blue, orange, white/brown, brown

C. White/orange, orange, white/green, green, white/blue, blue, white/brown, brown

D. White/brown, white/green, white/orange, blue, white/blue, orange, green, brown

190. You have three Virtual LANs (VLAN2, VLAN3, and VLAN4) with each implemented on three switches. A single router provides routing among the VLANs. All of the VLAN2 users connected to a common switch are complaining that they cannot access resources on other hosts within their own VLAN or on VLAN3 and VLAN4. Before today, they could connect to local and remote resources with no problem. What is the likeliest cause of the service interruption?

A. The router is malfunctioning and not routing among the VLANs.

B. VLAN2 is misconfigured.

C. The common switch to which the VLAN2 users are connected is not functioning.

D. VLAN3 and VLAN4 are misconfigured.

191. Alice is supporting a network that consists of four internal Local Area Networks (LANs) with 50 users each. Each internal LAN uses twisted-pair Gigabit Ethernet links that connect the users to a switch. Each of the four switches connects to a backbone router. All of the routers connect to the same backbone network, which has a single additional router to connect the company's network to the Internet, using a T-1 link. Users on one of the internal LANs are complaining that, when they came in this morning, they could not access the Internet or the other internal LANs, although they could access local resources with no problems. Which network component is the likeliest source of the problem in this scenario?

A. The router connecting the problem LAN to the backbone

B. The Internet router

C. The switch on the problem LAN

D. The cable on the backbone network

192. Alice is examining a captured sample of network traffic to create a network performance baseline for future reference. She notices that the sample contains a flood of multicast traffic, but she does not know why. After some investigation, she learns that there is video traffic on the network being transmitted as multicasts, but it is only intended for a particular group of users, not for everyone. However, since the multicast traffic is flooding the network, all of the hosts must process the packets, possibly resulting in performance degradation or even Denial-of-Service (DoS). Which of the following can Alice use to prevent the traffic from being processed by the unintended hosts?

A. Asymmetric routing

B. Flow control

C. Multipathing

D. IGMP snooping

193. Alice is supporting a network that consists of four internal Local Area Networks (LANs) with 50 users each. Each internal LAN uses twisted-pair Gigabit Ethernet links that connect the users to a switch. Each of the four switches connects to a backbone router. All of the routers connect to the same backbone network, which has a single additional router to connect the company's network to the Internet. Users on all of the internal LANs are complaining that, when they came in this morning, they could not access the Internet, although they could access resources on all of the LANs with no problems. Which network component is the likeliest source of the problem in this scenario?

    A. The router connecting the problem LAN to the backbone

    B. The Internet router

    C. The switch on the problem LAN

    D. The cable on the backbone network

194. Ed is implementing a web server farm on his company's network and has installed a router to create a screened subnet (or perimeter network) on which the web servers will be located. However, Ed now cannot access the web servers from his workstation on the internal network. Which of the following tasks will Ed have to complete before he can access the perimeter network from the internal network? (Choose all that apply.)

    A. Change IP addresses

    B. Change default gateway addresses

    C. Update the DNS records

    D. Change MAC addresses

195. Ralph has a wired home network with three Windows computers, a switch, and a cable modem/router that provides access to the Internet. One of the computers is able to connect to the other two, but it cannot connect to the Internet. Which of the following configuration parameters on the malfunctioning computer will Ralph most likely have to change to resolve this problem?

    A. IP address

    B. Subnet mask

    C. Default gateway

    D. MAC address

196. Ralph is a network administrator attempting to use his workstation to remote into a web server called WebServ1 on the screened subnet (perimeter network). However, the remote desktop client software is unable to establish a connection to the server. Ralph can see all of the computers on his local network and on the screened subnet. He tries using the ping utility to test WebServ1's Transmission Control Protocol/Internet Protocol (TCP/IP) functionality, and the ping test is successful. Ralph then calls his colleague Ed and has him try to connect to WebServ1 using the same remote access tool. Ed connects successfully. Which of the following could be the cause of the problem Ralph is experiencing?

    A. Name resolution failure

    B. Unresponsive service on the web server

    C. Blocked TCP/UDP ports on the web server

    D. Incorrect firewall settings on Ralph's workstation

197. A user calls the company's IT help desk to report that she has received an error message on her Windows workstation. The error states that her computer has an IP address that is duplicated on the network. Ralph is concerned that there might be a configuration problem with the DHCP servers on the network. He suspects that there are DHCP servers configured with scopes that overlap, resulting in two DHCP servers assigning the same IP addresses to different clients. He is worried that they are about to receive a flood of calls reporting the same problem. Alice reassures Ralph, telling him that it cannot be a DHCP problem, and that there must be two computers that are manually configured with the same IP address. How does Alice know this?

  A. Because Windows computers check the routing table before accepting an IP address from a DHCP server

  B. Because DHCP servers use DNS queries to check for duplicate IP addresses

  C. Because DHCP clients use ARP broadcasts to check for duplicate IP addresses

  D. Because it is only possible to have one DHCP server on a given subnet

198. A user, Ed, is reporting what appear to be intermittent traffic interruptions on his workstation. Sometimes he receives responses to his server requests, and sometimes not. It does not seem to be an Internet issue, because the problem also occurs with local server requests. While troubleshooting the problem, Ralph performs a series of packet captures and analyzes the network traffic. He discovers that all of the request messages generated by Ed's workstation have responses on the network, but in some cases, the responses are going to a workstation other than Ed's. Which of the following conditions could be causing this to happen?

  A. Duplicate IP addresses

  B. Blocked TCP/UDP ports

  C. Duplicate MAC addresses

  D. Incorrect host firewall settings

  E. Multicast flood

199. A user calls Alice at the IT help desk and reports that she is having intermittent problems accessing both local servers and Internet websites. Which of the following potential problems can Alice rule out immediately?

  A. Duplicate Media Access Control (MAC) addresses

  B. Duplicate Internet Protocol (IP) addresses

  C. Malfunctioning router

  D. Malfunctioning Domain Name System (DNS) server

200. The entire network at Adatum Corp. is unable to access the Internet. All of the users throughout the network are complaining that their browsers are displaying Domain Name System (DNS) failure messages. The company does not have an in-house network administrator, so they call Ralph at his consulting firm. Which of the following should be the first question that Ralph asks in his attempt to pinpoint the location of the malfunction?

  A. What browser are the users running?

  B. Where is the DNS server located?

  C. What technology is used to provide access to the Internet?

  D. What sites are the users attempting to access?

201. To save the company money and to provide some new hires with Gigabit Ethernet connectivity, Ralph has installed some new Category 5e (Cat 5e) cable runs, connecting his company's datacenter with a newly rented office at the far end of the building. However, the new users are complaining of intermittent connectivity problems. The company brings in a cabling contractor to investigate, and his diagnosis is attenuation. Which of the following will most likely be a sure solution to the problem?

 A. Repull the runs using Category 6 cable

 B. Shorten the cable runs

 C. Configure the hardware to run at a slower speed

 D. Install high-end network adapters in the workstations

202. Alice's network has been experiencing intermittent service slowdowns and outages ever since the company moved into their new building. She has tried every troubleshooting procedure she can think of and has not been able to determine the cause. One particular user, hoping to be the squeaky wheel that gets the grease, has taken to calling Alice every time he experiences a problem. One day, as she is working in the datacenter, Alice notices that the user calls her every time she hears an additional humming noise begin. After examining the doors in the hallway, Alice realizes that the racks containing her switches are located right next to the building's elevator machinery room. Which of the following conditions is probably causing the network communication problem?

 A. EMI

 B. NEXT

 C. FEXT

 D. Attenuation

203. Ralph is setting up a workstation for the company's new vice president. He has installed the computer in the VP's office and plugged the data cable into the wall plate. Then, back in the datacenter, he uses a patch cable to connect the corresponding port in the patch panel to a port in the network switch. However, the computer is unable to access the network. There are no complaints from other users. Which of the following could be the source of the problem? (Choose all that apply.)

 A. The DNS server is malfunctioning.

 B. The switch port is disabled.

 C. The NAT server is not functioning.

 D. The switch is configured to use port security.

204. Ralph is setting up a network connection for a new vice president, who is supplying his own laptop under the company's Bring Your Own Device (BYOD) policy. He plugs the computer into the wall plate, and the link pulse Light-Emitting Diode (LED) lights up. Then, back in the datacenter, he uses a patch cable to connect the corresponding port in the patch panel to a port in the network switch. Later, the VP calls Ralph to report that data transfers between his laptop and the network servers are extremely slow. Which of the following could explain the problem?

 A. There is a duplex mismatch between the laptop and the network switch.

 B. Ralph used a crossover cable to connect the laptop to the wall plate.

 C. The switch port is disabled.

 D. The network adapter drivers on the laptop are outdated.

205. While working in her company's datacenter, Alice notices that the Light-Emitting Diodes (LEDs) on most of the network switch ports are green, but there are some that are orange. Alice asks several people why this is so and receives a different answer from each one. Which one of the following answers is correct?

 A. The orange LEDs indicate that no device is connected to the switch port.

 B. The orange LEDs indicate that the connected device is experiencing an excessive number of collisions.

 C. The orange LEDs indicate that the device is connected to the switch at a relatively slow speed.

 D. The orange LEDs indicate that the connected devices are other switches, rather than workstations.

206. Alice's company is opening a new branch office, and Alice is responsible for building the domain controller for that office. She installs a new Windows server and configures it as a domain controller, and then ships it to the new office site. However, once it arrives and is connected to the home office network, the new domain controller fails to synchronize with the existing ones at the home office. Which of the following could be the cause of the problem?

 A. Incorrect time

 B. Server hardware failure

 C. Duplicate IP addresses

 D. Incorrect default gateway address

207. Ralph recently bought an old 10Base-T Ethernet hub at a garage sale and wants to use it to connect his various computers into a home network. He plugs three computers into the hub and finds that although two of his older computers can communicate with each other, his newest computer cannot connect to the network. Which of the following tasks will most likely resolve the problem?

 A. Configure the hub to run at 10 Mbps

 B. Configure the hub to run at 100 Mbps

 C. Configure the computer's network adapter to run at 10 Mbps

 D. Configure the computer's network adapter to run at 100 Mbps

208. Alice is troubleshooting a problem that some users are having connecting to an application server on the local network. While testing connectivity using the ping tool, she discovers that she can ping the server successfully using its computer name, but pinging the computer's fully qualified domain name (FQDN) fails. Which of the following is most likely the source of the problem?

 A. DNS

 B. DHCP

 C. EMI

 D. ACL

209. Alice is working on an older network with a Windows Internet Name Service (WINS) server, a Domain Name System (DNS) server, and an Internet router. A user is complaining that he suddenly cannot connect to hosts on other internal networks. The user is not having problems connecting to resources on his local network or the Internet. Alice asks the user whether anything is new or has been changed on the computer and discovers that he recently changed some Internet Protocol (IP) parameters. What should Alice do next?

   A. Verify that the router is up and running and properly configured

   B. Verify that the WINS server is up and running and properly configured

   C. Verify that the DNS server is up and running and properly configured

   D. Verify that the user's IP configuration settings are correct

210. Ralph has begun to receive calls from users reporting that they cannot access the local network or the Internet. Ralph checks their computers and discovers that all of the users with a problem have IP addresses in the 169.254.0.0/16 network, which is not the address used on Ralph's network. Which of the following might be the cause of the problem?

   A. The users have tried to modify their IP configuration settings.

   B. There is a rogue DHCP server somewhere on the network.

   C. The IP address leases assigned by the DHCP server have expired.

   D. The users' workstations have been infected by a form of malware.

211. Ralph has installed a new Category 5e (Cat 5e) cable run himself. He has attached keystone connectors to both ends of the cable, mounted the office-side connector to a wall plate, and mounted the datacenter connector into a patch panel. Then he took a patch cord and connected the patch panel port to an open port in one of the network switches. However, the Light-Emitting Diode (LED) on the switch port does not light. What should Ralph do?

   A. Repull the cable run using Category 6 cable

   B. Check the cable run for wiring faults

   C. Make sure the switch port is not disabled

   D. Plug a computer into the wall plate

212. A user calls Ed at the help desk to report that his computer is displaying a Duplicate IP Address error message. This puzzles Ed because all of the network workstations should be configured to obtain their Internet Protocol (IP) addresses from Dynamic Host Configuration Protocol (DHCP) servers. Ed asks the user if he has changed the Transmission Control Protocol/Internet Protocol (TCP/IP) configuration settings on the computer recently. The user says no. Ed then asks of anybody else uses the workstation. The user says no. However, when Ed runs the `ipconfig /all` command on the user's workstation, he sees that the DHCP Enabled setting reads No. What should Ed do next?

   A. Accuse the user of changing the TCP/IP settings and then lying about it

   B. Activate the DHCP client on the workstation and close the trouble ticket

   C. Begin an investigation into the possibility of a rogue DHCP server on the network

   D. Change the IP address on the workstation to one that is not already in use

213. Ralph is working with an Asymmetric Digital Subscriber Line (ADSL) router that has a switch module containing four Ethernet ports, all of which are assigned to the default VLAN1. Ralph can plug a laptop into one of the router's ports and access the Internet with no problems. Ralph now needs to connect the ADSL router to the company network, so that the wireless access points on the network can provide users with Internet access through the ADSL router. However, when Ralph plugs the router into a network switch port in VLAN4, the switch starts generating "Native VLAN mismatch detected" errors every minute. Which of the following steps should be part of the solution Ralph implements to stop the error messages? (Choose all that apply.)

A. Create a VLAN1 on the network switch

B. Create a VLAN4 on the ADSL router's switch module

C. Configure the network switch port connected to the router to use VLAN1

D. Configure the router port connected to the network switch to use VLAN4

214. Ralph is working with an Asymmetric Digital Subscriber Line (ADSL) router that has a switch module containing four Ethernet ports, all of which are assigned to VLAN2. Ralph can plug a laptop into one of the router's ports and access the Internet with no problems. Ralph now needs to connect the ADSL router to the company network. However, when Ralph plugs the router into a network switch port in VLAN4, the switch starts generating "Native VLAN mismatch detected" errors every minute. To correct the problem, Ralph attempts to create a VLAN4 on the router, but he receives a "Feature not licensed" error. Which of the following actions can Ralph take to resolve the problem? (Choose all that apply.)

A. Purchase a feature upgrade for the router

B. Create a VLAN2 on the switch

C. Configure the router to use VLAN1

D. Configure the switch to use VLAN1

215. Clients of Ralph's company are calling to complain that, when they try to access the company's website, they see an error message stating that the website has an untrusted security certificate. They are afraid that they are connecting to an unprotected site or that the site has been taken over by hackers. What must Ralph due to address this problem?

A. Obtain an SSL certificate from a trusted third-party company

B. Configure the web servers to generate a self-signed certificate

C. Install a certification authority on one of the network servers

D. Explain to the clients that it is safe to bypass the error message and proceed to the website

216. Ralph is a network administrator who has had a Windows user report difficulties accessing certain other computers on the network. Ralph determines that the user is only experiencing problems when trying to connect to a system on the far side of a router. Ralph therefore decides to inspect the routing table on the user's computer. Which of the following tools can he use to do this? (Choose all that apply.)

A. nbtstat

B. route

C. nslookup

D. netstat

217. A user calls Alice at the help desk to report that he cannot access the Internet. He can access systems on the local network, however. Alice examines the routing table on the user's workstation and sees the following. Which of the following commands must Alice run to correct the user's problem?

```
IPv4 Route Table
===========================================================================
Active Routes:
Network Destination  Netmask          Gateway  Interface     Metric
  127.0.0.0          255.0.0.0        On-link  127.0.0.1     331
  127.0.0.1          255.255.255.255  On-link  127.0.0.1     331
  127.255.255.255    255.255.255.255  On-link  127.0.0.1     331
  192.168.2.0        255.255.255.0    On-link  192.168.2.37  281
  192.168.2.37       255.255.255.255  On-link  192.168.2.37  281
  192.168.2.255      255.255.255.255  On-link  192.168.2.37  281
  224.0.0.0          240.0.0.0        On-link  127.0.0.1     331
  224.0.0.0          240.0.0.0        On-link  192.168.2.37  281
  255.255.255.255    255.255.255.255  On-link  127.0.0.1     331
  255.255.255.255    255.255.255.255  On-link  192.168.2.37  281
===========================================================================
Persistent Routes:
  None
```

A. route add 0.0.0.0 MASK 0.0.0.0 192.168.2.37 METRIC 25 IF 192.168.2.99

B. route add 0.0.0.0 MASK 255.255.255.0 192.168.2.99 METRIC 25 IF 192.168.2.37

C. route add 192.168.2.0 MASK 255.255.255.0 192.168.2.99 METRIC 25 IF 192.168.2.37

D. route add 0.0.0.0 MASK 0.0.0.0 192.168.2.99 METRIC 25 IF 192.168.2.37

218. Alice is working the IT help desk at her company, which has 500 inside salespeople who start work at 9:00 a.m. The users are running Windows 10 and obtaining their Internet Protocol (IP) address configuration settings from Dynamic Host Configuration Protocol (DHCP) servers. Every morning, Alice receives many trouble calls from users that are experiencing extremely slow performance after they first turn their computers on. Their performance gradually improves within an hour. Which of the following is the most likely cause of the slowdown?

A. Broadcast storm

B. Routing loop

C. Rogue DHCP server

D. Switching loop

E. Asymmetric routing

219. Alice is having trouble with a new fiber-optic cable run that has just been installed between two buildings on her company's campus. To confirm that there is a problem with the cables, Alice consults the wiring diagram provided by the cable installer and begins to calculate the optical power loss resulting from cable installation factors such as the type of cable used, the attenuation resulting from the length of the cable runs, and the number and type of splices. Which of the following terms describes the calculations that Alice is performing?

    A. Protocol analysis

    B. Routing loop

    C. Optical link budget

    D. Received Signal Strength Indication (RSSI)

220. Ralph is a network administrator for a company with several branch offices, each of which has a Windows domain controller. There have been problems lately with the domain controllers synchronizing their data, and Ralph suspects that the problem is related to the Network Time Protocol (NTP) settings on the servers. Examining the server logs on the various domain controllers, he sees multiple errors saying, "Server NTP service not synchronized." All of the other server functions are running normally. Which of the following could be the cause of the problem Ralph is experiencing?

    A. Name resolution failure

    B. Unresponsive database service on the servers

    C. Incorrect TCP/IP settings on the servers

    D. Incorrect firewall settings on the servers

Chapter

6

Practice Exam 1

1. Which of the following are the layers in the standard three-tier datacenter architecture? (Choose all that apply.)

    A. Core

    B. Intermediate

    C. Distribution

    D. Access

2. You are a new hire at Adatum Corp., and this is your first day on the job. You are setting up your workstation, but you are unsure whether you are permitted to install your favorite software on the company's computer. The Human Resources server has a large library of employee documents. Which of the following is a document that you might want to consult to determine whether personal software is allowed?

    A. SLA

    B. AUP

    C. NDA

    D. BYOD

3. You are working the help desk when a user calls and reports that she is unable to connect to the Internet. Which of the following steps would you be least likely to perform first when troubleshooting the problem?

    A. Check the configuration of the router connecting the Local Area Network (LAN) to the Internet.

    B. Ask the user if she can access resources on the local network.

    C. Check to see if anyone else is experiencing the same problem.

    D. Check the user's job title to see if she is an important person in the company.

4. Which of the following is not a means of preventing unauthorized individuals from entering a sensitive location, such as a datacenter?

    A. Key fobs

    B. Motion detection

    C. Biometric scans

    D. Identification badges

5. You are an IT consultant who has been contracted to install new computers on a client's Gigabit Ethernet network. You want the performance of the new computers to be as good as it can be, so you configure their network adapters to run at the full speed of 1 Gbps and to use full-duplex communication. You test the computers after installing them, and they function well. However, once the computers are in service, you begin getting complaints from the client of extremely poor network performance on the new machines. You return to the

site that evening and run some ping tests, but you do not detect any problem. You call in a colleague to perform a packet analysis, and she detects large numbers of packet collisions, late collisions, Cyclic Redundancy Check (CRC) errors, and runt frames. Which of the following could be the cause of the problem?

A. Damaged cables

B. Transmit/Receive (TX/RX) reversal

C. Duplex mismatch

D. Incorrect cable type

6. Which of the following is a wireless topology that does not require the use of an access point?

A. Star

B. Ad hoc

C. Bus

D. Infrastructure

7. You want to create a network in which computers from different departments are assigned to separate Virtual Local Area Networks (VLANs). You also want to be able to forward traffic between the VLANs so that each computer is capable of accessing any other computer. Which of the following will enable you to perform all these functions with a single device?

A. Load balancer

B. Virtual router

C. Multilayer switch

D. Broadband router

8. Which of the following are standard terms used in data loss prevention to describe specific data states? (Choose all that apply.)

A. Data on-line

B. Data at-rest

C. Data in-motion

D. Data in-use

9. Temporal Key Integrity Protocol (TKIP) is an encryption protocol that was introduced in the IEEE 802.11 wireless network standards to replace another protocol that was found to be easily penetrated. Which of the following 802.11 wireless security protocols uses TKIP for encryption?

A. AES

B. WEP

C. WPA

D. WPA2

10. You have been asked by your supervisor in the IT department to test some newly installed cable runs. She hands you the tool shown in the following figure. What is the function of the tool and how do you use it?

Reprinted from *CompTIA Network+ Study Guide: Exam N10-006, Third Edition* by Todd Lammle (Wiley, 2015)

   A. When you place the tool at one end of a wire, it generates a tone that can be detected at the other end.

   B. When you touch the end of the tool to a copper cable, you can detect and measure the electrical current flowing through it.

   C. When you connect the tool to the end of a fiber-optic cable, you can measure the length of the cable run.

   D. When you attach the tool to the end of a twisted-pair cable, it tests for crosstalk and other performance characteristics.

11. A multifactor authentication system consists of at least two different identifying criteria, typically falling into two of the following categories: something you have, something you do, something you know, and something you are. Which of the following authentication factors is an example of something you have?

   A. A password

   B. A fingerprint

   C. A smartcard

   D. A finger gesture

12. Which of the following are port numbers used for Structured Query Language (SQL) communications? (Choose all that apply.)

   A. 1433
   B. 3389
   C. 1521
   D. 3306

13. At a garage sale, you purchase some 802.11a wireless network adapter cards for desktop computers at a very low price. Your plan is to use them to expand your 802.11g home network. After installing one of the adapters in a computer, you attempt to connect to the network, but you cannot see the Service Set Identifier (SSID) in the list of available networks. You try installing a different adapter, thinking the first one might be broken, but the second one does not work either. What can you do to resolve the problem and connect the computer to your network?

   A. Configure the access point to use the 5 GHz frequency.
   B. Move the computer closer to the access point.
   C. Manually enter the SSID in the computer's wireless network client software.
   D. Nothing. 802.11a equipment cannot connect to an 802.11g network.

14. Parity is a fault tolerance technique used by disk storage arrays in which an additional parity bit is stored for a specified number of data bits. By using the parity information, the storage subsystem can calculate the values of bits that have been lost due to a disk failure, enabling the system to re-create the lost data. Redundant Array of Independent Disks (RAID) is a type of storage array that sometimes uses parity to provide fault tolerance. Which of the following RAID levels provide fault tolerance by using parity data? (Choose all that apply.)

   A. RAID 0
   B. RAID 1
   C. RAID 5
   D. RAID 6
   E. RAID 10

15. You are setting up an 802.11n wireless network using the 2.4 GHz frequency band. You plan to install three Wireless Access Points (WAPs). Which of the following channels should you use for your access points to avoid channel overlap that can result in interference? (Choose all that apply.)

   A. 1
   B. 4
   C. 6
   D. 8
   E. 11

16. Your supervisor has asked you to increase the security of the servers on your network. Which of the following procedures can be considered to be server hardening techniques? (Choose all that apply.)

   A. Upgrading server firmware

   B. Disabling unnecessary services

   C. Creating privileged user accounts

   D. Disabling unused TCP and UDP ports

17. You are working the IT help desk when a user calls to report that he cannot access the Internet, although he is able to connect to computers on the local network. At the user's workstation, you run the `ipconfig /all` command and examine the output. Which of the options is the most likely explanation for the user's problem, based on the following `ipconfig` results?

```
Windows IP Configuration

    Host Name . . . . . . . . . . . . : Client12
    Primary Dns Suffix  . . . . . . . :
    Node Type . . . . . . . . . . . . : Hybrid
    IP Routing Enabled. . . . . . . . : No
    WINS Proxy Enabled. . . . . . . . : No


Ethernet adapter Local Area Connection:

    Connection-specific DNS Suffix  . :
    Description . . . . . . . . . . . : PCIe Family Controller
    Physical Address. . . . . . . . . : 60-EB-69-93-5E-E5
    DHCP Enabled. . . . . . . . . . . : No
    Autoconfiguration Enabled . . . . : Yes
    Link-local IPv6 Address . . . . . : fe80::c955:c944:acdd:3fcb%2
    IPv4 Address. . . . . . . . . . . : 192.168.23.234
    Subnet Mask . . . . . . . . . . . : 255.255.255.0
    Lease Obtained. . . . . . . . . . : Monday, October 23, 2017 6:23:47 PM
    Lease Expires . . . . . . . . . . : Saturday, November 18, 2017 9:49:24 PM
    Default Gateway . . . . . . . . . : 192.168.216.99
    DHCPv6 IAID . . . . . . . . . . . : 241232745
    DHCPv6 Client DUID  . . . . . . . : 00-01-00-01-18-10-22-0D-60-EB-69-93-5E-E5
    DNS Servers . . . . . . . . . . . : 192.168.22.114
    NetBIOS over Tcpip. . . . . . . . : Enabled
```

   A. DHCP is not enabled.

   B. The Subnet Mask setting is incorrect.

   C. The Default Gateway setting is incorrect.

   D. The DNS Servers setting is located on another network.

18. Which of the following are typical examples of the Internet of Things (IoT)? (Choose all that apply.)

    A. A television remote control

    B. A key fob that unlocks your car

    C. A smartphone app for your home thermostat

    D. A remotely monitored cardiac pacemaker

    E. A refrigerator with an internal camera

19. When an internal Windows user logs on to an Active Directory domain, which of the following protocols authenticates the user?

    A. Kerberos

    B. WPA2

    C. RADIUS

    D. EAP-TLS

20. You are installing an ADSL router for your company's new branch office. The router has a switch module containing four Ethernet ports, all of which are assigned to the default VLAN1. When you plug a laptop into one of the Ethernet ports, you can access the Internet with no difficulties. You now need to connect the ADSL router to the company network so that the Wireless Access Points (WAPs) on the network can provide users with Internet access through the ADSL router. However, when you plug the router into a network switch port that is assigned to VLAN4, the switch starts generating "Native VLAN mismatch detected" errors once every minute. Which of the following steps should be part of the solution you implement to stop the error messages from appearing? (Choose all that apply.)

    A. Create a VLAN1 on the network switch.

    B. Configure the network switch port connected to the router to use VLAN1.

    C. Create a VLAN4 on the ADSL router's switch module.

    D. Configure the router port connected to the network switch to use VLAN4.

21. Which of the following steps will not help to prevent war driving attacks from compromising your wireless network? (Choose all that apply.)

    A. Configure your clients and access point to use WEP security.

    B. Configure your clients and access point to use WPA2 security

    C. Configure your access point not to broadcast its SSID.

    D. Configure your access point to use a longer SSID.

22. You have just created a new virtual machine using remote controls provided by a cloud service provider on the Internet. You then install Windows Server on the virtual machine and configure it to function as a web server. Which of the following cloud architectures are you using when you do this? (Choose all that apply.)

    A. IaaS

    B. PaaS

    C. SaaS

D. Public cloud

E. Private cloud

F. Hybrid cloud

23. It is your first day working for a consultant that does network cable installations. Your new boss hands you a spool of Category 6 cable, a bag of little clear plastic components, and the tool shown in the following figure. He then tells you to "get started on fives and tens." What is your new boss expecting you to do?

Reprinted from *CompTIA Network+ Study Guide: Exam N10-006, Third Edition* by Todd Lammle (Wiley, 2015)

A. Pull cable runs

B. Attach keystone connectors

C. Install a patch panel

D. Create patch cables

24. Which of the following well-known ports do you use to configure outgoing mail on a POP3 email client?

A. 110

B. 25

C. 143

D. 80

25. You are a consultant who has been hired to extend a network by a client that is still running thin Ethernet. Which of the following cable types will you have to bring with you to add thin Ethernet network segments?

    A. RG-8

    B. RG-58

    C. RJ45

    D. RJ11

26. Which of the following types of cable is never used to connect a workstation to an Ethernet network?

    A. Rollover

    B. Straight-through

    C. Crossover

    D. Plenum

    E. Shielded

27. Which of the following protocols does Internet Protocol Security (IPSec) use to provide data origin authentication by digitally signing packets before transmitting them over the network?

    A. AH

    B. SSL

    C. ESP

    D. RDP

28. You have constructed a network on which all of the computers are connected to a single switch. You then create Virtual Local Area Networks (VLANs) on the switch, corresponding to the company's departments, and add the switch port for each user workstation and department server to the appropriate VLAN. Later, users report that while they can access their departmental servers and the workstations of other users in the same department, they cannot communicate with any of the other departments. What is the problem, and what must you do to correct it?

    A. There is a faulty VLAN configuration on the switch. You must re-create all of the VLANs and configure each VLAN for routing.

    B. VLANs are limited to data link layer communication only. To enable communication between the VLANs, you must install a router or a layer 3 switch on the network and configure it to route traffic between the VLANs.

    C. The VLANs are using different data link layer protocols. You must configure the VLANs to use the same data link layer protocol in order for them to communicate with each other.

    D. One of the VLANs is configured to filter all of the other VLAN traffic for security purposes. You must change the filter on this one VLAN.

29. The TCP/IP term socket consists of which of the following elements? (Choose all that apply.)

   A. Port number

   B. MAC address

   C. IP address

   D. Subnet mask

30. You are installing a cable modem to provide your home network with access to the internet through your cable television provider. The cable modem is a multifunction device that the cable company says provides everything you need for a home network. Which of the following network functions does a home cable modem typically provide? (Choose all that apply.)

   A. DHCP server

   B. Wireless Access Point

   C. Broadband router

   D. Ethernet switch

   E. Proxy server

   F. RADIUS server

31. Which of the following Domain Name System (DNS) resource records is not used for forward name resolution?

   A. PTR

   B. CNAME

   C. AAAA

   D. MX

32. Which of the following are tasks that can be performed by a protocol analyzer that could provide potential intruders with information about the network? (Choose all that apply.)

   A. A protocol analyzer can decrypt protected information in packets captured from the network.

   B. A protocol analyzer can detect open ports on network systems and launch attacks against them.

   C. A protocol analyzer can display the IP addresses of the systems on the network.

   D. A protocol analyzer can display the application data in packets captured from the network.

33. Which of the following services are provided by a RADIUS server? (Choose all that apply.)

   A. Attenuation

   B. Authentication

   C. Assistance

   D. Authorization

   E. Accounting

34. Some users are having a problem connecting to an application server on their local network. You go to their department and start to troubleshoot the problem by testing connectivity using the ping tool at one of the user workstations. You discover that you can ping the server successfully using its computer name, but pinging the computer's fully qualified domain name (FQDN) fails. As a result of these tests, which of the following can you determine is the most likely source of the problem?

- **A.** EMI
- **B.** DHCP
- **C.** DNS
- **D.** ACL

35. You have been given the job of devising a plan to provide a 500-node private internetwork with access to the Internet. The primary objective of the project is to provide all of the network users with access to web and email services while keeping the client computers safe from unauthorized Internet users. There are two secondary objectives for the project: one is to provide a means of monitoring and regulating the users' Internet activities, and the other is to avoid having to manually configure IP addresses on each one of the client computers. You submit a proposal that calls for the use of private IP addresses on the client computers and a series of proxy servers with public, registered IP addresses, which are connected to the Internet. Which of the following statements about your proposed Internet access solution is true?

- **A.** The proposal satisfies the primary objective and both of the secondary objectives.
- **B.** The proposal satisfies the primary objective and one of the secondary objectives.
- **C.** The proposal satisfies the primary objective but neither of the secondary objectives.
- **D.** The proposal fails to satisfy both the primary and secondary objectives.

36. Which of the following cloud service models provides the consumer with the least amount of control over the cloud resources?

- **A.** IaaS
- **B.** PaaS
- **C.** SaaS
- **D.** IaaS, PaaS, and SaaS all provide the same degree of control.

37. The jumbo frame capability is associated with which networking protocol?

- **A.** Ethernet
- **B.** Internet Protocol (IP)
- **C.** Point-to-Point Protocol (PPP)
- **D.** Transmission Control Protocol (TCP)

38. You are working your company's IT help desk, where you are required to follow a specific troubleshooting protocol when handling calls from users. In which of the following trouble-shooting steps would you create a trouble ticket?

A. Establish a theory of probable cause

B. Verify full system functionality and, if applicable, implement preventive measures

C. Identify the problem

D. Test the theory to determine the cause

E. Document findings, actions, and outcomes

F. Implement the solution or escalate as necessary

G. Establish a plan of action to resolve the problem and identify potential effects

39. You are working your company's help desk when a user calls to report that he cannot access any of the data on his computer. He says that a message has appeared on his screen stating that all of his data has been encrypted by the FBI and that it will be decrypted only after he pays $768 in Bitcoin to an unknown address. The user wants to know if he is responsible for making the payment. Which of the following types of attacks has the user experienced?

A. Denial-of-Service

B. War driving

C. Ransomware

D. ARP poisoning

40. Which of the following Wide Area Network (WAN) services provide unequal amounts of upstream and downstream bandwidth? (Choose all that apply.)

A. SDSL

B. CATV

C. ADSL

D. FCoE

41. Network cable runs generally connect office endpoints, such as wall plates, to a central cabling nexus, which is typically where the runs are joined to a backbone network that links them together. Which of the following are terms for such nexuses where network cabling connections are found? (Choose all that apply.)

A. RDP

B. IDF

C. MDF

D. MTBF

42. Your supervisor has asked you to call the cabling contractor your company uses and make an appointment to install some new twisted-pair cable runs. In addition to asking how many cable runs you need pulled, the contractor asks you if you need plenum or PVC. Under which of the following conditions might the local building code require that a data network use plenum cable?

    A. When cable runs exceed the maximum length specified by the physical layer specification

    B. When cables must run through air ducts

    C. When cables run near to devices that generate electromagnetic interference (EMI)

    D. When multiple cables run through the same conduit

43. Which of the following is not a term for the process of combining the bandwidth of two or more network adapters to increase the overall speed of the connection and provide fault tolerance?

    A. Port aggregation

    B. Link aggregation

    C. Bonding

    D. Clustering

    E. NIC teaming

44. You have been asked by the director of the IT department to review the security status of the network device administration procedures currently in use. You know that network device hardening has as one of its first principles the use of secure protocols over insecure ones. Which of the following suggestions are examples of this principle that you should suggest to the director? (Choose all that apply.)

    A. Use WEP instead of WPA2.

    B. Use TKIP instead of AES.

    C. Use HTTPS instead of HTTP.

    D. Use SSH instead of Telnet.

45. The Simple Network Management Protocol (SNMP) works by processing information gathered from agents installed or embedded in network devices and displaying the information on a central console. Which of the following is the term used for the database in which SNMP agents store information about their properties?

    A. MIB

    B. Trap

    C. Syslog

    D. SIEM

46. When a web browser connects to a web server using an address with the `https://` prefix, the connection is secured using Transmission Control Protocol (TCP) and an encryption protocol. Which of the following are protocols that are typically used to secure communication between web servers and web browsers? (Choose all that apply.)

   A. TLS

   B. SSH

   C. DTLS

   D. SSL

47. A screened subnet is a segment that is exposed to the Internet and separated from the internal network by a firewall. Administrators typically use a screened subnet for servers that must be accessible by outside users, such as web and email servers. Which of the following is another term for a screened subnet?

   A. PEAP

   B. DMZ

   C. VLAN

   D. TKIP

48. Which of the following types of traffic is not exchanged by Remote Desktop clients and servers using the Remote Desktop Protocol (RDP)?

   A. Keystrokes

   B. Mouse movements

   C. Display information

   D. Application data

49. You have been engaged to design a Wireless Local Area Network (WLAN) for a site you have never seen. For that reason, you want the WLAN to be able to support both the 2.4 GHz and 5 GHz frequencies. Which of the following IEEE 802.11 WLAN standards should you look for when you are shopping for equipment that supports both frequencies? (Choose all that apply.)

   A. 802.11a

   B. 802.11b

   C. 802.11g

   D. 802.11n

   E. 802.11ac

   F. 802.11ax

50. Which of the following statements about multitenancy in a public cloud datacenter is not true?

   A. Multitenancy presents a potential security risk because other tenants are utilizing the same hardware.

   B. Multitenancy separates tenants by assigning each one its own virtual machine.

   C. Multitenancy reduces the cost of utilities and other overhead.

   D. Multitenancy introduces the possibility of competition for bandwidth with other tenants.

51. You have been asked to evaluate the security provided by the cryptographic algorithms in use on your network. Which of the following are not cryptographic algorithms used for file hashing? (Choose all that apply.)

A. RC4

B. MD5

C. AES

D. SHA

52. When starting her new position as a network administrator, Alice was given two user accounts. One account is intended for standard user activities, and another has the additional permissions needed for Alice to perform administrative tasks. This is an example of which of the following security concepts?

A. Zero day

B. Least privilege

C. Defense in depth

D. Multifactor authentication

53. You are in the process of troubleshooting a user's computer that is malfunctioning. Which step of the troubleshooting model involves replacing computer components until you have identified a faulty hardware device?

A. Establish a plan of action to resolve the problem

B. Duplicate the problem

C. Gather information

D. Verify full system functionality

E. Test the theory to determine the cause

F. Document findings, actions, and outcomes

G. Establish a theory of probable cause

54. An insider threat is most likely to be detectable by which of the following types of physical security?

A. Motion detection

B. Smartcards

C. Biometrics

D. Video surveillance

55. Which of the following network interface occurrences is considered to be a malfunction on a full-duplex Ethernet network but is not a malfunction on a half-duplex Ethernet network?

A. Runts

B. Late collisions

C. Giants

D. Collisions

56. A protocol analyzer is a tool that captures packets from a network and examines their contents. Which of the following Unix/Linux tools is a protocol analyzer?

  A. `nmap`

  B. `tcpdump`

  C. `pathping`

  D. `iptables`

57. A Storage Area Network (SAN) typically takes the form of a dedicated network used to provide servers with access to hard disk arrays and other storage devices. Which of the following statements about the differences between a SAN and Network Attached Storage (NAS) are true? (Choose all that apply.)

  A. NAS devices typically provide a filesystem, while SAN devices do not.

  B. NAS provides file-level storage access, whereas a SAN provides block-level storage access.

  C. NAS devices typically contain integrated iSCSI targets.

  D. SAN devices have an operating system, whereas NAS devices do not.

58. Your supervisor has just informed you that the CIO has hired an outside consultant to perform penetration testing on the company network. Which of the following best describes what you can expect the consultant to do?

  A. Evaluate the security conditions on the network

  B. Create computers or networks that are alluring targets for intruders

  C. Attempt to compromise the network's security measures

  D. Implement a new companywide security protocol

59. Your company is a contractor for the government that regularly works with highly sensitive defense data. To prevent this data from being compromised, the company's datacenter has various special security measures installed. All of the servers have crimped metal tags holding the cases closed. All of the hardware racks are locked in clear-fronted cabinets. All of the cable runs are installed in transparent conduits. These are all examples of which of the following types of physical security measure?

  A. Geofencing

  B. Port security

  C. Tamper detection

  D. Asset tracking

60. Wavelength division multiplexing is a technique for carrying multiple fiber-optic signals on a single network medium. There are several types of this multiplexing technique, including Coarse Wavelength Division Multiplexing (CWDM), Dense Wavelength Division Multiplexing (DWDM), and Bidirectional Wavelength Division Multiplexing (BWDM, or just WDM). Which of the following is one of the ways in which these types of multiplexing differ?

  A. They carry different numbers of channels on a single medium.

  B. They use different wavelength spacings.

  C. They provide different amounts of signal amplification.

  D. They use different forms of amplitude modulation.

61. Which of the following protocols use tunneling to establish secured links between TCP/IP systems? (Choose all that apply.)

A. L2TP

B. IPSec

C. MGRE

D. NAT

62. Your supervisor has given you a Class C network IP address and has asked you to create a network with 8 subnets and 30 hosts per subnet. Which of the following subnet masks will you have to use?

A. 255.255.255.128

B. 255.255.255.192

C. 255.255.255.224

D. 255.255.255.240

E. 255.255.255.248

F. 255.255.255.252

63. You are a consultant working at a client site. The client has supplied you with the Service Set Identifier (SSID) and the passphrase for the company's wireless network so that you can connect to it with your laptop. However, you are unable to establish a connection. Which of the following security measures might be preventing you from connecting your laptop to the network?

A. Geofencing

B. MAC filtering

C. Using WPA2

D. Disabling SSID broadcasts

64. You have just finished installing a new Category 5e cable run for the first time. After attaching keystone connectors to both ends of the cable, you mount the office-side connector to a wall plate and mount the datacenter connector into a patch panel. Then you take a patch cable and connect the patch panel port to an open port in one of the network switches. However, the link pulse LED on the switch port does not light as it is supposed to. What should you do next?

A. Repull the cable run using Category 6 cable.

B. Check the cable run for wiring faults.

C. Make sure the switch port is not disabled.

D. Plug a computer into the wall plate.

65. Devices on a TCP/IP network typically use the Address Resolution Protocol (ARP) to locate specific destinations on the local network by resolving IP addresses into Media Access Control (MAC) addresses (also known as hardware addresses). At which layer of the Open Systems Interconnection (OSI) model do these MAC addresses operate?

    A. Physical

    B. Data link

    C. Network

    D. Transport

66. Many network diagrams use Cisco symbols to illustrate the locations of and relationships between network components. Cisco symbols are standardized pictographs that illustrate the basic function of a network component. In a network diagram that uses Cisco symbols, what component does the symbol in the figure represent?

    A. A hub

    B. A switch

    C. A router

    D. A gateway

67. Address Resolution Protocol (ARP) poisoning is the deliberate insertion of fraudulent information into the ARP cache stored on computers and switches. Which of the following types of attack can be facilitated by ARP poisoning? (Choose all that apply.)

    A. Social engineering

    B. Man in the middle

    C. Evil twin

    D. Session hijacking

68. Recently, your network has been the target of numerous attack attempts. To gather information about the attackers, you have created a server that is designed to function as an enticing target but that does not provide access to any legitimately sensitive services or information. Which of the following is the term used to describe this technique?

    A. Spoofing

    B. DMZ

    C. Root guard

    D. Honeypot

69. You are a consultant working on a new client's network. The network has been in place for decades, and you have been given a diagram supplied by the original installer. The diagram says that the network computers are connected to a device called a multiport repeater. Which of the following devices can also be described as a multiport repeater?

A. Hub

B. Bridge

C. Switch

D. Router

70. When you run a port scanner on a server, which of the following is the result?

A. A list of the servers currently running user processes

B. A list of the computer's hardware ports that are currently in use

C. A list specifying the numbers of packets transmitted and received by each network adapter on the system

D. A list of open ports through which the system can be accessed

E. A list of the IP addresses used by all the devices on the local network

71. Your company has a seven-node failover cluster hosting databases on SQL Server. Each server has three network interface adapters installed in it. Two are standard Gigabit Ethernet adapters that provide the nodes with access to each other and clients with access to the cluster. One is a Fibre Channel adapter that provides the cluster nodes with access to a dedicated network that also hosts a large hard disk array. Which of the following terms describe the networks to which the cluster nodes are connected? (Choose all that apply.)

A. SAN

B. PAN

C. WAN

D. MAN

E. LAN

72. A Windows user calls you at the help desk and reports that he cannot connect to any hosts on either the local network or a remote network. This is the only report of its kind you have received today. You question the user about the problem and eventually learn that he has made some changes to his workstation's Internet Protocol (IP) settings. What should you do next?

A. Check the switches in the datacenter to see if they have logged any error messages.

B. Verify that the routers on the network are functioning.

C. Run the `ipconfig` command on the user's workstation to view its configuration.

D. Check the network's Domain Name System (DNS) server to see if it is resolving IP hostnames.

73. You are a network administrator attempting to use your workstation on the internal network to remotely control a web server called WebServ1 on the perimeter network. However, the remote desktop client software is unable to establish a connection to the server. You can see all the computers on your local network and on the perimeter network. You try using the ping utility to test the TCP/IP functionality of WebServ1, and the ping test is successful. You then call your colleague on the same internal network and have her try to connect to WebServ1 using the same remote access tool. She connects to WebServ1 successfully. Which of the following could be the cause of the problem you are experiencing?

   A.   Blocked TCP/UDP ports on the web server

   B.   Name resolution failure

   C.   Incorrect firewall settings on your workstation

   D.   Unresponsive service on the web server

74. The toolkit you were given when you began work for an IT consulting company contained the tool shown in the following figure. What is the function of this tool?

Reprinted from *CompTIA Network+ Study Guide: Exam N10-006, Third Edition* by Todd Lammle (Wiley, 2015)

   A.   When you touch the end of the tool to a copper cable, you can detect and measure the electrical current flowing through it.

   B.   When you place the tool at one end of a wire, it generates a tone that can be detected at the other end.

   C.   To connect a bulk cable to a keystone connector, you use the tool to punch each wire down into the correct receptacle on the connector.

   D.   When you connect the tool to the end of a fiber-optic cable, you can measure the length of the cable run.

75. You are designing a new wireless network based on the IEEE 802.11n standard. The equipment you have selected supports both the 2.4 GHz and 5 GHz frequencies, and you are undecided about which one to use. Which of the following are possible reasons why the 5 GHz frequency tends to perform better than the 2.4 GHz frequency on a Wireless Local Area Network (WLAN)? (Choose all.)

   A.   The 5 GHz frequency has more channels than the 2.4 GHz frequency.

   B.   The 5 GHz frequency conflicts with fewer common household devices than the 2.4 GHz frequency.

   C.   The 5 GHz frequency transmits at faster speeds than the 2.4 GHz frequency.

   D.   The 5 GHz frequency supports longer ranges than the 2.4 GHz frequency.

76. What is the name of the tool shown in the following figure?

Reprinted from *CompTIA Network+ Study Guide: Exam N10-006, Third Edition* by Todd Lammle (Wiley, 2015)

- **A.** Crimper
- **B.** Tone generator and locator
- **C.** Butt set
- **D.** Punchdown tool

77. Which of the following server applications uses two well-known port numbers, one for control traffic and one for data traffic?

- **A.** FTP
- **B.** SNMP
- **C.** NTP
- **D.** HTTP

78. You are configuring the computers on a new network, and you have been given the network address 10.26.0.0/13. Which of the following subnet mask values must you use when configuring the computers?

- **A.** 255.248.0.0
- **B.** 255.252.0.0
- **C.** 255.254.0.0
- **D.** 255.255.248.0
- **E.** 255.255.252.0
- **F.** 255.255.254.0

79. You are testing a twisted-pair cable run using a tone generator and locator. When you apply the tone generator to each of the first seven wires at one end of the cable, you successfully detect a tone on the corresponding pin at the other end. However, when you connect the tone generator to the eighth wire, you fail to detect a tone at the other end. Which of the following fault types have you discovered?

  A. Short circuit

  B. Open circuit

  C. Split pair

  D. Crosstalk

80. Which of the following functions are defined as occurring at the session layer of the Open Systems Interconnection (OSI) model? (Choose all that apply.)

  A. Data encryption

  B. Dialog control

  C. Datagram routing

  D. Dialog separation

81. You are working your company's IT help desk, and you have had several calls from users who are reporting problems with their Voice over Internet Protocol (VoIP) and streaming video connections. In each case, the audio or video connection experiences frequent dropouts in sound or video, causing frustrating interruptions. Which of the following terms describes a connectivity problem on a wired network that could cause these symptoms?

  A. Jitter

  B. Latency

  C. Bottleneck

  D. Attenuation

82. You are a consultant with a client who wants to have you install a wireless network with the highest throughput currently available. What can you tell your client is the fastest speed achievable by a Wireless Local Area Network (WLAN) using the currently ratified IEEE 802.11 standards?

  A. 54 Mbps

  B. 600 Mbps

  C. 1.3 Gbps

  D. 2.6 Gbps

83. A private network uses unregistered IP addresses that are not accessible from the Internet. For computers on the private network to access Internet servers, there must be a device that substitutes registered IP addresses for the unregistered ones. Which of the following devices are capable of performing this kind of IP address substitution? (Choose all that apply.)

  A. RADIUS server

  B. NAT router

  C. UTM appliance

  D. Proxy server

84. A user calls you at the technical support desk in the computer store where you work. He is installing a home network and is having trouble configuring the IP addresses for his computers. He starts reading off a list of the network addresses he has tried to use. Which of the following are valid IPv4 network addresses that the user can conceivably use to configure his computers? (Choose all that apply.)

A. 1.1.1.0

B. 9.34.0.0

C. 103.256.77.0

D. 229.6.87.0

85. Which of the following terms refers to a routing protocol that relies on hop counts to measure the efficiency of routes through an internetwork?

A. Link state protocol

B. Distance vector protocol

C. Edge gateway protocol

D. Interior gateway protocol

86. You have been hired by a client to connect two local area networks together, which are in different buildings 500 meters apart. The cable type you use must support Gigabit Ethernet data rates of 1000 megabits per second (Mbps) and provide a high level of resistance to electromagnetic interference (EMI). Which of the following cable types can you choose to meet the client's needs? (Choose all that apply.)

A. Single-mode fiber-optic cable

B. Thin coaxial cable

C. Multimode fiber-optic cable

D. Shielded Twisted Pair (STP) cable

E. Unshielded Twisted Pair (UTP) cable

87. You receive a call at the IT help desk from a user who has recently moved to a new office in the company building, down the hall from her old one. Since the move, she has only been able to access the company's wireless network with her laptop intermittently. The network is based on 802.11n equipment, and it is using the 2.4 GHz frequency and the WPA2 security protocol. The user never had a problem in her previous office location. Which of the following could not possibly be the cause of her problem? (Choose all that apply.)

A. The user's laptop is connecting to the wrong SSID.

B. The user's laptop is configured to use the 5 GHz frequency.

C. The user's new office is farther from the access point than her old one.

D. There are more intervening walls between the user's new office and the access point.

E. The user's laptop is configured with the wrong WPA2 passphrase.

88. Which of the following statements about static routing are not true? (Choose all that apply.)

   A. Static routes are automatically added to the routing table by routing protocols when a new network path becomes available.

   B. Static routes are manually configured routes that administrators must add, modify, or delete when a change in the network occurs.

   C. Static routes are a recommended solution for large internetworks with redundant paths to each destination network.

   D. Static routes are a recommended solution for small internetworks with a single path to each destination network.

   E. Static routes adapt to changes in the network infrastructure automatically.

89. Which layer of the Open Systems Interconnection (OSI) model has its own logical addressing system and is responsible for routing packets from one network to another?

   A. Physical

   B. Data link

   C. Network

   D. Transport

   E. Session

   F. Presentation

   G. Application

90. There are several marketing consultants working in your office for the first time, and they have approached you because they are unable to connect to the company's 802.11g wireless network with their laptops. They are selecting the correct Service Set Identifier (SSID) from the Available Networks list, but they still cannot connect, and there are no error messages of any kind. Which of the following tasks should you perform first to try to resolve the problem?

   A. Examine the area where the consultants are working for possible sources of signal interference.

   B. Change the frequency used by the wireless access point from 2.4 GHz to 5 GHz.

   C. Make sure that the consultants' laptops are configured to use the correct wireless security protocol.

   D. Check the network adapters in the laptops for channel overlap.

91. You are researching the various types of Storage Area Network (SAN) technologies currently available before making a purchasing recommendation to your IT director. Which of the following are genuine advantages of iSCSI over Fibre Channel? (Choose all that apply.)

   A. iSCSI can share the same network as standard Local Area Network (LAN) traffic; Fibre Channel cannot.

   B. iSCSI is routable, whereas Fibre Channel is not.

   C. iSCSI is less expensive to implement than Fibre Channel.

   D. iSCSI includes its own internal flow control mechanism; Fibre Channel does not.

92. In which of the following Domain Name System (DNS) transactions does the querying system generate an iterative query? (Choose all that apply.)

A. A DNS client extracts the server name www.adatum.com from a URL and sends it to its designated DNS server for resolution.

B. A client's DNS server sends a name resolution request to a root domain server to discover the authoritative server for the com top-level domain.

C. A client's DNS server sends a name resolution request to the com top-level domain server to find the authoritative server for the adatum.com domain.

D. A client's DNS server, which has been configured to function as a forwarder, sends the server name www.adatum.com from a URL to its Internet Service Provider's (ISP's) DNS server for resolution.

E. A client's DNS server sends a name resolution request to the adatum.com domain server to discover the IP address associated with the server name www.

93. A user approaches you as you are passing through his department and reports that he cannot access the Internet. After questioning him, you determine that he can access systems on the local network, however. You examine the routing table on the user's Windows workstation, and you see the problem. Which of the following commands must you run to correct the user's problem, based on the routing table display shown here?

```
IPv4 Route Table
===========================================================================
Active Routes:
Network Destination        Netmask          Gateway       Interface  Metric
          127.0.0.0        255.0.0.0        On-link       127.0.0.1     331
          127.0.0.1  255.255.255.255        On-link       127.0.0.1     331
    127.255.255.255  255.255.255.255        On-link       127.0.0.1     331
        192.168.2.0    255.255.255.0        On-link    192.168.2.37     281
       192.168.2.37  255.255.255.255        On-link    192.168.2.37     281
      192.168.2.255  255.255.255.255        On-link    192.168.2.37     281
          224.0.0.0        240.0.0.0        On-link       127.0.0.1     331
          224.0.0.0        240.0.0.0        On-link    192.168.2.37     281
    255.255.255.255  255.255.255.255        On-link       127.0.0.1     331
    255.255.255.255  255.255.255.255        On-link    192.168.2.37     281
===========================================================================
Persistent Routes:
  None
```

A. route add 192.168.2.0 MASK 0.0.0.0 192.168.2.37 METRIC 25 IF 192.168.2.99

B. route add 0.0.0.0 MASK 255.255.255.0 192.168.2.99 METRIC 25 IF 192.168.2.37

C. route add 192.168.2.0 MASK 255.255.255.0 192.168.2.99 METRIC 25 IF 192.168.2.37

D. route add 0.0.0.0 MASK 0.0.0.0 192.168.2.99 METRIC 25 IF 192.168.2.37

94. You are heading out to do a cabling job for a client who has coaxial and twisted-pair Ethernet networks at their facility. You want to bring connectors and cables to prepare for any eventuality. Which of the following connector types are typically associated with Ethernet networks? (Choose all that apply.)

A. N-type

B. BNC

C. F-type

D. RJ45

E. DB-9

95. When geofencing is used as part of a multifactor authentication system, which of the following best describes geofencing's role?

A. Somewhere you are

B. Something you do

C. Something you have

D. Something you know

96. Some organizations maintain alternative sites that they can use as datacenters should a disaster render the main datacenter unusable. Which of the following types of disaster recovery site can be made operational in the shortest amount of time?

A. A hot site

B. A warm site

C. A cold site

D. All of the site types require the same amount of preparation time.

97. Which of the following types of Virtual Private Network (VPN) connection is the best solution for connecting a home user to a corporate network?

A. Host-to-site

B. Site-to-site

C. Host-to-host

D. Extranet

98. Which of the following are valid reasons why the leaf and spine datacenter topology is superior to the standard three-tier topology? (Choose all the apply.)

A. The leaf and spine topology is less expensive to implement than the three-tier topology.

B. In a leaf and spine topology, all data flows require the same number of hops.

C. The leaf and spine arrangement uses a full mesh switching topology.

D. The leaf and spine topology uses software-defined networking to direct traffic, rather than blocking ports using the spanning tree protocol.

99. A baseline is a performance measurement for a device or system, taken under normal operating conditions, which you can use later to quantify any changes that might have taken place. Which of the following Windows applications would you most likely use to create a baseline of system or network performance?

   A. Syslog

   B. Event Viewer

   C. Network Monitor

   D. Performance Monitor

100. In most cases, a Denial-of-Service (DoS) attack refers to a deliberate attempt to overwhelm a server with incoming traffic. However, this is not always the case. Which of the following types of DoS attacks does not involve flooding a server with traffic?

   A. Amplified

   B. Distributed

   C. Permanent

   D. Reflective

Chapter

7

Practice Exam 2

1. Which of the following are technologies typically used for Personal Area Networks (PANs)? (Choose all that apply.)

   A. RFID

   B. Z-Wave

   C. ISDN

   D. NFC

   E. Bluetooth

2. Review the following figure. How many collision domains and broadcast domains are there in the network diagram?

   A. There are three collision domains and one broadcast domain.

   B. There is one collision domain and one broadcast domain.

   C. There are three collision domains and three broadcast domains.

   D. There are seven collision domains and three broadcast domains.

   E. There are nine collision domains and three broadcast domains.

3. Which of the following types of network devices can provide authentication services for multiple remote access servers using the device's own account database?

   A. NAS

   B. IDS

   C. NGFW

   D. RADIUS

4. You are designing the network for your company's new branch office, and you need a device on which administrators can create Virtual Local Area Networks (VLANs) and that will forward traffic between them. Which of the following types of devices can do this?

    A. Virtual router

    B. Multilayer switch

    C. Broadband router

    D. Load balancer

5. You are setting up a new network for which you have been given the IPv4 network address 10.61.0.0/19. You want to calculate the number of hosts you can create on each subnet. How many bits are allocated to the host identifier in an IPv4 address on this network?

    A. 5

    B. 8

    C. 13

    D. 21

6. The protocols that are responsible for the delivery of data packets to their final destinations on an internetwork operate at which layer of the Open Systems Interconnection (OSI) reference model?

    A. Application

    B. Session

    C. Transport

    D. Network

    E. Data link

7. Originally, Storage Area Networks (SANs) were dedicated solely to storage-based traffic. A Local Area Network (LAN) was also required for other types of traffic. Today, however, it is possible for SAN and LAN traffic to coexist on a single network medium. Which of the following SAN protocols are capable of sharing a network medium with standard LAN traffic? (Choose all that apply.)

    A. InfiniBand

    B. Fibre Channel

    C. iSCSI

    D. FCoE

8. Which of the following application layer protocols do not include a program that enables a user to log on to a remote network device and execute commands using a character-based interface? (Choose all that apply.)

    A. Telnet

    B. Simple Mail Transfer Protocol (SMTP)

    C. File Transfer Protocol (FTP)

    D. Domain Name System (DNS)

9. Many network diagrams use Cisco symbols to illustrate the locations of and relationships between network components. Cisco symbols are standardized pictographs that illustrate the basic function of a network component. In a network diagram that uses Cisco symbols, what component does the symbol in the figure represent?

   A. A hub
   B. A switch
   C. A router
   D. A gateway

10. You are planning an automated operating system deployment for 100 new Windows work-stations your company has received. You intend to configure the workstations to boot using Preboot Execution Environment (PXE), during which time the system will obtain an IP address from a Dynamic Host Configuration Protocol (DHCP) server and then download a boot image file from a Trivial File Transfer Protocol (TFTP) server. Which of the following well-known ports must you open on the firewall separating the workstations from the servers? (Choose all that apply.)

   A. 64
   B. 65
   C. 66
   D. 67
   E. 68
   F. 69

11. Your department is experiencing frequent delays as users wait for images to render using their outdated graphics software package. As a result, you submitted a change request for a new software product at the monthly meeting of the company's change management team. Now that the change request has been approved, it is time to implement the change. Which of the following administrative tasks will most likely be the change management team's responsibility during the implementation process? (Choose all that apply.)

   A. Notifying users
   B. Documenting all modifications made
   C. Authorizing downtime
   D. Designating a maintenance window

12. You are installing a new server that is equipped with two power supplies. The server's firmware enables you to set the mode in which the power supplies will be used. In which of the following modes must the dual power supplies be running for the system to be fault tolerant?

    A. Individual mode

    B. Combined mode

    C. Redundant mode

    D. Hot backup mode

13. The Domain Name System (DNS) defines a hierarchical name space, locations in which are reflected in fully qualified domain names (FQDNs). Which of the words in the FQDN www.paris.mydomain.org represents the bottommost layer in the DNS namespace's domain hierarchy?

    A. www

    B. paris

    C. mydomain

    D. org

14. The term *datagram* is typically used by protocols offering connectionless delivery service. Which of the following protocols use(s) the term *datagram* to describe the data transfer unit it creates? (Choose all that apply.)

    A. TCP

    B. IP

    C. UDP

    D. Ethernet

15. After using a tape backup solution for years, you have recently started backing up your server to an external hard disk drive. Your backup schedule calls for weekly full backups and daily incremental backups. In the past, performing a restore required multiple jobs, but now only a single job is needed. Why does performing incremental backups to a hard drive, rather than a tape drive, make it possible to restore a server with a single job, rather than multiple jobs?

    A. Because hard drives use a different block size than tape drives

    B. Because hard drives can transfer data faster than tape drives

    C. Because hard drives hold more data than tape drives

    D. Because hard drives are random access devices and tape drives are not

16. You have just received notification of a new software release for an application you are running on your servers. The release is intended to address a newly discovered security vulnerability. Which of the following is the correct term for a software release containing a fix designed to address one specific issue?

    A. An upgrade

    B. A patch

    C. A service pack

    D. An update

17. Twisted-pair cables consist of multiple pairs of wires within a sheath, with each pair of wires twisted together separately. Which of the following statements best explains the reason for the twists in twisted-pair cabling? (Choose all that apply.)

A. The twists help to prevent crosstalk in adjacent wire pairs.

B. The twists make it easier for installers to attach connectors to the cable ends.

C. The twists extend the cable's bend radius allowance, making it easier to install.

D. The twists limit the effects of electromagnetic interference (EMI) on the signals carried over the cable.

E. The twists help to prevent data collisions from occurring.

18. The figure shown here lists the processes currently running on a Linux workstation. Which of the following performance monitoring tools, provided in Linux and Unix operating systems, enables you to display information about processes that are currently running on a system?

```
  8:13am  up 2 min,   1 user,   load average: 0.16, 0.11, 0.04
  30 processes: 29 sleeping, 1 running, 0 zombie, 0 stopped
  CPU states:  0.0% user,   0.0% system,  0.0% nice, 100.0% idle
  Mem:    255524K av,   33296K used,  222228K free,       0K shrd,    5516K buff
  Swap:   530104K av,       0K used,  530104K free                   15852K cached

  PID USER     PRI  NI  SIZE  RSS SHARE STAT %CPU %MEM   TIME COMMAND
    1 root      9   0   544  544   472 S     0.0  0.2   0:04 init
    2 root      8   0     0    0     0 SW    0.0  0.0   0:00 keventd
    3 root      9   0     0    0     0 SW    0.0  0.0   0:00 kapm-idled
    4 root      9   0     0    0     0 SW    0.0  0.0   0:00 kswapd
    5 root      9   0     0    0     0 SW    0.0  0.0   0:00 kreclaimd
    6 root      9   0     0    0     0 SW    0.0  0.0   0:00 bdflush
    7 root      9   0     0    0     0 SW    0.0  0.0   0:00 kupdated
    8 root     -1 -20     0    0     0 SW<   0.0  0.0   0:00 mdrecoveryd
   78 root      9   0     0    0     0 SW    0.0  0.0   0:00 khubd
  289 root      2   0   528  528   448 S     0.0  0.2   0:00 vmware-guestd
  636 root      9   0   600  600   500 S     0.0  0.2   0:00 syslogd
  641 root      9   0  1100 1100   456 S     0.0  0.4   0:00 klogd
  655 rpc       9   0   596  596   504 S     0.0  0.2   0:00 portmap
  670 rpcuser   9   0   776  776   668 S     0.0  0.3   0:00 rpc.statd
  754 root      8   0   532  532   464 S     0.0  0.2   0:00 apmd
  803 root      9   0   648  648   544 S     0.0  0.2   0:00 automount
  815 daemon    9   0   584  584   508 S     0.0  0.2   0:00 atd
  865 root      8   0  1936 1936  1416 S     0.0  0.7   0:00 sendmail
```

A. netstat

B. dig

C. perfmon

D. top

19. You are contracting with a provider to obtain email services for the clients on your network, using their existing email servers in the public cloud. You do not need anything from the provider other than email. Which of the following service models will you be using?

A. PaaS

B. SaaS

C. IaaS

D. All of the above

20. Security Information and Event Management (SIEM) is a combination tool that uses information gathered from logs and network devices to provide a real-time analysis of the network's security condition. Which of the following SIEM processes performs searches for specific criteria, during specific time frames, in logs located on different computers?

A. Correlation

B. Retention

C. Data aggregation

D. Forensic analysis

21. When you start Dynamic Host Configuration Protocol (DHCP) client, it transmits DHCP-DISCOVER messages to locate and initiate contact with DHCP servers. Which of the following types of transmissions does the client use for this purpose?

A. Broadcast

B. Multicast

C. Anycast

D. Unicast

22. Virtual Private Networks (VPNs) use a technique called tunneling to secure traffic as it passes over a public network, such as the Internet. In some cases, the traffic within the VPN tunnel is also encrypted. Which of the following VPN protocols does not provide encryption within the tunnel?

A. L2TP

B. IPsec

C. PPTP

D. SSL

23. You are installing a wireless network in a site that has a great many 2.4 GHz wireless telephones. Which of the following wireless networking technologies can you use, which will never experience interference from the telephones? (Choose all that apply.)

A. IEEE 802.11b

B. IEEE 802.11g

C. IEEE 802.11ac

D. IEEE 802.11a

E. IEEE 802.11n

24. Which of the following is another term for a switch?

A. Multicast hub

B. Multiport repeater

C. Multiport bridge

D. Multihomed router

25. You are working at a client site with a managed router that includes a console port for administrative access, which you can use to connect a laptop and run a terminal program to access the device's interface. Which of the following is the best term for this type of access to the device?

    A. Client-to-site

    B. In-band

    C. BYOD

    D. Out-of-band

26. After some incidents of security breaches, you have been asked to draft a revised password policy for the company's users. Which of the following are typical elements of a corporate password policy? (Choose all that apply.)

    A. Frequent password changes

    B. Use of special characters

    C. Minimum password length

    D. Unique passwords

27. You have a laptop that requires you to hold your finger on a scanner pad before you can use it. A device equipped with a fingerprint scanner that authenticates the user is using which of the following types of technology?

    A. Tamper detection

    B. Biometrics

    C. Hand geometry

    D. Pattern recognition

28. You have been asked to locate the computers on a network which the previous consultant has configured with incorrect IPv6 addresses. Which of the following are not correctly formatted IPv6 addresses? (Choose all that apply.)

    A. fe00::c955:c944:acdd:3fcb

    B. fe00::b491:cf79:p493:23ff

    C. 2001:0:44ef68:23eb:99fe:72bec6:ea5f

    D. 2001:0:49e6:39ff:8cf5:6812:ef56

29. During a security evaluation by an outside contractor, you are asked whether your company uses a *fail open* or *fail closed* policy for the datacenter. You do not know what the contractor means. Which of the following physical security mechanisms can either *fail closed* or *fail open*?

    A. Door locks

    B. Motion detectors

    C. Honeypots

    D. Video cameras

30. Your company is concerned about the possibility of insider threats. Which of the following security measures can you use to monitor the specific activities of authorized individuals within sensitive areas?

A. Identification badges

B. Motion detection

C. Video surveillance

D. Key fobs

31. Ralph is troubleshooting a Windows server, and while doing so, he runs the following command: `ping 127.0.0.1`. The command completes successfully. What has Ralph proven by doing this?

A. That the computer's network adapter is functioning properly

B. That the computer's IP address is correct for the network

C. That the computer's TCP/IP networking stack is loaded and functioning

D. Nothing

32. Which of the following are not examples of multifactor authentication? (Choose all that apply.)

A. A system that requires a smart card and a PIN for authentication

B. A system that uses an external RADIUS server for authentication

C. A system that requires two passwords for authentication

D. A system that requires a password and a retinal scan for authentication

33. A user calls Ed at the help desk to report that he cannot access the Internet. He can access systems on the local network, however. Ed examines the routing table on the user's workstation and sees the following listing. Which statement explains why the user cannot access the Internet?

```
IPv4 Route Table
===========================================================================
Active Routes:
Network Destination    Netmask          Gateway    Interface      Metric
    127.0.0.0          255.0.0.0        On-link    127.0.0.1       331
    127.0.0.1          255.255.255.255  On-link    127.0.0.1       331
    127.255.255.255    255.255.255.255  On-link    127.0.0.1       331
    192.168.2.0        255.255.255.0    On-link    192.168.2.37    281
    192.168.2.37       255.255.255.255  On-link    192.168.2.37    281
    192.168.2.255      255.255.255.255  On-link    192.168.2.37    281
    224.0.0.0          240.0.0.0        On-link    127.0.0.1       331
    224.0.0.0          240.0.0.0        On-link    192.168.2.37    281
    255.255.255.255    255.255.255.255  On-link    127.0.0.1       331
    255.255.255.255    255.255.255.255  On-link    192.168.2.37    281
===========================================================================
Persistent Routes:
None
```

   A.   The routing table does not specify a loopback address.

   B.   The routing table does not specify a DNS server address.

   C.   The routing table does not specify a default gateway address.

   D.   The routing table contains two different routes to the 224.0.0.0 network.

34. Which of the following statements about single-mode fiber-optic cable are true? (Choose all that apply.)

   A.   Multimode cables use an LED light source, while single-mode cables use a laser.

   B.   Multimode cables can span longer distances than single-mode cables.

   C.   Multimode cables have a smaller core filament than single-mode cables.

   D.   Multimode cables have a smaller bend radius than single-mode, making them easier to install.

   E.   Multimode fiber-optic cables require a ground, whereas single-mode cables do not.

35. A user swipes a smartcard through the reader connected to a laptop and then types a password to log on to the system. Which of the following actions is the user performing?

   A.   Auditing

   B.   Accounting

   C.   Authorization

   D.   Authentication

36. Which of the following cabling topologies have never been used by standard Ethernet networks? (Choose all that apply.)

   A.   Bus

   B.   Ring

   C.   Star

   D.   Mesh

37. Pulling into your company parking lot at lunchtime, you notice a person without a company parking sticker on his car working at a laptop. You have seen this more than once, and you begin to suspect that unauthorized users are connecting to the company's Wireless Access Point (WAP) and gaining access to the network. Which of the following are steps you can take to prevent this from happening in the future? (Choose all that apply.)

   A.   Use Kerberos for authentication

   B.   Place the access point in a screened subnet

   C.   Disable SSID broadcasting

   D.   Implement MAC address filtering

38. Traffic shaping is a series of techniques that optimize the allocation of network bandwidth. Which of the following are techniques used in traffic shaping to prevent networks from being overwhelmed by data transmissions? (Choose all that apply.)

   A. Broadcast storming

   B. Bandwidth throttling

   C. Network Address Translation (NAT)

   D. Rate limiting

39. Multiprotocol switches are devices that perform functions associated with two different layers of the Open Systems Interconnection (OSI) reference model. Which two of the following layers are often associated with network switching? (Choose all that apply.)

   A. Application

   B. Presentation

   C. Session

   D. Transport

   E. Network

   F. Data link

   G. Physical

40. You are attempting to connect your new laptop to your company's wireless network. The Wireless Access Point (WAP) on the network has a Service Set Identifier (SSID) that is not broadcasted and uses WiFi Protected Access II (WPA2) for security. Which of the following describes what you must do to connect your laptop to the network?

   A. Select the SSID from a list and allow the client to automatically detect the security protocol.

   B. Type the SSID manually and then select WPA2 from the security protocol options provided.

   C. Type the SSID manually and allow the client to automatically detect the security protocol.

   D. Select the SSID from a list and then select WPA2 from the security protocol options provided.

41. Carrier Sense Multiple Access with Collision Avoidance (CSMA/CA) is a Media Access Control (MAC) mechanism designed to prevent two systems using the same network medium from transmitting at the same time. Which of the following IEEE standards calls for the use of CSMA/CA?

   A. 802.3

   B. 802.1X

   C. 802.11ac

   D. All of the above

42. A large enterprise network will—at a minimum—have demarcation points for telephone services and a connection to an Internet Service Provider's (ISP's) network. In many cases, these services will enter the building in the same equipment room that houses the backbone switch. Which of the following is the term used to describe this wiring nexus?

   A. MTBF

   B. IDF

   C. RDP

   D. MDF

43. You have configured your company's wireless network to enable clients to authenticate only when the signal strength of their connections exceeds a specified level. Which of the following terms best describes the security mechanism provided by this configuration?

   A. Geofencing

   B. Local authentication

   C. Motion detection

   D. Port security

44. Social engineering has become an increasingly serious problem on your company network. Which of the following is an effective method for preventing sensitive data from being compromised through social engineering?

   A. Install a firewall between the internal network and the Internet.

   B. Install an antivirus software product on all user workstations.

   C. Implement a program of user education and corporate policies.

   D. Use IPSec to encrypt all network traffic.

45. You have been given a Class B network IP address with which to configure the new network you are designing. Which of the following is the default subnet mask you should use for an IPv4 Class B network?

   A. 255.255.255.255

   B. 255.255.255.0

   C. 255.255.0.0

   D. 255.0.0.0

46. Alice's company has just started working with sensitive government data. To enhance the security of the datacenter, she has implemented some additional security measures. All of the servers now have crimped metal tags holding the cases closed. All of the hardware racks are locked in clear-fronted cabinets. All of the cable runs are installed in transparent conduits. These are all examples of which of the following physical security measures?

   A. Geofencing

   B. Tamper detection

   C. Port security

   D. Asset tracking

47. You have just installed a web server for your company, which is configured to host a public Internet site using the registered domain name `adatum.com`. The server's hostname in the Domain Name System (DNS) is www. The web server also has an administrative site, which you want to be able to access remotely. You have configured the administrative site to be encrypted and to use the port number 12354. Which of the following URLs must you use to access the administrative website from the Internet?

    A. `https://www.adatum.com:12354`

    B. `http://www.adatum.com`

    C. `https://www.adatum.com:80`

    D. `http://www.adatum.com:12354`

48. To prevent outside users from accessing your wireless network, you configure the access point not to broadcast the network's Service Set Identifier (SSID). However, you later discover that outsiders are still accessing the network. For which of the following reasons is disabling SSID broadcasts a relatively weak method of device hardening?

    A. Every access point's SSID is printed on a label on the back of the device.

    B. Attackers have software that can easily guess a network's SSID

    C. Attackers can capture packets transmitted over the network and read the SSID from them.

    D. Attackers have ways of connecting to the network without the SSID.

49. You are installing a web server farm in your corporate headquarters, which will be used to host websites for the corporation's subsidiaries, located all around the world. In which of the following cloud models does a single organization function as both the provider and the consumer of all cloud services?

    A. Private cloud

    B. Public cloud

    C. Ad hoc cloud

    D. Hybrid cloud

50. Your supervisor has recently begun using the terms *on-boarding* and *off-boarding*. With which of the following types of policies are these terms typically associated?

    A. Incident response

    B. Identity management

    C. Inventory management

    D. Data loss prevention

51. Virtual Private Networks (VPNs) use a data transmission technique called tunneling, which encapsulates a data packet within another packet for transmission over a network connection, typically using the Internet. The system also encrypts the entire encapsulated data packet for protection. Split tunneling is a variation of this method that provides which of the following advantages? (Choose all that apply.)

    A. Additional data integrity protection

    B. Access to local network devices while connected to the VPN

    C. Faster data transmission through multiplexing

    D. Conservation of VPN bandwidth

52. Your supervisor wants you to disable all of the ports on the network's switches that are not in use. You tell her that this is not necessary, and she wants to know why you think so. Which of the following are valid reasons not to disable unused switch ports? (Choose all that apply.)

    A. The unused ports are not patched in to wall jacks.

    B. The datacenter is already secured from unauthorized access.

    C. The switch is configured to use a MAC-based ACL.

    D. Leaving some ports enabled facilitates the on-boarding of new users.

53. Despite having imposed password policies on your network that compel users to change their passwords frequently, create passwords of a specific length, and use complex passwords, you have still had several reports of account penetrations. After investigating the incidents, you determine that the victims had all apparently shared a "tip" suggesting that users cycle through the names of their children, nephews, nieces, and other relatives when forced to create new passwords, changing letters to numbers as needed. Which of the following actions can you take to remedy the situation without creating a larger problem?

    A. Modify the password policies to force users to change passwords more frequently.

    B. Change the minimum password age policy to a larger value.

    C. Distribute a list of common passwords that are insecure, such as those based on names, birth dates, etc.

    D. Assign the users long passwords consisting of random-generated characters and change them often.

54. Which of the following network devices can employ Access Control Lists (ACLs) to restrict access? (Choose all that apply.)

    A. Routers

    B. Servers

    C. Switches

    D. Hubs

    E. Wireless Access Points

55. Which of the following terms is used to describe the threat mitigation technique of deploying individual applications and services on separate virtual servers so that no more than one is endangered at any one time, rather than deploying multiple applications on a single server?

   A. Network segmentation

   B. Geofencing

   C. VLAN hopping

   D. Role separation

56. Which of the following statements about Dynamic Host Configuration Protocol (DHCP) snooping are true? (Choose all that apply.)

   A. DHCP snooping is implemented in network switches.

   B. DHCP snooping prevents DNS cache poisoning.

   C. DHCP snooping detects rogue DHCP servers.

   D. DHCP snooping drops DHCP messages arriving over the incorrect port.

57. A user reports that she cannot connect to a server on her network. You want to identify the scope of the problem, so you try to reproduce the problem on the user's computer. The problem persists. No other users are reporting the same problem. What is the next logical step that you should perform to identify the affected area?

   A. Examine the server's configuration for the correct settings.

   B. Verify that the local router is forwarding traffic.

   C. Confirm that the switch the client is connected to is functioning.

   D. Perform the same task on another computer connected to the same segment.

58. On a wireless network, which of the following best describes an example of a captive portal?

   A. A web page stating that the data on a user's computer has been locked and will only be unlocked after payment of a fee

   B. A series of two doors with an intervening airlock through which people must pass before they can enter a secured space

   C. A dedicated switch port used to connect to other switches

   D. A web page with which a user must interact before being granted access to a wireless network

59. In the standard troubleshooting methodology, you begin by taking steps to identify the problem. After you have done this, which of the following steps should you perform next?

   A. Verify full system functionality

   B. Establish a theory of probable cause

   C. Establish a plan of action

   D. Implement the solution

60. The secured version of the Hypertext Transfer Protocol (HTTPS) uses a different well-known port from the unsecured version (HTTP). Which of the following ports are used by HTTP and HTTPS by default? (Choose all that apply.)

   A. 25

   B. 80

   C. 110

   D. 443

61. Which of the following are criteria typically used by load balancers to direct incoming traffic to one server out of a group of servers? (Choose all that apply.)

   A. Fastest response time

   B. Fastest processor

   C. Lightest load

   D. The next in an even rotation

62. You are responsible for a network that has a Domain Name System (DNS) server, a proxy server, and an Internet router. A user is reporting that she cannot connect to hosts on her own Local Area Network (LAN) or other internal LANs, and she also cannot access hosts on the Internet. No one else has reported a problem. What is the likeliest location of the issue preventing the user's access to the network?

   A. The router

   B. The DNS server

   C. The proxy server

   D. The user's computer configuration

63. Virtual Local Area Network (VLAN) hopping is a type of attack directed at network switches. Which of the following best describes how VLAN hopping is a potential threat?

   A. VLAN hopping enables an attacker to access different VLANs using 802.1q spoofing.

   B. VLAN hopping enables an attacker to scramble a switch's patch panel connections.

   C. VLAN hopping enables an attacker to change the native VLAN on a switch.

   D. VLAN hopping enables an attacker to rename the default VLAN on a switch.

64. You are a first-tier support technician working the IT help desk at your company. In your first hour of duty, you receive four trouble calls. Your job is to prioritize the calls based on their severity. Which of the following should be the problem that receives the lowest priority?

   A. A fatal error that causes a single computer to fail

   B. A problem with a mission-critical backbone router that affects an entire network

   C. A problem with an application server that affects a single Local Area Network (LAN)

   D. A problem with an order entry or customer service call center resource that affects an entire department, with multiple LANs

65. You are attempting to access a Domain Name System (DNS) server located on the other side of a router, but your attempt fails with an error stating that the destination port UDP 53 is unreachable. Your first step in troubleshooting the problem is to try using the `nslookup` utility to access that specific DNS server. This attempt also fails. Next, you use the `ping` utility with the DNS server's IP address. The `ping` test is successful, indicating that the server is up and running. Which of the following are possible causes of the problem? (Choose all that apply.)

    A. The TCP/IP host settings on your computer are improperly configured.

    B. The router connecting the networks is not running DNS and will not forward this type of datagram.

    C. There is a firewall blocking the DNS server's UDP port 53.

    D. The DNS process on the remote server is not running.

    E. The TCP/IP host settings on the DNS server are improperly configured.

66. Which of the following types of switches performs a Cyclic Redundancy Check (CRC) on an entire frame's contents prior to forwarding it out a port leading to the destination system?

    A. Packet filtering

    B. Cut-through

    C. Source route

    D. Store-and-forward

67. Which of the following attack types is not specifically targeted at wireless network clients?

    A. Logic bomb

    B. Deauthentication

    C. Evil twin

    D. War driving

68. You are having trouble installing a Wireless Local Area Network (WLAN) using IEEE 802.11b/g equipment in a new office complex. The wireless devices have trouble connecting to the access point, and when they do, they achieve only low speeds. When you use a WiFi analyzer to scan the 2.4 GHz frequency band, you see literally dozens of other networks in the area, spread across all of the available channels. Choose the tasks from the following list that you should perform to enable your wireless devices to connect to the network reliably and at their best possible speeds. (Choose all that apply.)

    A. Configure the access point to suppress SSID broadcasts.

    B. Configure all of the wireless network devices to use the 5 GHz band.

    C. Upgrade all of the network devices to the latest firmware.

    D. Configure all of the network devices to use WPA2 encryption with AES.

    E. Upgrade the access point and all of the wireless client devices to IEEE 802.11n.

69. Which Windows command-line utility produced the output shown here?

```
Interface: 192.168.2.24 --- 0x2
  Internet Address      Physical Address      Type
  192.168.2.2           d4-ae-52-bf-c3-2d      dynamic
  192.168.2.20          00-26-c7-7e-00-e0      dynamic
  192.168.2.22          00-90-a9-a2-43-8f      dynamic
  192.168.2.27          1c-c1-de-ca-1f-12      dynamic
  192.168.2.28          30-f7-72-38-e9-1d      dynamic
  192.168.2.255         ff-ff-ff-ff-ff-ff      static
  224.0.0.22            01-00-5e-00-00-16      static
  224.0.0.251           01-00-5e-00-00-fb      static
  224.0.0.252           01-00-5e-00-00-fc      static
  224.0.0.253           01-00-5e-00-00-fd      static
  239.255.255.250       01-00-5e-7f-ff-fa      static
  255.255.255.255       ff-ff-ff-ff-ff-ff      static
```

A. arp

B. ping

C. tracert

D. netstat

70. Your boss is working in the crawlspace under the floor of the datacenter, and he asks you to hand him the pliers. You hand him the tool shown in the following figure, and he throws it back at you. What is the real function of the tool shown in the figure?

Reprinted from *CompTIA Network+ Study Guide: Exam N10-006, Third Edition* by Todd Lammle (Wiley, 2015)

   A. When you connect the tool to pins in a punchdown block, you can access telephone circuits in order to test them or place telephone calls.

   B. When you attach the tool to one end of a wire, it generates a tone that can be detected at the other end.

   C. To attach a bulk cable end to an RJ45 connector, you use the tool to squeeze the connector closed, forcing the wire ends to contact the connector's pins.

   D. When you attach the tool to a copper cable, you can detect and measure the electrical current flowing through it.

71. You are starting work for a contractor that performs telecommunications cable installations. One of the tools in the kit you have been given is in the following figure. What is the name of the tool shown?

Reprinted from *CompTIA Network+ Study Guide: Exam N10-006, Third Edition* by Todd Lammle (Wiley, 2015)

   A. Crimper

   B. Punchdown tool

   C. Butt set

   D. Tone generator and locator

72. You are seeking to upgrade your company's IEEE 802.11b access point to one that provides faster transmission speeds for your newer workstations. Which of the following wireless networking standards are capable of supporting speeds faster than the 11 Mbps of 802.11b but that are still backward compatible with your existing IEEE 802.11b workstations? (Choose all that apply.)

   A. IEEE 802.11

   B. Bluetooth

   C. IEEE 802.11g

   D. IEEE 802.11a

   E. IEEE 802.11n

73. You are working on your company's screened subnet (also known as a perimeter network), which has five Linux web servers, a Cisco router, a CSU/DSU providing a leased line connection, and a Windows-based firewall on it. While trying to troubleshoot a network communications failure, you type the following command on one of the systems: `traceroute adatum.com`. Which of the following systems might you be working on? (Choose all that apply.)

A. The Cisco router

B. One of the Linux web servers

C. The CSU/DSU console

D. The Windows-based firewall

74. Which of the following are network topologies used by IEEE 802.11 Wireless Local Area Networks (WLANs)? (Choose all that apply.)

A. Bus

B. Mesh

C. Ad hoc

D. Star

E. Infrastructure

75. You have recently started a new job that enables you to telecommute from home, and you need a Wide Area Network (WAN) connection to the Internet. You will need to access the company network using a Virtual Private Network (VPN) connection to obtain client information, transfer files, and send email through the company servers. Your home is over 30 years old. The existing telephone wiring was not run through a conduit, and it seems to be deteriorating. You have cable television service, and your home is approximately 20,000 feet from the nearest telephone central office. You want to implement the fastest possible remote connection service, but cost is still a factor in the decision. Which WAN technology should you implement?

A. A standard modem-to-modem connection

B. A DSL (Digital Subscriber Line) connection

C. A broadband cable television (CATV) connection

D. A dedicated leased line (fractional T-1)

76. You are working the help desk at a local computer store, and you receive a call from a customer trying to set up a home network using computers running Windows 10 and wired Ethernet equipment. The customer reports that she cannot access the other two computers in the house from her workstation, nor can she access the Internet. You ask her to run the `ipconfig /all` command and read the results to you. She says that her IP address is 192.168.0.2, her subnet mask is 255.255.255.0, and her default gateway is 192.168.0.1. Which of the following is the most likely cause of the customer's problem?

A. The customer's network address cannot include a zero.

B. The customer has an incorrect subnet mask.

C. The customer's network cable is damaged or unplugged.

D. The customer has an incorrect default gateway address.

77. Some networks are designed with a switching fabric that contains redundant paths, for fault tolerance purposes. However, in this type of design, it is possible for packets to circulate endlessly around the network, which is called a switching loop. Which of the following protocols prevents network switching loops from occurring by shutting down redundant links until they are needed?

A. NAT

B. RIP

C. VLAN

D. STP

78. You are responsible for an internetwork that consists of four internal Local Area Networks (LANs) with 50 users each. Each internal LAN uses twisted-pair Gigabit Ethernet links that connect the users to a switch. Each of the four switches is connected to a separate router. All four routers connect to the same backbone network, which has a single additional router to connect the company's network to the Internet, using a T-1 Wide Area Network (WAN) link. Today, users on one of the four internal LANs are reporting that when they came in this morning, they could not access the Internet or resources on the other three internal LANs. However, they could access resources on their own LAN with no problems. Which network component is the likeliest source of the problem in this scenario?

A. The switch on the problem LAN

B. The Internet router

C. The router connecting the problem LAN to the backbone

D. The cable on the backbone network

79. You are negotiating an agreement with a provider for your company's email service. You have been told to require a 99.99 percent guaranteed rate of service reliability, but the provider is only willing to guarantee 99 percent. Eventually, you and the provider agree on a compromise of 99.9 percent. Which of the following documents will include the negotiated language on this particular point?

A. AUP

B. SLA

C. BYOD

D. NDA

80. Which of the following types of networking devices can split a single network into multiple collision domains while maintaining a single broadcast domain? (Choose all that apply.)

A. Switch

B. Bridge

C. Router

D. Hub

81. You have just finished installing a web server farm on your company's network, along with a router to create a screened subnet (perimeter network) on which the web servers are located. However, you now cannot access the web servers from your workstation on the internal network. Which of the following is not one of the tasks you will have to complete before you can access the screened subnet from the internal network?

    A. Change MAC addresses

    B. Change IP addresses

    C. Update the DNS records

    D. Change default gateway addresses

82. You are testing a twisted-pair cable run using a tone generator and locator. When you apply the tone generator to a particular pin at one end of the cable, you detect a tone on two pins at the other end. Which of the following faults have you discovered?

    A. Split pair

    B. Open

    C. Short

    D. Crosstalk

83. Your network has been experiencing intermittent service slowdowns and outages ever since the company moved into their new building. You have tried every troubleshooting modality you can think of, but you have not been able to determine the cause. One particular user, perhaps hoping to be the squeaky wheel that gets the grease, has taken to calling you every time he experiences a problem. One day, as you are working in the datacenter, you notice that the user calls every time you hear an additional humming noise. After examining the doors in the hallway, you realize that the racks containing the network switches are located right next to the elevator machinery room. Which of the following conditions is probably causing this intermittent network communication problem?

    A. Bottleneck

    B. EMI

    C. Latency

    D. Crosstalk

84. Ralph is installing a pair of redundant servers and must choose whether to run them in an active-active or active-passive configuration. Running the servers in an active-active configuration provides which of the following advantages that the same servers in an active-passive configuration do not? (Choose all that apply.)

    A. Fault tolerance

    B. Load balancing

    C. Data encapsulation

    D. Increased performance

85. You are starting work at a new company, and on your first day, you ask about wireless access for your laptop. You are given a Service Set Identifier (SSID) and a WiFi Protected Access II (WPA2) passphrase. Later, in the lunchroom, when you try to connect your laptop to the network, you cannot see the SSID you were given in the list of available networks, although you can see other networks. What should you do next to try to resolve the problem?

A. Move closer to the Wireless Access Point (WAP).

B. Move away from the microwave in the lunchroom.

C. Type in the WPA2 passphrase.

D. Type the SSID in manually.

86. You are responsible for a Wireless Local Area Network (WLAN) that consists of an 802.11n 2x2 access point and laptop computers with a variety of network adapters. Some of the laptops support 802.11n, most support 802.11g, and a few older models have 802.11b adapters. The WLAN is located in a large office building with many other wireless networks, and you are having trouble finding a channel on the 2.4 GHz band that is not congested with traffic. Scanning the 5 GHz band, you find relatively little traffic, so you reconfigure the access point to use a 5 GHz channel. The result is that some of the laptops are able to connect to the network, whereas others are not. What is the most likely reason for the connection failures, and what must you do to enable all the laptops to connect to the wireless network?

A. The 802.11b standard does not support communication using the 5 GHz band. You must replace the network adapters in those laptops with newer models for them to connect successfully.

B. The 5 GHz band does not support automatic channel selection. You must configure each laptop to use the same channel as the access point for all the laptops to connect successfully.

C. The 5 GHz band does not support Multiple Input, Multiple Output (MIMO) communications, so the 802.11n laptops are unable to connect to the network. You must replace the access point with an 802.11g unit for all the laptops to connect successfully.

D. The 802.11g and 802.11b standards do not support communication using the 5 GHz band. You must configure the access point to support 2.4 GHz for all the laptops to connect successfully.

87. In the Domain Name System (DNS), a zone is a contiguous area of the DNS namespace for which authority is delegated to one or more DNS servers. Which of the following DNS resource record types specifies the IP addresses of the authoritative DNS servers for a particular zone?

A. PTR

B. SRV

C. MX

D. NS

88. You are experiencing poor performance on your home 802.11n wireless network. You live in a large apartment complex, and when you run a WiFi analyzer, you see many other nearby networks using the often-recommended channels 1, 6, and 11 on the 2.4 GHz frequency. Using the 5 GHz frequency is not an option for your equipment. What should you do to improve the network's performance?

    A. Configure your equipment to use channel 10.

    B. Configure your equipment to use channel 9.

    C. Configure your equipment to use channel 5.

    D. Configure your equipment to use channel 2.

89. Your company's office building is having a fire inspection, and you are the only person on duty in the datacenter. The inspector from the fire department asks you where they can find documentation about all chemicals and equipment used in the company's datacenter. You lead the inspector to the director's office, but you are not sure what the documents he needs are called. Which of the following document types contains this information?

    A. MSDS

    B. NDA

    C. BYOD

    D. ESD

90. Which of the following Power over Ethernet (PoE) specifications supplies power to devices using the spare wire pair on a 10Base-T or 100Base-TX twisted-pair network?

    A. 4PPoE

    B. Alternative A

    C. Alternative B

    D. All of the above

91. The iSCSI storage area networking protocol uses clients called initiators and servers called targets. However, on many Storage Area Networks (SANs), there needs to be a way for the initiators to locate the targets. Which of the following technologies do iSCSI initiators use to locate iSCSI targets on the network?

    A. ICMP

    B. DNS

    C. iDNS

    D. iSNS

92. You are deploying an 802.11n wireless network for a client that is asking for the best possible security you can provide without deploying additional servers. When setting up the Wireless Access Point (WAP), you disable Service Set Identifier (SSID) broadcasts, select WiFi Protected Access with Pre-Shared Keys (WPA-PSKs), and configure Media Access Control (MAC) address filtering. Which of the following statements about the security of this arrangement is true?

A. You should not disable SSID broadcasts since this prevents users from connecting to the network.

B. The configuration is as secure as you can make it with the specified equipment.

C. You should use WiFi Protected Access II (WPA2) instead of WPA, since it is more resistant to certain types of attacks.

D. You should not use MAC address filtering since it exposes MAC addresses to possible attacks.

93. Which of the following connector types are used with fiber-optic cables? (Choose all that apply.)

A. DB-9

B. SC

C. BNC

D. ST

E. MTRJ

F. RJ11

94. Which of the following are available as Internet of Things (IoT) devices?

A. Refrigerators

B. Doorbells

C. Thermostats

D. Speakers

E. All of the above

95. You are designing an Ethernet network for your company's newest branch office. Your current task is to decide which Ethernet specification to use for the network, a decision that you know will determine what type of cabling you need to purchase and the topology with which the cable will be installed. Which layers of the Open Systems Interconnection (OSI) reference model apply to the cabling and topology elements of a network?

A. The application and transport layers

B. The transport and network layers

C. The network and data link layers

D. The data link and physical layers

96. You are troubleshooting a workstation that cannot access the network. The workstation is plugged into a wall plate that should provide it with access to a DHCP-equipped network using the 192.168.4.0/24 network address. No one else on that network is reporting a problem. You check that the patch cable is properly plugged into the workstation and the wall plate, which they are, and then run `ipconfig /all` on the workstation and examine the output. Which of the statements could be the explanation for the workstation's problem, based on the following `ipconfig` results?

```
Windows IP Configuration

    Host Name . . . . . . . . . . . . : Client12
    Primary Dns Suffix  . . . . . . . :
    Node Type . . . . . . . . . . . . : Hybrid
    IP Routing Enabled. . . . . . . . : No
    WINS Proxy Enabled. . . . . . . . : No


Ethernet adapter Local Area Connection:

    Connection-specific DNS Suffix  . :
    Description . . . . . . . . . . . : PCIe Family Controller
    Physical Address. . . . . . . . . : 60-EB-69-93-5E-E5
    DHCP Enabled. . . . . . . . . . . : Yes
    Autoconfiguration Enabled . . . . : Yes
    Link-local IPv6 Address . . . . . : fe80::c955:c944:acdd:3fcb%2
    IPv4 Address. . . . . . . . . . . : 169.254.203.42
    Subnet Mask . . . . . . . . . . . : 255.255.0.0
    Lease Obtained. . . . . . . . . . : Monday, October 23, 2017 6:23:47 PM
    Lease Expires . . . . . . . . . . : Saturday, November 18, 2017 9:49:24 PM
    Default Gateway . . . . . . . . . :
    DHCPv6 IAID . . . . . . . . . . . : 241232745
    DHCPv6 Client DUID.    . . . . . . . . : 00-01-00-01-18-10-22-0D-60-EB-69-93-5E-E5
    DNS Servers . . . . . . . . . . . : fec0:0:0:ffff::1%1
                                        fec0:0:0:ffff::2%1
                                        fec0:0:0:ffff::3%1
    NetBIOS over Tcpip. . . . . . . . : Enabled
```

A. The DNS server addresses are incorrect.

B. The Default Gateway address is missing.

C. The Subnet Mask value is incorrect.

D. The DHCP scope is exhausted.

97. A user calls you at the IT help desk and reports that she is having intermittent problems accessing both local servers and internet websites. Which of the following potential problems can you rule out immediately?

A. Malfunctioning Domain Name System (DNS) server

B. Duplicate Media Access Control (MAC) addresses

C. Duplicate IP addresses

D. Malfunctioning router

98. You have recently discovered a rogue Dynamic Host Configuration Protocol (DHCP) server on your network. After disabling the rogue server, you now need to terminate all of the rogue IP address leases currently held by DHCP clients on the network and then have them request new leases from the authorized DHCP server. Which of the following commands must you run on each client to do this? (Choose all that apply.)

A. `ipconfig /dump`

B. `ipconfig /lease`

C. `ipconfig /release`

D. `ipconfig /renew`

E. `ipconfig /discard`

99. Ralph is reading an article about datacenter design, and he is puzzled by references to east-west and north-south traffic. Which of the following statements best describes the difference between east-west and north-south traffic in a datacenter?

A. East-west is switch-to-switch traffic, while north-south is switch-to-router traffic.

B. East-west describes traffic between devices at the same layer of the Open Systems Interconnection (OSI) reference model, while north-south describes traffic between OSI model layers.

C. East-west traffic stays within the datacenter, while north-south traffic does not.

D. East-west is backbone traffic among switches and routers, while north-south is traffic to end systems, such as servers.

100. Which of the following attack types involves the modification of a legitimate software product?

A. War driving

B. Logic bomb

C. Evil twin

D. Social engineering

Appendix

Answers to Review Questions

Chapter 1: Networking Fundamentals

1. B. The Ethernet (or IEEE 802.3) protocol at the data link layer uses MAC addresses to identify computers on the local network. MAC addresses are coded into the firmware of physical network interface adapters by the manufacturer. The physical layer deals with signals and is not involved in addressing. The IP protocol at the network layer has its own addressing system. The transport layer protocols are not involved in addressing.

2. E. ISO developed and published the OSI model to serve as a conceptual model for software and hardware developers. The ITU-T, formerly known as the CCITT, coordinates the development and advancement of international telecommunication networks and services. ANSI is a private organization that administers and coordinates a United States–based standardization and conformity assessment system. The IEEE publishes standards that define data link and physical layer standards. These standards are referred to collectively as the 802 series.

3. C. Network layer protocols (such as IP) contain headers that specify logical addresses for end system communication and route datagrams across a network. The physical layer defines standards for physical and mechanical characteristics of a network. The data link layer uses media access control (MAC) or hardware addresses, not logical addresses. The transport layer uses port numbers, not logical addresses. Session layer protocols create and maintain a dialogue between end systems. Presentation layer protocols are responsible for the formatting, translation, and presentation of information. The application layer provides an entry point for applications to access the protocol stack and prepare information for transmission across a network.

4. B, C, D. Before the payload data generated by an application can be transmitted over a TCP/IP network, the system must encapsulate it by applying protocol headers and footers at three layers of the OSI model. The data link layer applies a header and footer to create an Ethernet frame. The network layer applies a header to create an IP datagram. The transport layer applies a TCP or UDP header to create a segment or datagram. The other model layers are involved in the payload transmission process, but they do not encapsulate the payload.

5. F. The presentation layer implements functions that provide formatting, translation, and presentation of information. No other layers of the OSI model translate and format application data.

6. D. A router connects networks at the network layer of the OSI model. Proxy servers operate at the application layer. Network interface adapters operate at both the data link and the physical layers. Hubs are physical layer devices.

7. G. The application layer provides an entry point for applications to access the protocol stack and prepare information for transmission across a network. All other layers of the OSI model reside below this layer and rely on this entry point.

8. E. The session layer is responsible for creating and maintaining a dialogue between end systems. This dialogue can be a two-way alternate dialogue that requires end systems to take turns transmitting, or it can be a two-way simultaneous dialogue in which either end system can transmit at will. No other layers of the OSI model perform dialogue control between communicating end systems.

9. B, C. The primary function of a switch is to process packets based on their media access control (MAC) addresses, which makes it a data link layer device. However, many switches can also perform routing functions based on IP addresses, which operate at the network layer.

10. D. There are two types of transport layer protocols: connection-oriented and connectionless. Connection-oriented protocols guarantee the delivery of data from source to destination by creating a connection between the sender and the receiver before any data is transmitted. Connectionless protocols do not require a connection between end systems in order to pass data. The physical layer does not use connectionless or connection-oriented protocols; it defines standards for transmitting and receiving information over a network. The data link layer provides physical addressing and final packaging of data for transmission. The network layer is responsible for logical addressing and routing. The session layer is responsible for creating and maintaining a dialogue between end systems. The presentation layer is responsible for the formatting, translation, and presentation of information. The application layer provides an entry point for applications to access the protocol stack and prepare information for transmission across a network.

11. A, B, C. The physical layer of the OSI model is associated with hubs, cables, and network interface adapters. The data link layer is associated with bridges and switches. The network layer is associated with routers. The transport, session, presentation, and application layers are typically not associated with dedicated hardware devices.

12. B. The only layer with a protocol (such as Ethernet) that adds both a header and a footer is the data link layer. The process of adding the headers and footers is known as data encapsulation. All other protocol layers that encapsulate data add just a header.

13. C. The Ethernet protocol that handles the addressing, transmission, and reception of frames operates at the data link layer. Each frame includes hardware addresses that identify the sending and receiving systems on the local network. Ethernet uses the CSMA/CD media access control method. Physical layer specifications include the transmission of signals in the form of electrical or light pulses to represent binary code, not frames. CSMA/CA is a data link layer media access control method used by wireless LAN protocols, but not Ethernet.

14. B. On a TCP/IP network, the Internet Protocol (IP) at the network layer is the protocol responsible for the delivery of data to its final destination. Data link layer protocols are only concerned with communication between devices on a Local Area Network (LAN) or between two points connected by a Wide Area Network (WAN) link. The session and application layers are not involved in the actual delivery of data.

15. D. Internet Protocol (IP), Internet Control Message Protocol (ICMP), and Internet Group Message Protocol (IGMP) are all network layer protocols. Internet Message Access Protocol (IMAP) is a mail protocol that operates at the application layer.

16. C. A connection-oriented transport layer protocol, such as Transmission Control Protocol (TCP), provides guaranteed delivery of data for upper layer applications. Connectionless protocols do not guarantee delivery of information and therefore are not a good choice. Guaranteed delivery of information is generally not a function of the data link, network, or application layer.

17. A. A hub functions only at the physical layer by forwarding all incoming signals out through all of its ports. Bridges and switches operate at the data link layer by selectively propagating incoming data. Routers operate at the network layer by connecting local area networks (LANs) and propagating only the traffic intended for another network, based on IP addresses.

18. A. The physical layer defines the mechanical and electrical characteristics of the cables used to build a network. The data link layer defines specific network (LAN or WAN) topologies and their characteristics. The physical layer standard that Alice will implement is dependent on the data link layer protocol she selects. The network, transport, and application layers are not concerned with cables and topologies.

19. E, F. In the TCP/IP suite, the functions of the session layer are primarily implemented in the transport layer protocols: Transmission Control Protocol (TCP) and User Datagram Protocol (UDP). The presentation layer functions are often implemented in application layer protocols, although some functions, such as encryption, can also be performed by transport or network layer protocols.

20. C. Transport layer protocols, such as Transmission Control Protocol (TCP) and User Datagram Protocol (UDP), have header fields that contain the port numbers of the applications that generated the data in the packet and which will receive it. The application, presentation, and network layers do not use port numbers.

21. E. The correct order of the OSI model layers, from top to bottom, is application, presentation, session, transport, network, data link, physical.

22. B. Switches and bridges are involved in Local Area Network (LAN) communications only and therefore primarily at the data link layer. They are not primarily associated with the physical, network, or transport layers, although some switches include network layer routing capabilities.

23. C. Flow control is a process that adjusts the transmission rate of a protocol based on the capability of the receiver. If the receiving system becomes overwhelmed by incoming data, the sender dynamically reduces the transmission rate. In the TCP/IP protocol suite, Transmission Control Protocol (TCP) is responsible for implementing flow control. TCP runs at the transport layer. None of the other layers listed have TCP/IP protocols that provide flow control.

24. A. The physical layer of the OSI model defines the standards for the physical and mechanical characteristics of a network, such as cabling (copper and fiber), connecting hardware (hubs and switches), and signaling methods (analog and digital). All of the other layers are not involved in the mechanical characteristics of the network.

25. D. The presentation layer provides a syntax translation service that enables two computers to communicate, despite their use of different bit-encoding methods. This translation service also enables systems using compressed or encrypted data to communicate with each other.

26. A. The physical layer of the OSI model defines the functions specific to the network medium and the transmission and reception of signals. All of the other layers are implemented in software and do not physically send or receive signals.

27. B. IP is a connectionless protocol that operates at the network layer of the OSI model. There are no connection-oriented protocols at this layer. The protocols at the transport layer include Transmission Control Protocol (TCP), which is connection-oriented, and User Datagram Protocol (UDP), which is connectionless.

28. A. An Ethernet network interface adapter functions at the data link layer by encapsulating network layer data for transmission over the network. It provides physical layer functions by providing the connection to the network medium and generating the appropriate signals for transmission. Network interface adapters do not operate at the network, transport, or application layer.

29. A, B. Hypertext Transfer Protocol (HTTP) and Simple Network Management Protocol (SNMP) operate at the application layer. Internet Control Message Protocol (ICMP) and Internet Group Management Protocol (IGMP) both operate at the network layer. User Datagram Protocol (UDP) operates at the transport layer.

30. B. The presentation layer of the OSI model is responsible for translating different kinds of syntax, including text-encoding systems, such as EBCDIC and ASCII. The application, session, and physical layers do not perform this function.

31. D. Internet Control Message Protocol (ICMP) operates at the network layer by sending operational and error messages. It does not encapsulate upper layer protocol data. Internet Protocol (IP) operates at the network layer, but it does encapsulate transport layer protocol data. Transmission Control Protocol (TCP) and User Datagram Protocol (UDP) are transport layer protocols that encapsulate upper layer protocol data. Address Resolution Protocol (ARP) does not encapsulate upper layer protocol data, but it is a data link layer protocol.

32. D. The TCP connection establishment exchange is a three-way handshake that uses TCP flags to specify the message type for each frame. The first frame contains a SYN flag from the client; the second frame contains the SYN and ACK flags from the server; and the last frame contains an ACK flag from the client.

33. C. The MTU is the largest amount of data (in bytes) that a protocol operating at a given layer of the OSI model can transmit in one packet. The MTU does not include any header and footer fields supplied by that protocol. For Ethernet, the maximum frame size is 1518 bytes, which includes 18 bytes of header and footer fields. Therefore, the MTU for Ethernet is 1500 bytes. Protocols operating at other OSI model layers can have different MTUs. For example, the typical MTU for an Internet Protocol (IPv4) implementation is smaller than that of Ethernet.

34. C. The termination phase of a TCP connection begins when either the client or the server sends a message containing the FIN control bit with a value of 1. The other control bits listed have nothing to do with the connection termination procedure, and there is no END bit.

35. A. A cable break in a bus topology would split the network into two halves, preventing the nodes on one side of the break from communicating with those on the other. In addition, both halves of the network would be left with one unterminated end, which would prevent the computers on each side of the break from communicating effectively. A cable break in a star or logical ring topology would only interrupt the connection of a single computer to the network. The mesh topology is not often used for LANs, but redundant network connections are a characteristic of mesh networks, which means that a single cable break would have no effect on the network.

36. D. A wired LAN is a group of computers within a small area, connected by a common network medium. A wired LAN can be configured using a ring, bus, or star topology.

37. B. A hybrid topology is a network that uses two or more of the basic topologies, connected together so that each workstation can communicate with all of the other workstations. Connecting four switches to a bus topology combines four-star networks in such a way that the workstations are all interconnected. Connecting a single workstation to a star and a bus network enables that workstation to access both networks, but it does not enable other workstations to access both topologies. Four workstations, each with a separate connection to the other three, is a mesh network topology, not a hybrid. Four connected switches expands the star topology, but it does not create a hybrid topology.

38. B. A Local Area Network (LAN), as the name implies, is a group of computers contained within a small geographic area. WANs (Wide Area Networks) connect LANs that are geographically distant. MANs (Metropolitan Area Networks) are not confined to a small area; they are typically larger than a LAN but smaller than a WAN. A Campus Area Network (CAN) typically includes a group of adjacent buildings, such as those of a corporation or university.

39. A. WANs (Wide Area Networks) connect LANs that are geographically distant. A LAN (Local Area Network), as the name implies, is a group of computers, not other LANs, and it is contained within a small area. MANs (Metropolitan Area Networks) connect LANs in a single metropolitan area; they are not confined to a small area. A MAN is typically larger than a LAN but smaller than a WAN. A Campus Area Network (CAN) typically includes a group of adjacent buildings, such as those of a corporation or university.

40. A. A bus topology requires terminating resistors at each end of the bus, to remove signals as they reach the end of the cable and prevent them from reflecting back in the other direction and interfering with newly transmitted signals. Star, ring, and mesh topologies do not require terminating resistors.

41. D. Virtually all of the new Ethernet networks installed today use the star or the hierarchical star topology, with one or more switches functioning as a cabling nexus.

42. A. A storage area network (SAN) is a network that is dedicated to carrying traffic between servers and storage devices. A Personal Area Network (PAN) provides communication among devices associated with a single person, such as smartphones. A Wide Area Network (WAN) is a network that connects devices or networks at different geographic locations. A Metropolitan Area Network (MAN) is a type of WAN that connects devices within a limited geographic area.

43. D. A Software-Defined Wide Area Network (SDWAN) is a technology that automates the configuration of WAN routers based on the current mix of traffic. It is therefore not suitable for use on a PAN. Bluetooth, Z-Wave, and near-field communication (NFC) are all short-range wireless technologies that are capable of providing communications between PAN devices.

44. A, C. WLANs can use the ad hoc topology, in which devices communicate directly with each other, or the infrastructure topology, in which the wireless devices connect to an access point. The bus and star topologies are used by wired networks only.

45. A. The first Ethernet networks used a physical layer implementation commonly known as Thick Ethernet or 10Base5. The network used coaxial cable in a bus topology. Later Ethernet standards use twisted pair cable in a star topology. Ethernet has never used a ring or mesh topology.

46. A, C. A hub or a switch can function as the cabling nexus at the center of an Ethernet star topology. Each of the devices on the network is connected by a cable to a hub or switch. Routers are used to connect networks to each other; they cannot function as the center of a star topology.

47. C. A mesh topology is one in which every node is directly connected to every other node, therefore providing complete redundancy through the network. In a star topology, each node is connected to a central nexus, providing each with a single path to the rest of the network. In a ring topology, each node is connected to two other nodes, providing two possible paths through the network. In a bus topology, nodes are chained together in a line, providing no redundancy.

48. A. 10Base2 is the physical layer specification for Thin Ethernet, which uses coaxial cable in a bus topology. 10Base-T, 100Base-TX, and 1000Base-T all use twisted pair cable in a star topology.

49. B, D. Personal area networks (PANs) connect devices associated with a single person, such as smartphones, and are nearly always wireless. Wireless Local Area Networks (WLANs) are wireless by definition. Wide Area Networks (WANs) typically span long distances and are typically wired, at least in part. Storage area networks (SANs) require high performance levels and are nearly always wired.

50. B. DWDM has become a popular technology in the construction of metro-optical networks because it addresses some of the scalability and cost restrictions of other optical technologies, such as Synchronous Optical Networks (SONETs). DSL, satellite, and cable providers do not typically use DWDM.

51. C. A peer-to-peer network calls for each workstation to maintain accounts for authenticating users that access their shared resources. On a client-server network, authentication is centralized. Peer-to-peer networks can be more difficult to administer than client-server networks, but they are not inherently less secure. Peer networks sharing copyrighted content on the Internet are illegal, but it is not illegal to share private resources on a peer-to-peer network. Workstations on a peer-to-peer network are not required to share their resources, but they are capable of it.

52. D. DSL technology provides higher data rates because it uses frequency ranges that are higher than the standard voice spectrum. DSL connections use 10 kHz and above, whereas the standard voice spectrum uses 300 Hz to 4 kHz. DSL does not use separate control circuits and does not perform CRC functions. Also, DSL technology is strictly digital and does not require an analog-to-digital conversion.

53. C. Rate-Adaptive Digital Subscriber Line (RADSL) technology can adjust its rate of transmission based on line conditions. High-bit-rate Digital Subscriber Line (HDSL), Very high-rate Digital Subscriber Line (VDSL), and Internet Digital Subscriber Line (IDSL) do not use rate adaptive transmission.

54. D. CATV networks use broadband signaling, which enables many signals to occupy the same channel. DSL and ISDN do not use broadband signaling. SONET is a physical layer standard that defines fiber-optic connections.

55. B. For this scenario, the best of the options given is a dedicated leased line connection. This is because the bandwidth requirements are constant, and the data transfer rates are high. To support the 40 Mbps data rate, Ed should recommend a T-3 dedicated leased line, running at 44.735 Mbps. Standard modem connections, CATV, and ADSL connections are all too slow.

56. D. In this scenario, the best solution is for Ralph to use his existing CATV service for the remote connection. CATV offers faster data rates than standard modem-to-modem service and supports VPN connections. A dedicated fractional T-1 line is expensive and is not typically used for remote user connections. Since Ralph's telephone lines are not run through conduit and the distance to the central office is more than 18,000 feet, he probably cannot use DSL technology, because it requires good-quality lines and close proximity to a central office.

57. A. PSTN is an analog, circuit-switched network. CATV, DSL, and SONET are all digital networks.

58. D. In a DSL connection, a signal splitter is needed at the customer site to separate the lower frequency voice range from the higher frequencies used by data traffic. The higher frequency signals are handled at the central office by a DSLAM device. Lower frequency signals carrying voice traffic are handled at the central office by a CODEC device. A signal terminator is not required by DSL.

59. B, C. There are two factors that affect DSL transmission rates. The first is the distance to the nearest central office, and the second is the condition and quality of the line. For DSL to achieve higher data rates, the site must be close to the central office and use good-quality lines for signal transmission. The other options are not factors relating to DSL transmission.

60. B. A demarcation point, or demarc, is the place where an outside telecommunications service meets a customer's private network, which is typically where the service enters the building. The demarc is also the place where the responsibility of the network administrator ends. If a problem occurs outside the demarc, it is up to the service provider to fix it. Inside the demarc, it is the network administrator's problem.

61. B. The word *symmetric* in Symmetric Digital Subscriber Line (SDSL) means that the service provides equal amounts of bandwidth in both directions. The *asymmetric* in Asymmetric Digital Subscriber Line (ADSL) means that the service provides more downstream bandwidth than upstream. Cable and satellite services are also asymmetric, providing more bandwidth downstream than upstream.

62. D. The network interface device (NID) at the demarcation point of a leased line can be a simple RJ-45 jack, but many service providers install smartjacks, which can also provide signal conversion, diagnostic testing, and other capabilities. Punchdown blocks, 110 blocks, and Channel Service Unit/Data Service Units (CSU/DSUs) are all telecommunications components located inside the demarc, on the subscriber's private network.

63. B, C. ISDN and DSL are both remote access technologies that enable users to transmit voice and data simultaneously. To do this, DSL splits the lower analog frequency (voice) range from the higher digital frequency (data) range, whereas ISDN provides multiple data channels (called B channels) that allow for both voice and data transmissions. Broadband cable television networks can often support simultaneous voice and data communications, but they use Voice over Internet Protocol (VoIP) to carry voice traffic over the Internet, not the PSTN. Dial-up connections and SONET do not support the simultaneous transmission of voice and data.

64. D. The demarc, or demarcation point, is the place where a service enters the building, and where the service provider's physical layer responsibility ends. The patch panel, the switch, and the firewall are all inside the network, and they are the responsibility of the subscriber.

65. E. A T-3 leased line connection is the equivalent of 28 T-1 connections. Each T-1 consists of 24 channels, so a T-3 has a total of 672 channels (28 × 24).

66. C. A T-3 leased line connection is the equivalent of 28 T-1 connections. Each T-1 consists of 24 channels, so a T-3 has a total of 672 channels (28 × 24), for an overall transfer rate of 44.736 Mbps.

67. B. The Synchronous Optical Networking (SONET) standard defines a base data transfer rate of 51.84 Mbps, which is multiplied at the various optical carrier levels. An OC-3 connection therefore runs at 155.52 Mbps, an OC-12 at 622.08 Mbps and so forth. The Synchronous Digital Hierarchy (SDH) is the European equivalent of SONET. Integrated Services Digital Network (ISDN) is a service that combines voice and data services using the Public Switched Telephone Network (PSTN), and Digital Subscriber Line (DSL) is a remote access technology that enables users to transmit voice and data simultaneously.

68. B. Multiprotocol Label Switching (MPLS) is a data transfer mechanism that assigns labels to individual packets, and then routes the packets based on those labels. Frame relay, Asynchronous Transfer Mode (ATM), Point-to-Point Protocol over Ethernet (PPPoE), and a Software-Defined Wide Area Network (SDWAN) do not assign labels to packets.

69. A, C. A Session Initiation Protocol (SIP) trunk provides a connection between the private and public domains of a unified communications network. A Voice over Internet Protocol (VoIP) gateway provides a connection between an IP network and the Public Switched Telephone Network (PSTN). Both of these provide a conduit between a subscriber's private network and the network furnished by a service provider. A Channel Service Unit/Data Service Unit (CSU/DSU) is a device that provides a router on a private network with access to a leased line. A smartjack provides signal conversion, diagnostic testing, and other capabilities to leased line subscribers. A Virtual Private Network (VPN) concentrator is a type of router that enables multiple client systems to access a network from remote locations.

70. A. Synchronous Digital Hierarchy (SDH) is the European equivalent of SONET. Optical carrier 3 (OC-3) is one of the SONET data rates. E-3 is the European equivalent of the T-3 connection in the United States. Asynchronous Transfer Mode (ATM) is a cell-switched protocol that is designed to carry voice, data, and video traffic by splitting it into uniform 53-byte cells.

71. B. A Channel Service Unit/Data Service Unit (CSU/DSU) is a device that provides a LAN router on a private network with access to a leased line WAN connection. Quad Small Form-factor Pluggable (QSFP) is a standard for a type of modular transceiver, often used on fiber-optic installations. A Session Initiation Protocol (SIP) trunk provides a connection between the private and public domains of a unified communications network, such as a LAN and the Public Switched Telephone Network (PSTN). An intrusion detection system/intrusion prevention system (IDS/IPS) is a network hardware or software security appliance that detects malicious activity and attempts to block it.

72. D. A subscription to part of the T-1 leased line is called a fractional T-1 service. This service enables you to purchase some of the 24 DS0 channels in a T-1 connection. An E-1 is the European version of a T-1. A B channel is part of an Integrated Services Digital Network (ISDN) service, not a T-1. An OC-1 is a fiber-optic connection on the Synchronous Optical Network (SONET) service.

73. B. MPLS is a data-carrying service that is often said to operate between the data link layer and the network layer. It is therefore sometimes called a layer 2.5 protocol. MPLS can be used to carry IP datagrams as well as Ethernet, Asynchronous Transfer Mode (ATM), and Synchronous Optical Network (SONET) traffic.

74. D. An OC-1 connection provides the fastest transfer rate at 51.84 Mbps. An E-1 connection is 2.048 Mbps. A T-3 is 44.736 Mbps, and a T-1 is 1.544 Mbps.

75. C. The Data Over Cable Service Interface Specification (DOCSIS) is a telecommunications standard that defines the manner in which data is to be transmitted over a cable television system. DOCSIS does not apply to dial-up modem, Digital Subscriber Line (DSL), or Integrated Services Digital Network (ISDN) connections.

76. B, C. Frame relay services offer permanent virtual circuits (PVCs) and switched virtual circuits (SVCs). SRV is a resource record type in the Domain Name System (DNS), and an Ultra-Physical Contact (UPC) is a type of fiber-optic cable connector.

77. C, D. Cable broadband and DSL subscribers typically connect to ISP networks that run Ethernet, but Ethernet has no built-in authentication or encryption mechanisms. PPP has the ability to use external authentication and encryption protocols, so by encapsulating PPP within Ethernet frames, users are able to log on to the ISP network securely. Leased lines, such as T-1s, and Synchronous Optical Network (SONET) connections do not use Ethernet connections, so they have no need for PPPoE.

78. C. A smartjack is a device located at the demarcation point of a leased line that can provide additional functions, such as signal conversion, diagnostic testing, and other capabilities. A Session Initiation Protocol (SIP) trunk is a connection to a Voice over Internet Protocol (VoIP) service provider. A media converter is a local area networking device that connects different cable types to the same network. An AAAA server provides authentication, authorization, accounting, and auditing services for remote access servers.

79. D. Frame relay is a packet switching service that uses a single leased line to replace multiple leased lines by multiplexing traffic through a cloud. Asynchronous Transfer Mode (ATM) uses a switched fabric, but it is not referred to as a *cloud*. A fractional T-1 is part of a leased line that connects two points, so there is no switching involved and no cloud. SONET is a physical layer standard that defines fiber-optic connections; it does not call for switching or use the term *cloud*.

80. D. All coaxial-based Ethernet networks, including Thin Ethernet, use a bus topology. All UTP-based Gigabit Ethernet networks use a star topology. Therefore, an upgrade from coaxial to UTP cable must include a change in topology from bus to star.

81. D. In most virtualization products, when you create multiple virtual machines on one host computer, they can communicate with each other internally using a built-in virtual switching capability. A computer with multiple network adapters can function as a router, but not as a switch. Layer 3 switches can provide virtual routers that connect VLANs together, but not virtual switches. The function that enables VLANs on different switches to communicate is called trunking, not virtual switching.

82. B. Type I virtualization does not require a host OS, whereas Type II virtualization does. Both Type I and Type II virtualization can use processors with hardware virtualization assistance, but only Type I requires it. The type of virtualization does not impose any limit on the number of virtual machines supported; any limitations are left to the individual implementation. Both Type I and Type II virtualization can share a single processor among virtual machines.

83. B. You can create Virtual Local Area Networks (VLANs) on a virtual switch, just as you can create them on many physical switches. In most cases, virtual components function just like their physical counterparts. Virtual NICs are components of virtual machines and therefore do not provide functions spanning entire networks. Virtual routers function at the network layer and virtual firewalls at the application layer, so neither of these can host VLANs, which operate at the data link layer.

84. B. Just like physical network interface cards (NICs), virtual NICs have 6 byte MAC addresses assigned to them, which enable them to be identified by data link layer protocols. Unlike physical NICs, however, it is typically an easy matter to modify a MAC address on a virtual NIC. Virtual switches, like physical switches, are not addressable devices, so they do not have MAC addresses on an unmanaged network. The hypervisor is the component on a host server that makes virtualization possible, so it does not require a MAC address. Virtual firewalls operate at the application layer, so they do not require data link layer MAC addresses. On a managed network, these devices have a MAC address to communicate with the management console, but addresses are not needed on an unmanaged network.

85. A. The hypervisor is the hardware or software component responsible for managing virtual machines and providing the virtualized hardware environment on which they run. Virtual servers and virtual switches are components that are part of the virtual network infrastructure enabled by the hypervisor. A Virtual Private Network (VPN) concentrator is a type of router that enables multiple remote clients to connect to a network; it has nothing to do with virtual networking.

86. C. A computer with a hypervisor, on which you can create virtual machines, is referred to as a host. The virtual machines themselves are called guests. Network Attached Storage (NAS) refers to a device containing shared drives that is connected to a network. A Storage Area Network (SAN) is a separate network dedicated to shared storage devices.

87. A. It is true that virtual switches can have unlimited ports, whereas physical switches are limited to the number of physical ports in the device. Both virtual and physical switches can support Virtual Local Area Networks (VLANs). Virtual switches can forward traffic to the host server. Physical switches do not always include layer 3 (routing) functionality.

88. E. A virtual firewall is a service or appliance that performs the same functions as a physical network firewall: packet filtering and monitoring. In a virtual environment, firewalls can take the form of software components installed on a guest virtual machine or a hypervisor host system. A firewall can also be incorporated into a virtual switch.

89. B. Frame relay is a packet switching service that uses a single leased line to replace multiple leased lines by multiplexing traffic through a cloud. The service can create virtual circuits connecting the subscriber's network to multiple destinations, eliminating the need for a dedicated leased line to each remote site. An E-1 is the European equivalent to a T-1 leased line, which does not replace multiple T-1s. Asynchronous Transfer Mode (ATM) is a cell-switching WAN technology, and Point-to-Point Protocol (PPP) is a protocol that provides a data link layer connection between two end systems. Neither is a replacement for multiple T-1s.

90. D. Network Address Translation (NAT) enables workstations on private networks to access the Internet by substituting a public IP address in packets generated with private addresses. Layer 2 Tunneling Protocol (L2TP), IPsec, and Multipoint Generic Routing Encapsulation (MGRE) are all protocols that encapsulate packets in an encrypted form within another protocol to secure the contents.

91. B. The NFV specification, published by the European Telecommunications Standards Institute (ETSI), calls for three main components: virtualized network functions (VNFs), which are software-based implementations of standard network services, such as firewalls and load balancers; a Network Functions Virtualization Infrastructure (NFVI), which is the hardware/software environment that hosts the VNFs; and a Network Functions Virtualization-Management And Orchestration (NFV-MANO) framework, which includes the elements required to deploy and administer the NFVI and the VNFs. The Network Functions Virtualization Industry Specification Group (NFV ISG) is the group within ETSI that develops the NFV specifications; it is not one of the three components.

92. A. The network medium provides the physical connection between networked computers. This connection can be made through a copper-based, fiber-optic, or wireless medium. The network medium is not a protocol, and it does not pass data packets; it only carries signals. The network medium does not process electrical or light pulses and convert them to data; it carries only the signals generated by transceivers.

93. D. Copper cables use electrical signals to transmit data. Fiber optic is a cable type, not a signal type. Microwave signals cannot be transmitted over copper cable. Infrared signals are used only for wireless networks.

94. E. The three organizations that collectively developed the T568b document, which defines the standard for a structured cabling system for voice and data communications, are the American National Standards Institute (ANSI), the Telecommunications Industry Association (TIA), and the Electronic Industries Association (EIA). All of the other options are not standards organizations or cabling standards.

95. D. The cable type and connector used to attach a television set to a CATV network is a coaxial cable with a screw-on F-type connector. Although CATV networks typically use fiber-optic cables and ST connectors for outdoor connections, they do not use fiber for internal connections to television sets. Coaxial cables with BNC connectors are most commonly used for Thin Ethernet LANs, not CATV network connections. Twisted pair cables and RJ-45 connectors are used for Ethernet LANs and telephone networks, but not CATV networks. AUI cables and vampire tap connectors are used for Thick Ethernet networks. Twinaxial cables are used for SATA 3.0 device and 100 Gbit Ethernet connections, but not for CATV connections.

96. A. The cable type used for Thick Ethernet segments is a coaxial cable called RG-8. RG-58 is used exclusively on Thin Ethernet segments. RJ-45 is a connector type used in twisted pair cabling for data networks. RJ-11 is a connector type used in twisted pair cabling for telecommunications networks.

97. B. RG-58 coaxial cable is used exclusively for Thin Ethernet segments. RG-8 cable is used for Thick Ethernet segments. RJ-45 is a connector type used in twisted pair cabling for data networks. RJ-11 is a connector type used in twisted pair cabling for telecommunications networks.

98. A. A 66 block is a type of punchdown block for telephone systems that was first introduced in 1962. By the year 2000, nearly all commercial telephone installations had begun using 110 blocks instead; 110 blocks are still in use, as are smartjacks and patch panels.

99. C. The Krone LSA-Plus is a proprietary telecommunications connector type commonly used in European installations. The 66 block is an outdated type of punchdown block for U.S. telephone systems. Multipoint Generic Routing Encapsulation (mGRE) is a technique for encapsulating network layer protocols; it is not a type of punchdown block. BIX (Building Industry Cross-connect) is a proprietary U.S. telecommunications connection system.

100. A, D. RG-6 and RG-59 are 75 ohm cables that are still used for cable television and similar connections. RG-8 and RG-58 are 50 ohm cables that were formerly used for Thick Ethernet and Thin Ethernet, respectively, but are no longer in general use.

101. A, B, C. Joining an APC to a UPC creates a mismatched connection that generates an extremely high rate of insertion loss (attenuation). APCs do generate more insertion loss than UPCs and less return loss (reflection). It is APCs, not UPCs, that use green boots or bodies on the connectors.

102. D. Bayonet-Neill-Concelman (BNC) is a type of connector used with coaxial cable. Subscriber Connector (SC), Mechanical Transfer-Registered Jack (MT-RJ), and Straight Tip (ST) are all types of fiber-optic connectors.

103. C. The Gigabit Interface Converter (GBIC) transceiver standard was first published in 1995 and defines a maximum data transfer rate of 1.25 Gbps. It was rendered all but obsolete by the Small Form-factor Pluggable (SFP) standard, introduced in 2001, which ran at the same maximum speed but was smaller in size. Subsequent variations on the standard, such as SFP+, Quad Small Form-factor Pluggable (QSFP), and QSFP+, defined devices with faster transfer rates.

104. B. There are two main types of twisted pair wiring used for data communications: Unshielded Twisted Pair (UTP) and Shielded Twisted Pair (STP). Both types can be used in a star topology. UTP and STP cables contain eight copper conductors twisted in four pairs. UTP and STP cables use RJ-45 connectors to connect end systems to switches, patch panels, and wall plates. RG-8 and RG-58 coaxial cable can only be used in a bus topology. Fiber-optic cable can be used in a star topology, but it uses either glass or plastic conductors and does not use RJ-45 connectors.

105. C. The twists in a twisted pair cable prevent the signals on the different wires from interfering with each other (which is called crosstalk) and also provide resistance to outside electromagnetic interference. The twists have no effect on collisions. The twists cannot completely eliminate the effects of EMI. Twists have nothing to do with the bend radius allowance for the cable.

106. A. A crimper or crimping tool is a jawed device that has a set of dies in it. Installers use a crimper to squeeze the two halves of an RJ-45 or RJ-11 connector together, with the wires inside securing the connector to the cable. Installers use a splicing tool to splice two cable segments together. There is no tool called a pigtail or a patch.

107. C. Thin Ethernet networks use a type of 50-ohm coaxial cable called RG-58, which is 0.195 inches in diameter and uses BNC connectors. 75-ohm coaxial cable with F connectors is used for cable television networks, and RG-8 coaxial is the cable that Thick Ethernet networks use.

108. B, C, E. Thin Ethernet networks use BNC connectors. Thick Ethernet networks use N-type connectors. All Unshielded Twisted Pair (UTP) Ethernet networks use RJ-45 connectors. F-type connectors are used with coaxial cable, typically for cable television installations. DB-9 connectors are commonly used for serial communications ports.

109. D. Thin Ethernet networks use a type of coaxial cable that runs from each computer to the next one, forming a bus topology. To connect the cable to the network computers, each network interface adapter has a T-connector attached to it, with two additional male BNC connectors, to which you connect two lengths of network cabling.

110. B, D, E. Fiber-optic cable connectors all function on the same basic principles, but there are a variety of form factors from which to choose, including Straight Tip (ST), Local Connector (LC), and Mechanical Transfer–Registered Jack (MT-RJ). RJ-11 is a twisted pair cable connector, and F connectors are for coaxial cable.

111. E. Thick Ethernet installations used a type of coaxial cable called RG-8. To connect a node to the network, installers ran a separate cable called an Attachment Unit Interface (AUI) cable from the computer to the RG-8 and connected it using a device called a vampire tap that pierced the sheathing to make contact with the conductors within. All of the other cable types listed use different types of connectors.

112. D. The cabling nexus in a telecommunications room is called a patch panel. A telepole is a tool used for installing cables. A backbone is a network that connects other Local Area Networks (LANs) together. A demarcation point, or demarc, is the location at which a telecommunication provider's service meets the customer's private network. A fiber distribution panel is used for fiber optic cable, not Unshielded Twisted Pair (UTP), connections.

113. A, C. Single-mode cables are capable of spanning longer distances than multimode because they have a narrower core diameter, reducing signal dispersion rates. Because the core consists of fewer (typically one or two) strands, single-mode cables are less flexible than multimode and cannot bend around corners as easily, making them more difficult to install. Because they use light impulses rather than electricity, all fiber-optic cables are completely immune to electromagnetic interference.

114. A, C, D. Voice telephone networks do not have performance requirements as strict as those of data networks, so they are less liable to suffer from crosstalk and other types of interference. As a result, installers often use larger UTP cables for telephone connections. UTP cables are available in configurations containing 25 wire pairs and 100 wire pairs in a single sheath, which enables installers to service multiple users with a single cable. The punchdown blocks for UTP data networks with 8P8C connectors are called 110 blocks. The older standard for punchdown blocks is the 66 block. Rarely used for data networking, 66 blocks are still found in many telephone service installations.

115. B, C. Single-mode cables have a smaller core filament and can span longer distances than multimode cables. Single-mode cables also use a laser light source, have a larger bend radius, and do not require a ground.

116. D. Installers use a punchdown block tool to connect the ends of bulk cable runs to jacks in wall plates and patch panels. A crimper or crimping tool is a jawed device that enables installers to squeeze the two halves of an RJ-45 or RJ-11 connector together, securing the connector to the cable. Installers use a splicing tool to splice two cable segments together. There is no tool called a pigtail.

117. A. Multimode fiber-optic cable best meets the client's needs. Fiber-optic cable supports the required 1000 Mbps data rate and can connect networks that are more than 1000 feet apart. Fiber-optic cable is immune to EMI. Although both multimode and single-mode fiber would meet the corporation's general needs, multimode is best in this scenario because it is less expensive than single-mode fiber. Twisted pair wiring (STP or UTP) meets the data rate and cost requirements but does not support connections longer than 100 meters. Thin coaxial cable does not support the data rate or distances longer than 185 meters.

118. A, B, C. BNC connectors are used for coaxial Thin Ethernet networks, and N-type connectors with Thick Ethernet. F-type connectors are used for coaxial cable television installations. Straight Tip (ST) connectors are used with fiber-optic cable, and RJ-11 connectors are used for telephone installations.

119. C. Either CAT6 or CAT6a UTP cable will provide the currently required 1 Gbps data rate, with a migration path to 10 Gbps in the future. The backbone cabling connecting the two LANs needs to be fiber optic, since it exceeds the distance limitations of twisted pair and coaxial cable. CAT5 cable conceivably runs at 1 Gbps; however, it does not run at 10 Gbps.

120.   D. The Thin Ethernet LAN is the network most endangered by the cable break. If a bus network is severed, all of the workstations on it are affected because the cable segments are no longer terminated at one end. The Gigabit Ethernet network uses a star topology, which means that only the one computer using the severed cable could be disconnected from the network. A FDDI double ring network can survive a single cable break without any workstations being affected.

121.   A. You use a punchdown block tool to connect the ends of bulk cable runs to jacks in wall plates and patch panels. The steps of the process are as follows:

1.   Strip some of the sheath off the cable end to expose the wires.

2.   Separate the twisted wire pairs at the ends.

3.   Strip a small amount of insulation off each wire.

4.   Insert the wires into the appropriate contacts in the jack.

5.   Press the bare wire down between the two metal contacts that hold it in place.

6.   Cut off the excess wire that protrudes past the contacts.

You must repeat the process of punching down for both ends of your internal cable runs.

122.   D. ST, SC, fiber LC, and MT-RJ are all connectors used with fiber-optic cables. F-type connectors are used with coaxial cables.

123.   D, E, F. Category 6a (CAT6a) twisted pair cable is a variant on CAT6 that enables you to create 10GBase-T networks with segments up to 100 meters long. Category 7 (CAT7) cable adds shielding both to the individual wire pairs and to the entire cable, for even greater resistance to crosstalk and noise. CAT7 supports 100-meter 10GBase-T segments as well. CAT8 cable supports bandwidth up to 2 GHz, making it even more suitable for 10GBase-T networks than CAT6a (500 MHz) or CAT7 (600 MHz). CAT5 and CAT5e are not suitable for use with 10GBase-T. You can use CAT6 for 10GBase-T, but it is limited to 55-meter segments.

124.   C, D. The DB-9 and DB-25 connectors were at one time ubiquitous on personal computers, providing peripheral connections to modems, printers, and other devices. They have since been largely eliminated in favor of USB. BNC connectors were used for Thin Ethernet networking, but they have been replaced by Unshielded Twisted Pair (UTP) cable with RJ-45 connectors. RJ-11 connectors are used for telephone connections.

125.   A. CAT3 cable was originally intended for use in voice-grade telephone networks but was later certified for use in data networks. CAT3 cable can support data transfer rates from 4 Mbps up to 100 Mbps (using the now-deprecated 100Base-T4 and 100VG-AnyLAN standards). Although this type of cable could run at 100 Mbps, it was seldom used at speeds greater than 10 Mbps. CAT5 cable was the primary replacement for CAT3, supporting data rates up to 100 Mbps. CAT5e and CAT6 are rated for data rates up to 1 Gbps, as on Gigabit Ethernet networks. CAT6 can even support 10 Gbps transfer rates over shorter distances.

126.   E. Because the company has few employees, a single location, and cost restrictions, the best solution is a star topology with prefabricated twisted pair cabling and an external installation method. The star topology uses a central switch. Prefabricated twisted pair cabling, with the connectors already attached, will keep the cost to a minimum. Since the employees are all located in the same building, with a common wall and a drop ceiling, the external installation method is the best choice. It is not possible to use a bus topology or coaxial cable for Gigabit Ethernet. Ed could use fiber-optic cable in a star topology for Gigabit Ethernet, but it is more difficult and expensive to install. An internal installation, which uses a combination of bulk cable and prefabricated cables, is more expensive than an external installation and is typically used for larger networks.

127. B, D. The main cable types used in LANs today are multimode fiber optic and unshielded twisted pair. Single-mode fiber optic is used primarily for long-distance Wide Area Network (WAN) connections, and coaxial cable is no longer used for LANs.

128. B, D, F. Coaxial cable has two conductors within the same sheath that share a common axis. These conductors are surrounded by an outer insulating sheath of either PVC or Teflon. Copper cables carry electrical signals. Only fiber-optic cables carry light pulse signals.

129. F. All twisted pair Gigabit Ethernet implementations require all four wire pairs to achieve 1000 Mbps transfer rates.

130. B, C, D. CAT5 cable was the original cable standard intended for transfer rates up to 100 Mbps. CAT5e and CAT6 support 100 Mbps and are also rated for data rates up to 1000 Mbps. All three of these standards also support the 10 Mbps transfer rate. CAT3 can support both 10 and 100 Mbps, but it requires four pairs for 100 Mbps.

131. A, B, D, E, F. Fiber-optic cable comes in two types: multimode and single-mode. Fiber-optic cables vary in light source (LED or laser), cable grade (glass or plastic), and size of the core conductor. Single-mode uses a higher-grade glass conductor with a laser light source. Multimode fiber uses an LED light source. Both types can use either ST or SC connectors to physically connect end devices to a fiber-optic network. Fiber-optic cable is used to extend networks over long distances. Fiber-optic cables do not use IDC connectors, which are intended for use with Shielded Twisted Pair (STP) cable.

132. A, D, F. The use of bulk cable with no connectors, wall plates, and rack-mounted patch panels are all characteristics of an internal wiring installation. Internal installations typically cover large geographic areas that require cabling through walls, ceilings, and around other obstacles, making the cabling difficult to move. Solid core wiring is used for longer cable runs, whereas shorter cable runs such as connections from node to wall plate use prefabricated stranded core cables with connectors attached.

133. B. 40GBase-T is a 40-gigabits-per-second (Gbps) Ethernet specification that calls for 4-pair CAT8 twisted pair cabling for lengths up to 30 meters. 10GBase-T and 100Base-TX do not require CAT8 cable, and 1000Base-SX is a fiber optic standard.

134. E. Ralph should use a mesh topology with redundant fiber-optic cable runs and an internal installation method. This will meet the requirements for connecting the LANs and providing redundancy and fault tolerance. Fiber-optic cable is immune to electromagnetic interference (EMI) and can span long distances. The internal installation method is most often used in larger networks, where end systems are geographically distant. The star topology will not fulfill the requirements since it provides no redundancy. Twisted pair cable cannot span distances more than 100 meters, and it is highly susceptible to EMI. Coaxial cable cannot span distances more than 500 meters, and it is also susceptible to EMI. The bus topology cannot use twisted pair cabling and does not support cable runs longer than 500 meters.

135. B. Although the design calls for an archaic technology, a Thin Ethernet network runs at 10 Mbps and can support 20 workstations over a maximum distance of 185 meters, thus achieving the primary goal. However, Thin Ethernet uses copper-based coaxial cable, which is susceptible to EMI, and it uses a bus topology, which is not tolerant of a cable break. Therefore, the solution does not achieve either of the secondary goals.

136. D. Fiber-optic cable is not more tolerant of cable breaks than UTP. Some fiber-optic networks are fault tolerant, but the Ethernet fiber-optic specifications are not. UTP cables connecting a computer to a switch can be no longer than 100 meters, making 200 meters the maximum distance between two computers. Connecting two buildings with a copper-based cable creates an electrical connection between them, which can be hazardous. Fiber-optic cable does not create an electrical connection. Fiber-optic cable is also unaffected by the EMI generated by manufacturing equipment.

137. A, B. FLP signals are an enhancement of the Normal Link Pulse (NLP) signals defined in the 10Base-T standard, which verify the integrity of the link. In 100Base-TX, the FLP signals retain that function, but they also enable multispeed devices to negotiate the speed at which they will operate. FLP signals do not indicate collisions or bad frames.

138. B. The 10GBase-CX4 specification calls for the use of a twinaxial copper cable with segments no longer than 15 meters. The10GBase-LR, 10GBase-ER, 10GBase-LX4, and 10GBase-SR specifications all call for fiber-optic cable.

139. D. The multispeed network interface adapters in the computers can run at 1 Gbps speed using the existing CAT5 cable, but the 100Base-T switch must be replaced with a 1000Base-T switch. While the network might run better with a cable upgrade, it is not immediately necessary. Replacing the network interface adapters is not necessary because the existing multispeed adapters can run at 1 Gbps if they are connected to a 1000Base-T switch.

140. C. 1000Base-T is the fastest Ethernet specification that can run on CAT5 UTP cable. 10GBase-T requires at least Category 5e (CAT5e) or Category 6 (CAT6) UTP cable. 100Base-TX can use CAT5 cable, but it runs at one-tenth the speed of 1000Base-T. 1000Base-LX and 1000Base-SX are fiber-optic specifications that cannot run on CAT5 UTP or any copper cable.

141. B, C, E. The three IEEE 10 Mbps standards for Ethernet are 10Base2, 10Base5, and 10Base-T. 10Base2 is limited to 185-meter segments; 10Base5 is limited to 500-meter segments; and 10Base-T is limited to 100-meter segments. The other options are not valid.

142. A, D. The first version of DIX Ethernet (Version 1) supported RG-8 thick coaxial cable in a bus topology. Version 2 added support for thin coaxial cable (RG-58) but was still limited to a bus topology. RG-10 and RG-14 are not Ethernet cable types.

143. D. The best solution in this scenario is to upgrade to 1000Base-T and replace the existing hubs with switches. 1000Base-T provides the fastest transfer speeds supported by the existing cable. Since users are complaining that the network is slow with the existing hubs, it makes sense to replace the shared hub environment with switches that offer dedicated bandwidth on each port. Any solution that does not replace the hubs would not address the users' complaints. 100Base-TX would provide a speed increase, but it runs at ~1/10 the speed of 1000Base-TX. Upgrading to 100Base-FX or 100Base-SX would require the cabling to be replaced with fiber optic, which would be very expensive.

144. A. Option A is the T568B pinout that Ralph should use when attaching connectors to the cables. Option B is the T568A pinout, which would also work but that Ralph has been instructed not to use. Options C and D are both incorrect and can result in excessive amounts of crosstalk.

145. B. The plier-like device is a crimper, which cable installers use to attach RJ45 connectors, like those in the bag, to lengths of bulk cable. This is the process of creating patch cables, which are used to connect computers to wall plates and patch panels to switches. The boss is telling Ralph to start making patch cables in 5-foot and 10-foot lengths. You do not use a crimper to attach keystone connectors, and the boss has not given Ralph the tools and components needed to pull cable runs or install a patch panel.

146. D. The types of wavelength division multiplexing use different spacing of the wavelengths they carry, which enables them to fit different numbers of channels on a single medium. WDM (or BWDM) carries two wavelengths for bidirectional communication. CWDM can carry up to 16 channels and DWDM 40 or 80 (depending on the spacing used). Various amplification technologies (including EFDA and Raman) can expand the amounts of usable wavelength in each type.

147. B. Network Address Translation (NAT) is a service that enables computers with unregistered IP addresses to access the Internet by substituting a registered address in packets as they pass through a router. The Dynamic Host Configuration Protocol (DHCP) is an IP address allocation service. Domain Name System (DNS) resolves domain and hostnames into IP addresses, and Network Time Protocol (NTP) enables network devices to synchronize their time settings.

148. C. A dual stack is an IP implementation that includes both IPv4 and IPv6 protocol stacks, operating simultaneously. A computer with two network adapters or connections to two network segments is often called multihomed. A computer with two installed operating systems is called a dual-boot system.

149. B. NAT works by modifying IP addresses, which are a network layer element. The data link layer is concerned only with communications on the local subnet and is not involved with NAT processing. Because NAT modifies only the IP packet headers, it works with any transport layer protocol. NAT also works with most TCP/IP applications because it operates below the application layer of the OSI model.

150. C. You cannot extend the IPv4 address beyond its 32-bit size, and you cannot remove bits from the network identifier, or the packets will not be routed properly. You must therefore create a subnet by borrowing bits from the host identifier.

151. B, C. IPv4 addresses with first byte values from 224 to 239 are Class D addresses, which are reserved for use as multicast addresses. Therefore, you cannot assign 229.6.87.3 to a host. Option C, 103.256.77.4, is an invalid address because the value 256 cannot be represented by an 8-bit binary value. The other options, 1.1.1.1 and 9.34.0.1, are both valid IPv4 addresses.

152. B. The value after the slash in a Classless Inter-Domain Routing (CIDR) address specifies the number of bits in the network identifier. An IPv4 address has 32 bits, so if 17 bits are allocated to the network identifier, 15 bits are left for the host identifier.

153. B, E. RFC 1918 defines the private address space as the following ranges:

- 10.0.0.0–10.255.255.255
- 172.16.0.0–172.31.255.255
- 192.168.0.0–192.168.255.255

Option B, 172:33:19:7, and Option E, 172.15.2.9, both fall outside the specified private Class B range, and are therefore not valid private addresses.

154. C. To create a network with 8 subnets and 30 hosts per subnet, Alice would have to allocate 3 of the 8 bits in the last octet for subnet identifiers. This would result in a binary value of 11100000 for the last octet in the subnet mask, which converts to a decimal value of 224.

155. A. A Class A address uses only the first octet as the network identifier, which yields a binary subnet mask of 11111111 00000000 00000000 00000000. In decimal form, the subnet mask is 255.0.0.0. The 255.255.0.0 mask is for Class B addresses, and 255.255.255.0 is for Class C addresses. Option D, 255.255.255.255, is the broadcast address for the current network.

156. B. According to RFC 3927, when a DHCP client cannot access a DHCP server, APIPA assigns it an address on the 169.254/16 network, the range of addresses for which is 169.254.0.0 to 169.254.255.255.

157. D. Address 127.0.0.1 is the designated IPv4 local loopback address, and as such, it is reserved. It falls between Class A, which has first octet values from 1 to 126, and Class B, which has first octet values of 128 to 191.

158. C. The address fe00::c955:c944:acdd:3fcb is correctly formatted for IPv6, with the double colon replacing three blocks of zeroes. Uncompressed, the address would appear as follows: fe00:0000:0000:0000:c955:c944:acdd:3fcb. Option A contains a nonhexadecimal digit. Option B contains only seven 16-bit blocks (and no double colon) instead of the eight required for 128 bits. Option D contains blocks larger than 16 bits.

159. B. All Class B addresses have first octet values between 128 and 191. The first octet range of a Class A address is 1 to 126, and the Class C first octet range is 192 to 223. Class D addresses have a first octet range of 224 to 239.

160. A. Variable-length subnet masking (VLSM) describes the process of subnetting an IPv4 network address by assigning an arbitrary number of host bits as subnet bits, providing administrators with great flexibility over the number of subnets created and the number of hosts in each subnet. Automatic Private IP Addressing (APIPA) is the process by which a DHCP client assigns itself an IP address when no DHCP servers are accessible. Virtual Local Area Networks (VLANs) are logical structures used to create separate broadcast domains on a large, switched network. Extended Unique Identifier-64 (EUI-64) is an addressing method used to create IPv6 link local addresses out of media access control (MAC) addresses.

161. B. The 14-bit prefix indicated in the network address will result in a mask with 14 ones followed by 18 zeroes. Broken into 8-bit blocks, the binary mask value is as follows:

11111111 11111100 00000000 00000000

Converted into decimal values, this results in a subnet mask value of 255.252.0.0.

162. A. In this scenario, the company has a Class C Internet Protocol (IPv4) address, which consists of 24 network bits and 8 host bits. The company wants 10 subnets and 14 hosts per subnet, so Ed must subdivide the 8 host bits into subnet and host bits. He can allocate 4 of the 8 host bits for subnets, enabling him to create up to 16 subnets. This leaves 4 bits for host addresses, enabling Ed to create 14 hosts per subnet.

163. E. The formula for calculating the number of subnets you can create using a subnet identifier of a given length is 2^x, where x is the number of bits in the subnet identifier. Therefore, with a 14-bit subnet, you can conceivably create 2^{14}, or 16,384, subnets.

164. C. In this scenario, the last byte of the IP address assigned to the company must be subdivided into 3 subnet bits and 5 host bits. The 3 subnet bits will give Alice up to 8 subnets, with 5 host bits for up to 30 hosts per subnet. The new subnet mask is 255.255.255.224. The 224 is the decimal equivalent of the binary value 11100000, which represents the 3 subnet bits and the 5 host bits.

165. D. To convert a MAC address to an Extended Unique Identifier (EUI-64), you split the 6-byte MAC address into two 3-byte halves and insert the 2-byte value FFFE in between, as follows:

001F9E FFFE FC7AD0

Then, you change the seventh bit in the first byte, the universal/local bit, from 0 to 1, indicating that this is a locally created address. This results in a binary first byte value of 00000010, which converts to 02 in hexadecimal.
Finally, you add the IPv6 link local prefix FE80::/10, resulting in the following complete address:

FE80::021F:9EFF:FEFC:7AD0

All of the other answers either insert the FFFE bytes in the wrong place or fail to change the universal/local bit.

166. A. A standard Class B address with a mask of 255.255.0.0 has 16 bits that can be used for subnets and hosts. To get 600 subnets, you must use 10 of the available bits, which gives you up to 1024 subnets. This leaves 6 host bits, which gives you up to 62 hosts per subnet, which exceeds the requirement of 55 requested by the client. Using 9 bits would give you only 510 subnets, while 11 bits would give you 2046 subnets but leave you only 5 bits for a maximum of 30 hosts, which is not enough.

167. C. The formula for calculating the number of hosts you can create using a host identifier of a given length is 2^x-2, where x is the number of bits in the host identifier. You cannot create a host with an address of all zeroes or all ones, which is why you subtract 2. On a network that uses 20 bits for network identification, 12 bits are left for the host identifier. Using those 12 bits, you can create $2^{12}-2$ or 4,094 host addresses.

168. B. With a Class B subnet mask of 255.255.248.0, the binary form of the third and fourth bytes is 11111000 00000000. There are 5 subnet bits, providing up to 32 subnets and 11 host bits, providing up to 2046 hosts.

169. A. The decimal value for 11111111 is 255, the value for 11100000 is 224, and the value for 00000000 is 0, so the mask is 255.255.224.0.

170. B. With a network address of 192.168.1.32 and 27 mask bits, the subnet mask value is 11111111.11111111.11111111.11100000 in binary form, or 255.255.255.224 in decimal form. This leaves 5 bits for the host identifier. The valid range of host bits is therefore 00001 (1) through 11110 (30). This gives you a range of 192.168.1.32 + 1 (33) through 192.168.1.32 + 30 (62).

171. C. To calculate the number of host addresses available, Alice must determine the number of host bits in the address, which is 10, raise 2 to that power, and subtract 2 for the network and broadcast addresses, which are unusable for hosts. The formula is therefore 2^x-2. $2^{10}-2=1022$.

172. B. When a DHCP client cannot access a DHCP server, APIPA assigns it a Class B address using the network address 169.254/16, which yields the address range 169.254.0.0 to 169.254.255.255.

173. D. Class D addresses are used for multicast transmissions. Class A, Class B, and Class C addresses are used for unicast transmissions. Class E is for experimental use only.

174. C. The address 10.1.0.253 is a proper address in the private address range 10.0.0.0 to 10.255.255.255. The address 192.167.9.46 falls outside the designated private IP address range, which is 192.168.0.0 to 192.168.255.255, and is therefore not a viable address on a private network. 172.16.255.255 is a broadcast address, which you cannot assign to a host. 225.87.34.1 falls in the Class D multicast address range and cannot be assigned to a single host.

175. B. The address given uses 20 bits to identify the network, leaving 12 bits for the host identifier. In binary form, therefore, the subnet mask value would be 11111111 11111111 11110000 00000000. The decimal value for 11111111 is 255, and the decimal value for 11110000 is 240. Therefore, the subnet mask is 255.255.240.0.

176. B. A /28 address leaves 4 bits for the host identifier. To calculate the number of hosts, Ed uses $2^4-2=14$. The first address on the subnet is therefore 192.168.2.33, and the fourteenth is 192.168.2.46.

177. A. 1.0.0.1 is a legitimate address that falls into Class A. Option B, 127.98.127.0, falls into the range of addresses reserved for use as loopback addresses (127.0.0.1 to 127.255.255.255). Option C, 234.9.76.32, falls into Class D, which is reserved for use as multicast addresses. Option D, 240.65.8.124, is a Class E address; that class is reserved for experimental use.

178. A. An IPv6 link local address is automatically assigned to each interface. Like Automatic Private IP Addressing (APIPA), it provides communication on the local network only. Global unicast addresses are routable; they are the functional equivalent of IPv4 registered addresses. Site local addresses are the equivalent of private IPv4 addresses. Anycast addresses are designed to transmit to any one host in a multicast group.

179. A, B. Unlike network address translation, port address translation uses a single public IPv4 address for all of the client workstations. Instead of assigning each workstation a unique address, PAT assigns each workstation a unique port number.

180. B. Stateless Address Auto-Configuration (SLAAC) is the means by which IPv6 systems self-generate link-local addresses with the prefix fe80::/64, much as IPv4 systems use APIPA to generate addresses. IPv6 systems can use DHCPv6 to obtain stateful (not stateless) addresses. An Extended Unique Identifier (such as EUI-64) is the format for a media access control (MAC) address.

181. A, D. Teredo and 6to4 are both tunneling protocols that were intended as transitional mechanisms, enabling the encapsulation of IPv6 datagrams within IPv4 packets. IPsec uses tunneling, but it is not used for the encapsulation of IPv6 traffic. Internet Control Message Protocol v6, like its ICMPv4 equivalent, enables routers and hosts to transmit informational and error messages; it does not use tunneling.

182. A. ICMPv6 hosts generate Router Solicitation messages and transmit them to the All Routers multicast address. Routers respond using Router Advertisement messages, which contain the prefix information that the host uses to generate a link-local address. Hosts do not have to learn the address of the nearest router, because they can use the All Routers multicast. Address conflict detection comes after the host has created a link-local address and does not use Router Solicitation and Router Advertisement messages. Hosts do not use Router Solicitation and Router Advertisement messages to encapsulate IPv4 packets.

183. B, D. A virtual IP address is an address that does not correspond to a physical network interface. Network Address Translation (NAT) uses virtual public IP addresses as substitutes for the private IP addresses associated with the client hosts. A network interface in a virtual machine is virtual as well, so the IP address associated with that interface must also be virtual. Dynamic Host Configuration Protocol (DHCP) and Automatic Private IP Addressing (APIPA) both can assign IP addresses to physical network interfaces; these addresses are therefore not virtual.

184. A. A subinterface is a logical (or virtual) network interface associated with a specific physical network interface. Devices (such as routers) can use multiple subinterfaces to connect to different subnets using a single physical network interface adapter. A subinterface is a logical device, so it is not one port on a physical network interface adapter or a physical adapter connected to a subnet. A subinterface is a complete logical interface, not just an IP address.

185. A. The default port for the Post Office Protocol (POP3) is 110. The default port for the Simple Mail Transfer Protocol (SMTP), the other protocol used by email clients, is 25. Port 143 is the default for the Internet Message Access Protocol (IMAP), a different email mailbox protocol that clients never use with POP3. Port 80 is the default for the Hypertext Transfer Protocol (HTTP), which is not used by POP3 email clients.

186. D. The File Transfer Protocol (FTP) uses two port numbers. It uses the first, port 21, for a control connection that remains open during the entire client/server session. The second port, 20, is for a data connection that opens only when the protocol is actually transferring a file between the client and the server. Network Time Protocol (NTP), Simple Network Management Protocol (SNMP), and Hypertext Transfer Protocol (HTTP) all use a single port on the server.

187. C. Ping uses the Internet Control Message Protocol (ICMP) to exchange messages with other systems. ICMP is also used to return error messages to sending systems. The User Datagram Protocol (UDP) and the Transmission Control Protocol (TCP) are both transport layer protocols that carry application layer data; Ping does not use either one. The Internet Group Management Protocol (IGMP) is used to create multicast groups; Ping does not use it.

188. B. The port numbers specified in a transport layer protocol header identify the application that generated the data in the packet or the application that will receive the data. Port numbers do not identify transport layer protocols, gateways, or proxy servers.

189. B. The IANA assigns values for well-known port numbers. The IEEE publishes Ethernet standards, among many others. The IETF develops standards for Internet technologies. The ISO developed the Open Systems Interconnection (OSI) model.

190. C. Port 80 is the default well-known port for HTTP. Port 22 is for the Secure Shell (SSH) protocol, port 20 is for File Transfer Protocol (FTP), and port 443 is for secured HTTP.

191. D. The well-known port for HTTPS is 443. Port 25 is for the Simple Mail Transfer Protocol (SMTP), port 80 is for unsecured HTTP, and port 110 is for the Post Office Protocol (POP3).

192. A. The Maximum Segment Size (MSS) field in the TCP Options subheader specifies the size (in bytes) of the largest segment a system can receive. The Window field indicates the amount of data (in bytes) that the receiver can accept. There are no MMS or WinMS fields in a TCP header.

193. A. The term for an IPv4 address and port number in combination is *socket*. An Organizationally Unique Identifier (OUI) identifies a manufacturer of networking hardware. A well-known port is a port number assigned to a specific application. A network address is the network identifier part of an IP address. A domain is a group of computers and other resources.

194. A, B. Internet Control Message Protocol (ICMP) and Internet Group Management Protocol (IGMP) are unusual in that they generate messages that are encapsulated directly within IP datagrams. Nearly all of the other TCP/IP protocols, including Simple Mail Transfer Protocol (SMTP) and Simple Network Management Protocol (SNMP), are encapsulated within one of the transport layer protocols—User Datagram Protocol (UDP) or Transmission Control Protocol (TCP)—which is encapsulated in turn within an IP datagram.

195. B. The Lightweight Directory Access Protocol (LDAP) is an application layer protocol used for managing and accessing information stored in directory services. Remote Desktop Protocol (RDP) is used to establish a graphical remote control session with another computer. Simple Network Management Protocol (SNMP) is used to carry information gathered by management agents distributed around a network to a central management server. Server Message Block (SMB) is the primary file sharing protocol used by Windows systems.

196. C, E. SMTP with TLS uses port number 587. POP3 over SSL uses port number 995. Port numbers 25 and 110 are used for SMTP and POP3 without encryption. Port number 995 is used for Internet Message Access Protocol (IMAP) over SSL.

197. D. The port number 3389 is used by the Remote Desktop Protocol (RDP) and is not involved in SQL communication. Port 1433 is used by SQL Server; 1521 is used by SQL-net; 3306 is used by MySQL.

198. B. Port number 514 is assigned to syslog, a Unix standard designed to facilitate the transmission of log entries generated by a device or process, such as the sendmail SMTP server, across an IP network to a message collector, called a syslog server. Port number 389 is assigned to the Lightweight Directory Access Protocol (LDAP). Port number 636 is assigned to LDAP over Secure Sockets Layer (SSL). Port number 993 is assigned to Internet Message Access Protocol (IMAP) over SSL.

199. A. Hypertext Transfer Protocol (HTTP) is the primary protocol used for web client/server communications. Hypertext Markup Language (HTML) is a coding language used to create web content. Simple Mail Transfer Protocol (SMTP) and File Transfer Protocol (FTP) can both be used in web communications, but neither is the primary protocol.

200. C. The Domain Name System (DNS) is a protocol that computers on a TCP/IP use to resolve host and domain names into the IP addresses they need to communicate. Dynamic Host Configuration Protocol (DHCP) and Bootstrap Protocol (BOOTP) are both IP address allocation protocols, and Simple Network Management Protocol (SNMP) carries information gathered by agents to a central management console.

201. B, D. The term *datagram* is typically used by protocols offering connectionless delivery service. The two main connectionless protocols in the TCP/IP suite are the Internet Protocol (IP) and the User Datagram Protocol (UDP), both of which use the term *datagram*. Ethernet uses the term *frame*, and Transmission Control Protocol (TCP) uses *segment*.

202. D. The default file sharing protocol used on all Windows operating systems is SMB. HTTP is the native protocol used by web clients and servers. NFS is the native file sharing protocol used on Unix/Linux networks. FTP is a protocol used for transferring files from one system to another. LDAP is a protocol for transmitting directory service information.

203. A. The receiving host uses the ACK bit to notify the sending host that it has successfully received data. The other control bits are not used to acknowledge receipt of information.

204. D. Two systems establishing a TCP connection exchange three messages before they begin transmitting data. The exchange of these synchronization messages is referred to as a three-way handshake. The other terms listed are not formally used to describe this exchange.

205. C, D, E. Dynamic Host Configuration Protocol (DHCP) servers use port numbers 67 and 68. The Trivial File Transfer Protocol (TFTP) uses port number 69. Neither protocol uses port 65 or 66.

206. B. TCP ports and UDP ports identify the application protocol or process that generated the information in a datagram. Client ports are chosen randomly from the range 1024 through 65,534. Server ports are well-known and are chosen from the range 1 through 1023.

207. C. Ephemeral client ports are in the range of 49152 through 65535. Well-known TCP and UDP server ports are in the range of 1 through 1023. Registered port numbers are in the range of 1024 to 49151.

208. A, D, E. UDP is a connectionless transport layer protocol. It has a small, 8-byte header and does not use packet sequencing or acknowledgments.

209. A, C. FTP uses two ports: one for control messages (port 21) and one for data transfers (port 20). Port 23 is used by Telnet. Port 53 is used by the Domain Name System (DNS). Port 69 is used by the Trivial File Transfer Protocol (TFTP).

210. C. The User Datagram Protocol (UDP) provides connectionless service at the transport layer. Transmission Control Protocol (TCP) provides connection-oriented service at the transport layer. Hypertext Transfer Protocol (HTTP) is an application layer protocol, and Address Resolution Protocol (ARP) is a data link layer protocol.

211. D. Well-known TCP and UDP server ports are in the range of 1 through 1023. Registered port numbers are in the range of 1024 to 49151. Ephemeral client ports are in the range of 49152 through 65535.

212. B, D. Ralph's traffic analysis should show the addition of the Simple Mail Transfer Protocol (SMTP), which handles incoming and outgoing Internet mail, and Internet Message Access Protocol (IMAP), which provides mailboxes for users that store their mail permanently on the server. POP3 is a mailbox protocol that enables users to download their messages and should therefore not be present on the network. SNMP is a network management protocol, and RIP is a routing protocol; neither of these carries email traffic.

213. F. An ephemeral port number is a temporary port supplied by a client to a server, for use during a single session or transaction. The allowed ephemeral port number values range from 49152 to 65535. The port values below 1024 are reserved for use as well-known ports, and the values from 1024 to 49151 are reserved for ports registered by specific manufacturers for their applications. Of these answers, 50134 is the only value that the client can use as an ephemeral port.

214. A. The Transmission Control Protocol (TCP) provides connection-oriented service at the transport layer, with guaranteed delivery. The User Datagram Protocol (UDP) provides connectionless service at the transport layer. Hypertext Transfer Protocol (HTTP) operates at the application layer, and Internet Protocol (IP) is a connectionless network layer protocol.

215. A. ARP relies on broadcast transmissions, which are not routable. It is therefore limited to use on the local subnet. DHCP also relies on broadcasts, but the ability to create DHCP relay agents makes it usable on an entire internetwork. DNS and SMTP do not rely on broadcasts and are therefore not limited to the local subnet.

216. B. No matter what protocol is used to encrypt a website, you must use the HTTPS:// prefix to access it. HTTP:// is for unencrypted sites, and TLS:// and HTLS:// are nonexistent prefixes.

217. A, B. Using the prefix HTTPS:// causes a web browser to use a different port number to establish a secure connection to the web server. Security is provided by encrypting all data using Secure Sockets Layer (SSL) or Transport Layer Security (TLS). However, SSL and TLS do not replace HTTP; they just augment it. The HTTPS:// prefix does not affect the IP address used to connect to the server.

218. D. Because the administrative site is encrypted, you must use the HTTPS:// prefix to access it. Because the administrative site uses the nondefault port number 12354, you must append that number to the server name with a colon.

219. A. Encapsulating Security Protocol (ESP) is a protocol in the TCP/IP suite that is capable of providing encryption services for IPsec. Authentication Header (AH) provides digital integrity services for IPsec, in the form of a digital signature. Secure Sockets Layer (SSL) is a security protocol that provides encrypted communications between web browsers and servers. MSCHAP is an authentication protocol used by remote access services.

220. B, C. Authentication Header (AH) is an IPsec protocol that provides authentication and digital integrity services. Encapsulating Security Protocol (ESP) provides encryption services for IPsec. Secure Shell (SSH) is a remote administration tool, and Secure Sockets Layer (SSL) is a security protocol that provides encrypted communications between web browsers and servers.

221. A. FTP does provide authentication capabilities, but passwords are transmitted over the network in clear text, which is an unacceptable security condition. FTPS adds security in the form of the Transport Layer Security (TLS) and Secure Sockets Layer (SSL) protocols. SFTP adds Secure Shell (SSH) security. File transfer speed and size limitations are not an issue.

222. A. FTP provides authentication capabilities, but it transmits passwords over the network in clear text, which is an unacceptable security condition. FTPS adds security in the form of the Transport Layer Security (TLS) and Secure Sockets Layer (SSL) protocols. SFTP adds Secure Shell (SSH) security. Both of these encrypt authentication passwords before transmitting them. Trivial File Transfer Protocol (TFTP) does not authenticate clients, so it does not transmit passwords at all.

223. D. Trivial File Transfer Protocol (TFTP) is a simplified version of FTP that does not authenticate clients, so systems booting with PXE can download boot images invisibly after being directed to a TFTP server by the Dynamic Host Configuration Protocol (DHCP). FTP, FTPS, and SFTP all require authentication and other interaction, which would be impractical for use with PXE.

224. C. Authentication Header (AH) is a protocol in the TCP/IP suite that provides digital integrity services, in the form of a digital signature, which ensures that an incoming packet actually originated from its stated source. Encapsulating Security Protocol (ESP) provides encryption services for IPsec. Secure Sockets Layer (SSL) is a security protocol that provides encrypted communications between web browsers and servers. MSCHAP is an authentication protocol used by remote access services.

225. A. Secure Sockets Layer (SSL) is the original security protocol for web servers and browsers and the predecessor of Transport Layer Security (TLS). Datagram Transport Layer Security (DTLS) is a protocol that provides the same encryption and other web server/browser security functions as TLS, but for User Datagram Protocol (UDP) traffic. Secure Shell (SSH) is a character-based tool that enables users to execute commands on remote computers. It does not provide web server or browser security.

226. B. Secure Sockets Layer (SSL) is the original security protocol for web servers and browsers and the predecessor of TLS. It was deprecated in 2015. Secure Shell (SSH) is a character-based tool that enables users to execute commands on remote computers. It does not provide web server or browser security like TLS and DTLS. IPsec is a set of security protocols that provide digital signing, encryption, and other services for network transmissions. It is not specifically designed for web security. Remote Desktop Protocol (RDP) is a component of Remote Desktop Services, a Windows mechanism that enables a client program to connect to a server and control it remotely. RDP is not a web security protocol.

227. B, D. When a client sends a name resolution query to its DNS server, it uses a recursive request so that the server will take on the responsibility for resolving the name. The only other use of recursive requests is in the case of a forwarder, which is configured to pass that responsibility on to another server. All of the other queries issued by the client's server to the various domain authorities are iterative queries.

228. A. Most wireless routers are designed to provide connecting workstations with IP addresses and other TCP/IP configuration parameters. Switches and bridges are data link layer devices, and hubs are physical layer devices, none of which are capable of providing clients with network layer IP addresses.

229. A, E. DHCP and BOOTP are both designed to allocate IP addresses to hosts. The primary difference between the two is that DHCP is capable of dynamic allocation and BOOTP is not. DNS resolves hostnames into IP addresses, and ARP resolves IP addresses into data link layer hardware (or MAC) addresses. FTP is designed to transfer files between systems and has no role in IP address allocation.

230. D. Like A and AAAA records, Pointer Records (PTRs) contain hostnames and IP addresses, but they are used for reverse name resolution—that is, resolving IP addresses into hostnames. A Mail Exchange (MX) record specifies the mail server that the domain should use. Canonical name (CNAME) records specify aliases for a given hostname. An AAAA resource record maps a hostname to an IPv6 address for name resolution purposes.

231. A. Dynamic Host Configuration Protocol (DHCP) can dynamically allocate IP addresses to clients and reclaim them when their leases expire. Bootstrap Protocol (BOOTP) and Reverse Address Resolution Protocol (RARP) can allocate addresses automatically or manually, but they cannot reclaim them. DHCP and BOOTP both support relay agents.

232. A, B, D, E. In a successful DHCP address allocation, the client issues DHCPDISCOVER broadcasts to locate servers, and the servers reply with DHCPOFFER messages containing addresses. Then, the client sends a DHCPREQUEST message to one server accepting an offered address, to which the server replies with a DHCPACK. DHCPNAK messages are only used in unsuccessful transactions, and DHCPRENEW, DHCPRELEASE, and DHCPINFORM messages are not used during the address allocation process.

233. D, E. In a successful DHCP address renewal transaction, the client issues a DHCPDREQUEST message, and the server replies with a DHCPACK. DHCPNAK messages are only used in unsuccessful transactions, and the other message types are not used during the address renewal process.

234. A. Reverse Address Resolution Protocol (RARP), Bootstrap Protocol (BOOTP), and Dynamic Host Configuration Protocol (DHCP) are all protocols that are designed to allocate IP addresses to clients. Address Resolution Protocol (ARP), on the other hand, resolves existing IP addresses into data link layer MAC (or hardware) addresses.

235. A. When a DNS server receives an iterative query, it responds immediately with the best information that it has available, or with an error message. It does not send queries to other servers.

236. D. The client component of the Domain Name System (DNS) is called the resolver. Requestor is a generic term for any system issuing requests, and only DNS servers can be authorities or forwarders.

237. C. The DNS Server Addresses parameter contains the addresses of servers that resolve domain names into IP addresses. Windows Internet Name Service (WINS) provides Network Basic Input/Output System (NetBIOS) name resolution. The Default Gateway parameter defines the local router to be used to access other networks. There is no such parameter as Subnet Gateway.

238. C. Stable is not a DHCP allocation method. DHCP supports three allocation methods: manual, dynamic, and automatic.

239. B. On a DHCP server, you create a scope that consists of a beginning and an ending IP address. Range, pool, and subnet are not technical terms for DHCP.

240. B, D. DHCP clients cannot contact servers on different networks to initiate an address assignment. Clients locate DHCP servers by transmitting broadcast messages, and broadcasts are limited to the local network. Relay agents forward the broadcast messages to other networks, enabling the server to assign IP addresses to clients on other subnets. DHCP does not require special licenses. DHCP uses User Datagram Protocol (UDP) transmissions, not TCP.

241. C. An AAAA resource record maps a hostname to an IPv6 address for name resolution purposes. A Mail Exchange (MX) record specifies the mail server that the domain should use. Pointer Records (PTRs) also contain hostnames and IP addresses, but they are used for reverse name resolution—that is, resolving IP addresses into hostnames. Canonical name (CNAME) records specify aliases for a given hostname.

242. B. A canonical name (CNAME) resource record specifies an alternative host name (or alias) for a system already registered in the DNS. By creating a CNAME record specifying the www name, the server can be addressed using either NE6 or www. Creating an additional A resource record will cause the server to be recognized using one name or the other, but not both. Modifying the existing A record will change the hostname. PTR resource records are used only for reverse name resolution.

243. A. The Router option specifies the addresses of routers on the local network, including the default gateway router. The Time Server option specifies the addresses of servers that provide time signals to the network. The Name Server option specifies the addresses of up to 10 name resolution servers (other than DNS servers) on the network. The LPR Server option specifies the addresses of line printer servers on the network.

244. B. DHCP clients use broadcasts to transmit DHCPDISCOVER messages on the local network. DHCP servers are then required to respond to the broadcasts. DHCP clients cannot use unicast, multicast, or anycast messages to initiate contact with DHCP servers, because they have no way of learning their addresses.

245. A. The Name Server (NS) resource record identifies the authoritative name servers for a particular DNS zone. Pointer Records (PTRs) are used to resolve IP addresses into hostnames. Mail Exchange (MX) records identify the mail servers for a particular domain. Service Records (SRVs) identify the designated servers for a particular application. The Start of Authority (SOA) record indicates the delegation of a domain's administrative control from its parent domain. A Text (TXT) record associates administrator-supplied text with a zone but performs no other function.

246. C. On a DHCP server, a reservation is a permanent IP address assignment to a specific MAC address. A scope is a range of IP addresses to be allocated to clients. An exclusion is a range of IP addresses that is to be excluded from a scope. A relay is a component that routes DHCP traffic between networks.

247. B. Dynamic allocation enables a Dynamic Host Configuration Protocol (DHCP) server to lease IP addresses to clients for a specific time interval. When the lease period expires, the client can renew it, if it is still using the address. If the address is no longer in use when the lease expires, it is returned to the scope of available leases for reallocation. Automatic allocation permanently assigns an IP address from the scope to a client. Manual and static allocation are two terms that describe the allocation of a specific IP address to a specific client.

248. B. Dynamic DNS (DDNS) is an addition to the DNS standards that eliminates the need for administrators to manually create certain DNS resource records. For example, when a DHCP server allocates an address to a client, DDNS creates a host (A) record containing the hostname of the client and the newly allocated IP address. Reverse name resolution is the process of looking up hostnames based on IP addresses. Automatic allocation is a DHCP process by which IP addresses are permanently assigned to clients. HOSTS is a text-based name resolution method that predates DNS.

249. C. IP address management (IPAM) is a system for planning, managing, and monitoring the IP address space for an entire enterprise network. IPAM provides links between the Dynamic Host Configuration Protocol (DHCP) and the Domain Name System (DNS) so that each is aware of the naming and addressing changes made by the other. DHCPv6 is an IPv6 version of the DHCP service, which enables it to allocate IPv6 addresses to network clients. HOSTS is a text-based name resolution method for individual systems that predates DNS. Automatic Private IP Addressing (APIPA) is the mechanism that enables a DHCP client to assign itself an address when no DHCP servers are accessible.

250. D. The term *stratum*, plus an integer, describes the distance in time of an NTP server from its time source in terms of the NTP server hierarchy. Stratum 0 represents an atomic clock or other precision timekeeping device. Stratum 1 represents an NTP server synchronized to within a few milliseconds of its Stratum 0 time source. Stratum 2 is a server synchronized to a Stratum 1 server, and so on. *Layer*, *path*, and *iteration* are not technical terms used by the NTP.

251. D. The Network Time Protocol (NTP) is used to synchronize computer clocks. Time signals can be provided by internal servers or time servers on the Internet. The Trivial File

Transfer Protocol (TFTP) is used to transfer files between systems without authentication. The Hypertext Transfer Protocol (HTTP) is used to exchange web traffic between clients and servers. The Simple Mail Transfer Protocol (SMTP) is used to transmit email traffic between clients and servers.

252. D. The topmost layer in the DNS hierarchy is represented by org, which is a top-level domain. mydomain is a second-level domain registered by a particular organization, paris is a subdomain within mydomain, and www is the name of a particular host in the paris.mydomain.org domain.

253. B. The Default IP Time-to-Live (TTL) option specifies the maximum number of seconds or hops allowed to an IP datagram before a router removes it from the network. This prevents datagrams from circulating endlessly. The Interface Maximum Transmission Unit (MTU) option specifies the maximum size of an IP datagram. The Address Resolution Protocol (ARP) cache timeout specifies how long entries containing the IP address assigned by the server can remain in the cache maintained by a client's ARP implementation. The Transmission Control Protocol (TCP) keepalive interval option specifies the number of seconds that the client should wait before transmitting a keepalive message over a TCP connection.

254. B, C. The external DNS server should contain records only for the resources that must be accessible from the Internet, such as web servers and public email servers. For security reasons, servers containing sensitive data, such as database servers and domain controllers, should be registered on the internal DNS server.

255. B. When there are no IP addresses available for lease in a DHCP scope, Automatic Private IP Addressing (APIPA) takes over, and the system self-assigns an address on the 169.254.0.0/16 network. Clients are not assigned a 0.0.0.0 address, nor are their requests forwarded to another DHCP server. Sharing IP addresses is not possible on a TCP/IP network.

256. B. Decreasing the lease time for the scope will cause abandoned IP addresses to be returned to the scope for reallocation more quickly, which would lessen the chances of exhausting the scope. Increasing the lease time will make scope exhaustion more likely. Installing another DHCP server or creating another scope will have no effect, because the limitation is the number of addresses allocated for the subnet.

257. A, B, D. DHCP relay, UDP forwarding, and IP helper are all router mechanisms that perform the same task, forwarding broadcast messages on one subnet to a specific IP address on another subnet as a unicast message. This enables DHCP clients to contact DHCP servers on another subnet to obtain IP addresses. Zone transfer is a DNS zone replication mechanism not used by DHCP clients or servers.

258. D. A zone transfer is a client/server transaction between two DNS servers in which one server requests a copy of the other server's entire zone database, to update its own. None of the other options are used for DNS database replication. Multi-master replication is a technique that enables two systems to exchange database information as needed to update each other. UDP forwarding is a router mechanism used by DHCP to forward broadcast messages on one subnet to a specific IP address on another subnet. An iterative query is a type of DNS message that transfers responsibility for a name lookup to another server.

259. A, C. iSCSI runs on a standard IP network, and Fibre Channel over Ethernet (FCoE) runs on a standard Ethernet network. Both of these protocols can share a network with LAN traffic, although the use of a Quality of Service (QoS) mechanism is usually recommended. Fibre Channel and InfiniBand both require a dedicated network medium that does not support LAN traffic.

260. C. Voice over Internet Protocol (VoIP) is a technology for the transmission of voice communications over IP networks; it is not a SAN protocol. Internet Small Computer Systems Interface (iSCSI), Fibre Channel over Ethernet (FCoE), and Fibre Channel are all SAN protocols.

261. E. The Internet Storage Name Service (iSNS) is an application that provides iSCSI initiators with automated discovery of targets located on the network. iSNS can also function as a discovery service for Fibre Channel devices. Active Directory, Internet Control Message Protocol (ICMP), and Domain Name System (DNS) are not capable of registering iSCSI targets. iWINS does not exist.

262. D. The current Fibre Channel standard calls for a maximum data transfer rate of 128 gigabits per second (Gbps), for a nominal throughput of 12,800 megabytes per second (MBps).

263. B. A NAS device is essentially a file server that connects to a network and provides users with access to shared files. A NAS is a single computer, so it cannot be associated with failover clustering. Just a Bunch of Disks (JBOD) is a simple storage array that provides block-level access to data, whereas NAS devices provide file-level access. Redundant Array of Independent Disks (RAID) is a fault tolerance technology that might be implemented in NAS devices, but it is not the device's primary function.

264. A, D. NAS devices are self-contained file servers that connect directly to a standard IP network. A NAS device provides file-level access to its storage devices and includes an operating system and a filesystem. NAS devices are typically not iSCSI targets.

265. A, B, D. Because it uses standard Ethernet hardware, Fibre Channel over Ethernet (FCoE) is far less expensive to implement than Fibre Channel, which requires a dedicated fiber-optic network. Because Fibre Channel requires a dedicated network, it cannot coexist with standard IP traffic, whereas FCoE can. Because it is encapsulated in Ethernet frames, FCoE is not routable on IP networks.

266. A, B, D. Common Internet File System (CIFS), Network File System (NFS), and Hypertext Transfer Protocol (HTTP) are all file sharing protocols supported by many NAS devices. Remote Direct Memory Access (RDMA) provides high-speed network data transfers, but it is not an application layer file sharing protocol.

267. C. iSCSI does not include its own flow control mechanism. It runs over a TCP connection, which is the protocol responsible for flow control. Because it runs on any IP network, iSCSI traffic is routable, and it is less expensive to implement. Fibre Channel requires a dedicated network using fiber-optic cable. iSCSI traffic can coexist with standard LAN traffic on a single network, although some type of Quality of Service (QoS) mechanism is frequently recommended.

268. A. InfiniBand is a high-end storage infrastructure technology that provides data transfer rates of up to 2.5 Gbps and scalable support for up to 64,000 devices. It is primarily used in high performance computing environments to replace older bus technologies connecting CPUs to storage arrays. Fibre Channel, Internet Small Computer System Interface (iSCSI), and Fibre Channel over Ethernet (FCoE) are all SAN technologies, but they are more commonly used in Local Area Network (LAN) environments.

269. A. The client side of an iSCSI implementation is called an *initiator*. The storage device to which the initiator connects is called a *target*. *Controller* and *adapter* are not terms used for iSCSI clients or servers.

270. A, B, C. iSCSI runs on a standard IP network; therefore, iSCSI messages are encapsulated using Transmission Control Protocol (TCP) at the transport layer, Internet Protocol (IP) at the network layer, and Ethernet at the data link layer. iSCSI does not use the User Datagram Protocol (UDP).

271. E. The Fibre Channel standard defines a unique, five-layer protocol stack that does not correspond to the OSI model layers. Therefore, Fibre Channel does not use Ethernet, nor does it use Transmission Control Protocol (TCP), Internet Protocol (IP), User Datagram Protocol (UDP), or any of the other TCP/IP protocols.

272. B. The Fibre Channel standard defines a five-layer networking stack, with layers numbered FC-0 to FC-4, that does not correspond to the layers of the OSI model. Internet Small Computer System Interface (iSCSI), Point-to-Point Protocol (PPP), and Remote Direct Memory Access (RDMA) all function within the standard OSI model layers.

273. A. Fibre Channel over Ethernet (FCoE) uses Ethernet frames in place of the bottom two layers (FC0 and FC1) of the Fibre Channel protocol stack. The remaining layers (FC2, FC3, and FC4) use the standard Fibre Channel protocols. FCoE does not use Transmission Control Protocol (TCP), Internet Protocol (IP), User Datagram Protocol (UDP), or any of the other TCP/IP protocols.

274. A. Ethernet uses jumbo frames to transfer large amounts of data more efficiently. On a packet-switched network, each packet requires header data, which adds to the network's transmission overhead. Splitting large files into a great many small packets can lead to so much overhead that network efficiency is impaired. Ethernet typically restricts frame size to 1500 bytes, but jumbo frames enable Ethernet systems to create frames up to 9000 bytes. Frames are data link layer protocol data units, so Internet Protocol (IP), operating at the network layer, is not involved in creating them. Fibre Channel and iSCSI are specialized storage area networking protocols that do not use jumbo frames.

275. B. The three-tier hierarchical architecture for datacenters consists of core, distribution, and access layers. The access layer in a datacenter contains servers, the distribution layer contains redundant switch connections, and the core layer provides high-speed transport between the switches. There is no intermediate layer in the architecture.

276. C. The leaf and spine topology uses a full mesh topology in its two layers of switches. This is more expensive than the three-tier topology, but it reduces latency by requiring the same number of hops in the path between any two routers. The use of software-defined networking provides adaptive path determination without the use of the Spanning Tree Protocol (STP) for layer 2 port blocking.

277. C. East-west traffic describes traffic flow within the datacenter, while north-south is traffic between devices inside the datacenter and outside devices. The terms *east-west* and *north-south* do not pertain to the OSI model layers or to specific devices used.

278. A. In a typical datacenter topology, racks contain servers that implement applications. A leaf switch at the top of the rack connects the servers in the rack together and also connects to a spine switch that links to the rest of the datacenter. The top-of-rack switches are not classified as backbone, spine, or core devices.

279. C. In an SDN architecture, the application layer is software, that is, the applications and services running on the network; the control layer is a centralized console through which administrators manage the applications; and the infrastructure layer consists of the switch and router hardware. Core is not one of the SDN layers.

280. E. The RFC 7426 document defines five planes in the SDN architecture: forwarding, operational, control, management, and application. Infrastructure is not one of the SDN planes.

281. B, F. In a colocated datacenter, a client houses its own servers and other hardware in a shared third-party facility. Therefore, Ralph's company would own the hardware in a branch office or colocated datacenter. A datacenter in a public cloud is easier to expand than the other options because it is simply a matter of creating additional virtual devices. A colocated datacenter would be less expensive to implement than a branch office datacenter, but the public cloud option would require the smallest initial outlay. The administrators would set up and manage the hardware in a branch office or colocated datacenter, but not in a public cloud datacenter. In a colocated datacenter, Ralph's company would share utility costs with other tenants. A public cloud facility is not necessarily more secure.

282. A. The Infrastructure as a Service (IaaS) model provides consumers with processing, storage, and networking resources that they can use to install and run operating systems and other software of their choice. Platform as a Service (PaaS) provides consumers with the ability to install applications of their choice on a server installed by the provider. Software as a Service (SaaS) provides consumers with access to specific applications running on the provider's servers. Desktop as a Service (DaaS) provides remote virtualization of the entire workstation desktop, instead of a single application.

283. C. The Software as a Service (SaaS) model provides consumers with access to a specific application running on the provider's servers. Infrastructure as a Service (IaaS) provides the consumers with processing, storage, and networking resources that they can use to install and run operating systems and other software of their choice. Platform as a Service (PaaS) provides consumers with the ability to install applications of their choice on a server installed by the provider. Desktop as a Service (DaaS) provides remote virtualization of the entire workstation desktop, instead of a single application.

284. A. The Infrastructure as a Service (IaaS) model provides the consumers with the most control, as the provider furnishes processing, storage, and networking resources that the consumer can use as needed. Platform as a Service (PaaS) provides consumers with the ability to install applications of their choice on a server furnished by the provider, but they have only limited control over the server and no control over the underlying resources.

Software as a Service (SaaS) and Desktop as a Service (DaaS) provide consumers with access to a specific application or an entire desktop environment running on the provider's servers, but the consumers have no control over the operating system, the servers, or the underlying resources.

285. A, D. Infrastructure as a Service (IaaS) provides consumers like Alice with processing, storage, and networking resources that they can use to install and run operating systems and other software of their choice. In the public cloud model, one organization or user functions as the provider, and another organization or user—in this case, Alice—consumes the services of the provider.

Platform as a Service (PaaS) provides consumers with the ability to install applications of their choice on a server furnished by the provider. Software as a Service (SaaS) provides consumers with access to a specific application running on the provider's servers. In a private cloud, the same organization that utilizes the cloud services is also the sole owner of the infrastructure that provides those services. A hybrid cloud is a combination of public and private infrastructure so that the consumer organization is only a partial owner of the infrastructure. A community cloud is a private cloud variant intended for specific business communities, such as the medical or legal fields.

286. B. In a private cloud, the same organization that utilizes the cloud services can also be the sole owner of the infrastructure that provides those services. A private cloud can also be owned by a third party, all or in part. In the public cloud model, one organization functions as the provider, and another organization consumes the services of the provider. A hybrid cloud is a combination of public and private infrastructure so that the consumer organization is only a partial owner of the infrastructure. There is no such thing as an ad hoc cloud model.

287. B. *Cloud bursting* is a common term for the offloading of excess traffic from private to public cloud resources when necessary to maintain satisfactory performance levels.

288. C. Software as a Service (SaaS) provides consumers with access to a specific application running on the provider's servers (in this case, an email service). Consumers have control over some of their email functions, but they have no control over the operating system, the servers, or the underlying resources. The Infrastructure as a Service (IaaS) model provides the consumers with access to processing, storage, and networking resources that the consumer can use as needed. Platform as a Service (PaaS) provides consumers with the ability to install applications of their choice on a server furnished by the provider. Desktop as a Service (DaaS) provides remote virtualization of the entire workstation desktop, instead of a single application.

289. C. A hybrid cloud consists of both public and private resources. One of its main advantages is that administrators can move services from private to public cloud servers and back again as needed, depending on the current workload. Public cloud resources require authentication, so while they might be less secure than a private cloud, they are not inherently insecure. The term *private cloud* refers to hardware resources that are owned and operated either by a single organization or a third party, regardless of their location. The various cloud delivery models do not impose specific hardware resource requirements.

290. B. The Platform as a Service (PaaS) model provides consumers with the ability to install applications of their choice on a server furnished by the provider. Infrastructure as a Service (IaaS) provides the consumers with processing, storage, and networking resources that they can use to install and run operating systems and other software of their choice. Software as a Service (SaaS) provides consumers with access to a specific application running on the provider's servers. Desktop as a Service (DaaS) provides remote virtualization of the entire workstation desktop, instead of a single application.

291. A, B, C. Multitenancy is a software architecture in which multiple tenants share a single instance of an application running in the cloud. Because tenants share a single application, there is a chance that data could be compromised. Because a single application instance is running in the cloud, the operational overhead is reduced compared to the use of individual virtual machines. Tenants share a finite amount of bandwidth, so the possibility exists for competition to occur, such as when one tenant is the target of a Denial of Service (DoS) attack. Multitenancy does not call for tenants to have individual virtual machines.

292. D. Infrastructure as Code (IaC) is a method of deploying and configuring cloud-based resources using script files. IaC deployment provides time and cost savings and improved elasticity and scalability by automating the virtual machine deployment process and also ensures a consistent deployment by using the same script for all newly deployed VMs. IaC does not encrypt the virtual machine configuration.

293. C. A cloud direct connection is a private link between the client's private network and the cloud service provider. This link is independent from any ISP connection used by the client organization for other traffic, so it ensures a consistent bandwidth for the hybrid cloud network. Using a different ISP or a leased line does not replace the entire connection; there are still potential bottlenecks. A VPN can provide better performance than a standard connection and greater security, but it is not as consistent (or as expensive) as a direct cloud connection.

Chapter 2: Network Implementations

1. D. Radio-frequency identification (RFID) uses tags containing data, frequently embedded in pets, which can be read using electromagnetic fields. Z-wave is a short-range wireless technology, frequently used for home automation. Bluetooth is a short-range wireless protocol, frequently used for computer peripherals and Personal Area Networks (PANs). Near-field communication (NFC) provides wireless communication over ranges of 4 cm or less, and it is often used for payment systems.

2. A. A key fob that unlocks your car is typically a short-range radio or infrared device that does not use the Internet for its communications. Each of the other examples describes a device with an IP address that uses the Internet to communicate with a controller or monitoring station.

3. D. A WAP is a device with a wireless transceiver that also connects to a standard cabled network. Wireless computers communicate with the WAP , which forwards their transmissions over the network cable. This is called an infrastructure topology. A star or bus network requires the computers to be physically connected to the network cable, and an ad hoc topology is one in which wireless computers communicate directly with one another.

4. C. The best choice is to replace the hubs with switches, since the network is relatively small, and cost is an issue. On the existing network, all users share the same 100 Mbps communication channel, and each computer must take turns transmitting. By replacing the hubs with switches, you provide each computer with a dedicated 100 Mbps connection to the switch, while reducing unnecessary traffic and collisions on the network. There is no such thing as a dedicated hub. Splitting the network into two routed LANs is not the best solution, because all users must share information on a constant basis. Also, cost is a factor, and routers are more expensive than switches. Replacing the hubs with a layer 3 switch and defining two VLANs with 20 users each is not a reasonable solution, because layer 3 switches are very expensive.

5. B. A bridge can split a single network into two collision domains, because it forwards only the packets that are destined for the other side of the bridge. The bridge forwards all broadcast packets, so it maintains a single broadcast domain. A hub maintains a single collision domain and a single broadcast domain. A switch creates a separate collision domain for each port, and a single broadcast domain for the entire network. A router creates two collision domains, but it does not forward broadcasts, so there are two broadcast domains as well. A repeater is a physical layer device that amplifies signals; it does not affect collision domains.

6. C, E. Broadband routers generally do not function as proxy servers, which are application layer devices used to regulate access to the Internet. They are also typically not Virtual Private Network (VPN) headends, which enable multiple remote VPN clients to connect to the network. Many broadband routers are also WAPs, enabling users to construct a LAN without a complicated and expensive cable installation. Many broadband routers have switched ports for connections to wired devices, such as printers and computers. Most broadband routers use DHCP to assign IP addresses to devices on the private network.

7. B, C. A repeater is a physical layer device that amplifies the signals entering it and transmits them again. A hub is a physical layer device that propagates incoming signals out through all of its ports. Switches and routers have physical layer elements but are primarily data link and network layer devices, respectively.

8. C. A modem (modulator/demodulator) is any device that converts analog signals to digital signals and digital signals back to analog signals. The digital device does not have to be a computer, and the analog device does not have to be the PSTN. There are many devices that are incorrectly referred to as modems, such as devices that connect a digital LAN to a digital WAN or all-digital devices that connect computers to the Internet.

9. C. Replacing routers with switches turns an internetwork into a single large subnet, and VLANs exist as logical elements on top of the switching fabric. Although VLANs are the functional equivalent of network layer subnets, the systems in a single VLAN are still connected by switches, not routers. Bridges connect network segments at the data link layer and selectively forward traffic between the segments. However, bridges do not provide a dedicated connection between two systems like a switch does, and they do not make it possible to convert a large, routed internetwork into a single switched network. Therefore, they have no role in implementing VLANs. Hubs are physical layer devices that propagate all incoming traffic out through all of their ports. Replacing the routers on an internetwork with hubs would create a single shared network with huge amounts of traffic and collisions. Hubs, therefore, do not connect the computers in a VLAN.

10. A. A firewall is a filter that can prevent dangerous traffic originating on one network from passing through to another network. A device that connects two networks together and forwards traffic between them is a router, not a firewall. A device that enables Internet network clients with private IP addresses to access the Internet is a description of a NAT router or a proxy server, not a firewall. A device that caches Internet data is a proxy server or caching engine, not a firewall.

11. B. Service-dependent filtering blocks traffic based on the port numbers specified in the transport layer header fields. Because port numbers represent specific applications, you can use them to prevent traffic generated by these applications from reaching a network. IP address filtering operates at the network layer. DPI scans the contents of packets, rather than their headers. NGFW defines a device with advanced protection capabilities; port number scanning is a basic firewall function.

12. A. A repeater is a physical layer device that regenerates incoming signals and retransmits them. A hub is a type of repeater that receives data through any one of its multiple ports and retransmits the data out through all of its other ports. Bridges and switches are data link layer devices, and routers are network layer devices. None of these three can be described as multiport repeaters.

13. C. Source route bridging was a technique used on Token Ring (and not Ethernet) networks, in which a Routing Information Field (RIF) in the packet header identified the network segments the packet should follow to reach its destination. Store and forward, transparent, and multiport bridges have all been used on Ethernet networks.

14. C, D. Most operating systems are capable of functioning as routers or firewalls. To route traffic, the system must have two network connections. A software firewall can be part of a computer's routing functionality, or it can be a stand-alone firewall that protects only the local system. Computers cannot function as hubs or switches, because multiple ports would be required, and standard network adapters do not implement those functions.

15. D. Service-dependent filtering blocks traffic based on the port numbers specified in the transport layer header fields. Because port numbers represent specific applications, you can use them to prevent traffic generated by these applications from reaching a network. IP address filtering enables you to limit network access to specific computers; it is not service dependent. Filtering based on hardware addresses provides the same basic functionality as IP address filtering, but it is more difficult to spoof hardware addresses than IP addresses. Filtering by protocol identifier enables you to block all traffic using TCP or UDP; it is not service dependent.

16. C. A personal firewall is an inexpensive way to protect an individual computer from Internet incursions. Installing a hardware firewall is a complex and expensive solution, not suitable for a small network. An IPS is a relatively expensive solution, suitable for larger networks. An IDS is also expensive, and connecting it to a switched port would not enable it to protect the other computers on the network. A port scanner is a device that performs scans on demand. It does not continuously monitor ports, and it does nothing to protect them.

17. B, C. Hubs operate at the physical layer and switches at the data link layer. Hubs and switches both create a single broadcast domain for all of the connected devices. Switches create a separate collision domain for each connected device, whereas hubs create a single collision domain. There are switches (but not hubs) with network layer (layer 3) functionality.

18. A, C. STP disables redundant links between switches that can allow packets to circulate end-lessly around the network. This is called a bridging loop. As a result of a bridging loop, the network can be flooded with broadcast traffic, which is called a broadcast storm. STP does nothing to prevent late collisions, which is an Ethernet timing problem, or crosstalk, which is a cabling fault.

19. B, C. A switch is essentially a multiport bridge. Both switches and bridges process incoming packets by scanning their data link layer hardware addresses and forwarding the packets out the port connected to the destination system. The primary difference between them is that switches have many ports, whereas bridges have only two. Hubs and routers are physical layer and network layer devices, respectively, and perform different functions.

20. B. The five functional levels in a distributed control system such as SCADA are field level, direct control, plant supervisory, production control, and production scheduling. Remote access is not one of the levels.

21. A. Cut-through switches are fast, because they look at only the first six bytes (the destina-tion Media Access Control, or MAC, address) when forwarding a frame. They do not per-form a cyclical redundancy check (CRC) on the entire frame's contents prior to forwarding it out a port leading to the destination. Source route is a bridging technique in which the source host, not the switch, determines the path a frame will take through a network to reach a destination. Store-and-forward switches take in the entire frame and verify its contents by performing a CRC calculation before forwarding it. There is no switch called a destina-tion switch.

22. B. Switches use Media Access Control (MAC) addresses to identify the ports associated with specific hosts. The switch reads the destination MAC address from each incoming packet and forwards it out through the port associated with that address. Switches are data link layer devices, so they do not use IP addresses or DNS names to forward packets. The Maximum Transmission Unit (MTU) value specifies the maximum size of data link layer frames; the switch does not use it to forward packets.

23. D. STP operates at the data link layer of the OSI model, so it works with hardware addresses, not IP addresses. Switches use STP to prevent redundant links from causing traffic loops on the network.

24. E. SOHO multifunction devices typically function as routers connecting the local network to an Internet Service Provider (ISP), switches providing wired connections to host devices, Dynamic Host Configuration Protocol (DHCP) servers assigning IP addresses, Domain Name System (DNS) servers resolving names into IP addresses, Network Address Translation (NAT) routers providing hosts with private IP addresses access to the Internet, and APs providing wireless devices with access to the network. They do not function as hubs.

25. B. The process by which STP populates its database with information about each port in a switch and designates the ports as forwarding or blocking is called convergence. Assimilation, tree-building, and listening are not terms for STP path evaluation.

26. A, B. All switches operate at the data link layer of the OSI model, but multilayer switches usually also function as routers, which are network layer devices. They are not usually trans-port or application layer devices.

27. C. A firewall that supports stateful packet inspection examines other network and transport layer header fields, looking for patterns that indicate damaging behaviors, such as IP spoofing, SYN floods, and teardrop attacks. Port number filtering is the most commonly used form of packet filtering; it is not the same as stateful packet inspection. Blocking traffic based on IP addresses prevents specific systems from accessing a network; stateful packet inspection is a much more complicated operation. Packet filtering based on protocol identifiers enables you to block TCP traffic; this is not stateful packet inspection.

28. B. Bridges are data link layer (layer 2) devices. Routing is a network layer (layer 3) function, so it is not a type of bridge. A store-and-forward, or simple, bridge examines each packet and decides whether to forward it to the connected network. A transparent bridge compiles a database of forwarding information, based on the packets it has processed previously. A multiport bridge provides connections to multiple networks; a switch is a type of multiport bridge.

29. A, C. IDSs can use anomaly-based detection to identify deviations from a known baseline of trustworthiness, or signature-based detection to locate specific malicious byte or instruction sequences. Behavior-based and statistic-based detection are not typical IDS methods.

30. B. Connecting subnets with routers at the network layer maintains the data link layer administrative boundaries that prevent broadcast transmissions from being propagated throughout the entire internetwork. Switching eliminates those data link layer boundaries, and administrators can use VLANs to simulate them. Because hubs propagate all of the traffic they receive out through all of their ports indiscriminately, they create no administrative boundaries. Firewalls are filtering devices that protect networks against malicious traffic; their functions are not related to VLANs. Switches are essentially multiport bridges that forward incoming traffic only to the device for which it is destined. Therefore, bridges are more closely related to eliminating administrative boundaries than to establishing them.

31. D. A simple media converter is a physical layer device that can connect different types of network media together, as long as they have the same speed and duplex settings. Because the converter simply retransmits the signals, the single-collision domain is maintained. Bridges and switches are data link layer devices that create multiple-collision domains. Routers are network layer devices that create separate collision and broadcast domains.

32. B. A switch is a data link layer device that essentially performs the function of a bridge for each device connected to one of its ports. It can therefore be described as a multiport bridge. Routers, hubs, and gateways are devices that operate at the network, physical, and application layers, respectively, so they cannot be described as bridges.

33. D. A gateway enables two devices using different protocols to communicate by performing translation and conversion services for them. Routers, hubs, and switches all require the same protocol at some of the OSI model layers.

34. A. Each port on a router defines a separate collision domain. Hubs forward all traffic to all of the connected nodes, so each network segment is a single-collision domain. Routers do not forward broadcasts, so each network segment is also a separate broadcast domain.

35. A, B, D. Routers are network layer devices that do not forward broadcast messages, so they create separate broadcast domains for each network. Switches do forward broadcasts, forming a single broadcast domain. Routers and switches can communicate using dedicated protocols. As data link layer devices, switches read only hardware addresses from packet frames; routers forward traffic based on the IP addresses in packets' IP headers.

36. A. Media converters will enable Ralph to join the multimode fiber-optic run to the UTP at both sides of the courtyard while maintaining a single network at minimum cost. Inexpensive small-business hubs and switches cannot join different media together. Routers can join different media, but they are more expensive, and they would separate the installation into three separate networks.

37. A. If the fifth computer is in a different VLAN from the other four, it would be unable to communicate with them. A switching loop would affect communication between all of the computers, not just the fifth one. An MTU black hole is a condition in which a system is unable to complete the Path MTU Discovery process, due to an intervening firewall. Because these five computers are all on the same LAN, they all have the same MTU, and Path MTU Discovery is not necessary. A virtual router would enable switched computers on different subnets to communicate with each other; it would not prevent them from communicating.

38. A. Security Information and Event Management (SIEM) systems can function as a central clearinghouse for information gathered by IDSs and other security processes. Next-Generation Firewall (NGFW), Remote Authentication Dial-In User Service (RADIUS), and Voice over IP (VoIP) are not systems that collect IDS information.

39. A. Hubs are network devices that simply receive signals through one port, electrically enhance them, and transmit them out through another port. Routers, switches, and bridges are capable of reading the signals and processing them, which classifies them as intelligent.

40. A, B. Adding a router splits the Ethernet LAN into two LANs, creating two separate broadcast domains. Each computer, therefore, has a smaller number of broadcast messages to process. Because the network is split by the router, the amount of unicast traffic on each subnet is reduced.

41. B. Standard hub ports have a crossover circuit, which ensures that the transmit signals at one end of the connection arrive at the receive pins at the other end. The uplink port in a hub bypasses the crossover circuit, so that two connected hubs do not have crossover circuits that cancel each other out. A connection between a standard port and an uplink port, using a standard cable, results in a single crossover, which is correct wiring. Each of the other solutions results in either two crossovers or no crossovers, which is incorrect.

42. D, E. By default, a switched LAN consists of a single broadcast domain. To create multiple broadcast domains, you can install routers to split the installation into two or more networks, because routers do not forward broadcasts. The other possibility is to create VLANs in the switches. Each VLAN is a separate broadcast domain. All of the other options would have no effect on the number of broadcast domains on the network.

43. B. Bridges and switches are data link layer devices that forward frames based on the destination MAC address contained in the frame. They operate in promiscuous mode, listening and processing all frames on each segment, and they build forwarding tables with this information. Forwarding tables are built based on source MAC addresses. Bridges are protocol independent; they are not involved with the upper layer protocols being carried on the LAN. Broadcast domains are defined by network layer devices, not data link layer devices.

44. C. A switch is best described as a multiport bridge, because it reads the hardware addresses of incoming packets and forwards them out through the port for the destination node. Although a switch does function at layer 2 of the OSI model (the data link layer), it is not a router, which connects networks together at layer 3 (the network layer). Hubs and repeaters are physical layer (layer 1) devices that are not capable of performing the functions of a switch.

45. E. The IoT consists of devices that are ordinarily passive, but which have been made intelligent by configuring them to participate on an IP network. All of the devices listed are available as "smart" devices that enable remote users to interact with them over the Internet.

46. C. The main reason why switches improve the efficiency of an Ethernet LAN is that they create a separate collision domain for each switched port, eliminating most collisions. Collisions result in packets having to be retransmitted, so fewer collisions means fewer retransmissions, which improves performance. Switches do not forward packets faster than hubs. Switches do forward broadcast transmissions. Switches do read hardware addresses, not IP addresses.

47. D. A collision domain is a LAN with a shared network medium, so that two devices transmitting at the same time generate a signal quality error, also known as a collision. Ethernet LANs connected by hubs create a shared medium, whereas switched networks create a separate collision domain for each connected node. Routers create separate collision domains. A group of computers able to receive broadcasts is the definition of a broadcast domain, not a collision domain. Overlong cables can precipitate collisions but do not define a collision domain.

48. A, C. VoIP uses the terms *terminal* and *endpoint* to refer to the device with which users make calls, including computers and telephone handsets. A VoIP gateway is the device that provides the conduit between an IP network and the Public Switched Telephone Network (PSTN). A VoIP private branch exchange (PBX) is a device that switches calls between endpoints on the local IP network and provides access to external Internet lines.

49. A. Hubs are physical layer devices that amplify and repeat signals out all ports except the one through which the data was received, regardless of the destination. Hubs are used to physically connect end systems to a star topology. Hubs typically provide an internal crossover circuit connection. Uplink ports are used to extend the distance of a star network, forming a hierarchical star.

50. A, D, E. Routers are network layer devices that use IP addresses to forward frames, not MAC addresses. Routers are protocol dependent. They must support the network layer protocol being routed. As a network layer device, a router defines networks (or LANs) that represent a separate broadcast domain. Routers do not build their routing tables or forward frames using MAC addresses.

51. A, B. The 100Base-TX specification specifies two hub types: Class I and II. Class I hubs perform signal translation; Class II hubs do not. A network can have only one Class I hub per collision domain; a network can have two Class II hubs per collision domain. The other options do not exist.

52. C. Routers store and maintain route information in a routing table that is stored in memory, not in a local text file. All of the other statements about routers are true.

53. D. The firewall is a conduit between the private network and the ISP's network (which provides access to the Internet), through which all traffic must pass. This ensures that the firewall has the opportunity to examine every packet that passes between the private network and the Internet and filter out those that are not authorized. If the firewall was located in the midst of the private internetwork, it would be possible for Internet computers to bypass the firewall and communicate directly with the private systems. Placing the firewall on the far side of the router would put it on the ISP's network, causing it to filter all of the ISP's traffic and not just that destined for the private network. Installing the firewall at the ISP's site would have the same effect as installing it on the far side of the router at the private network site.

54. A, B. The FTP protocol uses two well-known ports: 20 and 21. A firewall must have both of these ports open to admit FTP traffic. FTP does not require ports 22, 23, or 24.

55. D. A proxy server is an application layer service, because it receives Internet service requests from client computers, reads the application layer protocol data in each request, and then generates its own request for the same service and transmits it to the Internet server the client specifies. Only an application layer service can read and process the application layer data in network packets. A proxy server cannot be a data link layer device, because it can provide Internet access to an entire internetwork, while the data link layer is concerned with communications on a single subnet. Proxy servers cannot be network layer devices, because the network layer handles all internetwork packets indiscriminately and is unaware of what application generated the data carried inside the packets. The transport layer is not involved in processing application data, so proxy servers cannot be said to function at the transport layer.

56. B. DPI is a firewall technique that examines the data carried in packets and not just the protocol headers. While traditional firewalls typically do not support DPI, NGFWs often do. Stateful packet inspection, NAT, and VPN support are all features that are commonly supported by traditional firewall products.

57. C. Content filters are a firewall feature that examines the data inside packets, rather than their origin, to locate objectionable material. They do not scan IP addresses, nor do they detect typical types of malware. Content filters are not implemented in switches.

58. D. In most cases, a load balancing router works by processing incoming traffic based on rules set by the administrator. The rules can distribute traffic among a group of servers using various criteria, such as each server's current load or response time, or which server is next in a given rotation. Load balancers typically do not use the hardware configuration of the servers to direct traffic since this is a factor that does not change.

59. C. A VoIP gateway is a device that provides a conduit between an IP network and the Public Switched Telephone Network (PSTN). The gateway enables standard telephones connected to the PSTN to place calls using VoIP services on the Internet. A proxy server is an application layer device that provides web browsers and other client programs to access the Internet. A Virtual Private Network (VPN) headend enables multiple client systems to access a network from remote locations. A unified threat management (UTM) appliance typically performs VPN, firewall, and antivirus functions.

60. A, C. Network Address Translation (NAT) is a network layer device that converts the private IP addresses of all of a client's transmissions to registered IP address. NAT therefore works for all applications. A proxy server is an application layer device that performs the same type of conversion, but only for specific applications. A Remote Authentication Dial-In User Service (RADIUS) server can provide Authentication, Authorization, Accounting, Auditing (AAAA) services for remote access servers. It does not convert IP addresses. A unified threat management (UTM) appliance typically performs VPN, firewall, and antivirus functions. It too does not convert IP addresses.

61. A, B, C, E. HVAC sensors can measure temperatures and humidity in climate-controlled areas, such as datacenters; atmospheric pressure in devices like boilers and compressors; and occupancy, to control conditions based on the presence of people. Printers, cameras, door locks, and other physical access control devices are not part of an HVAC system.

62. B. A Virtual Private Network (VPN) headend is a type of router that enables multiple client systems to access a network from remote locations. Because the device provides an interface between networks, it is considered to be a type of router, not a switch, a gateway, or a bridge.

63. B. A virtual PBX is an arrangement in which a telephone company provides the PBX services to a customer but maintains the actual hardware at their own facility. The recent emphasis on cloud computing has led to a number of hosted PBX solutions that use Voice over IP (VoIP) to provide services to customers. QoS is a technique for prioritizing traffic by tagging packets based on their content. It is not a virtual PBX technique. The Cache Array Routing Protocol (CARP) enables proxy servers to exchange information; it does not provide virtual PBX services. In round-robin DNS, a DNS server contains multiple resource records for the same server name, each with a different IP address representing one of the computers running the server application. When a client resolves the server name, the DNS server accesses each of the resource records in turn so that each address theoretically receives the same number of visitors. This is not a virtual PBX technology.

64. C. Proxy servers provide network users with access to Internet services, and the unregistered IP addresses on the client computers protect them from unauthorized access by users on the Internet, which satisfies the first objective. The proxy servers also make it possible for network administrators to regulate users' access to the Internet, which satisfies one of the two secondary objectives. However, the proxy servers cannot assign IP addresses to the client computers, and the plan makes no mention of DHCP or another automatic TCP/IP configuration mechanism. Therefore, the plan does not satisfy the other secondary objective.

65. A, B. The Control and Provisioning of Wireless Access Points (CAPWAP) protocol and the Lightweight Access Point Protocol (LWAPP) are both protocols that enable wireless controllers to manage and control Access Points (APs). Lightweight Directory Access Protocol (LDAP) is used by directory services, and Point-to-Point Tunneling Protocol (PPTP) is used for virtual private networking.

66. B. In many enterprise wireless networks, the Access Points (APs) do not run a full operating system and are called thin or lightweight APs. The network also has a device called a wireless controller that performs some of the required tasks and manages the APs. A wireless endpoint is another term for a computer or other device that is a client on the wireless network. Hypervisors and demarcation points have nothing to do with wireless networking. A hypervisor creates and manages Virtual Machines (VMs) on a host server, and a demarcation point is the interface between a private network and an outside telecommunications service.

67. A. A multilayer switch is a network connectivity device that functions at both layer 2 and layer 3 of the OSI model. At layer 2, the device functions like a normal switch, providing individual collision domains to each connected node and enabling administrators to create multiple VLANs. At layer 3, the device also provides routing capabilities by forwarding packets between the VLANs. Virtual routers, load balancers, and broadband routers are strictly layer 3 devices that can route traffic but cannot create VLANs.

68. D. A Virtual Private Network (VPN) headend is a type of router that enables multiple client systems to access a network from remote locations. It does not distribute traffic among servers. A load balancer is a type of router that forwards traffic with a single IP address to multiple servers in turn. Round-robin DNS is a technique in which a DNS server resolves a name into several IP addresses, each in turn. A Network Load Balancing (NLB) cluster is a group of servers, all running the same application, that distribute incoming traffic among themselves.

69. B. A load balancer is a type of router that forwards traffic with a single IP address to multiple servers in turn. In most cases, a load balancing router works by processing incoming traffic based on rules set by the administrator. Because a load balancer works with IP addresses, it is a network layer device. Load balancers are not switches, gateways, or firewalls.

70. C. Next-Generation Firewalls (NGFWs) expand on the packet filtering capabilities of traditional firewalls by adding features such as DPI and IPSs, as well as inspection of encrypted traffic and antivirus scanning. Remote Authentication Dial-In User Service (RADIUS) servers can provide centralized Authentication, Authorization, Accounting, Auditing (AAAA) services. A CSU/DSU is a device that provides a router on a private network with access to a leased line. A proxy server is an application layer service that receives Internet service requests from client computers, reads the application layer protocol data in each request, and then generates its own request for the same service and transmits it to the Internet server the client specifies.

71. A. A private branch exchange (PBX) switches internal calls and provides access to external lines. A VoIP PBX performs the same tasks as a traditional PBX. A VoIP gateway is the device that provides the conduit between an IP network and the Public Switched Telephone Network (PSTN). A VoIP endpoint is a device that makes use of the VoIP system, such as a computer or handset. A multilayer switch is a data networking device that includes both switching and routing capabilities.

72. A. Because the client computers use private IP addresses, they are invisible to the Internet, so users outside the private network cannot see or access them. The proxy server has a public IP address so it can participate in service transactions with Internet servers. If the proxy server used a private IP address, it would not be able to access the Internet directly. If the clients used public IP addresses, they would be visible to the Internet and vulnerable to intrusion.

73. B, C. To provide clients with Internet access, a NAT or proxy server must have direct access to the Internet, which requires using a registered, or public, IP address. Both NAT and proxy servers function as the middleman in transactions between the client computers on a private network and Internet servers. The NAT or proxy server transmits the client's service request to the Internet server as though it was its own and, after receiving the reply, relays the response back to the client. Because NAT servers function at the network layer, clients can use any application to access the Internet through the server. Proxy servers, however, operate at the application layer and can provide Internet access only to certain types of client applications. Proxy servers are capable of caching web data for later use, because they are application layer devices that read the application layer protocol data in the message packets they receive. NAT servers are network layer processes that forward packets with no knowledge of the application layer information in their contents.

74. B, C, D. A multilayer switch typically operates at the data link, and network layers, assuming the functions of a switch and a router by using Media Access Control (MAC) addresses at the data link layer (layer 2) and IP addresses at the network layer (layer 3) to forward packets to their appropriate destinations. Some switches also function at the transport layer (layer 4) by distinguishing between User Datagram Protocol (UDP) and Transmission Control Protocol (TCP) traffic and using port numbers to forward packets.

75. A. Intrusion Detection Systems (IDSs) are designed to monitor network traffic for anomalies and send notifications to administrators. Uninterruptible power supplies (UPSs), Remote Authentication Dial-In User Service (RADIUS) servers, Denial-of-Service (DoS) attacks, and Remote Access Service (RAS) servers all have nothing to do with network monitoring.

76. C. Packet forwarding is a function typically associated with routers and is not a normal function of a UTM appliance. UTM appliances do typically perform VPN, firewall, and anti-virus functions.

77. B. Port mirroring is a feature found in some switches that takes the form of a special port that runs in promiscuous mode. This means that the switch copies all incoming traffic to that port, as well as to the dedicated destination ports. By connecting an IDS or protocol analyzer to this port, an administrator can access all of the network's traffic. Stateful packet inspection is a firewall feature that enables the device to examine network and transport layer header fields, looking for patterns that indicate damaging behaviors, such as IP spoofing, SYN floods, and teardrop attacks. Trunking is a switch feature that enables administrators to create VLANs that span multiple switches. Service-dependent filtering is a firewall feature that blocks traffic based on transport layer port numbers.

78. B. ACLs restrict access to network devices by filtering usernames, MAC addresses, IP addresses, or other criteria. Routers, switches, and WAPs all use ACLs to control access to them. Hubs are purely physical layer devices that relay electrical or optical signals. They have no way of controlling access to them.

79. B. The Default Gateway parameter specifies the address of the local router that the end system should use to access other networks. The WINS Server Addresses and DNS Server Addresses parameters are used to resolve names to IP addresses. There is no such parameter as Subnet Gateway.

80. A. The figure displays the format for a Routing Information Protocol (RIP) version 1 response packet. The figure does not show the packet format for RIPv2, Open Shortest Path First (OSPF), Enhanced Interior Gateway Routing Protocol (EIGRP), or Border Gateway Protocol (BGP).

81. A. EIGRP can support classless IPv4 addresses. It was designed to replace the Interior Gateway Routing Protocol (IGRP), which could not support classless addresses. All of the other options contain true statements.

82. A, B. Bandwidth throttling is a traffic shaping technique that prevents specified data streams from transmitting too many packets. Rate limiting is a traffic shaping technique that controls the transmission rate of sending systems. A broadcast storm is a type of network switching loop. NAT is a method by which private networks can share registered IP addresses. Neither of these last two is a traffic shaping technique.

83. D. Quality of Service (QoS) is a general term that refers to various mechanisms for prioritizing network traffic so that applications or data streams requiring a certain level of performance are not negatively affected by lower-priority transmissions. Port forwarding is a routing method that redirects traffic intended for one IP address and port number to another. Dynamic routing is a method by which routing tables are automatically updated with new information as the routing fabric of an internetwork changes. Virtual Local Area Networks (VLANs) are a means for partitioning a broadcast domain into discrete units that are functionally equivalent to physical LANs.

84. A, D. Routers that are running the RIPv1 routing protocol broadcast their entire routing tables every 30 seconds, regardless of whether there has been a change in the network. RIPv1 does not include the subnet mask in its updates, so it does not support subnetting.

85. A. Differentiated services (Diffserv) is a mechanism that provides Quality of Service (QoS) on a network by classifying traffic types using a 6-bit value in the differentiated services (DS) field of the IP header. Class of Service (CoS) is a similar mechanism that operates at the data link layer by adding a 3-bit Priority Code Point (PCP) value to the Ethernet frame. Traffic shaping is a means of prioritizing network traffic that typically works by delaying packets at the application layer. Quality of Service (QoS) is an umbrella term that encompasses a variety of network traffic prioritization mechanisms. Administrative distance is a value that routers use to select the most efficient route to a destination.

86. A, E. Administrators must manually add, modify, or delete static routes when a change in a network occurs. For this reason, static routes are not recommended for use in large internetworks where there are multiple paths to each destination network. Static routes are not automatically added by routing protocols and do not adapt to changes in a network.

87. A. RIPv1 does not include the subnet mask in its updates. RIPv2 supports subnetting and includes the subnet mask of each network address in its updates. OSPF and BGP both include the subnet mask within their updates.

88. D. Distance vector protocols rely on hop counts to evaluate the efficiency of routes. Link state protocols use a different type of calculation, usually based on Dijkstra's algorithm. The terms *interior gateway protocol* and *edge gateway protocol* do not refer to the method of calculating routing efficiency.

89. B. A single RIP broadcast packet can include up to 25 routes. If there are more than 25 routes in the computer's routing table, then RIP must generate additional packets.

90. A, C. OSPF is a link state routing protocol, which means that it does not rely solely on hop counts to measure the relative efficiency of a route. EIGRP is a hybrid protocol that can use link state routing. RIP is a distance vector routing protocol, meaning that it uses hop counts to measure route efficiency. BGP is an exterior gateway protocol that exchanges routing information among autonomous systems using path vectors or distance vectors.

91. A, B, D. OSPF does support CIDR. All of the other options contain true statements.

92. A. Convergence is the term for the process by which routers propagate information from their routing tables to other routers on the network using dynamic routing protocols. Distance vectoring, redistribution, and dissemination do not describe this process.

93. A. RIP is a distance vector protocol, which uses hop counts to measure the efficiency of routes. OSPF, BGP, and IS-IS are all link state protocols, which do not rely on hop counts.

94. A. Exterior Gateway Protocol (EGP) routes datagrams between autonomous systems. Interior Gateway Protocol (IGP) routes datagrams within an autonomous system. Routing Information Protocol (RIP) and Open Shortest Path First (OSPF) are examples of interior gateway protocols.

95. D. TTL is a value included in the IPv4 header that specifies the maximum number of hops the packet is allowed on the network. Each router processing the packet reduces the TTL value by one and discards the packet when the value reaches zero. OSPF is a routing protocol. MTU specifies the maximum size of a frame. Administrative distance is a value that routers use to select the most efficient route to a destination.

96. A, D. The `route` command was originally created to display a Unix or Linux system's routing table and modify its contents by adding, changing, and deleting static routes. The `ip` command is part of the `iproute2` command-line utility package, which has replaced `route` in many Unix and Linux distributions. Running `ip` with the `route` parameter can manipulate the routing table. The `traceroute` and `ifconfig` tools are not commands for manipulating the routing table.

97. A. Routers that use OSPF transmit the speed of each network interface with the other OSPF routers in the network. This enables the routers to evaluate the cost of various routes through the network and transmit packets using the route with the smallest cost value. The routers do not need to share information about the data link layer protocols or network media they use or their IP addresses.

98. B. BGP is a path vector routing protocol, not a link state routing protocol. All of the other options contain true statements.

99. A. The default route in an IPv4 routing table always has a destination address of 0.0.0.0. The other destinations are found in a routing table, but they are not the default route destination.

100. A. The figure displays the format for a Routing Information Protocol version 2 response packet. The figure does not show the packet format for RIPv1, Open Shortest Path First (OSPF), Enhanced Interior Gateway Routing Protocol (EIGRP), or Border Gateway Protocol (BGP).

101. D. The Border Gateway Protocol (BGP) is a highly scalable protocol used for routing both on private autonomous systems, where it is known as the Internal Border Gateway Protocol (iBGP) and maintains full mesh communication among all of the routers, and on the Internet, where it is known as the External Border Gateway Protocol (eBGP). Routing Information Protocol (RIP), Open Shortest Path First (OSPF), and Enhanced Interior Gateway Routing Protocol (EIGRP) do not have interior and exterior designations.

102. A, B. The Internet Protocol (IP) in both of its versions (IPv4 and IPv6) includes a TTL field in its message header that limits the number of times a packet can be routed on a network. Each router processing the packet reduces the TTL value by one until it reaches zero, after which it is discarded. The Internet Control Message Protocol (ICMP) and the Internet Group Management Protocol (IGMP) do not have a TTL field.

103. B. WAN optimization is not a form of traffic shaping, because it compresses data streams and transmits incremental file updates. Traffic shaping uses techniques like rate limiting, bandwidth throttling, and self-limiting to delay the transmission of specific types of data packets to optimize network performance.

104. A. Distributed switching describes a hierarchical switching architecture in which remote switches (departmental switches in this case) handle most of the network traffic, with a host switch used only for traffic between the remote locations. Port forwarding is a routing method that redirects traffic intended for one IP address and port number to another. Traffic shaping is a series of techniques that optimize the allocation of network bandwidth. Neighbor discovery is an IPv6 technique used to find addresses of devices and services on the local network. Flow control is a technique for regulating a system's transmission speed.

105. A. All half-duplex port connections on a store-and-forward switch represent a different collision domain. Full-duplex connections are not subject to collisions, so they do not define separate collision domains.

106. C. A Media Access Control (MAC) address is a 6-byte hexadecimal value, with the bytes separated by colons, as in 00:1A:6B:31:9A:4E. Option A, 10.124.25.43, is all decimals and uses periods; this is an IPv4 address. Option B, FF:FF:FF:FF:FF:FF, is a valid MAC address, but this value is reserved for use as a broadcast address. Option D, 03:AE:16:3H:5B:11, is not a valid hexadecimal address, which should contain only numerals and the letters A to F. Option E, fe80::89a5:9e4d:a9d0:9ed7, is too long for a MAC address; this is a valid IPv6 address.

107. B. The Spanning Tree Protocol (STP) prevents packets from endlessly looping from switch to switch due to redundant links. Creating redundant links is a good preventive against switch failure, but packets transmitted over multiple links can circulate from switch to switch infinitely. STP creates a database of switching links and shuts down the redundant ones until they are needed. Routing Information Protocol (RIP) propagates routing table information. A Virtual Local Area Network (VLAN) is an organizational tool that operates within switches by creating multiple broadcast domains. Network Address Translation (NAT) is a routing method that enables private networks to share registered IP addresses. Address Resolution Protocol (ARP) is a protocol that discovers a system's MAC address by broadcasting its IPv4 address.

108. A, B. When connecting an MDI port to an Auto-MDI-X port, it is possible to use either a straight-through or a crossover cable because the Auto-MDI-X port can self-adjust to implement the necessary crossover circuit if it is needed. MDI and Auto-MDI-X ports are used only with twisted pair cables, so there is no need for coaxial or fiber optic cables.

109. B. The Neighbor Discovery Protocol (NDP) is a network layer protocol that defines five new Internet Control Message Protocol version 6 (ICMPv6) packet types, which enable IPv6 systems to locate resources on the network, such as routers and DNS servers, as well as autoconfigure and detect duplicate IPv6 addresses. Border Gateway Protocol (BGP) is an exterior gateway protocol that is designed to exchange routing information among autonomous systems. Open Shortest Path First (OSPF) is a link state routing protocol that enables routers to exchange routing table information. Power over Ethernet (PoE) is a general term for standards defining mechanisms for power delivery over Ethernet cables, along with data signals.

110. B. IEEE 802.1Q is a standard defining a mechanism (called Ethernet trunking by some manufacturers) that identifies the Virtual Local Area Network (VLAN) to which a packet belongs by inserting an extra 32-bit field into its Ethernet frame. IEEE 802.1P is a standard that defines a mechanism for implementing Quality of Service (QoS) at the data link layer by adding a 3-bit field into Ethernet frames. IEEE 802.1X is a standard defining an authentication mechanism called Port-based Network Access Control (PNAC). IEEE 802.1AB is a standard defining the Link Layer Discovery Protocol (LLDP). IEEE 802.1AX is a specification for the Link Aggregation Control Protocol (LACP), which is a mechanism for combining physical ports into a single logical channel.

111. C. Stations on a CSMA/CD network first check the medium to see if it is idle. If they detect an idle medium, they begin transmitting. If two or more devices transmit at the same time, a collision occurs. Immediately after a collision occurs, the two stations involved stop transmitting. After that, they send out a jam signal. Then, the two stations back off for a random interval, and the transmission process begins again.

112. A. For CSMA/CD to function properly, a system must detect a packet collision while it is transmitting the packet. If cable segments are too long, the packet might leave the transmitting system before the collision is detected, resulting in a late collision, which cannot be retransmitted. Incorrect pinouts, too many systems, and excessive collisions typically will not prevent the collision detection system from occurring.

113. B. After transmitting their jam signals, the two systems wait for a randomized interval. This is to prevent them from retransmitting their packets at the same time, resulting in another collision. It is not necessary for the systems to reassemble, rebuffer, or recalculate checksums for their packets.

114. C. Replacing routers with switches turns an internetwork into a single large subnet, and Virtual Local Area Networks (VLANs) exist as logical elements on top of the switching fabric. Although VLANs are the functional equivalent of network layer subnets, the systems in a single VLAN are still physically connected by switches, not routers. Bridges connect network segments at the data link layer and selectively forward traffic between the segments. However, bridges do not provide a dedicated connection between two systems like a switch does, and they do not make it possible to convert a large, routed internetwork into a single switched network. Therefore, they have no role in implementing VLANs. Hubs are physical layer devices that propagate all incoming traffic out through all of their ports. Replacing the routers on an internetwork with hubs would create a single shared broadcast domain with huge amounts of traffic and many collisions. Hubs, therefore, do not connect the computers in a VLAN.

115. A. Collisions are a normal occurrence on an Ethernet network; they occur when two nodes transmit at exactly the same time. There need not be a network fault for collisions to occur. When collisions occur, the nodes involved retransmit their packets so that no data is lost. Collisions are a phenomenon of data link layer protocols; they have nothing to do with IP addresses, which are network layer constructs.

116. D. Collisions are a normal occurrence on an Ethernet network, but late collisions are not normal. Late collisions occur when two packets collide after one or more finishes transmitting. Packet retransmissions, collision detection, and jam signals are all normal occurrences on an Ethernet network.

117. B. Connecting subnets with routers at the network layer maintains the data link layer administrative boundaries that prevent broadcast transmissions from being propagated throughout the entire internetwork. Switching eliminates those data link layer boundaries, and administrators can use Virtual Local Area Networks (VLANs) to simulate them. Because hubs propagate all of the traffic they receive out through all of their ports indiscriminately, they create no administrative boundaries. Domains are logical groups of network devices defined by the Domain Name System (DNS). Their functions are not related to VLANs in any way. Switches are essentially multiport bridges that forward incoming traffic only to the device for which it is destined. Therefore, bridges are more closely related to eliminating administrative boundaries than to establishing them.

118. B, D. The computers in a single Virtual Local Area Network (VLAN) can be located anywhere on a switched network, irrespective of the switches' physical configuration. A broadcast message generated by a computer in a VLAN is transmitted to all of the other computers in that VLAN only, just as if the systems were physically located on a separate LAN or subnet. Unicast transmissions between computers on a switched network do not require VLANs, because the switches create what amounts to a direct connection between the two systems. VLANs are needed only for communication processes that require the use of broadcasts, which if transmitted without VLANs, would flood the network. Even though they are a purely logical construction, VLANs function just like physical subnets and require routers for communication between them. Routing capabilities are often integrated into switches to enable communication between VLANs.

119. A, D. Every network device has a unique hardware address coded into its network interface adapter, and administrators can use these addresses to select the devices that will be part of a specific Virtual Local Area Network (VLAN). When VLANs are implemented inside the switch, selecting the ports to which specific computers are attached is a simple way to identify the computers in a particular VLAN. IP addresses are layer 3 (network layer) constructs, so they do not apply to layer 2 (data link layer) devices like switches. Although DNS names do uniquely identify computers on a network, DNS is an application layer process and has nothing to do with the switching and routing processes, which occur at the data link and network layers. Therefore, you cannot use DNS names to identify the computers in a VLAN.

120. C. VLANs are data link layer Local Area Networks (LANs) defined within switches. Only devices (and users) connected to ports belonging to the same VLAN can communicate with each other until a layer 3 device, such as a router or a layer 3 switch, is added to the network. Re-creating and reconfiguring the VLANs will not correct this problem. Traffic filters are usually implemented on routers. VLANs do not have to use the same data link protocol.

121. D. Ethernet uses jumbo frames at the data link layer to transfer large amounts of data more efficiently. Ethernet typically restricts frame size to 1500 bytes, but jumbo frames enable Ethernet systems to create frames up to 9000 bytes. Frames are protocol data units associated only with the data link layer, so they do not apply to the network, transport, or application layer.

122. C, D. Home and small office networks typically consist of a single subnet and require only a basic switch without the advanced Virtual Local Area Network (VLAN) capabilities that enable administrators to create separate subnets. Most home and small office networks have a Dynamic Host Configuration Protocol (DHCP) server that assigns IP addresses and other TCP/IP configuration settings to clients. The DHCP server can be integrated into a broadband router or another Internet access sharing solution. Most home and small office networks support Network Address Translation (NAT), enabling them to use private IP addresses and still access the Internet. 10GBase-T is the designation for UTP-based 10 Gigabit Ethernet, which is an advanced standard for network interface adapters often found in servers.

123. A, B. To join ports on different switches into one VLAN, you designate a trunk port on each switch for the traffic between switches. Initially, the native VLAN uses the default VLAN1 for trunk traffic, and that traffic is left untagged. Untagged traffic is susceptible to attacks using double-tagged packets. When you configure the native VLAN to use tagging, this makes it impervious to double-tagging. Changing the native VLAN does not create root guards or Bridge Protocol Data Unit (BPDU) guards, and all traffic continues to be switched, not routed.

124. C. The IEEE 802.1q protocol is responsible for VLAN tagging, a procedure that enables network switches to support VLANs. Through the insertion of VLAN identifier tags into frames, switches can determine which VLAN each packet is destined for and forward it to the correct ports. IEEE 802.3x is one of the standards for wired Ethernet networks. IEEE 802.1X is a standard that defines a Port-based Network Access Control (PNAC) mechanism used for authentication on wireless and other networks. IEEE 802.11ac is a standard defining the physical and data link layer protocols for wireless networks.

125. B. When in-band switch management traffic, such as that generated by a Secure Shell (SSH) connection to a switch, uses the native VLAN, it is untagged by default. This is because the native VLAN is at first the default VLAN1, which is not tagged by the 802.1q protocol, leaving it open to certain types of double-tagging attacks. When you tag the native VLAN traffic, it is rendered immune to double-tagging. The default VLAN cannot be renamed, and SSH traffic is already encrypted by the sending workstation. Changing the native VLAN does not move the management traffic off that VLAN, although many authorities advocate the creation of a separate VLAN dedicated to in-band management traffic.

126. D. Ethernet implementations, such as 100Base-TX, which use separate wire pairs for transmitting and receiving data, require a crossover circuit to ensure that the transmit pins on each end of a connection are wired to the receive pins at the other end. This crossover circuit can be implemented in a patch cable—called a crossover cable—or by a switch port. Switches with auto-medium-dependent interface crossover (MDI-X) ports can detect the need for a crossover circuit and implement it automatically in the port. This eliminates the need for crossover cables. Auto-medium-dependent interface crossover (MDI-X) ports do not eliminate the need for 8P8C connectors, connections between switches, or straight-through cables.

127. B. When connecting an MDI port to an MDI-X port, the necessary crossover circuit is implemented in the MDI-X port. Therefore, the connection needs a straight-through cable, and there is no need for a crossover cable. MDI and MDI-X ports are used only with twisted pair cables, so there is no need for coaxial or fiber optic cables.

128. C. When implemented in an Ethernet switch, port security uses port-by-port MAC address filtering to allow only one MAC address to access each switch port. Blacklisting blocks the MAC addresses on the list from using all of the ports on the switch. Whitelisting allows the listed MAC addresses to use any port on the switch. MAC address spoofing is a method for defeating port security, blacklists, or whitelists.

129. D. When transmitting voice traffic on a network along with data traffic, the voice traffic should have priority, to ensure the quality of the stream. Separating data and voice traffic on separate VLANs enables switches to assign voice traffic a higher priority by applying appropriate tags to the voice packets. Separate VLANs are not needed to prevent packet conflicts or to encrypt either voice or data packets.

130. C. The Transmission Control Protocol (TCP) protocol uses a flow control technique in which the receiving system creates a window of a specific size and allows the transmitting system to send packets until that window is full. When the window is full, the sender stops transmitting. The receiver then sends back an acknowledgment packet that specifies the next packet it expects to receive from the sender. The User Datagram Protocol (UDP), Hypertext Transfer Protocol (HTTP), and Domain Name System (DNS) do not use the sliding window technique or any other form of flow control.

131. B. The Alternative B PoE variant can use the spare wire pair in a CAT 5 or better 10Base-T or 100Base-TX cable to supply power to connected devices. The Alternative A and 4PPoE variants cannot use the spare wire pair in this manner; they supply power using the wire pairs that carry data at the same time. For Gigabit Ethernet or faster installations, Alternative B is also capable of using the data wire pairs.

132. C. Whitelisting is the process of using MAC filtering to specify the hardware addresses of devices that are permitted to access a wireless network. Blacklisting, by contrast, is making a list of addresses that are denied access to the network.

133. A, B. Bridge Protocol Data Units (BPDUs) are messages that switches running the STP exchange to learn about the available paths through a switched network and the states of other switches. Switches should only receive BPDUs through ports that are connected to other switches. BPDU guard is a feature that prevents BPDU messages from arriving through ports connected to end systems, such as computers, thus preventing an attacker from manipulating the STP topology. A root guard affects the behavior of the STP by enforcing the selection of root bridge ports on a switched network. Without root guards, there is no way for administrators to enforce the topology of a network with a redundant switching fabric.

134. A. The IEEE 802.11ac standard, like all of the wireless LAN standards in the 802.11 working group, uses CSMA/CA for MAC. The 802.1X standard defines an authentication mechanism and does not require a MAC mechanism. The IEEE 802.3 (Ethernet) standard uses Carrier-Sense Multiple Access with Collision Detection (CSMA/CD).

135. C. An infrastructure topology uses a Wireless Access Point (WAP) to connect wireless devices to a wired network. An ad hoc topology connects wireless devices to each other, without connecting to a wired network. The star and bus topologies do not support wireless devices.

136. D. An ad hoc topology describes wireless computers that communicate directly with each other, without the need for any hardware other than their wireless network adapters. The ad hoc topology therefore does not require a router, an Internet connection, an Access Point (AP), or a special antenna.

137. A, E. IEEE 802.11b, 802.11g, 802.11n, and 802.11ax networks can use the 2.4 GHz frequency band for their transmissions, which can experience interference from a wireless telephone using the same frequency. IEEE 802.11a and IEEE 802.11ac, however, use the 5 GHz band, which will not experience interference from a 2.4 GHz phone.

138. B. IEEE 802.11g supports transmission speeds up to 54 Mbps, and it is backward compatible with 802.11b equipment. IEEE 802.11 cannot run at 54 Mbps, and while 802.11a can, it is not compatible with 802.11b. IEEE 802.11n cannot run at 54 Mbps, though it can run at faster speeds. Bluetooth is not compatible with any of the IEEE 802.11 standards.

139. C, D, E. The IEEE 802.11n, 802.11ac, and 802.11ax standards include MIMO, which enables them to effectively multiplex signals using multiple antennae. This capability was first introduced in the 802.11n standard, so the 802.11a and 802.11b/g standards do not support it.

140. C. Time Division Multiple Access (TDMA) is a communication technique that splits a frequency into multiple time slots, enabling it to carry multiple data streams. Commonly used in 2G cellular systems, the major U.S. carriers no longer use it in their 3G systems. Code Division Multiple Access (CDMA), Global System for Mobile Communications (GSM), and Long-Term Evolution (LTE) are alternative communications techniques that are currently used by the major U.S. cellular carriers.

141. B. The IEEE 802.11b standard calls for DSSS signal modulation. All of the other standards listed call for Orthogonal Frequency-Division Multiplexing (OFDM) encoding.

142. D. By placing a unidirectional antenna against an outside wall, you can limit network access to users inside the structure. Unidirectional antennae provide greater signal strength than omnidirectional antennae, enabling their signals to penetrate more interior walls. It is possible to focus a unidirectional antenna to a wider or narrower signal pattern.

143. B. The IEEE 802.11n and 802.11ac standards support a transmission technique called Multiple Input, Multiple Output (MIMO), which combines the bandwidth of multiple data streams to achieve greater throughput. IEEE 802.11n and 802.11ac do use the 5 GHz band, but this in itself does not yield greater transmission speeds. The specified standards do not call for the use of DSSS modulation, nor do they sacrifice range for speed. In fact, 802.11n and 802.11ac networks can achieve greater ranges than the previous technologies.

144. A, C, D. The 5 GHz frequency has 23 channels available in the United States, while the 2.4 GHz frequency has only 11. Many household devices, such as cordless telephones, use the 2.4 GHz frequency band, but relatively few devices use the 5 GHz band. Higher frequencies typically support faster transmission speeds, because with all other conditions equal, they can carry more data in the same amount of time. The 5 GHz frequency typically has a shorter range than 2.4 GHz, because it is less able to penetrate barriers.

145. A, C. Upgrading the devices to 802.11n will enable them to use the 5 GHz band and evade the traffic generated by the surrounding networks. Configuring the devices to use the 5 GHz band will provide many more channels to choose from and will avoid the interference from the surrounding 2.4 GHz networks. The type of encryption that a wireless network uses has no bearing on the ability of the devices to avoid the interference generated by surrounding networks. Suppressing SSID broadcasts will not help the devices to connect to the network. Upgrading the firmware on the devices is not likely to have any effect on the connection problems when they are the result of interference from other networks.

146. C. The 802.11ac standard defines a wireless LAN running at a speed of up to 1.3 gigabits per second (Gbps). None of the other ratified 802.11 standards call for speeds beyond 600 megabits per second (Mbps). No currently ratified standard enables speeds of 2.6 Gbps.

147. D. The Multiple Input, Multiple Output (MIMO) technology introduced in the IEEE 802.11n standard enables wireless devices to transmit and receive signals using multiple antennae simultaneously. The Multiuser MIMO (MU-MIMO) variant defined in the 802.11ac standard advances this technique by enabling wireless devices to transmit multiple frames to different users simultaneously, using multiple antennae. Carrier-Sense Multiple Access with Collision Avoidance (CSMA/CA) is a Media Access Control (MAC) mechanism used by all 802.11 networks. Channel bonding is a wireless networking technique that combines channels to increase bandwidth.

148. A. Wireless LAN regulations call for 22 MHz channels in the 2.4 GHz band that are spaced 5 MHz apart, which means that they overlap. Channels 1, 6, and 11 are the only three channels that are distant enough from each other not to overlap. Therefore, they do not interfere with each other. Channels 1, 6, and 11 do not differ from the other channels in their bandwidth or their transmission range. Each wireless device can be set to use only one channel. Therefore, channels 1, 6, and 11 cannot all be the default setting.

149. C. Wireless networks using equipment based on the IEEE 802.11n standard can span indoor distances of up to 175 feet at speeds up to 600 Mbps. An 802.11ac network can run at faster speeds—up to 1.3 Gbps—but it is limited to approximately 115-foot distances. Networks using 802.11g equipment can span 150 feet, but they run at only a maximum of 54 Mbps. An 802.11a network cannot span more than 75 feet, and it runs at no more than 54 Mbps.

150. A. Multiple Input, Multiple Output (MIMO) calls for the use of two or more antennae, enabling wireless devices to effectively multiplex signals, thereby increasing their transmission speeds. Time Division Multiple Access (TDMA) is a communication technique that splits a frequency into multiple time slots, enabling it to carry multiple data streams. A Personal Area Network (PAN) provides communication among devices associated with a single person, such as smartphones. Ant+ is a wireless protocol that is typically used to monitor data gathered by sensors, such as those in cardiac pacemakers.

151. D. Using a technique called channel bonding, the 802.11ac standard defines the combination of up to eight 20 MHz channels, for a total possible channel width of 160 MHz. The 802.11n standard can bond up to two channels, for a 40 MHz width. Earlier standards are limited to a single 20 MHz channel.

152. A, E. The IEEE 802.11a and IEEE 802.11ac standards can use the 5 GHz band only. IEEE 802.11b and IEEE 802.11g can use the 2.4 GHz band only. IEEE 802.11n can use either the 2.4 or 5 GHz band.

153. B. The IEEE 802.11ac standard provides the greatest possible throughput, at up to 1.3 Gbps. The 802.11n standard runs at speeds up to 600 Mbps. The 802.11a and 802.11g standards run at up to 54 Mbps. The 802.11b standard runs at up to 11 Mbps.

154. D. Only the 802.11n standard defines wireless LAN devices that can support both 2.4 GHz and 5 GHz frequencies. The 802.11a and 802.11ac standards use only 5 GHz, and the 802.11b and 802.11g standards use only 2.4 GHz.

155. C. The 802.11ac standard supports Multiple Input, Multiple Output (MIMO) through the use of up to eight antennae on a single device. 802.11n is the only earlier 802.11 standard that supports MIMO, but it can only use a maximum of four antennae.

156. C. The Service Set Identifier (SSID) is the name that you use when connecting to a wireless network. A Basic Service Set (BSS) refers to the wireless network itself, consisting of a single AP and a number of clients. An Extended Service Set (ESS) consists of two or more BSSs, using multiple APs. The Basic Service Set Identifier (BSSID) is the MAC address of the Access Point associated with a BSS.

157. A, B. Devices conforming to the IEEE 802.11a and 802.11g standards can only use a single 20 MHz channel. IEEE 802.n devices can use channel bonding to join two channels together and achieve an aggregate channel width of 40 MHz. IEEE 802.11ac devices can bond up to eight channels, for an aggregate width of 160 MHz.

158. A. Wireless range extenders are physical layer devices that receive signals from Wireless Access Points (WAPs) and network adapters and retransmit them, enabling devices to connect that are farther apart than the network would normally support. Because the extenders do not process the packets in any way, but just retransmit the signals, they do not operate at any layer above the physical.

159. C. WPA2 is the most secure of the wireless protocols, providing the greatest degree of network device hardening. WiFi Protected Access (WPA) was created to replace the insecure Wired Equivalent Privacy (WEP) protocol, and WPA2 was created to replace the Temporal Key Integrity Protocol (TKIP) used in the first version of WPA with Advanced Encryption Standard (AES). Extensible Authentication Protocol (EAP) is a framework for the encapsulation of authentication messages.

160. B. WPA was created to replace the insecure Wired Equivalent Privacy (WEP) protocol and used Temporal Key Integrity Protocol (TKIP) with the RC4 cipher for encryption. Counter Mode with Cipher Block Chaining Message Authentication Code Protocol (CCMP) with Advanced Encryption Standard (AES) is an encryption protocol that is used with the WiFi Protected Access II (WPA2) security protocol. Extensible Authentication Protocol (EAP) is a framework for the encapsulation of authentication messages. EAP is used on wireless networks and point-to-point connections and supports dozens of different authentication methods, including Transport Layer Security (TLS). It is not the encryption protocol used with WPA. Terminal Access Controller Access Control System Plus (TACACS+) is a protocol designed to provide AAA services for networks with many routers and switches.

161. B. WiFi Protected Access (WPA) was created to replace the insecure Wired Equivalent Privacy (WEP) protocol and used the Temporal Key Integrity Protocol (TKIP) with the RC4 cipher. WPA was replaced by WPA2, which uses Counter Mode with Cipher Block Chaining Message Authentication Code Protocol (CCMP) with Advanced Encryption Standard (AES) for encryption. Extensible Authentication Protocol (EAP) is a framework for the encapsulation of authentication messages.

162. A. WiFi Protected Access (WPA) is a wireless security protocol that was designed to replace the increasingly vulnerable Wired Equivalent Privacy (WEP). WPA added an encryption protocol called Temporal Key Integrity Protocol (TKIP). This too became vulnerable, and WPA2 was introduced, which replaced TKIP with the stronger CCMP-Advanced Encryption Standard (CCMP-AES). Extensible Authentication Protocol and 802.1X do not provide encryption.

163. D. TKIP augments the existing WEP encryption key, making it longer, enabling it to be changed for every packet, and enabling WPA to be deployed without replacing network adapter or Access Point (AP) hardware. TKIP does continue to support the use of PSKs.

164. B. To use the WPA2 protocol with a PSK, the client and the Access Point (AP) must both be configured with the same passphrase. The base key, the serial number, and the MAC address are all components that WPA2 uses to generate the encryption key for each packet.

165. C. A replay attack is one in which an attacker utilizes the encryption key found in a previously captured packet to gain access to the network. Because TKIP generates a unique encryption key for every packet, it prevents this type of attack from being successful.

166. C. WiFi Protected Access (WPA) is a wireless security protocol that was designed to replace the increasingly vulnerable Wired Equivalent Privacy (WEP). WPA added an encryption protocol called Temporal Key Integrity Protocol (TKIP). This too became vulnerable, and WPA2 was introduced, which replaced TKIP with CCMP-Advanced Encryption Standard (CCMP-AES).

167. A. Wired Equivalent Privacy (WEP) was the first wireless LAN security protocol to achieve widespread use in commercial products. This protocol was soon found to be vulnerable to attack, and it was replaced by WiFi Protected Access (WPA), which added a stronger encryption protocol called Temporal Key Integrity Protocol (TKIP). This too became vulnerable, and WPA2 was introduced, which replaced TKIP with a different type of encryption, called CCMP-Advanced Encryption Standard (CCMP-AES).

168. A. WPA2 adds Counter Mode Cipher Block Chaining Message Authentication Code Protocol - Advanced Encryption Standard (CCMP-AES), a new symmetric key encryption algorithm that strengthens the protocol's security. Multiple-input and multiple-output (MIMO) is a multiplexing technology added to the IEEE 802.11n standard, not to WPA2. Wired Equivalent Protocol (WEP) is the predecessor to WPA; it is not part of WPA2. Temporal Key Integrity Protocol (TKIP) is the encryption algorithm used in the first version of WPA; it was not added in the second version.

169. B. WiFi Protected Access 2 (WPA2) will provide the maximum security for the wireless network, in part because it uses long encryption keys that change frequently. Wired Equivalent Privacy (WEP) has a number of vulnerabilities, including short, unchanging encryption keys, that make it less secure than WPA. IPsec is a network layer security standard that does not provide the security needed for IEEE 802.11 wireless networks. Transport Layer Security (TLS) is a protocol that encrypts data exchanged by web servers and clients at the application layer. It does not provide adequate security for wireless LANs. Layer 2 Tunneling Protocol (L2TP) is a virtual private networking protocol; it does not provide adequate security for wireless networks.

170. C. Counter Mode with Cipher Block Chaining Message Authentication Code Protocol (CCMP) with Advanced Encryption Standard (AES) is an encryption protocol that is used with the WiFi Protected Access II security protocol. WPA was created to replace the insecure Wired Equivalent Privacy (WEP) protocol, and WPA2 was created to replace the Temporal Key Integrity Protocol (TKIP) used in the first version of WPA. Extensible Authentication Protocol (EAP) is a framework for the encapsulation of authentication messages.

171. A. Counter Mode with Cipher Block Chaining Message Authentication Code Protocol (CCMP) with Advanced Encryption Standard (AES) is an encryption protocol that is used with the WiFi Protected Access II (WPA2) security protocol. WPA was created to replace the insecure Wired Equivalent Privacy (WEP) protocol, and WPA2 was created to replace the Temporal Key Integrity Protocol (TKIP) used in the first version of WPA. Extensible Authentication Protocol (EAP) is a framework for the encapsulation of authentication messages. EAP is used on wireless networks and point-to-point connections and supports dozens of different authentication methods, including Transport Layer Security (TLS). It is not the encryption protocol used with WPA2. Terminal Access Controller Access Control System Plus (TACACS+) is a protocol designed to provide AAA services for networks with many routers and switches.

172. C. Wired Equivalent Protocol (WEP) and WiFi Protected Access II (WPA2) are both wireless security protocols that control access to the network and provide encryption, using protocols like Advanced Encryption Standard (AES). These protocols do not provide authentication services, however. Extensible Authentication Protocol (EAP) is a framework for the encapsulation of authentication messages. Its many variants provide support for the use of smartcards and other authentication factors, such as biometrics, in addition to traditional passwords.

173. C, D. WPA-Enterprise, also known as WPA-802.1X, can use the Extensible Authentication Protocol (EAP) to support various types of authentication factors and requires a Remote Authentication Dial-In User Service (RADIUS) server. WPA-Personal, also known as WPA-PSK (Pre-Shared Key), is intended for small networks and does not require RADIUS.

174. A. WPA-Personal, also known as WPA-PSK, is intended for small networks and requires a PSK. WPA-Enterprise, also known as WPA-802.1X, uses the Extensible Authentication Protocol (EAP) to support various types of authentication factors and requires a Remote Authentication Dial-In User Service (RADIUS) server.

175. A. TKIP uses the RC4 stream cipher for its encryption. Advanced Encryption Standard (AES) is used with CCMP on version 2 of the WiFi Protected Access (WPA2) security protocol, not version 1 (WPA), which uses TKIP. Secure Hash Algorithm (SHA) is a file hashing algorithm, not used for wireless network encryption.

176. C. CCMP (Counter Mode Cipher Block Chaining Message Authentication Code Protocol), is based on the Advanced Encryption Standard (AES) and is the encryption protocol used with the WiFi Protected Access II (WPA2) security protocol on wireless networks. CCMP is not used with version 1 of the WPA protocol or with Wired Equivalent Privacy. 802.1X is an authentication protocol, not used for encryption.

177. C. CCMP (Counter Mode Cipher Block Chaining Message Authentication Code Protocol) is based on the Advanced Encryption Standard (AES) and is the encryption protocol used with the WiFi Protected Access II (WPA2) security protocol on wireless networks. CCMP is not based on the Temporal Key Integrity Protocol (TKIP), which uses RC4 as its stream cipher. 802.1X is an authentication protocol, not used for encryption.

178. D. An SSID that is not broadcast is not detectable by clients, so you must type it in manually. Security protocols are also not detectable, so you must configure the clients to use the same protocol you selected on the client.

179. A. Wired Equivalent Privacy (WEP) was one of the first commercially available security protocols for wireless LANs, but it was soon found to be easily penetrated and was replaced by WiFi Protected Access (WPA) and then WPA2. Extensible Authentication Protocol (EAP) is a framework for the encapsulation of authentication messages.

180. B. WPA uses the Temporal Key Integrity Protocol (TKIP) for encryption. It does not use Advanced Encryption Standard (AES), which eventually replaced TKIP in WPA2. Secure Hash Algorithm (SHA) and Message Digest 5 (MD5) are both file hashing algorithms, not used for wireless network encryption.

181. B. Wired Equivalent Privacy (WEP), which was one of the first commercially successful security protocols for wireless LANs, enabled administrators to choose between open and shared key authentication. The open option enabled clients to connect to the network with an incorrect key. The shared option required the correct key, but it also exposed the key to potential intruders. The correct option is to not use WEP at all, as it was easily penetrated and subsequently replaced by WiFi Protected Access (WPA) and then WPA2. Extensible Authentication Protocol (EAP) is a framework for the encapsulation of authentication messages. None of the other three provides a choice between open and shared key options.

182. B. WiFi Protected Access (WPA) is a wireless security protocol that was designed to replace the increasingly vulnerable Wired Equivalent Privacy (WEP). WPA added an encryption protocol called Temporal Key Integrity Protocol (TKIP). This too became vulnerable, and WPA2 was introduced, which replaced TKIP with an Advanced Encryption Standard protocol (CCMP-AES).

183. D. Open System Authentication enables any user to connect to the wireless network without a password, which actually increases the security of the protocol. This is because most WEP implementations use the same secret key for both authentication and encryption. An intruder that captures the key during the authentication process might therefore penetrate the data encryption system as well. By not using the key for authentication, you reduce the chances of the encryption being compromised. The use of short, 40-bit encryption keys was mandated at the time by U.S. export restrictions. Later protocols used keys at least 128 bits long. The initialization vector (IV) is a randomized value appended to the shared secret to ensure that the cipher never encrypts two packets with the same key. The relatively short IV that WEP uses results in a reasonable probability of key duplication, if an attacker captured a sufficient number of packets. Shared secrets that do not change provide attackers with more time to crack them. The lack of a mechanism to automatically change WEP shared secrets weakened the protocol considerably.

184. C. WPA2 was introduced when the earlier version of WiFi Protected Access (WPA) was determined to be increasingly vulnerable to attack. WPA used an encryption protocol called Temporal Key Integrity Protocol (TKIP). WPA2 replaced TKIP with an Advanced Encryption Standard (CCMP-AES) protocol.

185. B. Wired Equivalent Privacy (WEP) was one of the first commercially available security protocols for wireless LANs. WEP requires 24 bits of the encryption key for the initialization vector, substantially weakening the encryption. WEP was soon found to be easily penetrated and was replaced by WiFi Protected Access (WPA) and then WPA2. Extensible Authentication Protocol (EAP) is a framework for the encapsulation of authentication messages.

186. B, C, D. Roaming from one AP to another without interruption requires that the APs all use the same SSID, the same security protocol, and the same passphrase. The APs will not function properly if they have the same IP address.

187. D. The 5G cellular network specification calls for maximum theoretical download speeds of 10 gigabits per second, although the actual speed realized will be less.

188. A, B. 5G networks can operate on three frequency bands—low, medium, and high—with the high frequencies having the fastest speeds and reduced range. 4G devices cannot function on 5G networks.

189. C. IEEE 802.1X is a standard that defines a port-based Network Access Control (PNAC) mechanism used for authentication on wireless and other networks. IEEE 802.11ac and 802.11n are standards defining the physical and data link layer protocols for wireless networks. IEEE 802.3x is one of the standards for wired Ethernet networks.

190. A, D. Disabling SSID broadcasting prevents a wireless network from appearing to clients. The clients must specify the SSID to which they want to connect. MAC address filtering is a form of Access Control List (ACL) that is maintained in the AP and contains the addresses of devices that are to be permitted to access the network. Both of these mechanisms make it more difficult for unauthorized devices to connect to the Access Point (AP). Kerberos is an authentication protocol used by Active Directory, and relocating the AP to a DMZ will not resolve the problem.

191. D. WAPs use the layer 2 MAC addresses coded into devices in their ACLs. Usernames, IP addresses, and device names can easily be impersonated.

192. A, B. There are two methods for identifying packets carrying voice traffic: by recognizing the MAC address of the sending system as a voice device, and by recognizing packets that have already been tagged as voice VLAN traffic. It is not possible to identify voice traffic using IP addresses or DNS names.

Chapter 3: Network Operations

1. A, E. An SNMP-based network management system consists of three components: a management console software product installed on a network computer, agents installed on the devices you want to manage, and MIBs for each of the agents. Because the switches support SNMP management and already have agents, they have MIBs also. Therefore, all you have to do is purchase the network management software and install the console on a network computer.

2. A, C. SNMP version 1, the original version, used an unencrypted community string. SNMPv2 added better security, but it was not backward compatible with the version 1 community string. A revised version, SNMP2c, added backward compatibility. SNMPv3, the one most often seen today, includes more advanced security and does not use a community string.

3. B, C. SNMP is not the name of a network management product; it is just the name of the protocol that provides a framework for the interaction of the various components in a network management product. SNMPv1 uses a community string, but SNMPv2 does not. The interim version SNMPv2c retains the community string from version 1 in place of the new version 2 security system. When you see a network interface adapter, switch, router, access point, or other device that purports to be managed or that claims to have network management capabilities, this usually means that the device includes an SNMP agent. Most of today's network management products do support SNMPv3. In addition, many network management products that implement SNMPv3 also include support for the earlier, unprotected versions, such as SNMPv1 and SNMPv2c.

4. C. The utility shown in the figure is the Windows Event Viewer, which displays the contents of the system, application, setup, and security logs, as well as others.

5. A. Syslog is a standard designed to facilitate the transmission of log entries generated by a device or process, such as the sendmail Simple Network Management Protocol (SMTP) server, across an Internet Protocol (IP) network to a message collector, called a syslog server. Netstat is a program that displays status information about a system's network connections; it does not provide logging services. SNMP is a protocol that carries network management information from agents to a central console; it was not created specifically for sendmail. The Cache Array Routing Protocol (CARP) enables proxy servers to exchange information; it does not provide logging services.

6. A. The best solution is to implement Simple Network Management Protocol (SNMP). This includes a management console, agents, and Management Information Bases (MIBs). SNMP allows you to track statistical network information (historical and current) and produce reports for baseline analysis and troubleshooting. Some SNMP products also allow you to track software distribution and metering. Protocol analyzers are best used for troubleshooting problems in real time and are not used for software distribution and metering. Performance Monitor is a tool that allows you to track performance statistics for one system at a time and does not include software distribution and metering. There is no such product as a network traffic monitor.

7. A. Security Information and Event Management (SIEM) is a product that combines two technologies: security event management (SEM) and security information management (SIM). Together, the two provide a combined solution for gathering and analyzing information about a network's security events. Simple Network Management Protocol (SNMP) is a technology that gathers information about managed devices.

8. C, D. Security Information and Event Management (SIEM) is a product type that combines two technologies: security event management (SEM) and security information management (SIM). Together, the two provide a combined solution for gathering and analyzing information about a network's security events. Simple Network Management Protocol (SNMP) is a technology that gathers information about managed devices. Syslog is a standard designed to facilitate the transmission of log entries generated by a device or process, such as the sendmail Simple Network Management Protocol (SMTP) server, across an Internet Protocol (IP) network to a message collector, called a syslog server. Neither SNMP nor syslog capabilities are typically included in SIEM products.

9. D. A protocol analyzer provides information about network traffic; it does not interpret web server logs. Most web servers maintain logs that track the Internet Protocol (IP) addresses and other information about all hits and visits. The logs are stored as text files and contain a great deal of information, but in their raw form, they are difficult to interpret. Therefore, it is common practice to use a traffic analysis application that reads the log files and displays their contents in a more user-friendly form, such as tables and graphs.

10. B. A baseline is a record of a system's performance under real-world operating conditions, captured for later comparison as conditions change. The workload during a baseline capture should be genuine, not simulated or estimated.

11. B. If a server is using all of its network bandwidth, then the most logical solution is to add more. You can do this by installing a second network adapter and connecting it to a different subnet. The other solutions could conceivably address the problem, but their success is less likely.

12. A. Performance monitoring utilities typically provide statistics on the Central Processing Unit (CPU), memory, network, and disk usage, but not computer temperature monitoring.

13. A. Every syslog message includes a single-digit severity code. Code 0 is the most severe, indicating an emergency that has rendered the system unusable. Severity code 1 is an alert message, indicating that immediate action is needed. Severity code 2 is a critical condition message, and code 3 is an error condition. Code 4 is a warning message.

14. B. Every syslog message includes a single-digit severity code. Severity code 1 is an alert message, indicating that immediate action is needed. Code 0 is the most severe, indicating an emergency that has rendered the system unusable. Severity code 2 is a critical condition message, and code 3 is an error condition. Code 4 is a warning message.

15. D. Every syslog message includes a single-digit severity code. Code 6 indicates that the message is purely informational. Code 0 is the most severe, indicating an emergency that has rendered the system unusable. Severity code 2 is a critical condition message, and code 4 is a warning message. Code 7 is used strictly for debugging.

16. D. Messages that SNMP agents send to consoles when an event needing attention occurs are called traps. *Alerts* and *notifications* are terms for the messages that the console sends to administrators. A ping is an Internet Control Message Protocol (ICMP) echo request message sent from one TCP/IP computer to another.

17. D. The term *rollback* refers to the process of uninstalling or downgrading an update patch; it has nothing to do with monitoring a network interface. An interface monitor does typically display the number of transmission errors that occur on an interface, the amount of the available bandwidth that the interface is using, and the number of packets that have been dropped due to errors or discards.

18. B, C. The packet drops displayed by an interface monitor are caused by errors, such as malformed or unreadable packets, or discards, which are packets that are dropped because they are destined for another interface. Resets and overflows are not reasons for packet drops.

19. D. Performance baselines characterize hardware performance, so the OS update history would be of little or no use for future comparisons. A baseline typically consists of CPU, memory, disk, and network performance statistics.

20. C, D. Logs frequently contain sensitive information, so securing them with the appropriate permissions is an essential part of log management. Logs also can grow to overwhelm the storage medium on which they are stored, so cycling is a technique for managing log size by configuring it to delete the oldest record each time a new one is added. Rollback and utilization are not log management tasks.

21. B. In SIEM, forensic analysis is a process of searching logs on multiple computers for specific information based on set criteria and time periods. Data aggregation is a process of consolidating log information from multiple sources. Correlation is the process of linking logged events with common attributes together. Retention is the long-term storage of log data.

22. A. In SIEM, data aggregation is a process of consolidating log information from multiple sources. Forensic analysis is a process of searching logs on multiple computers for specific information based on set criteria and time periods. Correlation is the process of linking logged events with common attributes together. Retention is the long-term storage of log data.

23. C. When individual packets in a data stream are delayed, the resulting connectivity problem is called jitter. Although this condition might not cause problems for asynchronous applications, real-time communications, such as Voice over Internet Protocol (VoIP) or streaming video, can suffer interruptions, from which the phenomenon gets its name. Latency describes a generalized delay in network transmissions, not individual packet delays. Attenuation is the weakening of a signal as it travels through a network medium. A bottleneck is a condition in which all traffic is delayed, due to a faulty or inadequate component.

24. **A, B, C, D.** All of these occurrences are malfunctions on a full-duplex Ethernet network. Runt frames occur when a network interface generates packets that are smaller than the 64-byte minimum allowable length. Giants occur when frames are larger than the 1518-byte maximum allowable length. Collisions are normal on a half-duplex network, but on a full-duplex network, collisions are considered to be malfunctions. Late collisions occur when network cables are too long.

25. **B, C.** Jitter is a connectivity problem on wired networks that is caused by individual packets that are delayed due to network congestion, different routing, or queuing problems. When individual packets in a data stream are delayed, the resulting connectivity problem is called jitter. While this condition might not cause problems for asynchronous applications, such as email and instant messaging, real-time communications, such as Voice over Internet Protocol (VoIP) or streaming video, can suffer intermittent interruptions, from which the phenomenon gets its name.

26. **A.** Syslog is a standard designed to facilitate the transmission of log entries generated by a device or process, such as the sendmail SMTP server, across an Internet Protocol (IP) network to a message collector, called a syslog server. Network Monitor (Netmon) is a protocol analyzer. Netstat is a program that displays status information about a system's network connections. Top is a utility to display system processes. None of these provide logging services.

27. **A.** System logs document the server's startup activities and the ongoing status of its services and device drivers. When a problem occurs or the server's status changes, the system logs can provide information about what happened and when.

28. **D.** On a Windows system, information about services, including successful service starts and failures, is recorded in the System event log. The Application, Security, and Setup logs typically do not contain this type of information.

29. **A.** Performance Monitor is a Windows application that can create logs of specific system and network performance statistics over extended periods. Such a log created on a new computer can function as a baseline for future troubleshooting. Event Viewer is a Windows application for displaying system log files; it cannot create a performance baseline. Syslog is a log compilation program originally created for Unix systems; it does not create performance baselines. Network Monitor is a protocol analyzer. Although it can capture a traffic sample that can function as a reference for future troubleshooting efforts, this ability cannot be called a performance baseline.

30. **B.** Humidity prevents the buildup of static electricity that can cause discharges that damage equipment. Humidity levels of 50 percent or lower can cause equipment to be susceptible to electrostatic shock.

31. **C.** When you enable audit policies on Windows systems, you can specify whether to audit successful or failed events (or both), including access attempts. This audit information is recorded in the Security event log. The System, Application, and Setup events logs typically do not record both successful and failed access attempts.

32. C. A Management Information Base (MIB) is the database on an SNMP console where all of the information gathered from the network is stored. A trap is an alert message that SNMP agents send to the network management console. Syslog is a standard for message logging components. Security Information and Event Management (SIEM) is a combination tool that uses information gathered from logs and network devices to provide a real-time analysis of the network's security condition.

33. A. Runts and giants are typically the result of a network interface adapter malfunction. Runt frames occur on an Ethernet network when a network interface generates packets that are smaller than the 64-byte minimum allowable length. Giants occur when frames are larger than the 1518-byte maximum allowable length. Collisions are normal on a half-duplex network, but runts and giants are not. Late collisions occur when network cables are too long. Electromagnetic interference is a likely cause of Cyclic Redundancy Check (CRC) errors, but not runts and giants.

34. C. Electromagnetic interference is the likely cause of CRC errors. A network interface adapter malfunction can cause runts and giant frames. Collisions are normal on a half-duplex network, but CRC errors are not. Late collisions occur when network cables are too long, but they do not cause CRC errors.

35. C. The netstat utility can display the incoming and outgoing packets for a specific network interface, as well as other statistics, depending on the operating system. Top and ifconfig are Unix/Linux utilities, and Nbtstat is a Windows tool.

36. B. Netflow is a network traffic monitoring feature first introduced in Cisco routers in 1996. Netmon, Netstat, and Nbtstat are all operating system utilities, not router features.

37. E. Jumbo frames is a feature supported by some Ethernet implementations that enable frames to exceed the 1500-byte maximum data payload defined in the IEEE 802.3 standard. Runt frames, giant frames, Cyclical Redundancy Check (CRC) errors, and encapsulation errors are all types of errors typically reported in network interface diagnostics.

38. D. Cyclical Redundancy Checks (CRCs) are faults that occur when data does not arrive at its destination in the same state as when it was sent; they are not Simple Network Management Protocol (SNMP) components. Management Information Bases (MIBs), traps, and Object Identifiers (OIDs) are all components of a Simple Network Management Protocol (SNMP) implementation.

39. C. Unless there is a specific known threat at the datacenter location, radon is not one of the environmental factors that typically can affect equipment uptime and that needs to be monitored. Temperature, humidity, flooding, and static electricity, however, are factors that should be monitored in a datacenter, as variations of these elements can result in equipment damage and downtime.

40. A, D. Link states and Dijkstra's algorithm are used by link state routing protocols, such as Open Shortest Path First (OSPF) and Intermediate System – Intermediate System (IS – IS). Routing Information Protocol (RIP) and Enhanced Interior Gateway Routing Protocol (EIGRP) are distance vector protocols, which do not use link states. Border Gateway Protocol (BGP) is a distance vector protocol and an exterior (not interior) gateway protocol.

41. A. A network map is a depiction of network devices, not drawn to scale, with additional information added, such as IP addresses and link speeds. In most cases, network maps are automatically created by a software product, such as Nmap, that scans the network and creates a display from the information it discovers. The term *network diagram* is most often used to refer to a manually created document containing pictograms of network devices, with lines representing the connections between them. The diagram might be roughly similar to the actual layout of the site, but it is usually not drawn to scale. A cable diagram is a precise depiction of the cable runs installed in a site. Often drawn on an architect's floor plan or blueprint, the cable diagram enables network administrators to locate specific cables and troubleshoot connectivity problems. A Management Information Base (MIB) is a component of a network management system that is based on the Simple Network Management Protocol (SNMP) and contains information about only one device; it does not depict all of the devices on the network.

42. C. A cable diagram is a precise depiction of the cable runs installed in a site. Often drawn on an architect's floor plan or blueprint, the cable diagram enables network administrators to locate specific cables and troubleshoot connectivity problems. A network map is a depiction of network devices, not drawn to scale, with additional information added, such as IP addresses and link speeds. In most cases, network maps are automatically created by a software product, such as Nmap, that scans the network and creates a display from the information it discovers. The term *network diagram* is most often used to refer to a manually created document containing pictograms of network devices, with lines representing the connections between them. The diagram might be roughly similar to the actual layout of the site, but it is usually not drawn to scale. A Management Information Base (MIB) is a component of a network management system that is based on the Simple Network Management Protocol (SNMP) and contains information about only one device; it does not depict all of the devices on the network.

43. C. Devices designed to fit into IT equipment racks typically have heights measured in units. One unit equals 1.75 inches. Most rack-mounted devices are one (1U), two (2U), or four units (4U) tall.

44. A. A reputable cable installer should supply a cable diagram that indicates the locations of all the cable runs on a plan or blueprint of the site. You should be able to use this to determine which ports go with which wall plates. A busy cable installer is unlikely to remember specific details about an installation performed years ago. Using a tone generator and locator is an effective way to associate ports and wall plates, but it can be incredibly time consuming and is certainly not the easiest method. A cable certifier can test the cable run for faults, measure its length, and perform other tests, but it cannot specify which wall plate goes with which port, unless you entered that information yourself earlier.

45. B. ISO 19770 is a family of IT Asset Management (ITAM) standards that defines procedures and technology for the management of software and related assets in a corporate infrastructure. ISO 19770-2 defines the creation and use of SWID tags, which are XML files containing management and identification information about a specific software product. The other standards define other ITAM elements, such as compliance with corporate governance (ISO 19770-1) and resource utilization measurement (ISO 19770-4).

46. A, C. A large enterprise network will—at minimum—have demarcation points for telephone services and a connection to an Internet Service Provider's (ISP's) network. In many cases, these services will enter the building in the same equipment room that houses the backbone switch. This room is then called the Main Distribution Frame (MDF). An Intermediate Distribution Frame (IDF) is the location of localized telecommunications equipment such as the interface between the horizontal cabling and the backbone. Mean Time Between Failure (MTBF) and Remote Desktop Protocol (RDP) are not locations of network wiring.

47. C. Rack diagrams use vertical measurement called units, each of which is 1.75 inches. Most rack-mounted devices are one (1U), two (2U), or four units (4U) tall.

48. A. The symbol shown in the figure represents a network switch. It is not a router, a hub, or a gateway.

49. A, C. A physical diagram, in this case, represents the actual physical locations of the cable drops connected to the patch panels. A logical diagram uses artificial divisions that correspond to the organization of the company.

50. C. IDF diagrams should be based on an architect's plan whenever possible so that actual lengths and locations of cable runs can be documented. In situations where an architect's plan is not available, a detailed sketch, drawn to scale, can be acceptable. Photographs, models, and reports are impractical for this purpose.

51. A, B, C. MDF and IDF documentation should take into account the power sources available at the locations, the HVAC equipment needed to keep the temperature and humidity levels under control, and the distances the cable runs must span. This type of documentation is typically used for installation and troubleshooting purposes, so the costs of components and services are unnecessary and can be covered elsewhere.

52. C. Patch panel ports and wall plates should be labeled when the cable runs are attached to them. Labeling them at any earlier time can result in cable runs being connected incorrectly.

53. A. A large enterprise network will—at minimum—have demarcation points for telephone services and a connection to an Internet Service Provider's (ISP's) network. In many cases, these services will enter the building in the same equipment room that houses the backbone switch. This room is then called the Main Distribution Frame (MDF). An Intermediate Distribution Frame (IDF) is the location of localized telecommunications equipment such as the interface between the horizontal cabling and the backbone. Mean Time Between Failure (MTBF), Remote Desktop Protocol (RDP), and Memorandum of Understanding (MOU) are not locations of network wiring.

54. A, B, C, D. A change management team typically requires thorough documentation for all requested changes, specifying exactly what is needed; how the change will affect the current workflow, both to the direct recipients of the change and the rest of the organization; and what ramifications might come from the change.

55. B. A single rack unit is 1.75 inches, or 44.5 mm. Option A, 1.721 inches, is the height used for many components that are one rack unit tall, leaving a small space between components for easy insertion and removal.

56. A, C. The change management team is usually not responsible for tasks directly involved in the implementation of the changes they approve. Therefore, they would not be the ones to notify users exactly when the change will take place or document the procedure afterward. They would, however, be responsible for providing a maintenance window, during which the change must occur, and authorizing any downtime that would be needed.

57. E. ISO 19770 is a family of IT Asset Management (ITAM) standards that defines procedures and technology for the management of software and related assets in a corporate infrastructure. ISO 19770-5 provides a general overview of the functions provided by the standards and their benefits to an IT infrastructure. The other standards define other ITAM elements, such as compliance with corporate governance (ISO 19770-1), creation and use of software ID (SWID) tags (ISO 19770-2), and resource utilization measurement (ISO 19770-4).

58. D. The standard unit height for IT equipment racks is 1.75 inches, which is the equivalent of one unit. Four units would therefore be 7 inches.

59. D. The main purpose of a wiring schematic is to indicate where cables are located in walls and ceilings. A physical network diagram identifies all of the physical devices and how they connect together. Asset management is the identification, documentation, and tracking of all network assets, including computers, routers, switches, and so on. A logical network diagram contains addresses, firewall configurations, Access Control Lists (ACLs), and other logical elements of the network configuration.

60. B, D. A physical network diagram identifies all of the physical devices and how they connect together. A logical network diagram contains IP addresses, firewall configurations, Access Control Lists (ACLs), and other logical elements of the network configuration. Both physical and logical network diagrams can be created automatically or manually. It is the physical network diagram that contains the information needed to rebuild the network from scratch.

61. B. The symbol shown in the figure represents a network router. It is not a switch, a hub, or a gateway.

62. C. An Intermediate Distribution Frame (IDF) is the location of localized telecommunications equipment such as the interface between a horizontal network, which connects to workstations and other user devices, and the network backbone. A large enterprise network will typically have demarcation points for telephone services and a connection to an Internet Service Provider's (ISP's) network. In many cases, these services will enter the building in the same equipment room that houses the backbone switch. This room is then called the Main Distribution Frame (MDF). Mean Time Between Failure (MTBF), Service Level Agreements (SLAs), and Memoranda of Understanding (MOUs) are not locations of network wiring.

63. C. The standard width of an equipment rack in a data center is 19 inches. Network hardware manufacturers use this width when designing rack-mountable components.

64. C. The symbol shown in the figure represents a network hub. It is not a switch, a router, or a gateway.

65. A. Datacenters typically mount components in racks, 19-inch-wide and approximately 6-foot-tall frameworks in which many networking components are specifically designed to fit. A rack diagram is a depiction of one or more racks, ruled out in standardized

1.752-inch rack units, and showing the exact location of each piece of equipment mounted in the rack. Network maps, wiring schematics, and logical diagrams are documents that define the relationships between components, not their precise locations. A business continuity plan describes the organization's disaster prevention and recovery policies. An audit and assessment report is a document—often prepared by a third party—that summarizes the organization's security posture.

66. B. Network diagrams typically specify device types and connections, but network maps can also include IP addresses, link speeds, and other information. Network maps diagram the relationships between devices, and provide information about the links that connect them, but they are not drawn to scale and usually do not indicate the exact location of each device. Although universal accessibility would be desirable, there are individuals who should not have access to network maps and other documentation, including temporary employees and computer users not involved in IT work. A network map includes all networking devices, not just cable runs and endpoints.

67. B. A Material Safety Data Sheet (MSDS) is a document created by manufacturers of chemical, electrical, and mechanical products, specifying the potential dangers and risks associated with them, particularly in regard to exposure or fire. A properly documented network should have MSDS documents on file for all of the chemical and hardware products used to build and maintain it. MSDSs can be obtained from the manufacturer or the Environmental Protection Agency (EPA). Electrostatic discharges (ESDs), Non-Disclosure Agreements (NDAs), Bring Your Own Device (BYOD) policies, and standard operating procedures (SOPs) are not concerned with the chemical composition of cleaning compounds.

68. D. A privileged user agreement specifies the abilities and limitations of users with respect to the administrative accounts and other privileges they have been granted. Remote access policies specify when and how users are permitted to access the company network from remote locations. A Service Level Agreement (SLA) is a contract between a provider and a subscriber that specifies the guaranteed availability of the service. Acceptable Use Policies (AUPs) specify whether and how employees can utilize company-owned hardware and software resources.

69. A. Remote access policies specify when and how users are permitted to access the company network from remote locations. A Service Level Agreement (SLA) is a contract between a provider and a subscriber that specifies the guaranteed availability of the service. Acceptable Use Policies (AUPs) specify whether and how employees can utilize company-owned hardware and software resources. A privileged user agreement specifies the abilities and limitations of users with respect to the administrative accounts and other privileges they have been granted.

70. B. Acceptable Use Policies (AUPs) specify whether and how employees can utilize company-owned hardware and software resources. AUPs typically specify what personal work employees can perform, what hardware and software they can install, and what levels of privacy they are permitted when using company equipment. A Service Level Agreement (SLA) is a contract between a provider and a subscriber. A Non-Disclosure Agreement (NDA) specifies what company information employees are permitted to discuss outside the company. A Bring Your Own Device (BYOD) policy specifies how employees can connect their personal devices to the company network.

71. D. A Bring Your Own Device (BYOD) policy specifies the personal electronics that employees are permitted to use on the company network and documents the procedures for connecting and securing them. A Service Level Agreement (SLA) is a contract between a provider and a subscriber that specifies the percentage of time that the contracted services are available. Acceptable Use Policies (AUPs) specify whether and how employees can utilize company-owned hardware and software resources. A Non-Disclosure Agreement (NDA) specifies what company information employees are permitted to discuss outside the company.

72. C. A Non-Disclosure agreement (NDA) specifies what company information employees are permitted to discuss outside the company. A Service Level Agreement (SLA) is a contract between a provider and a subscriber that specifies the percentage of time that the contracted services are available. Acceptable Use Policies (AUPs) specify whether and how employees can utilize company-owned hardware and software resources. A Memorandum of Understanding (MOU) is a document outlining an agreement between two parties that precedes the signing of a contract. A Bring Your Own Device (BYOD) policy specifies the personal electronics that employees are permitted to use on the company network and documents the procedures for connecting and securing them.

73. A, B, C, D. The longer the password, the more difficult it is to guess. Corporate policies typically require passwords of a minimum length. A larger character set also makes a password more difficult to guess, so requiring upper- and lowercase, numeric, and special characters is common. Changing passwords forces the attack process to start over, so policies typically require frequent password changes and prevent users from reusing passwords.

74. C. Requiring unique passwords can prevent users from thwarting a password change policy by reusing the same passwords over and over. Password length, password character sets, and password change interval maximums can do nothing to thwart a frequent password change policy.

75. A, C, D. Account lockout threshold specifies the number of incorrect logon attempts that are allowed before the account is locked out. Account lockout duration is the amount of time that an account remains locked out. Reset account lockout threshold counter specifies the amount of time before the number of incorrect attempts is reset to zero. Account lockout policies typically do not include a setting that regulates the amount of time allowed between logon attempts.

76. B. Account lockouts limit the number of incorrect passwords that a user can enter. This prevents intruders from using a brute force attack to crack the account by trying password after password. After a specified number of incorrect tries, the account is locked for a specified length of time or until an administrator unlocks it.

77. C, D. Data in motion and data in transit are the terms used to describe network traffic. Data in use describes endpoint actions, and data at rest describes data storage.

78. A. Data in use is the data loss prevention term used to describe endpoint access, such as a user loading data into an application. Data in motion is the term used to describe network traffic. Data at rest describes data storage. Data in process is not one of the standard data loss prevention terms.

79. B. Data at rest describes data that is currently in storage while not in use. Data in motion is the term used to describe network traffic. Data in use describes endpoint actions working with the data, and data on disk is not one of the standard data loss prevention terms.

80. A. Data online is not one of the standard data loss prevention terms. Data at rest is a data loss prevention term that describes data that is currently in storage while not in use. Data in motion is the term used to describe network traffic. Data in use describes endpoint actions.

81. D. On-boarding and off-boarding are identity management processes in which users are added or removed from an organization's identity and access management (IAM) system. This grants new users the privileges they need to use the network, modifies their privileges if they change positions, and revokes privileges when they leave the company. On-boarding and off-boarding are not data loss prevention, incident response, inventory management, disaster recovery, or business continuity processes.

82. C. On-boarding and off-boarding are identity management processes in which users are added or removed from an organization's identity and access management (IAM) system. Off-boarding revokes a user's privileges when he or she leaves the company. The term *off-boarding* does not refer to cluster management, disconnecting a switch, or retiring workstations.

83. A. After a change is requested, approved, scheduled, and performed, everyone involved should be notified, and the entire process should be documented for future reference.

84. B, C, D. The U.S. government controls exports of sensitive software and other technology as a means to maintain national security interests and foreign policy agreements. Three U.S. agencies have the authority to issue export licenses: the Department of State, the Department of Commerce, and the Department of the Treasury. Individual software developers do not have the authority to impose their own export controls.

85. B. While incident response policies might include the process of responding to an incident and identifying and documenting its cause, the primary function of incident response policies is to ensure that the same incident does not happen again.

86. D. Material Safety Data Sheets (MSDSs) are documents created by manufacturers of chemical, electrical, and mechanical products, which specify the potential risks and dangers associated with them, particularly in regard to flammability and the possibility of toxic out-gassing. A properly documented network should have MSDS documents on file for all of the chemical and hardware products used to build and maintain it. MSDSs can be obtained from the manufacturers or the Environmental Protection Agency (EPA). Electrostatic discharges (ESDs), Non-Disclosure Agreements (NDAs), and Bring Your Own Device (BYOD) policies are not concerned with the dangers inherent in building contents.

87. D. Software and hardware upgrades are typically not part of an AUP, because they are handled by the company's IT personnel. An AUP for a company typically includes a clause indicating that users have no right to privacy for anything they do using the company's computers, including email and data storage. An AUP usually specifies that the company is the sole owner of the computer equipment and any proprietary company information stored on it or available through it. The AUP also prohibits the use of its computers or network for any illegal practices, typically including spamming, hacking, or malware introduction or development.

88. A, B. Clauses regarding company property, including the copyrights and patents for the work performed for the company, typically do appear in an AUP but not in the privacy clause. This information would be more likely to appear in an ownership clause. The privacy clause commonly explains that the company has the right to access and monitor anything stored on its computers.

89. D. Once a network infrastructure has been partially or completely destroyed, it is no longer a matter of incident response; the responsibility passes over to the disaster recovery plan, which requires a different set of policies. Stopping, containing, and remediating an incident are all considered incident response policies.

90. A, B, D. Attacks, hardware failures, and crashes are all events that can be addressed by incident response policies that define what is to be done to analyze and remediate the problem. An electrical fire is typically not something that would be addressed by an IT department's incident response team; it is a job for trained firefighters. Once the fire is out, the company's response falls under the heading of disaster recovery.

91. B. The process of adding a user's personal device and allowing it to access the company network is called on-boarding. Removing the personal device from the network would be called off-boarding. In-band and out-of-band are terms defining methods for gaining administrative access to a managed network device.

92. C. A fail closed policy for the datacenter specifies that any open doors should lock themselves in the event of an emergency. To support this policy, the datacenter will have to have a self-contained fire suppression system, which uses devices such as fire detectors and oxygen-displacing gas systems.

93. B, C, D, E. While securing the area to prevent contamination of evidence, documenting the scene with photographs or video, collecting any evidence that might be visible, and cooperating with the authorities are tasks that are likely to be in the company's incident response policy. Turning off the server most certainly would not, because this could disturb or delete evidence of the crime.

94. A. Although all of the options are characteristics of a strong password, the definition of a complex password is one that expands the available character set by using a mixture of upper- and lowercase letters, numerals, and symbols. The larger the character set used to create passwords, the more difficult they are to guess.

95. A. A history requirement in a password policy prevents users from specifying any one of their most recently used passwords. Although creating passwords using the names of relatives and historical figures is not recommended, it is not something that is easy to prevent. Each user maintains his or her own password history; there is no conflict with the passwords of other users.

96. C. A brute-force password attack is one in which the perpetrator tries as many passwords as possible in an effort to guess or deduce the right one. Account lockout policies are intended to prevent this type of attack by limiting the number of incorrect password attempts.

97. A, B, D. A brute-force password attack is one in which the perpetrator tries as many passwords as possible in an effort to guess or deduce the right one. Password length and complexity policies produce passwords that are harder to guess, making the attack statistically less likely to succeed. Account lockout policies are intended to prevent brute-force attacks by limiting the number of incorrect password attempts. Password history policies do not help to prevent brute-force attacks.

98.   C. An IT asset disposal policy typically includes procedures to be performed on assets that have reached the end of their system life cycle and that are ready for final processing. This includes the wiping of all data, the completion of inventory records, and the possible recycling of the asset. The policy assumes that all data requiring preservation has already been preserved before the asset is submitted for disposal. Therefore, data preservation procedures are not needed at this phase.

99.   A. A Service Level Agreement (SLA) is a contract between a provider and a subscriber that specifies the percentage of time that the contracted services are available. Acceptable Use Policies (AUPs) specify whether and how employees can utilize company-owned hardware and software resources. A Non-Disclosure Agreement (NDA) specifies what company information employees are permitted to discuss outside the company. A Bring Your Own Device (BYOD) policy specifies the personal electronics that employees are permitted to use on the company network and documents the procedures for connecting and securing them.

100.   D. An ISP provides subscribers with access to the Internet. The applications that the subscriber uses on the internet are typically not part of the SLA. An SLA does typically specify exactly what services the ISP will supply, what equipment the ISP will provide, and the technical support services the ISP will furnish as part of the agreement.

101.   A. A Service Level Agreement (SLA) is a contract between a provider and a subscriber that specifies the percentage of time that the contracted services are available. Mean Time Between Failure (MTBF) is a hardware specification that estimates how long a particular component can be expected to function. Acceptable Use Policies (AUPs) specify whether and how employees can utilize company-owned hardware and software resources. Mean Time to Repair (MTTR) specifies the average time it will take to repair a specific hardware company when it malfunctions.

102.   A, B, D. The technical support clause of an SLA typically defines the type of support that the provider will furnish, the time service for support, and the amount of support that is included in the contract, as well as the cost for additional support. An SLA will typically guarantee service ability in the form of a percentage, but this refers to problems at the provider's end and is not a customer technical support matter.

103.   A. Traffic shaping is a technique for prioritizing packets by buffering packets that are not time sensitive for later transmission. You can use this technique to give VoIP packets priority over other types of traffic. Load balancing can conceivably improve the performance of a server, but it cannot help to relieve traffic congestion on the Internet link. The traffic congestion is on the Internet connection, not the LAN, so upgrading to Gigabit Ethernet will not help. SNMP is a protocol used by network management products; it will not relieve the traffic congestion problem.

104.   B. A server with dual power supplies can run in one of two modes: redundant or combined. In redundant mode, both power supplies are capable of providing 100 percent of the power needed by the server. Therefore, the server can continue to run if one power supply fails, making it fault tolerant. In combined mode, both power supplies are needed to provide the server's needs, so a failure of one power supply will bring the server down. Individual mode and hot backup mode are not terms used for this purpose.

105. C. If a server is connected to two building circuits, it can continue to function if the breaker for one circuit trips and remains uncorrected. All of the other options will bring the server down unless additional redundancies are in place.

106. C. Windows Server Backup cannot back up data to magnetic tape drives. However, it can back up to local hard disks, optical disks, and remote shares.

107. C. RAID is a technology for storing data on multiple hard disk drives, providing fault tolerance, increased performance, or both. The various RAID levels provide different levels of functionality and have different hardware requirements. RAID 5 combines disk striping with distributed storage of parity information, which provides fault tolerance. The parity information enables the array to rebuild a disk whose data has been lost. RAID 0 uses data striping only (blocks written to each disk in turn), which does not provide any form of fault tolerance. RAID 1 provides fault tolerance through disk mirroring. RAID 10 creates fault-tolerant mirrored stripe sets.

108. B. Power redundancy is a general term describing any fault tolerance mechanism that enables equipment to continue functioning when one source of power fails. A UPS is a device that uses battery power, not a generator. The term *dual power supplies* refers to the power supply units inside a computer, not a separate generator. The term *redundant circuits* refers to multiple connections to the building's main power, not to a generator.

109. C. Redundant Array of Independent Disks (RAID) is a technology for storing data on multiple hard disk drives, providing fault tolerance, increased performance, or both. The various RAID levels provide different levels of functionality and have different hardware requirements. RAID 5 combines disk striping (blocks written to each disk in turn) with distributed storage of parity information, for fault tolerance. RAID 0 provides data striping only. RAID 1 provides disk mirroring. RAID 10 creates mirrored stripe sets.

110. C. Mean Time Between Failures (MTBF) is a hardware specification used to predict the approximate lifetime of a component. It does not refer to any type of fault tolerance mechanism. Port aggregation, clustering, and Uninterruptible Power Supplies (UPSs) are all mechanisms that provide fault tolerance in the event of network adapter, server, and power failures, respectively.

111. B. Load balancing is a method of distributing incoming traffic among multiple servers. Network Address Translation (NAT) is a routing mechanism that enables computers on a private network to share one or more public Internet Protocol (IP) addresses. It is therefore not a load balancing method. Domain Name System (DNS) round-robin, multilayer switching, and content switching are all mechanisms that enable a server cluster to share client traffic.

112. A. A content switch is an application layer device, which is what renders it capable of reading the incoming Hypertext Transfer Protocol (HTTP) and Hypertext Transfer Protocol Secure (HTTPS) messages. HTTP is an application layer protocol. Multilayer switches do not operate above the transport layer. Failover clustering and (DNS) round-robin are both techniques for distributing incoming traffic without actually processing it.

113. B, D. It is an online UPS that runs devices using battery power all the time so that there is no gap to the power supplied to devices during a failure. It is a standby UPS that switches devices to battery power during a main power failure. Both online and standby UPSs provide only enough power for an orderly shutdown of the devices.

114. B. Online UPSs run devices from the battery all the time, while simultaneously keeping the battery charged. There is therefore no switchover gap when a power failure occurs. Online UPSs do not necessarily run longer than standby UPSs, nor do they provide more protection again power spikes and sags. Both online and standby UPSs can be managed devices.

115. A, B, D, E. Bonding, link aggregation, port aggregation, and Network Interface Card (NIC) teaming are all terms for the same basic technology, in which the bandwidth of multiple network adapter connections is joined to speed up transmissions. The technology also enables the network communication to continue if one of the adapters should be disconnected. Clustering refers to combining servers into a single unit, not network adapters.

116. B. In a network load balancing cluster, each computer is referred to as a host. Other types of clusters use other terms. For example, in a failover cluster, each computer is called a node. The terms *server* and *box* are not used in clustering.

117. C. Highly available systems often have redundant failover components that enable them to continue operating even after a failure of a router, switch, hard disk, server, or other component. Backups, snapshots, and cold sites can all contribute to a system's high availability, but they do not function automatically.

118. A. Redundant Array of Independent Disks (RAID) is a technology for storing data on multiple hard disk drives, providing fault tolerance, increased performance, or both. The various RAID levels provide different levels of functionality and have different hardware requirements. RAID 0 uses data striping only (blocks written to each disk in turn), which does not provide any form of fault tolerance. RAID 1 provides disk mirroring, RAID 5 combines disk striping with distributed storage of parity information, and RAID 10 creates mirrored stripe sets—these three levels all provide fault tolerance.

119. A, B. A high availability virtual IP address implementation is when multiple servers are identified by a single address, enabling all of the servers to receive incoming client traffic. In the case of server clustering and network load balancing arrangements, the cluster itself has a unique name and IP address, separate from those of the individual servers. Clients address themselves to the cluster, not to one of the servers in the cluster. NAT is not a high availability technology, and NIC teaming does not use virtual IP addresses.

120. C. Cold, warm, and hot backup sites differ in the hardware and software they have installed. A cold site is just a space at a remote location. The hardware and software must be procured and installed before the network can be restored. It is therefore the least expensive and takes the most time. A warm site has hardware in place that must be installed and configured. A hot site has all of the necessary hardware already installed, configured, and ready to go in the event of a disaster. A warm site is more expensive than a cold site, and a hot site is the most expensive and takes the least amount of time to be made operational.

121. D. A cloud site is the least expensive to implement. Cold, warm, and hot backup sites differ in the hardware and software they have installed, but they all require the maintenance of a facility for a new datacenter. A cold site is just a space at a remote location. The hardware and software must be procured and installed before the network can be restored. It is therefore the least expensive of the cold, warm, and hot options and takes the most time. A warm site has hardware in place that must be installed and configured. A hot site has all of the necessary hardware already installed, configured, and ready to go in the event of a disaster. A warm site is more expensive than a cold site, and a hot site is the most expensive and takes the least amount of time to be made operational. A cloud site is a virtual facility maintained with a cloud service provider. The cloud site does not require physical space or physical hardware, so it is therefore the least expensive.

122. B. The Recovery Time Objective (RTO) specifies the amount of time needed to restore a server from the most recent backup if it should fail. This time interval depends on the amount of data involved and the speed of the backup medium. A Recovery Point Objective (RPO) specifies how much data is likely to be lost if a restore from backups should be necessary. This figure is based on the frequency of the backups and the amount of new data generated by the system. Business contingency planning (BCP) is an umbrella term for procedures enacted to keep the organization functioning in the event of a disaster. A Management Information Base (MIB) is a database used by Simple Network Management Protocol (SNMP) systems.

123. B. Mean Time to Failure (MTTF) refers to devices that will eventually fail once and then be discarded, rather than repaired. Mean Time Between Failure (MTBF), Mean Time to Repair (MTTR), and Mean Down Time (MDT) all refer to devices that will eventually fail and then be repaired and reused.

124. A, D. If one of the server's power supplies fails, the other will continue to function. If the building's backup generator fails, the server will continue to run as long as the building still has outside power. If the UPS fails, the server will go down. If the breaker for the building power circuit trips, the server will run only as long as the UPS battery holds out.

125. B. UPSs can provide servers with battery backup power, but usually only for a few minutes, so that the servers can be powered down safely, without the potential for data corruption or loss. UPSs cannot keep servers running for two hours. UPSs can protect against power spikes, but that is not their primary function. A computer power supply failure will bring a server down, regardless of the presence of a UPS.

126. A, B, D. If one of the server's power supplies fails, the other will continue to function. If the UPS fails, the server will continue to use the power supply plugged into the wall socket. If the building's backup generator fails, the server will continue to run as long as the building still has outside power. If the breaker for the building power circuit trips, the server will run only as long as the UPS battery holds out.

127. A, B, C, D. If one of the server's power supplies fails, the other will continue to function. If one of the UPSs fails, the server will continue to run using the other. If one of the building power circuit breakers trips, the server will continue to run using the other one. If the building's backup generator fails, the server will continue to run as long as the building still has outside power.

128. C. The archive bit that backup software uses to perform incremental and differential jobs is a file attribute, so this is the most commonly used filter type. It is possible to filter files based on their names, their extensions, and their size, but these are not used as often as the archive file attribute.

129. A. Cold, warm, and hot backup sites differ in the hardware and software they have installed. A cold site is just a space at a remote location. The hardware and software must be procured and installed before the network can be restored. It is therefore the least expensive. A warm site has hardware in place that must be installed and configured. A hot site has all of the necessary hardware installed and configured. A warm site is more expensive than a cold site, and a hot site is the most expensive.

130. D. Load balancing refers to the distribution of traffic between two or more channels. Port aggregation combines ports into a single logical channel with a single Media Access Control (MAC) address and provides greater throughput. Port aggregation also provides fault tolerance in the event of a port failure.

131. D. A cluster is a group of computers configured with the same application that function as a single unit. The cluster can function as a fault tolerance mechanism by failing over from one server to the next, when necessary, or provide load balancing by distributing traffic among the servers.

132. B. NIC teaming enables you to combine the functionality of two Network Interface Cards (NIC) in one connection. However, when you configure a NIC team to use an active/passive configuration, one of the network adapters remains idle and functions as a fault tolerance mechanism. If the other NIC should fail, the passive NIC becomes active. In this configuration, NIC teaming does not provide load balancing, server clustering, or traffic shaping.

133. D. Redundant Array of Independent Disks (RAID) level 1 is a fault tolerance mechanism that is also known as disk mirroring. A storage subsystem writes data to two or more disks at the same time so that if a disk fails, the data remains available. Because data is written to the disks at the same time, this RAID level does not provide load balancing. NIC teaming balances a network traffic load among two or more Network Interface Cards (NICs), whereas server clustering and Domain Name Service (DNS) round-robin balance a traffic load among multiple servers.

134. D. Cold, warm, and hot backup sites are a disaster recovery mechanism that enables a network to be activated at a remote location when a catastrophe occurs. The temperature refers to the sites readiness to assume the role of the network. A cold site is just a space at a remote location. The hardware and software must be procured and installed before the network can be restored. A warm site has hardware in place that must be installed and configured. It takes less time to restore the network than at a cold site, but more than at a hot site. A hot site has all of the necessary hardware installed and configured. The network can go live as soon as the most recent data is restored.

135. A. Mean Time Between Failure (MTBF) specifies how long you can expect a device to run before it malfunctions. For a hard disk, this specification indicates the life expectancy of the device. A Service Level Agreement (SLA) and an Acceptable Use Policy (AUP) are not specifications associated with hard disk drives. Mean Time to Repair (MTTR) can conceivably be specified for a hard disk, but hard disk drives in a RAID array are typically replaced, not repaired.

136. B, D. Redundant Array of Independent Disks (RAID) is a technology for storing data on multiple hard disk drives, providing fault tolerance, increased performance, or both. The various RAID levels provide different levels of functionality and have different hardware requirements. RAID 1 provides disk mirroring, and RAID 10 creates mirrored stripe sets. Both provide fault tolerance by maintaining two copies of every stored file, for a usable disk space percentage of 50 percent. Some mirroring configurations store more than two copies of each file, for even less usable space. RAID 0 provides data striping only, with no fault tolerance. RAID 5 combines disk striping (blocks written to each disk in turn) with distributed storage of parity information, for fault tolerance with a usable disk space percentage of at least 66 percent.

137. D. Disk mirroring and disk duplexing both use multiple hard disk drives to store duplicate copies of all data. However, disk duplexing calls for each disk to be connected to a separate controller so that the data remains available despite a disk failure or a disk controller failure.

138. B. Redundant Array of Independent Disks (RAID) is a technology for storing data on multiple hard disk drives, providing fault tolerance, increased performance, or both. The various RAID levels provide different levels of functionality and have different hardware requirements. RAID 1 provides disk mirroring for fault tolerance and requires two or more disk drives. RAID 0 provides data striping only, with no fault tolerance. RAID 5 combines disk striping (blocks written to each disk in turn) with distributed storage of parity information for fault tolerance, but it requires a minimum of three disk drives. RAID 10 creates mirrored stripe sets and requires at least four disk drives.

139. B, D. Redundant Array of Independent Disks (RAID) is a technology for storing data on multiple hard disk drives, providing fault tolerance, increased performance, or both. The various RAID levels provide different levels of functionality and have different hardware requirements. RAID 1 and RAID 10 both use disk mirroring to provide fault tolerance, which does not require parity data. RAID 0 uses data striping only (blocks written to each disk in turn), which does not provide any form of fault tolerance. RAID 5 combines disk striping with distributed storage of parity information.

140. C. Differential backups use the archive bit to determine which target files to back up. However, a differential backup does not reset the archive bit. Full backups do not pay attention to the archive bit, because they back up all of the files. A full backup, however, does clear the archive bit after the job is completed. Incremental backups also use the archive bit to determine which files have changed since the previous backup job. The primary difference between an incremental and a differential job, however, is that incremental backups clear the archive bit so that unchanged files are not backed up. There is no such thing as a supplemental backup job.

141. C. The generational media rotation system uses the terms *grandfather*, *father*, and *son* to refer to backup jobs that are run monthly, weekly, and daily. The jobs can be full, incremental, or differential, and the terms have nothing to do with whether the backup medium is a hard disk, optical, or any type of tape drive.

142. A, C. Windows Server Backup can perform full backups and incremental backups. It does not support differential backups, and there is no backup job called a supplemental.

143. A. A snapshot is a read-only copy of a data set taken at a specific moment in time. By creating a snapshot and then backing it up, you can be sure that no data corruption has occurred due to version skew. A hot site is an alternative network location in which all hardware and software is installed and ready. Incrementals and differentials are types of backup jobs.

144. D. Version skew can occur when a data set changes while a system backup is running. A file written to a directory that has already been backed up will not appear on the backup media, even though the job might still be running. This can result in unprotected files, or worse, data corruption. A snapshot is a read-only copy of a data set taken at a specific moment in time. By creating a snapshot and then backing it up, you can be sure that no data corruption has occurred due to version skew. Incrementals and differentials are types of backup jobs, and iteration is not a specific storage technology.

145. C. An incremental backup is a job that backs up all of the files that have changed since the last backup of any kind. Therefore, to restore a system that failed on Monday at noon, you would have to restore the most recent full backup from the previous Wednesday and the incrementals from Thursday, Friday, Saturday, and Sunday.

146. B. An autochanger is a robotic device containing one or more removable media drives, such as magnetic tape or optical disk drives. The robotic mechanism inserts and removes media cartridges automatically so that a backup job can span multiple cartridges, increasing its overall capacity.

147. D. An incremental backup is a job that backs up all of the files that have changed since the last backup of any kind. Therefore, to restore a system that failed on Tuesday at noon, you would have to restore the most recent full backup from the previous Saturday and the incrementals from Sunday, Monday, and Tuesday morning.

148. B. A differential backup is a job that backs up all the files that have changed since the last full backup. Therefore, to restore a system that failed on Tuesday at noon, you would have to restore the most recent full backup from the previous Wednesday and the most recent differential from Monday.

149. C. Data is stored on tape drives in a linear fashion. Once you write backup data to a tape, you cannot selectively replace individual files. When you perform a restore job, you might have to restore the most recent full backup, followed by incremental backups, which over-writes some of the full backup files with newer ones. Hard disk drives are random access devices, meaning that individual files can be written to and read from any location on the disk. When you perform incremental backup jobs to a hard disk, the software can restore data using any version of each file that is available. Data capacity, transfer speed, and block size are not relevant.

150. C. Simple Network Monitoring Protocol (SNMP) is a means of tracking the performance and functionality of network components. Software or firmware components called agents are embedded in network devices and communicate with a central monitoring console. SNMP does not provide fault tolerance. An Uninterruptible Power Supply (UPS) is a battery backup device that enables a computer to continue functioning in the event of a power failure. Redundant Array of Independent Disks (RAID) level 1 is a disk mirroring mechanism that provides fault tolerance by maintaining duplicate copies of all stored data. Clustering is a mechanism by which multiple servers function as a single unit, running the same application, so that if a server should fail, the others continue to function.

151. B. A PDU for a datacenter performs the same basic function as an office power strip, but it typically has a larger power input. It does not necessarily have more outlets or a larger power output.

152. A, D. A backup of a firewall's state includes its configuration as well as other elements, such as templates and policies. The state therefore contains more data than the configuration.

153. D. Hydrofluorocarbon (HFC) 125 is a heat-absorbing gas that is frequently used for fire suppression systems. Many large datacenters include HFC-125 total flooding fire suppression systems because the products resulting from the flame retardation process are less toxic than carbon dioxide and do not damage electric and electronic equipment as water and foam do.

154. A, B, D. CMR is a technique in which routers transmit data packets using multiple routes to the destination. This provides load balancing and improved performance by spreading the transmission among multiple paths and a measure of fault tolerance because a failure of one route only endangers part of the data. Data encapsulation is not involved in the CMR process.

155. C. FHRPs provide a fault tolerant default gateway for network hosts by automatically failing over to an alternative router address in the event of a router failure. Protocols such as Virtual Router Redundancy Protocol (VRRP) and Hot Standby Router Protocol (HSRP) create a virtual router that hosts use for their default gateway. The virtual router contains the addresses of multiple physical routers, to which it sends packets transmitted by the hosts. This provides fault tolerance in the event that a router fails, and in some cases provides load balancing as well. FHRPs do not affect the hosts' IP addresses, subnet masks, or DNS server addresses.

156. D. FHRPs provide a fault tolerant default gateway for network hosts by automatically failing over to an alternative router address in the event of a router failure. The Reverse Address Resolution Protocol (RARP) is a deprecated Internet Protocol (IP) address assignment protocol; it is not an FHRP. Common Address Redundancy Protocol (CARP), Virtual Router Redundancy Protocol (VRRP), and Hot Standby Router Protocol (HSRP) are all FHRPs.

157. C. This redundant switch arrangement can result in broadcast storms, which are caused by packets being read by multiple switches as originating on different networks. The result is endless circulation of packets from switch to switch.

158. A, B, D. Configuring the router to split incoming packets between the two firewalls provides load balancing and a resulting performance increase. If one firewall should fail, the parallel arrangement enables the other one to take over the processing of all incoming packets, providing fault tolerance. Two firewalls in parallel does not provide additional security.

159. A, D. In an active-active configuration, servers can balance the incoming client load between them. Because the active servers are all servicing clients, the overall performance of the cluster is increased. Both active-active and active-passive configurations provide fault tolerance. Data encapsulation is not a factor in either configuration.

160. D. Access to the Internet can be interrupted by a failure on the Internet Service Provider's (ISP's) network, by a failure on the Wide Area Network (WAN) provider's network, or by a router failure on the local network. Building redundancy into all of these elements is the best way to ensure continuous access to the Internet.

Chapter 4: Network Security

1. B, E, F. Servers that must be accessible both from the internal network and from the Internet are typically located in an area of the enterprise called a screened subnet, a perimeter network, or a demilitarized zone (DMZ). This area is separated from both the Internet and the internal network by firewalls, which prevents unauthorized Internet users from accessing the internal network. Intranet is another term for the internal network. Edge Gateway Protocol (EGP) is a type of routing protocol, and stateless is a type of firewall; neither apply to this definition.

2. C. Windows networks that use AD DS authenticate clients using the Kerberos protocol, in part because it never transmits passwords over the network, even in encrypted form. Remote Authentication Dial-In User Service (RADIUS) is an authentication, authorization, and accounting service for remote users connecting to a network. Windows does not use it for internal clients. WiFi Protected Access 2 (WPA2) is a security protocol used by wireless Local Area Network (LAN networks. It is not used for AD DS authentication. Extensible Authentication Protocol-Transport Layer Security (EAP-TLS) is a remote authentication protocol that AD DS networks do not use for internal clients.

3. C, D. Multifactor authentication combines two or more authentication methods and reduces the likelihood that an intruder would be able to successfully impersonate a user during the authentication process. A password and a retinal scan is an example of a multifactor authentication system. A smartcard and a PIN, which is the equivalent of a password, is an example of multifactor authentication because it requires users to supply something they know and something they have. Multifactor authentication refers to the proofs of identity a system requires, not the number of servers used to implement the system. Therefore, the use of a Remote Authentication Dial-In User Service (RADIUS) server is not an example of multifactor authentication. A system that requires two passwords is not an example of multifactor authentication, because an attacker can compromise one password as easily as two. A multifactor authentication system requires two different forms of authentication.

4. A. The Extensible Authentication Protocol (EAP) is the only Windows remote authentication protocol that supports the use of authentication methods other than passwords, such as smartcards. MS-CHAPv2 is a strong remote access authentication protocol, but it supports password authentication only. Users cannot use smartcards. The Challenge Handshake Authentication Protocol (CHAP) is a relatively weak authentication protocol that does not support the use of smartcards. The Password Authentication Protocol (PAP) supports only cleartext passwords, not smartcards.

5. B. Multifactor authentication combines two or more authentication methods, requiring a user to supply multiple credentials. This reduces the likelihood that an intruder would be able to successfully impersonate a user during the authentication process. The term multifactor does not refer to the number of resources, devices, or groups with which the user is associated.

6. C, D. Accounting and auditing are both methods of tracking and recording a user's activities on a network, such as when a user logged on and how long they remained connected. Authentication is the confirmation of a user's identity, and authorization defines the type of access granted to authenticated users.

7. A. Authentication is the process of confirming a user's identity. Passwords are one of the authentication factors commonly used by network devices. Authorization defines the type of access granted to authenticated users. Accounting and auditing are both methods of tracking and recording a user's activities on a network, such as when a user logged on and how long they remained connected.

8. A. Authentication is the process of confirming a user's identity. Fingerprints and other biometric readers are one of the authentication factors commonly used by network devices. Authorization defines the type of access granted to authenticated users. Accounting and auditing are both methods of tracking and recording a user's activities on a network, such as when a user logged on and how long they remained connected.

9. A. Kerberos is a security protocol used by Active Directory that employs a system of tickets to authenticate users and other network entities without the need to transmit credentials over the network. IEEE 802.1X does authenticate by transmitting credentials. Temporal Key Integrity Protocol (TKIP) and Lightweight Directory Access Protocol (LDAP) are not authentication protocols.

10. C. Auditing of authentication activities can record both successful and unsuccessful logon attempts. Large numbers of logon failures can indicate attempts to crack passwords. Auditing tracks the time of authentication attempts, sometimes enabling you to detect off-hours logons that indicate an intrusion. Auditing does not record the passwords specified during authentications, so it cannot identify patterns of unsuccessful guesses.

11. A. Authentication is the process of confirming a user's identity. Smartcards are one of the authentication factors commonly used by network devices. Authorization defines the type of access granted to authenticated users. Accounting and auditing are both methods of tracking and recording a user's activities on a network, such as when a user logged on and how long they remained connected.

12. A. Multifactor authentication combines two or more authentication methods and reduces the likelihood that an intruder would be able to successfully impersonate a user during the authentication process. A password (something you know) and a retinal scan (something you are) is an example of a multifactor authentication system. A smartcard and a PIN, which is the equivalent of a password, is another example of multifactor authentication because it requires users to supply something they know and something they have. Multisegment, multimetric, and multifiltered are not applicable terms in this context.

13. A. Network Access Control (NAC) is a mechanism that defines standards of equipment and configuration that systems must meet before they can connect to the network. Lightweight Directory Access Protocol (LDAP) provides communication between directory service entities. Remote Authentication Dial-In User Service (RADIUS) is an authentication, authorization, and accounting service for remote users connecting to a network. Temporal Key Integrity Protocol (TKIP) with the RC4 cipher is an encryption protocol used on wireless networks running the WiFi Protected Access (WPA) security protocol.

14. C. SSO uses one set of credentials and requires the user to supply them only once to gain access to multiple resources. Same sign-on also uses a single set of credentials, with one password, but the user must perform individual logons for each resource. Neither SSO nor same sign-on calls for multifactor authentication.

15. C. Biometrics is a type of authentication factor that uses a physical characteristic that uniquely identifies an individual, such as a fingerprint or a retinal pattern. Biometrics is therefore best described as something you are, as opposed to something you know, something you have, or something you do.

16. B. Something you have refers to a physical possession that serves to identify a user, such as a smartcard. This type of authentication is typically used as part of a multifactor authentication procedure because a smartcard or other physical possession can be lost or stolen. A fingerprint would be considered something you are, a password is something you know, and a finger gesture is something you do.

17. D. Terminal Access Controller Access Control System Plus (TACACS+) is a protocol designed to provide Authentication, Authorization, and Accounting (AAA) services for networks with many routers and switches, enabling administrators to access them with a single set of credentials. It was not designed to provide AAA services for wireless networks, Active Directory, or remote dial-in users.

18. B, C. A PIN, like a password, is something you know, and a thumbprint, or any other biometric factor, is something you are. An example of something you have would be a smartcard, and an example of something you do would be a finger gesture.

19. D. The act of drawing on the screen with your finger is a gesture, which is an example of something you do. A PIN or a password is something you know; a thumbprint, or any other biometric factor, is something you are; and a smartcard is an example of something you have.

20. D. Something you do refers to a physical action performed by a user, such as a finger gesture, which helps to confirm his or her identity. This type of authentication is often used as part of a multifactor authentication procedure because a gesture or other action can be imitated. A fingerprint would be considered something you are, a password is something you know, and a smartcard is something you have.

21. C. Something you know refers to information you supply during the authentication process, such as a password or PIN. This is the most common type of authentication factor because it cannot be lost or stolen unless the user violates security policies. A fingerprint would be considered something you are, a finger gesture is something you do, and a smartcard is something you have.

22. A. Something you are refers to a physical characteristic that uniquely identifies an individual, such as a fingerprint or other form of biometric. This type of authentication is often used as part of a multifactor authentication procedure because a biometric element can conceivably be compromised. A finger gesture would be considered something you do, a password is something you know, and a smartcard is something you have.

23. B. NAC is a set of policies that define security requirements that clients must meet before they are permitted to connect to a network. 802.1X is a basic implementation of NAC. Remote Authentication Dial-In User Service (RADIUS) and Terminal Access Controller Access Control System Plus (TACACS+) are Authentication, Authorization, and Accounting (AAA) services. They are not NAC implementations themselves, although they can play a part in their deployment. Lightweight Directory Access Protocol (LDAP) provides directory service communications.

24. C. An 802.1X transaction involves three parties: the supplicant, which is the client attempting to connect to the network; the authenticator, which is a switch or access point to which the supplicant is requesting access; and the authentication server, which is typically a Remote Authentication Dial-In User Service (RADIUS) implementation that verifies the supplicant's identity. There is no party to the transaction called an authorizing agent.

25. D. An 802.1X transaction involves three parties: the supplicant, which is the client attempting to connect to the network; the authenticator, which is a switch or access point to which the supplicant is requesting access; and the authentication server, which is typically a Remote Authentication Dial-In User Service (RADIUS) implementation that verifies the supplicant's identity. The supplicant is not involved in issuing certificates.

26. C. An 802.1X transaction involves three parties: the supplicant, which is the client attempting to connect to the network; the authenticator, which is a switch or access point to which the supplicant is requesting access; and the authentication server, which is typically a Remote Authentication Dial-In User Service (RADIUS) implementation that verifies the supplicant's identity. The authenticator is not involved in issuing certificates.

27. C. The authentication server role is typically performed by a Remote Authentication Dial-In User Service (RADIUS) server. In an 802.1X transaction, the supplicant is the client attempting to connect to the network, the authenticator is a switch or access point to which the supplicant is requesting access, and the authentication server verifies the client's identity.

28. B, C. Remote Authentication Dial-In User Service (RADIUS) and Terminal Access Controller Access Control System Plus (TACACS+) are both services that provide networks with AAA. 802.1X provides only authentication, and Lightweight Directory Access Protocol (LDAP) provides communication between directory service entities.

29. A. Remote Authentication Dial-In User Service (RADIUS) was originally conceived to provide AAA services for Internet Service Providers (ISPs), which at one time ran networks with hundreds of modems providing dial-up access to subscribers. Terminal Access Controller Access Control System Plus (TACACS+) is a protocol that was designed to provide AAA services for networks with many routers and switches, but not for dial-up connections. Kerberos and Lightweight Directory Access Protocol (LDAP) are not AAA services.

30. A. Remote Authentication Dial-In User Service (RADIUS) uses User Datagram Protocol (UDP) ports 1812 and 1813 or 1645 and 1646 for authentication, whereas Terminal Access Controller Access Control System Plus (TACACS+) uses Transmission Control Protocol (TCP) port 49.

31. B. Terminal Access Controller Access Control System Plus (TACACS+) is a protocol designed to provide AAA services for networks with many routers and switches, enabling administrators to access them with a single set of credentials. Remote Authentication Dial-In User Service (RADIUS) provides AAA services, but not for routers and switches. Kerberos and Lightweight Directory Access Protocol (LDAP) are not AAA services.

32. C. Authorization is the process of determining what resources a user can access on a network. Typically, this is done by assessing the user's group memberships. Authentication is the process of confirming a user's identity. Accounting is the process of tracking a user's network activity. Access control is the creation of permissions that provide users and groups with specific types of access to a resource.

33. A. Authentication is the process of confirming a user's identity by checking credentials, such as passwords, ID cards, or fingerprints. Authorization is the process of determining what resources a user can access on a network. Accounting is the process of tracking a user's network activity. Access control is the creation of permissions that provide users and groups with specific types of access to a resource.

34. B. Accounting is the process of tracking a user's network activity, such as when the user logged on and logged off and what resources the user accessed. Authentication is the process of confirming a user's identity by checking credentials. Authorization is the process of determining what resources a user can access on a network. Access control is the creation of permissions that provide users and groups with specific types of access to a resource.

35. B, D. In a public key infrastructure, data encrypted with a user's public key can only be decrypted with the user's private key, and data encrypted with a user's private key can only be decrypted with the user's public key. This enables the system to provide both message encryption and nonrepudiation. If data encrypted with a user's public key could be decrypted with that same public key, the system would provide no security at all. If data encrypted with a user's private key could be decrypted with that same private key, the user could only send secure messages to him- or herself.

36. A. A Remote Authentication Dial-In User Service (RADIUS) server can provide Authentication, Authorization, and Accounting (AAA) services for remote access servers. Intrusion Detection Systems (IDSs), Next-Generation Firewalls (NGFWs), and Network Attached Storage (NAS) devices do not provide authentication services.

37. B. The Integrity element of the CIA triad prevents data from being modified by unauthorized users. Confidentiality is protection against unauthorized viewing of data. Availability provides users with access to the data they need.

38. C. Systems that use local authentication have user accounts stored on the computer, enabling users to log on without the need for any network communication. Systems that use Remote Authentication Dial-In User Service (RADIUS) or Kerberos for authentication require network communication. A password and a retinal scan is an example of a multifactor authentication system, which might or might not be local.

39. B. A honeypot is a computer configured to function as bait for attackers, causing them to waste their time penetrating a resource that provides no significant access. A demilitarized zone (DMZ) is the part of a network where administrators locate servers that must be accessible from the Internet. A root guard provides protection to switch ports. Spoofing is an attack technique in which an intruder modifies packets to assume the appearance of another user or computer.

40. A. A honeypot or honeynet is a type of mitigation technique that takes the form of a computer or network configured to function as bait for attackers, causing them to waste their time penetrating a resource that provides no significant access.

41. D. Penetration testing is when an outside consultant is engaged to attempt an unauthorized access to protected network resources. Testing by an internal administrator familiar with the security barriers would not be a valid test. While having a consultant examine the network's security from within can be useful, this is not a penetration test. Computers or networks that are alluring targets for intruders are called honeypots or honeynets.

42. C, D. A network segment that is separated from the internal network by a firewall and exposed to the Internet is called a screened subnet, a demilitarized zone (DMZ), or a perimeter network. Administrators typically use a screened subnet for servers that must be accessible by outside users, such as web and email servers. For security reasons, domain controllers and Dynamic Host Configuration Protocol (DHCP) servers should be located on internal network segments.

43. B. A vulnerability is a weakness, whether in software or hardware, of which an exploit is designed to take advantage. Neither term is specific to hardware or software.

44. A. Security Information and Event Management (SIEM) is a product that combines two technologies: security event management (SEM) and security information management (SIM). Together, the two provide a combined solution for gathering and analyzing information about a network's security events. Simple Network Management Protocol (SNMP) is a technology that gathers information about managed devices. SEIM and SEM/SIM are not correct abbreviations for Security Information and Event Management.

45. B. Your supervisor's concern is that the disgruntled technician might take advantage of his access to devices and facilities to sabotage the network. When an individual takes advantage of information gathered during his or her employment, it is called an internal (or insider) threat. An external threat is one originating from a non-employee. Social engineering is a form of attack in which an innocent user is persuaded by an attacker to provide sensitive information via email or telephone. A logic bomb is a code insert placed into a legitimate software product that triggers a malicious event when specific conditions are met. War driving is an attack method that consists of driving around a neighborhood with a computer, scanning for unprotected wireless networks.

46. C. A zero-day vulnerability is a serious software problem with a potential for exploitation in a newly released software product. The vulnerability has not yet been discovered, addressed, or patched by the software's developer, but it has been discovered by potential attackers. A zero-day vulnerability is one that has not yet been patched or fixed.

47. B. The Common Vulnerabilities and Exposures (CVE) database is a resource that assigns identifier numbers to known security issues found in software products. By searching the database, Ralph can learn about the vulnerabilities that have already been found in the products he is evaluating. The Confidentiality - Integrity - Availability (CIA) triad lists important information security concepts, but it does not provide information about specific products. Stock Keeping Units (SKU) are product identifiers that do not involve security issues. Security Information and Event Management (SIEM) is a product that gathers and analyzes information about a network's security events, but it would not help Ralph discover vulnerabilities in the products he is evaluating.

48. C. Role-based access control works by assigning permissions to specific jobs or job roles. Each new user can then be associated with a role and receive the necessary permissions automatically. When a user leaves a job, removing them from their role revokes the permissions associated with it. Least privilege, zero trust, and defense in depth are all theoretical security concepts, but they are not descriptive of Alice's practice in this regard.

49. C. Least privilege is the practice of only providing users with the permissions they need to perform their designated tasks and no more. For her standard activities, Alice is given an account that does not have administrative permissions, because she does not need those permissions to perform standard tasks. The administrative account has the additional permissions needed for Alice to perform administrative tasks. The intention is for Alice to use that account only for those administrative tasks. Zero-day is a type of vulnerability; multifactor authentication calls for users to supply two identifying factors; defense in depth refers to the use of multiple security mechanisms to provide additional protection. None of these three options refers to the use of multiple user accounts.

50. D. Lateral movement is when a user gains basic access to a network by legitimate means and then uses it to gain unauthorized access to other resources inside the network. A zero trust provides full protection for all sensitive resources, even from users already inside the network. A zero trust architecture does not protect against zero-day vulnerabilities, which are exploits in software; external threats; or deauthentication, which is a type of Denial-of-Service (DoS) attack.

51. E. Social engineering is a means for gaining unauthorized access to a network by convincing users to disclose passwords or other sensitive information; it is not part of a defense in depth strategy. Defense in depth can include physical protection, such as access control vestibules; division of resources using network segmentation, separation of duties, or screened subnets; and deceptive lures, such as honeypots.

52. A, C. A threat assessment should estimate the potential severity of a threat, such as the damage that the loss of a specific resource can cause to the organization. The assessment should also estimate the likelihood of a particular threat occurring, as the organization will have to devote more attention to the more likely threats. An assessment of the organization's current posture (or status) with regard to a specific threat and the mitigation techniques used to counter it are both elements that come later in the risk management process, after the threat assessment has been completed.

53. B. A process assessment is an examination of an existing procedure to determine its compliance with a specific set of goals that can include cost, quality, and timeliness. A vendor assessment is an examination of the organization's relationship with a specific business partner. Business assessment and risk assessment are more general terms that can include process assessments.

54. B. Ransomware is a type of attack in which a user's access to his or her data is blocked unless a certain amount of money is paid to the attacker. The blockages can vary from simple screen locks to data encryption. War driving is an attack method that consists of driving around a neighborhood with a computer, scanning for unprotected wireless networks. Denial-of-Service (DoS) is a type of attack that overwhelms a computer with traffic, preventing it from functioning properly. Address Resolution Protocol (ARP) poisoning is the deliberate insertion of fraudulent information into the ARP cache stored on computers and switches.

55. A, C. Spoofing is the process of modifying network packets to make them appear as though they are transmitted by or addressed to someone else. One way of doing this is to modify the Media Access Control (MAC) address in the packets to one that is approved by the MAC filter. An on-pass (or man-in-the-middle) attack is one in which an attacker intercepts network traffic, reads the traffic, and can even modify it before sending it on to the destination. Denial-of-Service (DoS) is a type of attack that overwhelms a computer with traffic, preventing it from functioning properly, whereas a logic bomb is a code insert placed into a legitimate software product that triggers a malicious event when specific conditions are met. Neither of these last two involves modifying network packets.

56. C. A logic bomb is a code insert placed into a legitimate software product that triggers a malicious event when specific conditions are met. Social engineering is the practice of obtaining sensitive data by manipulating legitimate users, such as by pretending to be someone with a genuine need for that data. War driving is an attack method that consists of driving around a neighborhood with a computer, scanning for unprotected wireless networks. An evil twin is a fraudulent access point on a wireless network that mimics the Service Set Identifier (SSID) of a legitimate access point, in the hope of luring in users.

57. B, C. Configuring the access point not to broadcast its Service Set Identifier (SSID) will prevent an unsophisticated war driving attacker from seeing the network. Configuring your equipment to use WiFi Protected Access II (WPA2) security will make it difficult for a war driver who detects your network to connect to it. The SSID is just an identifier; its length has no effect on security. Wired Equivalent Privacy (WEP) is a security protocol that has been found to have serious weaknesses.

58. B. War driving is an attack method that consists of driving around a neighborhood with a computer, scanning for unprotected wireless networks. When a war driver locates a wireless network and marks it for other attackers, it is called war chalking. There are no such attacks as war tagging and war signing.

59. B. Bluesnarfing is an attack in which an intruder connects to a wireless device using Bluetooth, for the purpose of stealing information. Bluejacking is the process of sending unsolicited messages to a device using Bluetooth. The other options do not exist.

60. D. Although a DoS attack typically involves traffic flooding, any attack that prevents a server from functioning can be called a DoS attack. A permanent DoS attack is one in which the attacker actually damages the target system and prevents it from functioning. This can be a physical attack that actually damages the hardware, or the attacker can disable the server by altering its software or configuration settings. Flood-based attacks include the Distributed Denial-of-Service (DDoS) attack, one in which the attacker uses hundreds or thousands of computers controlled by malware and called bots or zombies, to send traffic to a single server or website in an attempt to overwhelm it and prevent it from functioning. An amplified DoS attack is one in which the messages sent by the attacker require an extended amount of processing by the target servers, increasing the burden on them more than simpler messages would. A reflective DoS attack is one in which the attacker sends requests containing the target server's IP address to legitimate servers on the Internet, such as Domain Name System (DNS) servers, causing them to send a flood of responses to the target.

61. B. Distributed Denial-of-Service (DDoS) attacks use hundreds or thousands of computers that have been infected with malware, called bots or zombies, to flood a target server with traffic in an attempt to overwhelm it and prevent it from functioning. A reflective DoS attack is one in which the attacker sends requests containing the target server's IP address to legitimate servers on the Internet, such as Domain Name System (DNS) servers, causing them to send a flood of responses to the target. Neither attack type causes a computer to flood itself.

62. A. An amplified DoS attack is one in which the messages sent by the attacker require an extended amount of processing by the target servers, increasing the burden on them more than simpler messages would. Reflective and distributed DoS attacks use other computers to flood a target with traffic. A reflective DoS attack is one in which the attacker sends requests containing the target server's IP address to legitimate servers on the Internet, such as Domain Name System (DNS) servers, causing them to send a flood of responses to the target. A Distributed Denial-of-Service (DDoS) attack is one in which the attacker uses a botnet consisting of hundreds or thousands of computers, controlled by malware and called bots or zombies, to send traffic to a single server or website in an attempt to overwhelm it and prevent it from functioning. A permanent DoS attack is one in which the attacker actually damages the target system and prevents it from functioning.

63. A, B, C. A brute-force attack is one in which an attacker uses repeated guesses to find a password, an open port, or some other type of sensitive data. A Denial-of-Service (DoS) attack floods a target server with traffic so that it is unable to function normally. While both of these attack types can be mounted using specialized software, they can also be the work of a lone attacker using nothing more than the tools provided on a standard workstation. Social engineering is the practice of obtaining sensitive data by contacting users and pretending to be someone with a legitimate need for that data. It requires nothing more than a telephone or an email client. Phishing is the term for an attack that uses bogus emails or websites designed to infect users with some type of malware.

64. B, C. Deauthentication is a type of Denial-of-Service (DoS) attack in which the attacker targets a wireless client by sending a deauthentication frame that causes the client to be disconnected from the network. The object of the attack is often to compel the client to connect to a rogue access point called an evil twin. An evil twin is a fraudulent access point on a wireless network that mimics the Service Set Identifier (SSID) of a legitimate access point, in the hope of luring in users. A logic bomb is a code insert placed into a legitimate software product that triggers a malicious event when specific conditions are met. Address Resolution Protocol (ARP) poisoning is the deliberate insertion of fraudulent information into the ARP cache stored on computers and switches. Neither of these last two is specifically targeted at wireless clients.

65. A. Social engineering is the practice of obtaining sensitive data by contacting users and pretending to be someone with a legitimate need for that data. No software or hardware solution can prevent it; the only way is to educate users on the potential dangers and establish policies that inform users what to do when they experience a social engineering attempt. Social engineering is not a virus or other form of malware, so an antivirus product has no effect against it. Social engineering is not implemented in network traffic, so a firewall cannot filter it. Social engineering is not implemented in network traffic, so IPSec cannot protect it.

66. B, C. Reflective and distributed DoS attacks use other computers to flood a target with traffic. A reflective DoS attack is one in which the attacker sends requests containing the target server's IP address to legitimate servers on the Internet, such as DNS servers, causing them to send a flood of responses to the target. A Distributed Denial-of-Service (DDoS) attack is one in which the attacker uses hundreds or thousands of computers, controlled by malware and called bots or zombies, to send traffic to a single server or website in an attempt to overwhelm it and prevent it from functioning. An amplified DoS attack is one in which the messages sent by the attacker require an extended amount of processing by the target servers, increasing the burden on them more than simpler messages would. A permanent DoS attack is one in which the attacker actually damages the target system and prevents it from functioning.

67. C. Virtual Area Network (VLAN) hopping is a method for sending commands to switches to transfer a port from one VLAN to another. This can enable the attacker to connect his or her device to a potentially sensitive VLAN. VLAN hopping does not modify the switch's patch panel connections, only its VLAN assignments. It is not possible to rename a switch's default VLAN. VLAN hopping does not enable an attacker to change a switch's native VLAN.

68. B, D. War driving is an attack method that consists of driving around a neighborhood with a computer, scanning for unprotected wireless networks. It therefore requires nothing more than a vehicle and a wireless-equipped computer. The term *driving* in war driving refers to driving a vehicle, not a screw; a screwdriver is therefore not required. War driving uses a wireless computer or other device to scan for open networks; a telephone is therefore not required. War driving is a means for locating unprotected networks; it does not require a credit card number, nor does it involve stealing them.

69. A. Spoofing is the process of modifying network packets to make them appear as though they are transmitted by or addressed to someone else. One way of doing this is to modify the Media Access Control (MAC) address in the packets to one that is approved by the MAC filter. Brute-force is the method of repeated guessing, which is impractical with MAC addresses. A Domain Name System (DNS) works with IP addresses, not MAC addresses. War driving is the process of looking for unprotected Wireless Access Points (WAPs).

70. C. A Distributed Denial-of-Service (DDoS) attack is one in which the attacker uses hundreds or thousands of computers, controlled by malware and called bots or zombies, to send traffic to a single server or website in an attempt to overwhelm it and prevent it from functioning. An amplified DoS attack is one in which the messages sent by the attacker require an extended amount of processing by the target servers, increasing the burden on them more than simpler messages would. A reflective DoS attack is one in which the attacker sends requests containing the target server's IP address to legitimate servers on the Internet, such as Domain Name System (DNS) servers, causing them to send a flood of responses to the target. A permanent DoS attack is one in which the attacker actually damages the target system and prevents it from functioning.

71. A. An amplified DoS attack is one in which the messages sent by the attacker require an extended amount of processing by the target servers, increasing the burden on them more than simpler messages would. A reflective DoS attack is one in which the attacker sends requests containing the target server's IP address to legitimate servers on the Internet, such as Domain Name System (DNS) servers, causing them to send a flood of responses to the target. A Distributed Denial-of-Service (DDoS) attack is one in which the attacker uses hundreds or thousands of computers, controlled by malware and called bots or zombies, to send traffic to a single server or website in an attempt to overwhelm it and prevent it from functioning. A permanent DoS attack is one in which the attacker actually damages the target system and prevents it from functioning.

72. A, D. Smurf attacks rely on routers to forward broadcast traffic. Routers no longer forward broadcast messages, so smurf attacks have been rendered ineffective. In the same way, Virtual Area Network (VLAN) hopping, which is a method for sending commands to switches to transfer a port from one VLAN to another, is rarely seen because switches are now designed to prevent them. A logic bomb is a code insert placed into a legitimate software product that triggers a malicious event when specific conditions are met. Phishing is the term for a bogus email or website designed to infect users with some type of malware. Both of these are still commonly used attack types.

73. D. Although DoS attacks typically involve traffic flooding, any attack that prevents a server from functioning can be called a DoS attack. A permanent DoS attack is one in which the attacker actually damages the target system and prevents it from functioning. This can be a physical attack that damages the hardware, or the attacker can disable the server by altering its software or configuration settings. A Distributed Denial-of-Service (DDoS) attack is one in which the attacker uses hundreds or thousands of computers, controlled by malware and called bots or zombies, to send traffic to a single server or website in an attempt to overwhelm it and prevent it from functioning. An amplified DoS attack is one in which the messages sent by the attacker require an extended amount of processing by the target servers, increasing the burden on them more than simpler messages would. A reflective DoS attack is one in which the attacker sends requests containing the target server's IP address to legitimate servers on the Internet, such as Domain Name System (DNS) servers, causing them to send a flood of responses to the target.

74. C. Distributed Denial-of-Service (DDoS) attacks use hundreds or thousands of computers that have been infected with malware, called bots or zombies, to flood a target server with traffic, in an attempt to overwhelm it and prevent it from functioning. A reflective DoS attack is one in which the attacker sends requests containing the target server's IP address to legitimate servers on the Internet, such as Domain Name System (DNS) servers, causing them to send a flood of responses to the target. A reflective attack does not require infected computers; it takes advantage of the servers' native functions. An amplified DoS attack is one in which the messages sent by the attacker require an extended amount of processing by the target servers, increasing the burden on them more than simpler messages would. A permanent DoS attack is one in which the attacker actually damages the target system and prevents it from functioning.

75. D. Domain Name System (DNS) poisoning is a type of attack in which an attacker adds fraudulent information into the cache of a DNS server. Then, when a client attempts to resolve the name of a website or other server, the DNS server supplies the incorrect IP address, causing the client to access the attacker's server instead. An evil twin is a rogue Wireless Access Point (WAP) on a network. Address Resolution Protocol (ARP) poisoning is the deliberate insertion of fraudulent information into the ARP cache stored on computers and switches, which can interfere with the resolution of IP addresses into Media Access Control (MAC) addresses on a local level. Spoofing is the process of modifying network packets to make them appear as though they are transmitted by or addressed to someone else.

76. B. Domain Name System (DNS) poisoning is a type of attack in which an attacker adds fraudulent information into the cache of a DNS server. This can interfere with the name resolution process by causing a DNS server to supply the incorrect IP address for a specified name. The process of resolving an IP address into a Media Access Control (MAC) address can be interfered with by Address Resolution (ARP) poisoning. DNS has nothing to do with passwords or switching.

77. C. A vulnerability is a potential weakness in a system that an attacker can use to his or her advantage. An exploit is a hardware or software element that is designed to take advantage of a vulnerability. A mitigation is a form of defense against attacks on system security. A honeypot is a computer configured to function as bait for attackers, causing them to waste their time penetrating a resource that provides no significant access.

78. D. A logic bomb is a code insert placed into a legitimate software product that triggers a malicious event when specific conditions are met. The terminated administrator might have created code designed to trigger the deletions after the administrator's departure from the company. Social engineering is a form of attack in which an innocent user is persuaded by an attacker to provide sensitive information via email or telephone. The Address Resolution Protocol (ARP) is responsible for resolving IP addresses into Media Access Control (MAC) addresses. ARP poisoning is the deliberate insertion of fraudulent information into the ARP cache stored on computers and switches. An evil twin is a fraudulent access point on a wireless network.

79. B, C. Address Resolution Protocol (ARP) poisoning is the deliberate insertion of fraudulent information into the ARP cache stored on computers and switches. This can enable an attacker to intercept traffic intended for another system. In an on-path (man-in-the-middle) attack, the attacker can read the intercepted traffic and even modify it before sending it on to the destination. In a session hijacking attack, the attacker can use the intercepted traffic to obtain authentication information, including passwords. An evil twin is a fraudulent access point on a wireless network. Social engineering is a form of attack in which an innocent user is persuaded by an attacker to provide sensitive information via email or telephone.

80. B. A replay attack is one in which an attacker utilizes the information found in previously captured packets to gain access to a secured resource. In many cases, the captured packets contain authentication data. In this way, the attacker can make use of captured passwords, even when they are encrypted and cannot be displayed. The other options all describe valid attack methodologies, but they are not called replay attacks.

81. B. This is a classic example of a phishing scam. In all likelihood, the link in the email Ed received has taken him not to the real website of his bank, but rather a duplicate created by an attacker. By supplying his logon credentials, he is in effect giving them to the attacker, who can now gain access to his real bank account. Social engineering is the practice of obtaining sensitive data by contacting users and pretending to be someone with a legitimate need for that data. A logic bomb is a code insert placed into a legitimate software product that triggers a malicious event when specific conditions are met. Spoofing is the process of modifying network packets to make them appear as though they are transmitted by or addressed to someone else.

82. A, C, D. An evil twin is a fraudulent access point on a wireless network that mimics the Service Set Identifier (SSID) of a legitimate access point, in the hope of luring in users. War driving is an attack method that consists of driving around a neighborhood with a computer, scanning for unprotected wireless networks. Deauthentication is a type of Denial-of-Service (DoS) attack in which the attacker targets a wireless client by sending a deauthentication frame that causes the client to be disconnected from the network. Phishing is an attack type that is targeted at all users, not just wireless ones.

83. C, D. A DoS attack is one designed to prevent a target from fulfilling its function. While ping floods are a common form of server DoS attacks, physically damaging the server hardware also prevents it from performing its function. Therefore, this too is a type of DoS attack. Capturing packets and rogue access points are not typically described as DoS attacks.

84. A. A zombie (or bot) is a computer that has been infected by malware—usually some form of Trojan—which an attacker can control remotely, causing the computer to flood a target system with traffic. An attack using multiple zombies is known as a Distributed Denial-of-Service (DDoS) attack. The other options are not examples of zombies.

85. C. Ransomware is a type of attack in which a user's access to his or her computer or data is blocked unless a certain amount of money is paid to the attacker. The blockages can vary from simple screen locks to data encryption.

86. B. Social engineering is the practice of obtaining sensitive data by contacting users and pretending to be someone with a legitimate need for that data. No computer equipment is required, and no software or hardware solution can prevent it; the only way is to educate users on the potential dangers and establish policies that inform users what to do when they experience a social engineering attempt. Denial-of-Service (DoS) is a type of attack that overwhelms a computer with traffic, preventing it from functioning properly. A brute-force or dictionary attack is one in which an attacker uses repeated guesses to find a password, an open port, or some other type of sensitive data. Phishing is the term for a bogus email or website designed to infect users with some type of malware.

87. B. A brute-force attack (also called a dictionary attack) is one in which an attacker uses repeated guesses to find a password, an open port, or some other type of sensitive data. Brute-force does not refer to a physical attack. Flooding a server with traffic created by zombies is a Distributed Denial-of-Service (DDoS) attack. Deploying an unauthorized access point is an evil twin attack.

88. A. An evil twin is a fraudulent access point on a wireless network, which an intruder can use to obtain passwords and other sensitive information transmitted by users. War driving is the term for seeking out open wireless networks. Social engineering is a form of attack in which an innocent user is persuaded by an attacker to provide sensitive information via email or telephone. Spoofing is the process of modifying network packets to make them appear as though they are transmitted by or addressed to someone else.

89. C. Social engineering is the term for a type of attack in which a smooth-talking intruder contacts a user and convinces him or her to disclose sensitive information, such as account passwords. An on-path (man-in-the-middle) attack is one in which an attacker intercepts network traffic, reads the traffic, and can even modify it before sending it on to the destination. Spoofing is the process of modifying network packets to make them appear as though they are transmitted by or addressed to someone else. An evil twin is a fraudulent access point on a wireless network.

90. B. Operating system updates and patches are frequently released to address newly discovered exploits that make computers vulnerable to malware infestation. Applying updates on a regular basis can help to mitigate the impact of malware. Updates and patches typically cannot mitigate Denial of Service (DoS) attacks, and they have no effect on nontechnical dangers such as social engineering or dangers that apply to switches, such as port security hazards.

91. D. The term *social engineering* refers to various methods that attackers can use to gain access to secured resources by manipulating authorized users, either physically or digitally. An evil twin is a rogue access point deliberately connected to the network for malicious purposes, so it is not a form of social engineering. Piggybacking and tailgating typically refer to the practice of closely following an authorized individual through a physical security barrier, such as a locked door or a guarded entrance. Shoulder surfing is a method of gathering sensitive information by passing behind a user and looking at their monitor. Phishing is a digital form of social engineering in which a user is duped into disclosing sensitive information by a faked email or other communication.

92. B. Extensible Authentication Protocol (EAP) is a framework for the encapsulation of authentication messages. EAP is used on wireless networks and point-to-point connections and supports dozens of different authentication methods. WiFi Protected Access (WPA) is a wireless encryption standard. Temporal Key Integrity Protocol (TKIP) is an encryption algorithm. Transport Layer Security (TLS) is an encryption protocol used for Internet communications.

93. A. Extensible Authentication Protocol (EAP) and 802.1X are both components of an authentication mechanism used on many wireless networks. EAP and 802.1X do not themselves provide authorization, encryption, or accounting services.

94. A, B. Protected Extended Authentication Protocol (PEAP) encapsulates EAP inside a Transport Layer Security (TLS) tunnel. Flexible Authentication via Secure Tunneling (FAST) also establishes a TLS tunnel to protect user credential transmissions. EAP-TLS uses TLS for encryption, but not for tunneling. EAP-PSK uses a preshared key to provide an authentication process that does not use encryption.

95. C. *Geofencing* is the generic term for a technology that limits access to a network or other resource based on the client's location. In wireless networking, geofencing is intended to prevent unauthorized clients outside the facility from connecting to the network. Local authentication is an application or service that triggers an authentication request to which the user must respond before access is granted. Port security is a method for protecting access to switch ports. Motion detection is a system designed to trigger a notification or alarm when an individual trespasses in a protected area.

96. A. Geofencing is a mechanism that is intended to prevent unauthorized clients outside the facility from connecting to the network. The mechanism can take the form of a signal strength or power level requirement, a GPS location requirement, or strategic placement of the antennae for wireless access points. The other options listed are not descriptions of typical geofencing technologies.

97. C. As part of a public key infrastructure (PKI), digital certificates are associated with a key pair, consisting of a public key and a private key. The certificate is issued to a person or computer as proof of its identity. A signature does not associate a person or computer with a key pair. An exploit is a hardware or software element that is designed to take advantage of a vulnerability. Resource records are associated with the Domain Name System (DNS).

98. A, D. The Protected Extensible Authentication Protocol (PEAP) and EAP Flexible Authentication via Secure Tunneling (EAP-FAST) both use TLS tunneling to secure authentication transmissions. EAP Password (EAP-PWD) and EAP-MP5 do not use TLS for tunneling or any other purpose.

99. A, B, C, E. Encryption, authentication, Media Access Control (MAC) filtering, and antenna placement are all techniques for hardening a wireless network against attack. Social engineering is a type of attack in which an intruder contacts a user and convinces him or her to disclose sensitive information, such as account passwords; it is not specifically associated with wireless networks.

100. A. There are no policies that can prevent users from creating easily guessed passwords. The only action that can help is to educate users on the fact that attackers are frequently able to guess passwords by using information such as familiar names and dates. Forcing more frequent password changes would not compel users to alter their method for choosing passwords, nor would increasing the password history value. Assigning random passwords would address the issue, but user complaints and forgotten passwords would likely create greater problems than it would solve.

101. A, C, D. Access points, switches, and routers all require authentication to access their administrative interfaces, and most have a standard username and password configured at the factory. The purchaser can modify the default credentials, but many people fail to do so. Windows servers do not have default credentials assigned; the installer is prompted to specify an Administrator password during the setup process.

102. A, D. Secure Shell (SSH) and Telnet are both remote terminal programs, but Telnet passes instructions (including passwords) in cleartext, whereas SSH is encrypted. Hypertext Transfer Protocol Secure (HTTPS) is the encrypted version of Hypertext Transfer Protocol (HTTP). In both of these cases, the suggested substitute is more secure. However, Temporal Key Integrity Protocol (TKIP) provides less secure encryption than Advanced Encryption Standard (AES), and Wired Equivalent Protocol (WEP) is less secure than WiFi Protected Access 2 (WPA2).

103. B, C. Servers and switches are both devices on which unused ports can be a security hazard, but they use the term port differently. Servers have application layer ports that permit specific types of service traffic to enter the server. Switches have ports to which administrators can connect computers and other devices. Both can provide attackers with unauthorized access to the device. It is not possible to disable hub ports, and the Wireless Access Points (WAPs) used on enterprise networks typically have only a single port.

104. B. Disabling SSID broadcasts is a way of hiding the presence of a wireless network, but if an intruder knows that a network is there, it is a simple matter to capture packets transmitted by the wireless devices and read the SSID from them. It is not possible to connect to a wireless network without the SSID. SSIDs are set by the administrator of the access point; they are not printed on the device's label. SSIDs can be found relatively easily but guessing them is no easier than guessing a password.

105. C. Upgrading the UEFI or BIOS firmware on a server typically does not enhance its security, so it cannot be considered a form of server hardening. Disabling services and ports that are not in use reduces the attack surface of a server, and creating privileged user accounts reduces the chance that privileged accounts will be compromised. Therefore, these are all forms of server hardening.

106. A, D. If there is no way for unauthorized people to access the datacenter, then there is no danger of someone plugging a device into a port that is left enabled. If the switch uses an Access Control List (ACL) that specifies the Media Access Control (MAC) addresses of systems permitted to connect to it, then there is no need to disable unused ports. However, disabling the ports is probably far easier than creating and maintaining the ACL. Ports that are not patched in can still be compromised at the switch location. Enabling ports is not difficult, so accommodating new users is not a valid reason for leaving them enabled.

107. D. The "Passwords must meet complexity requirements" policy includes a provision that new passwords cannot include the user's account name or full name. If the full name is delimited by spaces or punctuation, the individual words cannot appear in the password either. The other options do not prevent the use of common passwords.

108. D. Deauthentication is a type of Denial-of-Service (DoS) attack in which the attacker targets a wireless client by sending a deauthentication frame that causes the client to be disconnected from the network. It is therefore not a method for hardening an access point. Upgrading the device's firmware to apply security fixes, changing the default administrative credentials applied at the factory, and frequent Pre-Shared Key (PSK) changes are all means of hardening the security of an access point.

109. C. *Network hardening* is a term used to describe any method of making it more difficult for intruders to penetrate. In many cases, network hardening techniques are based on education rather than technology. Compelling users to create passwords that are difficult to guess is one example of this. Mitigation techniques are methods for reducing the severity of an attack. Multifactor authentication calls for the use of two different identity confirmation mechanisms, such as a password and a fingerprint. Access control is a technique for creating a list of approved users or systems.

110. A, B. Administrator is the default administrative user account in Windows, and root is the administrative account in Linux. Control and admin are not privileged user accounts provided with the operating systems.

111. B, D. Virtual Local Area Networks (VLANs) can be used to isolate systems on a separate network segment. A demilitarized zone (DMZ), also called a screened subnet or a perimeter network, is a network segment accessible from the Internet and separated from the internal network by a firewall. Both of these are methods for isolating systems to prevent security breaches from spreading beyond their bounds. Access Control Lists (ACLs) and Network Access Control (NAC) are both methods for enhancing network security, but they are not segmentation methods.

112. D. Dynamic Host Configuration Protocol (DHCP) snooping is a feature found in some network switches that prevents rogue DHCP servers from assigning IP addresses to clients. It can also detect when DHCP release or decline messages arrive over a port other than the one on which the DHCP transaction originated. The other options are all techniques that are applicable to servers.

113. B. ACLs define the type of access granted to authenticated users. This process is known as authorization. Authentication is the confirmation of a user's identity. Accounting and auditing are both methods of tracking and recording a user's activities on a network.

114. C. Role separation is the practice of creating a different virtual server for each server role or application. In addition to providing other benefits as well, this forces intruders to mount attacks on multiple servers to disable an entire network. Geofencing is a technique for limiting access to a wireless network. Network segmentation describes the process of creating multiple Virtual Local Area Networks (VLANs) or deploying firewalls to isolate part of a network. VLAN hopping is a type of attack in which an intruder sends command messages to a switch to transfer a port from one VLAN to another.

115. B. Role separation is the practice of creating a different virtual server for each server role or application. In addition to providing other benefits as well, this forces intruders to mount attacks on multiple servers to disable an entire network. Switches, routers, and access points do not use this technique.

116. D. An implicit deny is a policy that denies access to a resource by default, without a rule defining that denial. Creating a new rule denying access is an explicit deny. If anyone was able to access the server remotely by default, that would be an implicit allow. An explicit allow is a rule granting specific users remote access.

117. A. Dynamic Host Configuration Protocol (DHCP) snooping is a process in which the switch examines DHCP traffic to determine the IP addresses that DHCP servers have assigned to specific MAC addresses. DAI detects ARP poisoning attempts by comparing the IP-and-MAC address pairs in ARP packets with those in the DHCP snooping table it has compiled. The switch then discards packets with address pairs that do not match. Secure SNMP Secure Network Protocol (SNP), Domain Name Server (DNS) name resolution, and Neighbor Discovery Protocol (NDP) are not used to implement DAI.

118. D. Dynamic Host Configuration Protocol (DHCP) snooping is a feature found in some network switches that prevents rogue DHCP servers from assigning IP addresses to clients. It can also detect when DHCP release or decline messages arrive over a port other than the one on which the DHCP transaction originated. Although DHCP snooping can prevent DHCP clients from being assigned an incorrect IP address, it does not directly prevent the poisoning of Domain Name System (DNS) server caches with erroneous information.

119. A. Although DHCP is an application layer service that uses the User Datagram Protocol (UDP) transport layer protocol to assign network layer IP addresses, DHCP snooping is a data link layer process in which a network switch examines incoming DHCP traffic to determine whether it originates from an authorized server and is arriving over the correct port.

120. C. By flooding a switch with packets containing many different false Media Access Control (MAC) addresses, an attacker can cause the legitimate entries in the switch's MAC table to be aged out of the device and replaced with bogus entries. When the destinations of incoming packets are not found in the table, the switch broadcasts them throughout the network, where they can be more readily captured and compromised. A flood guard is a mechanism that prevents confirmed MAC addresses in the table from being replaced. A flood guard in a switch cannot protect against Domain Name System (DNS) poisoning, war driving, or evil twin attacks.

121. B. A root guard affects the behavior of the Spanning Tree Protocol (STP) by enforcing the selection of root bridge ports on a switched network. Without root guards, there is no way for administrators to enforce the topology of a network with a redundant switching fabric. Root guards do not affect the Extensible Authentication Protocol (EAP), the Lightweight Directory Access Protocol (LDAP), or the Address Resolution Protocol (ARP).

122. A. File integrity monitoring (FIM) is a process that typically consists of a comparison of files in their current state to a known baseline copy stored elsewhere. The comparison can be direct, or it could involve the calculation of checksums or other types of file hashes. The object of the comparison is to detect changes in documents, both in content and in sensitive areas, such as credentials, privileges, and security settings, which might indicate the presence of a potential or actual security breach. Role separation applies to the deployment of applications on servers. Deauthentication is a type of wireless network attack. Tamper detection is a term used to describe a physical security measure for hardware. Router Advertisement (RA) guard is a feature found on certain switches that prevents the misuse of RA messages to redirect traffic.

123. C. Digital signatures can be used for the following functions: authentication, to confirm that data originated from a specific individual; nonrepudiation, to prevent the sender from denying the data's origin; and integrity, to confirm that the data has not been modified in transit. Segmentation is not a function of digital signatures.

124. A, B, C. Because only Ralph possesses the private key, only he could have signed and encrypted it. Although it is possible for someone other than Alice to have decrypted the document while it was in transit, using Ralph's public key, that individual could not have modified it and encrypted it again.

125. B, D. Because anyone can obtain Ralph's public key, the document could have been created and encrypted by anyone. However, because only Ralph possesses the private key that can decrypt the document, he can be sure that no one else has opened it while it was in transit.

126. A. Firmware is a type of software permanently written to the memory built into a hardware device. A firmware patch overrides the read-only nature of this memory to update the software. Driver updates, feature updates, and vulnerability patches are typically applied to software products, such as applications and operating systems.

127. A. A patch is a relatively small update that is designed to address a specific issue, often a security exploit or vulnerability. Patches do not add features or new capabilities; they are fixes targeted at a specific area of the software. Updates, upgrades, and service packs are larger packages that might include new features and/or many different fixes.

128. C. Rolling back, the process of uninstalling a patch to revert to the previous version of the software, is not part of the patch evaluation process. The evaluation process for new patches in a corporate environment usually consists of a research stage, in which you examine the need and purpose for the patch; a testing stage, in which you install the patch on a lab machine; and a backup of the production systems to which you will apply the patch.

129. D. *Rollback* is a term used in change management to describe the process of reversing a change that has been made, to restore the original configuration. In the case of patch management, a rollback is the process of uninstalling a recently installed software update. The terms *backslide*, *downgrade*, and *reset* are not used to describe this procedure.

130. D. MAC address filtering enables administrators to configure an access point to allow only devices with specific addresses to connect; all other traffic is rejected. Access points broadcast their presence using a Service Set Identifier (SSID), not a MAC address. MAC address filtering protects WLANs when implemented in an access point, not a firewall. MAC address filtering does not call for the modification of addresses in network packets. MAC filtering does not isolate clients from the network.

131. D. Geofencing is the generic term for a technology that limits access to a network or other resource based on the client's location. It is therefore best described as somewhere you are. A finger gesture would be considered something you do, a password is something you know, and a smartcard is something you have.

132. A. Wireless Access Points (WAPs) typically include the ability to maintain an Access Control List (ACL), which specifies the Media Access Control (MAC) addresses of devices that are permitted to connect to the wireless network. The technique is known as MAC address filtering. Remote Authentication Dial-In User Service (RADIUS) servers, domain controllers, and smartcards typically do not include MAC filtering capabilities.

133. A, C. NTFS files and folders all have ACLs, which contain Access Control Entries (ACEs) that specify the users and groups that can access them and the specific permissions they have been granted. Wireless Access Points (WAPs) have ACLs that contain Media Access Control (MAC) addresses of the devices that are permitted to connect to the wireless network. Lightweight Directory Access Protocol (LDAP) and Kerberos are protocols that provide directory service communication and authentication, respectively. Neither one uses ACLs.

134. A. Media Access Control (MAC) filtering takes the form of an Access Control List (ACL) on the wireless network's access points, listing the MAC addresses of all the devices that are to be permitted to access the network. If the MAC address of Alice's laptop is not included in the ACL, she will be unable to connect to the network. Alice has been given the SSID of the network, so she should be able to connect, even if the access points are not broadcasting the SSID. Geofencing is intended to prevent users outside the office from accessing the network, so this should not be the problem. Alice has been given the passphrase for the network, so she should be able to configure WiFi Protect Access 2 (WPA2) on her laptop. Alice is not using a separate guest network, so this is not preventing her from connecting.

135. B. A captive portal is a web page displayed to a user who is attempting to access a public wireless network. The user typically must supply credentials, provide payment, or accept a user agreement before access is granted. A captive portal does not refer to a switch port, a secured entryway to a room, or a type of extortionate computer attack.

136. A. A web page that prompts users for payment, authentication, or acceptance of a EULA is a captive portal. Ransomware is a type of attack that extorts payment. Port security and root guards are methods for protecting access to switch ports.

137. B. Port isolation, also known as Private Virtual Local Area Network (VLAN), is a feature in some switches that enables administrators to restrict selected ports to a given uplink, essentially creating a separate, secondary VLAN that is isolated from the switch's default, primary VLAN. Screened subnets (also called perimeter networks or demilitarized zones [DMZs]), frame relay, and VPNs are not switching techniques.

138. B, C. Because many IoT devices are mobile or located in unprotected areas, a firewall is not a viable protection mechanism for all of them, nor is the practice of placing them on separate network segments. Network security mechanisms such as access control policies and centralized gateways providing authentication and authorization could conceivably be incorporated into a general IoT security standard.

139. B, D. The default Virtual Local Area Network (VLAN) on most switches has the ID VLAN 1, not VLAN 0, and it cannot be renamed or deleted. The default VLAN does not have to be created by the administrator; it is the one to which all ports are assigned in the default configuration.

140. D. Control plane policing uses Quality of Service (QoS) policies to block, allow, or impose rate limits on the traffic processed by the router or switch. Internet Protocol Security (IPSec) is a network layer security mechanism that encrypts or authenticates traffic. 802.1X is a network authentication mechanism. Router Advertisement (RA) Guard is a feature found on certain switches that prevents the misuse of RA messages to redirect traffic. Virtual Local Area Network (VLAN) hopping is a method for sending commands to switches to transfer a port from one VLAN to another.

141. B. VPN typically enables remote clients to connect to a VPN router at a central site, much like the star topology of a Local Area Network (LAN), in which computers are all connected to a central switch. Dynamic Multipoint Virtual Private Network (DMVPN) is a technology that creates a mesh topology between the remote VPN sites, enabling the remote sites to connect directly to each other, rather than to the central VPN server. A VPN concentrator is a type of router that enables multiple client systems to access a network from remote locations. A Session Initiation Protocol (SIP) trunk provides a connection between the private and public domains of a unified communications network. Multiprotocol Label Switching (MPLS) is a data transfer mechanism that assigns labels to individual packets, and then routes the packets based on those labels. Clientless VPN creates an encrypted tunnel to a server using a browser, without the need to install additional client software.

142. C. Point-to-Point Tunneling Protocol (PPTP) is considered to be obsolete for VPN use because of several serious security vulnerabilities that have been found in it. IPSec, Layer 2 Tunneling Protocol (L2TP), and Secure Sockets Layer/Transport Layer Security (SSL/TLS) are all still in use.

143. C. Layer 2 Tunneling Protocol (L2TP) is used to create the tunnel forming a VPN connection, but it does not encrypt the traffic passing through the tunnel. To do this, it requires a separate protocol that provides encryption, such as Internet Protocol Security (IPSec). Point-to-Point Tunneling Protocol (PPTP) and Secure Sockets Layer (SSL) are both capable of encrypting tunneled traffic.

144. A, B, C. Although the computers do not have to use hardware made by the same manufacturer, both must use the same basic type of WAN connection, such as a leased line, a modem and PSTN line, or an Internet connection. Both of the computers must also use the same data link layer protocol, such as PPP, to establish a remote network connection. Most remote network connections use some form of authentication mechanism, even if it is nothing more than the exchange of a username and cleartext password. To establish the remote network connection, both computers must be configured to use the same type of authentication, even if it is no authentication at all. As long as all of the other elements are in place, such as the physical layer connection and the protocols, there is no need for both of the computers involved in a remote network connection to be running the same operating system.

145. C. Secure Shell (SSH) is a character-based tool that enables users to execute commands on remote computers. It does not provide web server/browser security. Secure Sockets Layer (SSL) is a security protocol that provides encrypted communications between web browsers and servers. Transport Layer Security (TLS) is an updated security protocol that is designed to replace SSL. Datagram Transport Layer Security (DTLS) is a security protocol that provides the same basic functions as TLS, but for User Datagram Protocol (UDP) traffic.

146. D. An extranet VPN is designed to provide clients, vendors, and other outside partners with the ability to connect to your corporate network with limited access. A host-to-site VPN is a remote access solution, enabling users to access the corporate network from home or while traveling. A site-to-site VPN enables a branch office to connect to the home office using the Internet rather a more expensive Wide Area Network (WAN) connection. A host-to-host VPN enables two individual users to establish a protected connection to each other.

147. B. Trivial File Transfer Protocol (TFTP) is typically used to download boot image files to computers performing a Preboot Execution Environment (PXE) startup. It is not used for remote control. Remote Desktop Protocol (RDP) is used by Remote Desktop Services in Windows to provide clients with graphical control over servers at remote locations. Secure Shell (SSH) and Telnet are both character-based tools that enable users to execute commands on remote computers.

148. A. RDP is a component of Remote Desktop Services, a Windows mechanism that enables a client program to connect to a server and control it remotely. RDP does not carry actual application data; it just transfers keystrokes, mouse movements, and graphic display information. Because the client program does not participate in the application computing on the server, it is known as a thin client. RDP does not provide clientless virtual private networking, encrypted tunneling, or unauthenticated file transfers.

149. B. A site-to-site VPN enables one network to connect to another, enabling users on both networks to access resources on the other one. This is usually a more economical solution for branch office connections than a Wide Area Network (WAN) link. A host-to-site VPN is a remote access solution, enabling users to access the corporate network from home or while traveling. A host-to-host VPN enables two individual users to establish a protected connection to each other. An extranet VPN is designed to provide clients, vendors, and other outside partners with the ability to connect to a corporate network with limited access.

150. C. EAP is the only authentication protocol included with Windows 10 that supports hardware-based authentication, so this is the only viable option. PAP transmits passwords in cleartext and is therefore not a viable option, as is CHAP, because it must store passwords using reversible encryption. MSCHAPv2 provides sufficient password protection but does not support the hardware-based authentication needed for smartcard use.

151. B, C. Remote Desktop Protocol (RDP) is a component of Remote Desktop Services, a Windows mechanism that enables a client program to connect to a server and control it remotely. RDP does not carry actual application data; it just transfers keystrokes, mouse movements, and graphic display information. Virtual Network Computing (VNC) is a similar desktop sharing system that is platform independent and open source. Secure Shell (SSH) and Telnet are character-based remote control solutions.

152. D. The term *virtual desktop* does not refer to a projection device that can display a computer desktop on a screen. A virtual desktop can be a realization of a computer monitor in a virtual reality environment; a virtualized desktop larger than the monitor, which users can scroll to view all parts of the display; or a cloud-based service provided by Microsoft Azure that provides users with access to their desktops using remote devices.

153. A, B, C. RDP is a component of Remote Desktop Services, a Windows mechanism that enables a client program to connect to a server and control it remotely. RDP does not carry actual application data; it just transfers keystrokes, mouse movements, and graphic display information.

154. A, B, C. VNC is a graphical desktop sharing system that uses a protocol called Remote Frame Buffer (RFB) to connect a client to a server and control it remotely. VNC does not transmit actual application data; it just transfers keystrokes, mouse movements, and graphic display information.

155. A, C. Telnet is a character-based remote-control protocol and application that is available on virtually all computing platforms. Because it is strictly character based, Telnet clients transmit only keystrokes and receive only character-based display information from the server.

156. C. Remote Desktop Gateway is a Windows Server role that enables remote users outside the network to establish a Remote Desktop Protocol (RDP) connection without the need for a Virtual Private Network (VPN) connection. The gateway does not provide multiple Remote Desktop client access to one workstation, Remote Desktop client access to multiple workstations, or access to workstations without a Remote Desktop client.

157. B, C. Out-of-band management uses a dedicated channel to devices on the network. This means that the device to be managed does not require an IP address. The channel provides access to the BIOS or UEFI firmware and makes it possible to reinstall the operating system on a remote computer. Telnet, SSH, and VNC are not out-of-band management tools.

158. C. Out-of-band management refers to the use of an alternative communications channel to a network device. The channel can be a modem connection, a direct cable connection, a wireless or cellular connection, or a dedicated Ethernet connection.

159. A, C, D, F. A computer requires four components to establish a remote connection. First, a physical-layer Wide Area Network (WAN) connection is needed. Second, the two systems must share common protocols from the data link layer and above. Third, if TCP/IP is being used to establish a remote session, then TCP/IP parameters must be configured on the systems. Fourth, host and remote software are needed. The remote client must have software that enables it to establish a remote session, and the server must have software that enables it to receive and grant remote sessions. Microsoft RAS supports both client and server remote access software; however, this is not a required component since other types of software can be used. PPTP is a tunneling protocol and is not a required component for establishing a remote session.

160. B. When users connect to a remote network using VPN, they become a participant on that network, which includes using the remote network's Internet connection. Therefore, when a user opens a browser, the application passes the user's requests through the VPN tunnel to the remote server, which uses the default gateway and Internet connection at the remote site to connect to the desired address. This is inherently slower than connecting the browser directly to the Internet from the client computer.

161. D. A site-to-site VPN connection connects two remote Local Area Networks (LANs) together, enabling users on either network to access the other one. The typical configuration would consist of two VPN concentrators, one at each site, functioning as the endpoints of the connection.

162. C. A client-to-site VPN connection connects a single workstation to a remote Local Area Network (LAN), enabling the workstation user to access the remote network's resources. The typical configuration would consist of a standalone workstation and a VPN concentrator at the network site functioning as the endpoints of the connection.

163. B, C. The two most common types of TLS/SSL VPN connection are TLS/SSL portals, which provide users with access to selected remote network resources through a standard website, and TLS/SSL tunnels, which require the client web browser to run an active control, typically using Java or Flash. TLS/SSL client and TLS/SSL gateway are not common TLS/SSL VPN connections.

164. A. A host-to-host VPN connection connects two individual workstations at different locations, enabling the users on each workstation to access the other one through a secure tunnel. The typical configuration would consist of two workstations, one at each site, functioning as the endpoints of the connection.

165. A. The term *out-of-band* is used to describe any type of management access to a device that does not go through the production network. Plugging a laptop into the console port avoids the network, so it is considered to be an example of out-of-band management. In-band management describes an access method that goes through the production network. Client-to-site is a type of Virtual Private Network (VPN) connection, and Bring Your Own Device (BYOD) is a policy defining whether and how users are permitted to connect their personal devices to the network.

166. A, B. Because the two endpoints of a VPN are connecting to local Internet Service Providers (ISPs), the ongoing connection costs are typically much less than a long-distance WAN connection. However, in most cases, a VPN is slower because it is affected by Internet bandwidth use and other factors. VPN connections are not inherently less secure than WANs, and they are not necessarily more difficult to maintain.

167. B, C, D. Any method of connecting to a router, switch, or other managed device that does not use the production network is considered to be out-of-band management. This includes connecting a computer or terminal directly to the device, using a point-to-point modem connection, or consolidating dedicated ports on all of the devices by connecting them to an isolated switch. Logging on remotely using a workstation on the production network would be considered in-band management.

168. C. VNC supports many operating systems, can run through a web browser, and is free. However, it is not any faster than the competing products.

169. A. Telnet (TELetype NETwork) was the first TCP/IP terminal emulation program, but it is rarely used today because of its limitations. It is character-based only, and it transmits all data as cleartext, which is insecure. Secure Shell (SSH) addresses the security problem, but it too is character-based. Windows Terminal Services and Virtual Network Computing (VNC) were both created to provide graphical terminal emulation.

170. A, C, D. Tunneling is the process of encapsulating a data packet within another packet. The system then encrypts the entire data packet. Message integrity enables the recipient to detect any data tampering. Authentication ensures that only the intended recipient can access the data. There is no applicable technique called socketing.

171. B, C. A basic VPN typically uses full tunneling, in which all of the system's network traffic is encapsulated and encrypted for transmission. Split tunneling is a variation of this method in which only part of the system's traffic uses the VPN connection; the rest is transmitted over the network in the normal manner. Administrators can select which applications and devices use the VPN. Split tunneling can conserve Internet bandwidth used by the VPN and provide access to local services without the need for encapsulation. Split tunneling does not provide additional data integrity protection or improved performance through multiplexing.

172. C. Telnet transmits keystrokes in cleartext, including usernames and passwords. It is therefore insecure. Secure Shell (SSH) improves on the performance of Telnet by encrypting the passwords and other data it transmits over the network. Like Telnet, SSH is free and does not support graphical terminal emulation. SSH is also no faster than Telnet.

173. A. RDP is the client/server protocol created for use with Windows Terminal Services, now known as Remote Desktop Services. It is not used with VNC, Citrix products, or Telnet.

174. B, C. In this scenario, each user wants the fastest service available to connect to the corporate network over a VPN connection. Of all the services listed here, the only ones that will meet this requirement are DSL and CATV Internet. CATV and DSL Internet connections support high data rates and can be used to connect using a VPN tunnel, so they meet the speed requirement. Each user can use his or her existing CATV connection or use an existing telephone line to install DSL. Once the line is installed, each user needs to install and configure a VPN client on his or her computer and configure it to use L2TP and IPSec. Modem connections are slow—the maximum upstream speed is 33.6 Kbps, and the downstream is 56 Kbps. ISDN's maximum transfer rate for Basic Rate Interface (BRI) is 128 Kbps.

175. D. Extensible Authentication Protocol (EAP) is a shell protocol used with Point-to-Point Protocol (PPP), which enables systems to support various types of authentication mechanisms. The primary advantage of EAP is that it enables a computer to use mechanisms other than passwords for authentication, including public key certificates, smartcards, badge readers, and biometric devices, such as fingerprint scanners. Password Authentication Protocol (PAP) and Challenge Handshake Authentication Protocol (CHAP) support only password authentication. Point-to-Point Tunneling Protocol (PPTP) is a Virtual Private Network (VPN) protocol, not an authentication protocol.

176. C. The technology that uses human physical characteristics to authenticate users is called biometrics. Biometric devices can identify users based on fingerprints, retinal pattern, voice prints, and other characteristics.

177. A. Bar coding the new computers enables the IT department to record their locations, status, and conditions throughout their life cycle, a process known as asset tracking. Bar codes are not used for tamper detection and device hardening. Port security refers to switches, not computers.

178. C. An insider threat by definition originates with an authorized user. Smartcards, motion detection, and biometrics will only detect the presence of someone who is authorized to enter sensitive areas. Video surveillance, however, can track the activities of anyone, authorized or not.

179. D. The terms *fail close* and *fail open* refer to the default position of an electric or electronic door lock when there is a power failure. Security is often a trade-off with safety, and in the event that an emergency occurs, cutting off power, whether secured doors are permanently locked or left permanently open, is a critical factor. These terms do not apply to motion detectors or video cameras. A honeypot is a computer configured to lure potential attackers; it is not a physical security mechanism.

180. F. Smart lockers are available with a wide variety of authentication mechanisms, ranging from relatively unsecure PINs, Near Field Communication (NFC), and Bluetooth devices; to high-security biometric scans and radio-frequency identification (RFID) tags.

181. A, C. Closed-circuit television cameras are part of a self-contained system in which the cameras feed their signals to dedicated monitors, usually located in a security center. IP cameras are standalone devices that transmit signals to a wireless access point. While CCTV cameras can only be monitored by users in the security center, or another designated location, IP cameras can be monitored by any authorized user with a web browser. Lightweight Directory Access Protocol (LDAP) is a directory services protocol, and Network Access Control (NAC) is a service; neither one is a type of video surveillance device.

182. A. Social engineering is the practice of obtaining sensitive data by manipulating legitimate users, such as by pretending to be someone with a genuine need for that data. Because it is not a technological vulnerability, the only means of preventing this type of attack is to educate and train users to recognize potential threats. War driving is an attack method that consists of driving around a neighborhood with a computer, scanning for unprotected wireless networks. A logic bomb is a code insert placed into a legitimate software product that triggers a malicious event when specific conditions are met. An evil twin is a fraudulent access point on a wireless network that mimics the Service Set Identifier (SSID) of a legitimate access point, in the hope of luring in users.

183. C. A door that is configured to fail open reverts to its unsecured state—open—when an emergency occurs. This must be a carefully considered decision, as it can be a potential security hazard. However, configuring the door to fail closed is a potential safety hazard in the event of a fire or other disaster.

184. C. The technology that uses human physical characteristics to authenticate users is called biometrics. Biometric devices can identify users based on fingerprints, retinal pattern, voice prints, and other characteristics.

185. A, B, C. Biometric scans, identification badges, and key fobs are all means of distinguishing authorized from unauthorized personnel. Motion detection cannot make this distinction.

186. A. Video surveillance can monitor all activities of users in a sensitive area. With properly placed equipment, event-specific actions, such as commands entered in a computer, can be monitored. Identification badges, key fobs, motion detection, and locking cabinets can indicate the presence of individuals in a sensitive area, but they cannot monitor specific activities.

187. A, C, E. A radio-frequency identification (RFID) device is a small chip that can be electronically detected by a nearby reader. The chip can contain small amounts of data, such as the authentication credentials needed to grant an individual access to a secured area. Key fobs, proximity cards (prox cards), and smart lockers can use RFIDs to enable users to unlock a door by waving the device near a reader. Keycard locks typically require the card to be inserted into a reader and typically use magnetic strips to store data. Cypher locks rely on data supplied by the user—that is, the combination numbers.

188. B, D. Possession of the key fob is something you have, but the key fob could be lost or stolen, so its security is confirmed by entering a PIN, something you know. Unless the user both lost the key fob and shared the PIN, the device remains secure.

189. A, C. Key fobs and proximity cards (prox cards) often use radio-frequency identification (RFID) devices to enable users to unlock a door by waving the device near a reader. Keycard locks typically use magnetic strips to store data and require the card to be physically inserted into a reader. Cypher locks rely on data manually supplied by the user—that is, the combination numbers.

190. B, D. Video surveillance can conceivably prevent an evil twin attack, which takes the form of a rogue access point deliberately connected to the network for malicious purposes. Video surveillance can also help to prevent insider threats by monitoring the activities of authorized users. Video surveillance cannot prevent social engineering, which involves nothing more than communicating with people, or brute-force attacks, which are usually performed remotely.

191. D. When a false positive occurs during a biometric authentication, a user who should not be granted access to the secured device or location is granted access. A false negative is when a user who should be granted access is denied access.

192. A. All of the mechanisms listed are designed to make any attempts to tamper with or physically compromise the hardware devices immediately evident. This is therefore a form of tamper detection. Asset tracking is for locating and identifying hardware. Geofencing is a wireless networking technique for limiting access to a network. Port security refers to network switch ports.

193. C. The technology that uses human physical characteristics to authenticate users is called biometrics. Biometric devices can identify users based on fingerprints, retinal pattern, voice prints, and other characteristics.

194. D. A tailgater is a type of intruder who enters a secure area by closely following an authorized user. Most people are polite enough to hold the door open for the next person without knowing if they are authorized to enter. A tailgater is therefore not an intrusion prevention mechanism. Identification badges, locks, and key fobs are methods of preventing intrusions.

195. A. Identification badges, key fobs, and access control vestibules (mantraps) are all physical security mechanisms, in that they prevent unauthorized personnel from entering sensitive areas, such as datacenters. These mechanisms are not used for data file security, asset tracking, or switch port security.

196. C, D. Biometrics and smartcards are both means of preventing intrusions, whereas motion detection and video surveillance are mechanisms for detecting them.

197. B. A door that is configured to fail closed reverts to its secured state—locked—when an emergency occurs. This must be a carefully considered decision, since it can be a potential safety hazard in the event of a fire or other disaster. However, configuring the door to fail open is a potential security hazard.

198. B. An entrance arrangement in which people must close one door before they can open the next one is called an access control vestibule or mantrap. Security personnel can evaluate potential entrants while they are in the vestibule and detain attempted intruders there.

199. A, D. Deleting files on a hard disk drive leaves them available for retrieval, even though they appear to be gone. A disk wipe utility deletes all of the files on the hard drive and then overwrites the entire disk with zeroes, rendering all files unretrievable. Ralph can then reinstall the operating system to prepare the computer for sale. Performing these two steps eliminates the need to uninstall applications, delete data files manually, or perform a factory reset.

200. C. Terminal Access Controller Access Control System Plus (TACACS+) is a protocol that was designed to provide AAA services for networks with many routers and switches. AAA stands for Authentication, Authorization, and Accounting, but not administration.

Chapter 5: Network Troubleshooting

1. A. The first step in troubleshooting is to identify the problem by establishing symptoms related to the network issue being reported. In this step, problems are typically reported as trouble tickets, which are prioritized based on the severity of the problem. You complete the other steps after the trouble ticket has been prioritized and is being investigated.

2. C. A systemwide error is a problem that renders an individual user's system (computer) completely unusable. All the other problems listed would affect more than one system or user.

3. D. Any problem that affects all the users on the network is a networkwide problem and should be given the highest priority. An example of this would be a problem with an Internet router. All other problems listed do not affect the entire network.

4. B. In this scenario, only one user is reporting a problem. Therefore, the likeliest next step is to perform the same task on another computer attached to the same segment. If Ed can perform the task successfully, the problem most likely lies within the user's computer or the connection to the switch. Since no other users are reporting the same problem, the server and switches on the network are probably up and functioning. Checking the router is not necessary since the user and server are on the same network.

5. A. The first step in troubleshooting is to identify the problem by establishing symptoms related to the network problem being reported. In this step, you ask the user many questions to identify and define the symptoms of the problem and prioritize the trouble ticket. Although you might continue to ask the user questions throughout the troubleshooting process, this is typically associated with the first step of the troubleshooting process.

6. C. After identifying the problem, the next step is to establish a theory for the probable cause of the problem. After that, you can test your theory, establish a plan of action, implement a solution, verify the functionality of the system, and document the entire process.

7. B. The second step in troubleshooting is to attempt to duplicate a problem and develop a theory of its probable cause. As you troubleshoot a problem, you then test your theory to confirm your findings. You complete the other troubleshooting steps after the specific cause has been identified.

8. D. Replacing components by guesswork could resolve the problem through chance, but it would more likely be a waste of time and hardware. When Ralph's first theory is disproven, the next logical step would be to devise another theory. This could conceivably involve reinterviewing the users or escalating the issue to a senior technician. If the theory had been confirmed, the next step would be to devise a plan of action to resolve the problem.

9. C. In troubleshooting, one of the first steps in the process of identifying the problem is to question the obvious, such as whether the computer is plugged in or switched on. It would be unlikely that the user would know her computer's IP address or what updates had been installed when the screen is blank. Questioning whether other people have used the computer might come up later, but it will be little help at this stage of the troubleshooting process.

10. B. If a problem lies within a specific server or other network component that prevents many users from working, it is a shared resource problem. A problem that lies within resources that provide services to the entire network is a networkwide problem. Systemwide problems put a specific computer out of commission, preventing a user from getting any work done. An application problem is a problem that affects only a single user's access to a device or application.

11. A. Since only one user is reporting the problem, and he had admitted to making changes to his IP configuration, Alice should probably start by checking the configuration using the `ipconfig` command. If the router, DNS server, or WINS server were causing the problem, more than one user would be experiencing difficulties.

12. A. Since only one user is reporting the problem, the user's computer and its configuration are the likeliest suspect components. A DNS, proxy, or router problem would affect more than one user.

13. C. Alice is using a top-to-bottom approach, based on the Open Systems Interconnection (OSI) reference model. She begins at the top of the model (the application layer) by checking the system's email capabilities, and then proceeds downwards to check the computer's IP configuration (at the network layer), the local network connectivity (the data link layer), and the computer's cables (the physical layer). A bottom-to-top approach would begin with the cables. The divide-and-conquer approach and questioning the obvious would not involve the steps Alice took in the order that she took them.

14. A. There are many possible causes for the problem that are more likely than a router configuration error, so this is not something Alice would check first. Asking if the user can access the local network attempts to isolate the problem. If she cannot, the problem could be in her computer; if she can, then the problem lies somewhere in the Internet access infrastructure. If other users are experiencing the problem, then the issue should receive a higher priority, and Alice knows that the problem does not lie in the user's computer. While it might not be the first thing she checks, it is a political reality that higher ranking users often get preferential treatment.

15. B. Documenting everything you discover and everything you do is a crucial part of the troubleshooting method that must begin before you take any other action whatsoever. However, it appears as the last step in the troubleshooting methodology.

16. E. The first step in troubleshooting involves identifying the problem and creating a trouble ticket. You complete the other troubleshooting steps after the trouble ticket has been prioritized.

17. D. During the troubleshooting process, you must establish whether anything has changed. This typically involves asking the user whether any new or existing hardware or software has been installed or reconfigured.

18. C. After you have established a theory of probable cause, you can try to test the theory by replacing hardware components one by one until you find the faulty device.

19. D, F. Verifying that a router is functioning and forwarding traffic and verifying that a client's IP configuration is correct are not considered general troubleshooting steps. You might perform these two steps as a subset of general troubleshooting steps.

20. A, C. When a network problem or incident is reported, documentation begins. Proper documentation makes it easier for a first-tier support technician to prioritize and to escalate the call to senior technicians, if necessary.

21. B, D. When establishing priorities, networkwide problems take precedence over departmental problems, and problems with shared resources take precedence over individual desktop problems.

22. A, B, D. First-tier technicians are generally less experienced than second-tier technicians. First-tier technicians are the first point of contact for users. They receive and prioritize help desk calls and escalate problems to second-tier technicians, if necessary. First-tier technicians generally handle individual desktop problems, whereas second-tier technicians troubleshoot mission-critical network components such as routers and switches.

23. C. A problem that affects the entire network should be given highest priority. This includes a mission-critical backbone router. Problems that affect multiple LANs or an entire department are generally given the next highest priority. An application problem that affects a shared application server on a LAN should be given the next highest priority. A problem with a single user's computer should be given the lowest priority if the other problems have been reported.

24. B. A problem that affects the entire network should be given highest priority. This includes a mission-critical backbone router. Problems that affect multiple LANs or an entire department are generally given the next highest priority. An application problem that affects a shared application server on a LAN should be given the next highest priority. A problem with a single user's computer should be given the lowest priority if the other problems have been reported.

25. D. After you identify a problem and establish and test a theory of its probable cause, you must create a plan of action to resolve the problem and identify any potential effects (positive or negative) your solution might have. Then, you implement your solution, test the results, and finish documenting the incident.

26. G. The last step of the troubleshooting process is to document the solution and explain to the user what happened and why. In reality, documentation should begin when the problem is reported, and the documentation should be updated throughout the troubleshooting process.

27. A, D. The first stage of the troubleshooting process calls for Alice to identify the problem by gathering information. Learning about who is reporting the problem and what has changed since the server was last accessible can provide Alice with information that could help her determine whether the problem is located in the users' workstations, somewhere in the network, or in the server itself. The other options are intended to test a theory about a probable cause, a troubleshooting stage that comes later.

28. A. Because the multiple problems seem to be unrelated, Alice should handle them individually by creating a separate trouble ticket for each one and prioritizing each one. None of the problems seem to be severe enough to warrant escalation, nor should it be necessary to replace the computer. While it would be possible to send a technician to address all of the problems at once, it would be more efficient to assign each its own priority and handle it like any other trouble call.

29. B. The first phase of the troubleshooting process is gathering information. Learning whether the printer is accessible over the network can help Alice to isolate the location of the problem and develop a theory of probable cause. Installing drivers, checking switches, and upgrading firmware are all part of a later phase in the troubleshooting process: testing a theory to determine the cause of the problem.

30. A. A wiremap tester consists of a main unit that connects to all eight wires of a UTP cable at once and a loopback device that you connect to the other end, enabling you to test all of the wires at once. A wiremap tester can detect opens and shorts, as well as transposed wires. However, it cannot detect split pairs because, in that fault, the pins are properly connected.

31. D. The first and most essential test that installers must perform on every cable run is a continuity test, which ensures that each wire on both ends of the cable is connected to the correct pin and only the correct pin. If a pin on one end of a cable run is connected to two or more pins on the other end, the cable has a short circuit.

32. A. A rollover cable is a type of null modem cable, usually flat and light blue in color, with the pinouts reversed on either end, to enable a terminal to communicate with a router or switch through the device's dedicated console port. None of the other options are suitable for this purpose. A straight through cable is the standard network cable used to connect a computer to a switch. A crossover cable is designed to connect two network adapters directly. A plenum cable is a type of cable intended for use within air spaces and has an outer sheath that does not produce toxic fumes when it burns. A shielded cable is intended to protect signals from electromagnetic interference. A tap is a device used to branch a coaxial cable to two devices.

33. A. A straight through cable is the standard network patch cable used to connect a computer to a wall plate. A crossover cable is designed to connect two network adapters directly. A rollover cable is used to enable a terminal to communicate with a router or switch through the device's console port. A plenum cable is a type of cable intended for use within air spaces that has an outer sheath that does not produce toxic fumes when it burns.

34. C. The technique that provides this capability is called time-domain reflectometry (TDR). The tester transmits a signal over the cable and measures how long it takes for a reflection of the signal to return from the other end. Using this information and the cable's nominal velocity of propagation (NVP)—a specification supplied by the cable manufacturer—the device can calculate the length of a cable run. The other devices listed do not work in this way.

35. B. A short circuit is a wiring fault indicating that a pin at one end of a cable run is connected to two pins at the other end. To correct the problem, you must replace the connector with the faulty wiring. None of the other suggestions are solutions for a wiring fault.

36. C. All of the suggested tools are capable of associating wall plates with the correct patch panel ports, but the tone generator and locator is by far the most inexpensive solution.

37. D. Telephone cable technicians have their own specialized tools, such as the butt set, a one-piece telephone handset with alligator clips that enables its operator to connect to a line anywhere that the cables are accessible.

38. B, D. The punchdown tool is critical to this operation. In one motion, the tool strips the insulation off of the wire, presses it down into the connector, and cuts off the excess at the end. A wire stripper simplifies the task of preparing the cable for the connection process. A crimper is used only for attaching connectors to patch cables. Pigtail splicers and fusion splicers are used only on fiber-optic networks.

39. A. An optical loss test set (OLTS) identifies signal loss in fiber-optic cabling. A time-domain reflectometer (TDR) measures electrical signals in copper-based cabling, not light signals. Tone generator and locator tools and wiremap testers are used in copper-based cabling installations, not fiber-optic cabling.

40. B. You can use a cable certifier to identify a variety of cable performance characteristics, typically including cabling lengths, signal attenuation, crosstalk, propagation delay, delay skew, and return loss, in addition to providing all the functionality of a wiremap tester. The other tools listed are dedicated to a single testing modality and do not test for crosstalk.

41. B. Plenum cable is a type of cable intended for use within building air spaces (called plenums) that has an outer sheath that is more resistant to high temperatures and does not produce toxic fumes when it burns. The use of plenum cable has no effect on EMI or the type of traffic on the cable, nor is it required for low temperature areas.

42. D. An Optical Time Domain Reflectometer (OTDR) is a device that transmits light pulses over a fiber-optic network and measures the time interval and strength of the returning pulse, to measure the length of the cable run. An OTDR can be used to locate fiber-optic cable breaks, as well as characterize a cable run's reflectance, optical return loss, and other characteristics. Multimeters, tone generators, and wiremap testers are all devices that work only with copper networks.

43. C. A butt set is a one-piece telephone handset with alligator clips that enables its operator to connect to a telephone line anywhere that the cables are accessible. They are used by telephone cable technicians, but generally not by installers of network data cables. The other options are all standard tools used by data networking cable installers.

44. B. A crimper is a plier-like device that cable installers use to create patch cables by attaching RJ45 connectors to lengths of bulk cable. Installers use a punchdown tool, not a crimper, to attach a cable end to a keystone connector. It is not always necessary to purchase a crimper for each cable type. Some crimpers are designed for a single cable/connector combination, but there are many that have replaceable bits, supporting a variety of cables and connectors. Making patch cables yourself can represent a false economy. Buying bulk cable and connectors and making patch cables yourself can conceivably be cheaper than purchasing prefabricated cables. However, when you factor in the time needed to attach the connectors, the learning curve required to attach the connectors correctly, and the failure rate requiring the re-application of connectors, it might be more economical to purchase prefabricated patch cables in quantity instead.

45. A, C. Cable certifiers can detect all of the faults that tone generators and wiremap testers can detect, and they can do a great deal more, such as specify whether a cable run meets the performance specifications defined in a cable standard. When testing a new cable type, the specifications defined in the cable standard must be added to the device. Cable certifiers are far more expensive than most other cable testing solutions. Cable certifiers are available that support various cable media, including copper and fiber optic.

46. C, D. Alice can use a tone generator and locator or a wiremap tester to identify and test cable connections. By connecting the tone generator or the remote wiremap unit to one end of a cable run, she can use the locator or the master wiremap unit to find the other end. This can enable her to identify a starting point and an ending point for a cable run. A loopback adapter is used to test the transmission and reception capabilities of a port. A packet sniffer captures and analyzes network traffic; it cannot identify cables.

47. B, D. A crimper is a device used for attaching connectors to patch cables. A wire stripper, while not essential to the process, can simplify the task of preparing the cable. A punchdown tool is used for attaching keystone connectors to cable ends, for use in wall plates and patch panels. A standard set of pliers is not used in the process of attaching connectors.

48. B. Crimpers and punchdown tools are relatively simple and inexpensive mechanical devices that cable installers use to connect bulk cable to connectors. A wiremap tester is an electronic device for cable testing, but it is still relatively simple. A cable certifier is a complex electronic device that can perform a battery of tests on a cable run, confirm that the cable conforms to the required wiring standards, and maintain records of the testing procedure. Cable certifiers are by far the most expensive of the devices listed.

49. C. The device shown in the figure is a multimeter, which is used to measure the electric current on a copper conductor, such as an Unshielded Twisted Pair (UTP) network. This tool is not capable of performing any of the tasks described in the other options.

50. B. The device shown in the figure is a punchdown tool, used to connect Unshielded Twisted Pair (UTP) cable ends to the keystone connectors used in modular wall plates and patch panels. After lining up the individual wires in the cable with the connector, one uses the tool to press each wire into its slot. The tool also cuts the wire sheath to make an electrical contact and trims the end of the wire. This tool is not capable of performing any of the tasks described in the other options.

51. A. The device shown in the figure is a tone generator and locator, used to test Unshielded Twisted Pair (UTP) wiring and detect certain basic wiring faults. This tool is not capable of performing any of the tasks described in the other options.

52. B. The device shown in the figure is a crimper, which is used to create patch cables by attaching connectors to both ends of a relatively short length of bulk cable. This tool is not capable of performing any of the tasks described in the other options.

53. A. The device shown in the figure is a butt set, a basic tool of telephone installers and line workers. By connecting the clips to pins in a punchdown block, you can access telephone circuits in order to test them or place telephone calls.

54. B, C. A crimper is a plier-like tool that cable installers use to attach RJ45 connectors to patch cables. A punchdown tool is a tool that cable installers use to attach keystone connectors to cable ends, for use in wall plates and patch panels. A telepole is a device used to run cables through walls, floors, and ceilings, but since the cable runs have already been pulled, Ralph will not need this tool. A pigtail splicer is a tool used only in fiber-optic cable installations.

55. A. The failure to detect a tone on a wire indicates that there is either a break in the wire somewhere inside the cable or a bad connection with the pin in one or both connectors. This condition is called an open circuit. A short is when a wire is connected to two or more pins at one end of the cable. A split pair is a connection in which two wires are incorrectly mapped in exactly the same way on both ends of the cable. Crosstalk is a type of interference caused by signals on one wire bleeding over to other wires.

56. B. A short is when a wire is connected to two or more pins at one end of the cable or when the conductors of two or more wires are touching inside the cable. This would cause a tone applied to a single pin at one end to be heard on multiple pins at the other end. An open circuit would manifest as a failure to detect a tone on a wire, indicating that there is either a break in the wire somewhere inside the cable or a bad connection with the pin in one or both connectors. A split pair is a connection in which two wires are incorrectly mapped in exactly the same way on both ends of the cable. Crosstalk is a type of interference caused by signals on one wire bleeding over to other wires.

57. C. A split pair is a connection in which two wires are incorrectly mapped in exactly the same way on both ends of the cable. Each pin on one end of the cable is correctly wired to the corresponding pin at the other end, but the wires inside the cable used to make the connections are incorrect. In a properly wired connection, each twisted pair should contain a signal wire and a ground wire. In a split pair, it is possible to have two signal wires twisted together as a pair. This can generate excessive amounts of crosstalk, corrupting both of the signals involved. Because all of the pins are connected properly, a tone generator and locator cannot detect this fault. An open circuit would manifest as a failure to detect a tone on a wire, indicating that there is either a break in the wire somewhere inside the cable or a bad connection with the pin in one or both connectors. A short is when a wire is connected to two or more pins at one end of the cable or when the conductors of two or more wires are touching inside the cable. Transposed pairs is a fault in which both of the wires in a pair are connected to the wrong pins at one end of the cable. All three of these faults are detectable with a tone generator and locator.

58. C. A split pair is a connection in which two wires are incorrectly mapped in exactly the same way on both ends of the cable. Each pin on one end of the cable is correctly wired to the corresponding pin at the other end, but the wires inside the cable used to make the connections are incorrect. In a properly wired connection, each twisted pair should contain a signal wire and a ground wire. In a split pair, it is possible to have two signal wires twisted together as a pair. This can generate excessive amounts of crosstalk, corrupting both of the signals involved. Open circuits, shorts, and transposed pairs interfere with cable performance but do not make it more susceptible to crosstalk.

59. D. A split pair is a connection in which two wires are incorrectly mapped in exactly the same way on both ends of the cable. Each pin on one end of the cable is correctly wired to the corresponding pin at the other end, but the wires inside the cable used to make the connections are incorrect. In a properly wired connection, each twisted pair should contain a signal wire and a ground wire. In a split pair, it is possible to have two signal wires twisted together as a pair. This can generate excessive amounts of crosstalk, corrupting both of the signals involved. Because all of the pins are connected properly, a tone generator and locator cannot detect this fault, and neither can a wiremap tester or a multimeter. However, a cable certifier is a highly sophisticated electronic device that can detect all types of cable faults, including split pairs, as well as measure cable performance characteristics.

60. C, D. A time-domain reflectometer (TDR) is a device that determines the length of a cable by transmitting a signal at one end and measuring how long it takes for a reflection of the signal to return from the other end. Using this information and the cable's nominal velocity of propagation (NVP)—a specification supplied by the cable manufacturer—the device can calculate the length of a cable run. In a cable with a break in its length, a TDR calculates the length of the cable up to the break. Cable certifiers typically have time-domain reflectometry capabilities integrated into the unit. A tone generator and locator or a multimeter cannot locate a cable break.

61. C. Of the options provided, the only possible source of the problem is that the cable runs are using a cable type not rated for Gigabit Ethernet. Some older buildings might still have Category 3 cable installed, which was used in the original twisted-pair Ethernet specification. Cat 3 is unsuitable for use with Gigabit Ethernet in many ways and can result in the poor performance that Alice is experiencing. A cable installation with runs wired using different pinout standards will not affect performance as long as each run uses the same pinouts at both ends. Gigabit Ethernet will not function at all if only two wire pairs are connected. The transceivers are located in the equipment that Alice's company brought from the old location, so they are not mismatched.

62. B. Ralph can use a tone generator and locator to locate the correct cable associated with each office connection. By connecting the tone generator to one end of a cable run, he can use the locator to find the other end. A cable certifier identifies a variety of cable performance characteristics, typically including cabling length, signal attenuation, and crosstalk. An Optical Time Domain Reflectometer (OTDR) is a device for measuring the lengths and other characteristics of fiber-optic cables. A multimeter is a device for measuring the electric current on a copper cable.

63. B. An optical loss test set (OLTS) is the term for the combination of an optical light source and an optical power meter. The optical power meter by itself cannot be used to test the cable runs when there are no devices connected to them. An Optical Time Domain Reflectometer (OTDR) is a device for measuring the lengths and other characteristics of fiber-optic cables. A multimeter is a device for measuring the electric current on a copper cable.

64. C. A split pair is a connection in which two wires are incorrectly mapped in exactly the same way on both ends of the cable. In a properly wired connection, each twisted pair should contain a colored signal wire and a striped ground wire. In a split pair, it is possible to have two signal wires twisted together as a pair. This can generate excessive amounts of crosstalk, corrupting both of the signals involved. Because all of the pins are connected properly, a tone generator and locator cannot detect this fault. An open circuit would manifest as a failure to detect a tone on a wire, indicating that there is either a break in the wire or a bad connection in one or both connectors. A short is when a wire is connected to two or more pins or when the conductors of two or more wires are touching. Transposed pairs is a fault in which both of the wires in a pair are connected to the wrong pins at one end of the cable. All three of these faults are detectable with a tone generator and locator.

65. C. Attenuation is the weakening of a signal as it travels long distances, whether on a wired or wireless medium. The longer the transmission distance, the more the signal weakens. Absorption is the tendency of a wireless signal to change as it passes through different materials. Latency is a measurement of the time it takes for a signal to travel from its source to its destination. Crosstalk is a type of interference that occurs on wired networks when a signal bleeds over to an adjacent wire.

66. B, C. Dirt on fiber-optic cable connectors can reduce the strength of the signal, resulting in decibel loss. Excessive cable length can result in greater attenuation and weaker signals due to the decibel loss. Electromagnetic interference and signal crosstalk are both factors that can affect copper cable transmissions, but not fiber optic.

67. A, B, C. There should be no collisions at all on a full-duplex network, so collisions indicate that at least one side of the connection is trying to operate in half-duplex mode. Ethernet running over twisted-pair cable, in its original half-duplex mode, detects collisions by looking for data on the transmit and receive pins at the same time. In full-duplex mode, data is supposed to be transmitted and received at the same time. In a duplex mismatch, in which one side of a connection is configured to use full duplex and the other end is configured to use half duplex, the full-duplex communications originating from one side look like collisions to the half-duplex side. The half-duplex adapter transmits a jam signal as a result of each collision, which causes the full-duplex side to receive an incomplete or damaged frame, which are perceived as runts or through Cyclic Redundancy Check (CRC) errors. Both sides then start to retransmit frames in a continuing cycle, causing network performance to diminish.

Ping tests do not detect a duplex mismatch, because ping only transmits a small amount of data in one direction at a time. The mismatch only becomes apparent when the systems transmit large amounts of data.

68. B, D, E. A speed mismatch on a wired network only occurs when two devices are configured to use a specific transmission speed and those speeds are different. In that case, network communication stops. For network communication to occur on a twisted-pair network, transmit (TX) pins must be connected to receive (RX) pins. If the connections are reversed, no communication occurs. If the switch port to which a computer is connected is bad, there will be no network communication. Bottlenecks and duplex mismatches will slow down network communications, but they will not stop them completely.

69. A, C. A bottleneck is a component involved in a network connection that is not functioning correctly, causing a traffic slowdown that affects the entire network. A duplex mismatch occurs when one side of a connection is configured to use full duplex and the other end is configured to use half duplex. When this occurs, the full-duplex communications on the one side look like collisions to the half-duplex side. The half-duplex adapter transmits a jam signal as a result of each collision, which causes the full-duplex side to receive an incomplete frame. Both sides then start to retransmit frames in a continuing cycle, causing network performance to diminish drastically. A speed mismatch or a Transmit and Receive (TX/RX) reversal will stop network communication completely.

70. B. Attenuation is the weakening of a signal as it travels long distances, whether on a wired or wireless medium. The longer the transmission distance, the more the signal weakens. Cable length specifications are designed in part to prevent signals from attenuating to the point at which they are unviable. Jitter, crosstalk, and electromagnetic interference (EMI) are all conditions that can affect the performance of a wired network, but they are not directly related to the length of the cable.

71. B, C. The Gigabit Ethernet standards call for switches and network adapters to support autonegotiation by default, which enables devices to communicate and select the best network speed and duplex mode available to them both. Therefore, speed mismatches and duplex mismatches no longer occur unless someone modifies the speed or duplex settings to incompatible values on one or both devices.

72. D. Fluorescent light fixtures and other devices in an office environment can generate magnetic fields, resulting in electromagnetic interference (EMI). When a copper-based cable runs too near to such a device, the magnetic fields can generate an electric current on the cable that interferes with the signals exchanged by network devices. Jitter, crosstalk, and attenuation are all conditions that can affect the performance of a wired network, but they are not directly related to the cables' proximity to light fixtures.

73. C. The link pulse LED indicates the adapter is connected to a functioning hub or switch. The speed LED specifies the data rate of the link. The collision LED lights up when collisions occur. There is no status LED on a network interface adapter.

74. C. The Alternative B PoE variant can use the spare wire pairs in a Category 5 (Cat 5) or better 10Base-T or 100Base-TX cable to supply power to connected devices. The Alternative A and 4PPoE variants cannot use the spare wire pair in this manner; they supply power using the wire pairs that carry data at the same time. For Gigabit Ethernet or faster installations, Alternative B is capable of using the data wire pairs.

75. C. Jitter is defined as delays in the transmission of individual network packets. For audio or video transmissions, jitter can result in dropped words or frames. For data file transmissions, jitter can require retransmission of packets.

76. A, B, C, D. The 1000Base-SX standard calls for multimode cable with a maximum length of approximately 500 meters, while the new cable run is 4,000 meters and uses single-mode cable. The 1000Base-SX transceiver will also be incompatible with the 1000Base-BX10 transceiver at the other end. 1000Base-BX10 uses wavelengths from 1,300 to 1,600 nanometers (nm), whereas 1000Base-SX uses wavelengths of 770 to 860 nm.

77. A. There should be no collisions on a full-duplex network, so the problem is clearly related to the duplexing of the communications. Ethernet running over twisted-pair cable, in its original half-duplex mode, detects collisions by looking for data on the Transmit and Receive (TX/RX) pins at the same time. In full-duplex mode, data is supposed to be transmitted and received at the same time. When one side of a connection is configured to use full duplex, as Alice's new computers are, and the other end is configured to use half duplex (as the switches must be), the full-duplex communications on the one side look like collisions to the half-duplex side. The half-duplex adapter transmits a jam signal as a result of each collision, which causes the full-duplex side to receive an incomplete frame. Both sides then start to retransmit frames in a continuing cycle, causing network performance to diminish drastically. The ping tests do not detect a problem, because ping only transmits a small amount of data in one direction at a time. The other options would likely cause the ping tests to fail as well. The solution to the problem is to configure all of the devices to autonegotiate their speed and duplex modes.

78. B, E. One possible cause of the problem is that the DNS process on the remote server is corrupted or not running. Another possible cause is that there is a firewall blocking access to the server's Unshielded Twisted Pair (UTP) port 53. Both of these would render the port unreachable. The Transmission Control Protocol/Internet Protocol (TCP/IP) client on the server is operating, as verified by the ping utility. This means that the IP host configurations on Ralph's computer and on the DNS server are both functioning. The router does not need to be running DNS to forward datagrams.

79. A, B. Both Telnet and FTP are protocols that include command-line client applications, with Telnet providing terminal emulation and FTP file transfer functionality. SNMP and DNS are both application layer protocols, but neither one includes a program. Nslookup has a command-line interface, but it executes commands on the local system, not a remote one.

80. D. The Windows tracert tool transmits a series of ICMP messages with incrementing Time to Live (TTL) values, which identify each router on the path that the packets take through the network. Ping uses ICMP, but it does not manipulate TTL values. Netstat, Route, Nslookup, and Hostname do not use ICMP messages, nor do they manipulate TTL values when performing their normal functions.

81. B. If Alice suspects that a DNS server is not resolving hostnames, she should try connecting to a remote host using the Internet Protocol (IP) address instead of the name. If she can connect, she knows that all internal Local Area Network (LAN) components and the Internet gateway are functioning, and the remote host is functioning. The problem most likely lies within the DNS server itself. If Alice cannot connect to a remote host using the IP address, the problem is not the DNS server. She would need to do more testing to isolate the problem device and the affected area. `ipconfig` is a workstation command that enables you to verify the local IP configuration; it is not used to test a DNS server's functionality. Using the `ping` command will only tell you whether the computer hosting the DNS service is functioning at the network layer of the Open Systems Interconnection (OSI) model; it will not test the DNS service functionality. The `tracert` (or `traceroute`) command is used to identify the hop-by-hop path taken to reach a destination; it does not allow you to test functionality above the network layer of the OSI model.

82. B, E. `nslookup` and `dig` are both command-line utilities that you can direct to a specific DNS server and then generate queries that display resource record information the program retrieves from the server. `netstat` displays information about networking protocols, whereas `nbtstat` displays information derived from the system's Network Basic Input/Output System (NetBIOS) over Transmission Control Protocol/Internet Protocol (TCP/IP) implementation. `arp` is a tool that you can use to display and manage a system's Address Resolution Protocol (ARP) table entries. `netstat`, `nbtstat`, and `arp` are not able to display resource record information.

83. D. Running the `arp` utility with the −a parameter on a Windows system displays the contents of the Address Resolution Protocol (ARP) cache. The cache contains records of the Internet Protocol (IP) addresses on the network that `arp` has resolved into Media Access Control (MAC) addresses. The `ping`, `tracert`, `netstat`, and `hostname` utilities are not capable of producing this output.

84. B. The Windows `tracert` utility functions by transmitting a series of Internet Control Message Protocol (ICMP) Echo Request messages to a specified destination with incrementing Time to Live (TTL) values. Each successive message reaches one hop farther on the route to the destination before timing out. The `tracert` display therefore lists the names and addresses of the routers that packets must traverse to reach the destination. The `ping`, `netstat`, `arp`, and `hostname` utilities are not capable of producing this output.

85. A. The Windows `ping` utility functions by transmitting a series of Internet Control Message Protocol (ICMP) Echo Request messages to a specified destination. The destination system responds with ICMP Echo Reply messages that are listed in the output display. The `tracert`, `netstat`, `arp`, and `hostname` utilities are not capable of producing this output.

86. C. Running the Windows `netstat` utility with no parameters generates a list of the workstation's active connections. The `ping`, `tracert`, `arp`, and `hostname` utilities are not capable of producing this output.

87. B. Like `traceroute` and `tracert`, `pathping` is capable of generating a list of the routers that packets pass through on the way to a specific destination system. `pathping` also displays the percentage of lost packets for each hop, which `traceroute` and `tracert` cannot do. The `ping`, `netstat`, and `route` utilities are not capable of displaying route traces.

88. C. The `traceroute` (or `tracert`) utility can locate a malfunctioning router by using an Echo Request messages with incrementing Time to Live (TTL) values. `ifconfig` is a network configuration utility for Unix and Linux systems; `ping` can test connectivity to another Transmission Control Protocol/Internet Protocol (TCP/IP) system, but it cannot locate a malfunctioning router; and `netstat` displays information about network connections and traffic but cannot locate a malfunctioning router.

89. E. All Windows ping transactions use Internet Control Message Protocol (ICMP) messages. ICMP messages are encapsulated directly within Internet Protocol (IP) datagrams; they do not use transport layer protocols, such as User Datagram Protocol (UDP). Ping transactions to destinations on the local network are encapsulated within Ethernet frames. On Unix and Linux, ping uses UDP, which is also encapsulated in IP datagrams.

90. B. The netstat utility can display the routing table, along with other types of network traffic and port information. The arp utility is for adding addresses to the Address Resolution Protocol (ARP) cache; it cannot display the routing table. The ifconfig command displays Transmission Control Protocol/Internet Protocol (TCP/IP) configuration information on Unix and Linux systems; it cannot display the routing table. Telnet is a terminal emulation program; it cannot display the routing table.

91. C. Running ping with the -l parameter enables you to specify the size of the messages sent to the target—in this case, 2028 bytes. The -n parameter enables you to specify the number of messages the ping tool should transmit—in this case, 11. Combining these two parameters generates the output in the figure. The -t parameter causes the ping tool to transmit messages until manually halted.

92. C. The arp -a command displays the entries in the ARP table stored in its cache. The arp -d command is for deleting entries, and the arp -s command is for adding entries. The arp -c command is not a valid option.

93. B. The nslookup tool enables you to generate DNS request messages from the command line and send them to a specific DNS server. The other options listed are not DNS utilities.

94. A. On a Unix or Linux host, the ifconfig command displays the system's current IP configuration settings and parameters. ipconfig is a Windows command-line utility that performs the same basic function. The other options are command-line utilities that do not display IP configuration information.

95. B. Running the ping tool with the -t parameter causes it to send messages to the target continuously until it is manually stopped. The -n parameter specifies the number of messages the ping tool should transmit. The -i parameter specifies the time-to-live (TTL) value of the messages ping transmits. The -a parameter resolves an Internet Protocol (IP) address specify as the target to a hostname.

96. B. The arp -d command is for deleting cache entries, and by running it with the asterisk wildcard, the command deletes all of the entries in the cache. The arp -a command displays the entries in the ARP table stored in its cache, and the arp -s command is for adding entries. The arp -c * command is not a valid option.

97. D. The nmap utility is capable of scanning a system for open ports that might be a security hazard. The tcpdump, dig, iptables, and iperf utilities cannot do this.

98. C, D. ping and tracert are both utilities that test network layer characteristics using ICMP messages. ping tests the network layer functionality of the host, and traceroute displays the path to the host through the internetwork. ipconfig and netstat do not use ICMP messages.

99. C. Running the `ping` tool with the `-i` parameter specifies the TTL value of the messages that `ping` transmits. The `-t` parameter causes the `ping` tool to send messages to the target continuously until it is manually stopped. The `-n` parameter specifies the number of messages the `ping` tool should transmit. The `-a` parameter resolves an Internet Protocol (IP) address specified as the target to a hostname.

100. B. Ralph wants to store and view only the traffic relating to the hosts that are experiencing problems. The best way to do this is to set a capture filter. Capture filters determine what is stored in the buffer. Display filters only determine what is displayed from the contents of the buffer. You do not set a trap on an analyzer—you set traps on Simple Network Management Protocol (SNMP) agents. Also, there is no need to configure both a capture filter and a display filter. If you set a capture filter that blocks all other traffic from entering the buffer, the display filter would be redundant.

101. A, D. Ralph can use the `ping` and `traceroute` tools to verify the network layer functionality of the application server and the router. The `ping` tool tests the network layer through the exchange of Internet Control Message Protocol (ICMP) Echo and Echo Reply messages. The `traceroute` tool can verify that there is a functioning path between the users' workstations and the application server. The `route` tool is used to administer the routing table on the local machine. The `arp` tool is used to view a computer's Internet Protocol to Media Access Control (IP to MAC) address resolution table stored in memory.

102. C. A protocol analyzer copies all network traffic, interprets the protocol headers and fields, and displays the output. The Event Viewer displays system, application, and security event logs on a single computer. There is no network troubleshooting tool called a traffic monitor. A management console is a remote monitoring and management device that queries Simple Network Management Protocol (SNMP) agents.

103. E. Of the utilities listed, `tcpdump`, `dig`, `iptables`, and `ifconfig` are all tools that run on Unix or Linux systems only. The `route` utility runs on both Unix or Linux and Windows.

104. A. `nslookup` is a command-line utility that generates Domain Name System (DNS) resource record requests and sends them to a specific DNS server. The output shown here first specifies the name and address of the DNS server to which the request was sent, and then the response to the request, containing the name to be resolved and the Internet Protocol (IP) addresses contained in the server's resource record for that name. The `pathping`, `netstat`, and `route` utilities cannot perform DNS queries.

105. A. Running the `ping` tool with the `-n` parameter specifies the number of messages the tool should transmit with each execution. The `-t` parameter causes the `ping` tool to send messages to the target continuously until manually stopped. The `-i` parameter specifies the Time to-Live (TTL) value of the messages that `ping` transmits. The `-a` parameter resolves an Internet Protocol (IP) address specified as the target to a hostname.

106. A, E. The `ping` and `nslookup` utilities can both run on Windows, Unix, or Linux systems. The `traceroute` command runs only on Unix or Linux, although there is a Windows version called `tracert`. The `ifconfig` and `iptables` commands only exist on Unix and Linux systems.

107. D. The `ifconfig` command runs only on Unix and Linux systems. The `ping` and `netstat` utilities run on Windows, Unix, or Linux systems. The `ipconfig` and `tracert` commands run only on Windows, although there is a Unix/Linux version of `tracert` called `traceroute`.

108. B. The `ipconfig` command runs only on Windows, although there is a similar Unix or Linux-only command called `ifconfig`. The `ping` and netstat utilities run on Windows, Unix, or Linux systems. The `traceroute` utility runs only on Unix or Linux systems, although there is a Windows version called `tracert`.

109. B, D. Both Linux and the Cisco IOS operating systems have the `traceroute` utility. Windows has a version of the utility, but it is called `tracert`. The CSU/DSU cannot run a `traceroute` command.

110. B. The `netstat -s` command displays packet counts and other traffic statistics for the IPv6, IPv4, ICMP, TCP, and UDP protocols. The `netstat -a` command displays all of a workstation's current connections and ports on which it is listening. The `netstat -e` command displays Ethernet statistics, such as the number of bytes and packets sent and received. The `netstat -r` command displays the computer's routing table.

111. A. Running `netstat` with the `-e` parameter on a Windows workstation displays Ethernet statistics, including the number of bytes and packets the workstation has sent and received. The `ipconfig` command displays Transmission Control Protocol/Internet Protocol (TCP/IP) configuration data; it does not display network traffic statistics. The `tcpdump` and `iptables` commands both run only on Unix and Linux workstations.

112. A, B, D. Windows, Linux, and the Cisco IOS operating systems all include the `ping` utility. The CSU/DSU cannot run a `ping` command.

113. B. The Internet Protocol (IP) address 127.0.0.1 is a dedicated loopback address that directs outgoing IP traffic directly into the incoming IP traffic buffer. A successful ping test using that address indicates that the computer's Transmission Control Protocol/Internet Protocol (TCP/IP) stack is functioning properly, but the traffic never reaches the network adapter or the network, so the test does not confirm that the adapter is functioning or that the computer has a correct IP address for the network.

114. B, C. The Internet Protocol (IP) address 127.0.0.1 is a dedicated loopback address that directs outgoing IP traffic directly into the incoming IP traffic buffer. The hostname localhost resolves to the 127.0.0.1 address on every TCP/IP system. Ed can therefore ping either the hostname or the IP address to test that his TCP/IP stack is functional. Loopback is not a hostname for the loopback address, and 127.0.0.0 is a network address, not a host address, so it will not work in this situation.

115. B. `ipconfig` is a Windows command that displays a computer's current IP address and Transmission Control Protocol/Internet Protocol (TCP/IP) configuration settings, including whether the computer has obtained its address from a DHCP server. The `ifconfig` command displays the same information for Unix and Linux systems. `msinfo32` is a Windows program that generates a graphical display of the computer's hardware and software configuration, but not its IP address and TCP/IP settings. The `tracert` command in Windows displays the path that packets take through the internetwork to reach a specified destination, but it does not display DHCP information.

116. B, C, D. When you run the `netstat` command without any switch options, it displays the computer's active connections. Running `netstat -e` displays the computer's interface statistics. Running `netstat -r` displays the routing table. There is no `netstat` switch that displays the computer's connection state.

117. B. The `route print` command displays both the IPv4 and IPv6 routing tables. To display only the IPv6 routing table, you add the `-6` parameter to the `route print` command. `route list` and `route list -6` are not valid commands.

118. C. Running the Windows `netstat` command with the `-e` parameter displays Ethernet statistics, including the number of bytes and packets that have been transmitted and received. The `ping`, `tracert`, and `arp` utilities are not capable of producing this output.

119. B. Running the `arp -e` command on a Linux system displays the contents of the Address Resolution Protocol (ARP) cache in the format shown here. The `arp -a` command displays the cache using an alternative format. The `arp -d` command is for deleting cache entries, and the `arp -s` command is for creating cache entries.

120. D. The `arp -s` command enables you to create a cache record specifying the Media Access Control (MAC) address and its associated Internet Protocol (IP) address. The `arp -N` command enables you to display the ARP cache entries for a specified network interface. The `arp -d` command is for deleting cache entries. The `arp -a` command displays the entries in the ARP table stored in its cache.

121. C. The `tcpdump` utility is a command-line tool that captures network packets and displays their contents. The `iptables`, `nmap`, and `pathping` utilities cannot capture and analyze packets. `iptables` manages Unix/Linux kernel firewall rules, `nmap` is a port scanner, and `pathping` is a Windows route tracing tool.

122. C. A NetFlow analyzer is a tool that can collect network traffic data and analyze how bandwidth is being used and who is using it. A protocol analyzer is also a tool that captures network packets, but for the purpose of analyzing their contents. A bandwidth speed tester measures a network's internet access speed. An Internet Protocol (IP) scanner lists the IP addresses that are in use on a network.

123. B. The destination system is the last one listed in the trace. By averaging the response times of 99, 106, and 108 milliseconds (ms), you can calculate the average response time: 104.33 ms.

124. B. The `dig` utility in Linux can display the authoritative Domain Name System (DNS) servers for a particular domain when you specify the domain name and the ns (name server) parameter. The `netstat`, `nslookup`, and `route` commands cannot generate this particular output.

125. D. On Unix and Linux systems, the `traceroute` utility tests Transmission Control Protocol/Internet Protocol (TCP/IP) connectivity by transmitting User Datagram Protocol (UDP) messages. This is unlike the `tracert` utility on Windows systems, which uses Internet Control Message Protocol (ICMP) messages. Neither version uses TCP or Hypertext Transfer Protocol (HTTP).

126. B. To access the Internet, the workstation's routing table must include a default gateway entry, which would have a Network Destination value of 0.0.0.0. A workstation's routing table does not specify the address of a Domain Name System (DNS) server. The loopback and 224.0.0.0 multicast addresses are normal routing table entries.

127. D. A protocol analyzer is a tool that enables a user to view the contents of packets captured from a network. In Ed's case, if IPSec is properly implemented, he should be able to see that the data in packets captured from his workstation is encrypted. A packet sniffer is a tool that captures packets for the purpose of traffic analysis but cannot view their contents. In practice, however, packet sniffer and protocol analyzer capabilities are usually integrated into a single tool. A port scanner examines a system, looking for open Transmission Control Protocol (TCP) and User Datagram Protocol (UDP) ports, and a multimeter is a tool that reads voltages on electrical circuits. An Internet Protocol (IP) scanner queries the network for the IP addresses currently in use and gathers information about the devices using them. None of these tools can examine packet contents.

128. A. A packet sniffer is a tool that captures packets for the purpose of traffic analysis but cannot view their contents. A protocol analyzer is a tool that enables a user to view the contents of packets captured from a network. In practice, however, packet sniffer and protocol analyzer capabilities are often integrated into a single tool. Both tools can function in promiscuous mode to capture packets from an entire network.

129. B, E. The `ipconfig /release` command terminates the current DHCP address lease. Then, the `ipconfig /renew` command causes the client to begin the process of negotiating a new lease, this time with an authorized DHCP server. `dump`, `lease`, and `discard` are not valid `ipconfig` parameters.

130. D. The correct syntax for the Windows `route add` command is to specify the destination network address, followed by the subnet mask for the destination network, followed by the address of the router interface on the local network that provides access to the destination network. The other options do not specify the correct addresses in the syntax.

131. C. The correct syntax for the Windows `route add` command is to specify the destination network address, followed by the subnet mask for the destination network, followed by the address of the router interface on the local network that provides access to the destination network. Therefore, 192.168.87.226 is the address of the router interface on the internal network, where Ralph's workstation is located.

132. C. Port scanning identifies open ports on a single computer, whereas port sweeping scans multiple computers for a single open port. War driving and bluejacking are methods of attacking wireless networks.

133. D. A protocol analyzer captures frames and displays their contents, including the header fields created by the protocols at the various Open Systems Interconnection (OSI) model layers. To interpret the exchanges between the computers on the network, you must be familiar with the protocols and how they operate. Protocol analyzers are useful tools in the hands of experienced network administrators, but they can also be used for malicious purposes, such as displaying unencrypted passwords and other confidential information in the captured packets. The difference between analyzers and sniffers is that analyzers read the internal contents of the packets they capture, parse the individual data units, and display information about each of the protocols involved in the creation of the packet, while sniffers look for trends and patterns in the network traffic without examining the contents of each packet.

134. A, B. nmap is a command-line utility that scans a range of IP addresses, runs a series of scripts against each device it finds, and displays a list of the open ports it finds on each one. Nessus is similar to nmap in that it also scans a range of IP addresses to find open ports, but it then proceeds to mount attacks against those ports, to ascertain their vulnerability. Network Monitor is a protocol analyzer or packet sniffer, which is a program that captures network traffic samples and analyzes them. It is not a port scanner. Performance Monitor is a program that displays statistics for specific system and network performance criteria. It is not a port scanner.

135. B. The top utility displays performance information about the currently running processes on a Unix/Linux system. netstat is a tool that enables you to view active network connections and Transmission Control Protocol/Internet Protocol (TCP/IP) traffic statistics. It does not measure system performance. There is no Unix or Linux tool called monitor or cpustat.

136. B. Protocol analyzers report the total number of frames seen compared to the number of frames that were accepted. If a capture filter is in place, there will be a discrepancy between these two values. Only frames that meet the capture criteria will be accepted by the analyzer and placed in the buffer for later display. Protocol analyzers place good and bad frames into the buffer as long as they meet the capture criteria. If only good frames were placed in the buffer, there would be no way to identify problems.

137. B. A port scanner examines a system for open endpoints, accessible using the Transmission Control Protocol (TCP) or User Datagram Protocol (UDP), which intruders can conceivably use to gain access to the system from the network.

138. B. A port is a numbered service endpoint identifying an application running on a Transmission Control Protocol/Internet Protocol (TCP/IP) system. A port scanner examines a system for open endpoints, accessible using the TCP or User Datagram Protocol (UDP) at the transport layer, which intruders can conceivably use to gain access to the system from the network.

139. B. The ports that a port scanner examines are the system endpoints identified by port numbers in Transmission Control Protocol (TCP) and User Datagram Protocol (UDP) headers. An open port provides network access to an application running on the computer, which can conceivably be exploited by an intruder.

140. C. A packet analyzer is capable of looking at the data inside packets, which in the case of packets generated by Telnet and FTP, can contain passwords in clear text. Packet sniffers analyzer traffic patterns, vulnerability scanners search for open ports, and Trivial File Transfer Protocol (TFTP) servers transfer boot files to Dynamic Host Configuration Protocol (DHCP) client workstations. Telnet is itself a terminal emulator and does not display packet contents.

141. A. Protocol analyzers capture packets from the network and interpret their contents including the display of the application layer payload, which can include confidential information. Protocol analyzers can display the Internet Protocol (IP) addresses of systems on the network, but this is not as great a security threat. Protocol analyzers cannot decrypt the protected information it finds in captured packets. Vulnerability scanners detect open ports and launch attacks against them; protocol analyzers do not do this.

142. B. Microsoft Assessment and Planning Toolkit (MAP Toolkit) is a free application that performs an agentless inventory of a network and uses the information to create reports on specific scenarios, such as whether computers are prepared for an operating system upgrade. Nessus, Nmap, and Microsoft Baseline Security Analyzer (MBSA) are all tools that include vulnerability scanning but that have other capabilities as well.

143. D. Port scanning, the process of looking for open Transmission Control Protocol (TCP) and User Datagram Protocol (UDP) ports that are exploitable by attackers, is one of the many functions that qualifies as a type of vulnerability scanning. Network mapping, the remediation of vulnerabilities, and penetration testing, which is the process of deliberately performing a planned attack, are not considered vulnerability scanning techniques.

144. A. Once the frames are in the buffer, Alice can configure a display filter to block the unwanted frames from view. This does not delete them from the buffer. Since the capture was already performed, there is no need to restart the capture. Configuring a capture filter will not meet the requirements, because the filter will eliminate the other frames completely from the buffer. It is not possible to delete specific frames from an analyzer buffer.

145. A. The 802.11b standard calls for a maximum speed of 11 Mbps, so there is nothing that Ralph can do to increase his network's speed except purchase new equipment.

146. A, C, E. The 2.4 GHz band used by Wireless Local Area Networks (WLANs) consists of channels that are 20 (or 22) MHz wide. However, the channels are only 5 MHz apart, so there is channel overlap that can result in interference. Channels 1, 6, and 11 are the only channels that are far enough apart from each other to avoid any overlap with the adjacent channels. Channels 4 and 8 are susceptible to overlap.

147. A. Specifying the wrong passphrase for the encryption protocol is the most common cause of a failure to connect to the network with no indication of an error. Incorrect antenna placement and channel overlap could result in a weak signal or no signal, either of which would be indicated in the Available Networks list. An incorrect Service Set Identifier (SSID) is not likely to be the error, as long as Ralph selected the AP from the list.

148. B, D, E. Interference resulting from channel overlap, a weak signal due to incorrect antenna polarization, and signal loss due to antenna cable attenuation could render the workstation unable to make contact with the AP. An incorrect passphrase would not be the problem unless Ralph had already seen the AP and attempted to connect to it. An incorrect Service Set Identifier (SSID) would be the problem only if Ralph had already attempted to manually enter an SSID.

149. C. A patch antenna is a flat device that transmits signals in a half-spherical pattern. By placing the antenna against the building's outer wall, Ralph can provide coverage inside the building and minimize coverage extending to the outside. A dipole antenna is another name for the omnidirectional antenna usually provided with an AP. A unidirectional antenna directs signals in a straight line, which would not provide the coverage Ralph needs. A Yagi antenna is a type of unidirectional antenna.

150. A, D. Greater distance from the AP or interference from intervening walls can both cause a weakening of wireless signals, resulting in the intermittent connectivity that Trixie is experiencing. An incorrect Service Set Identifier (SSID) would prevent Trixie's laptop from ever connecting to the network. An omnidirectional antenna generates signals in every direction, which would not account for Trixie's problem.

151. B. It is possible that the WAP has been configured to not broadcast the network's SSID as a security measure, so Alice should first attempt to access it by typing the SSID in manually. She would not be able to type in the WPA2 passphrase until she is connecting to the SSID. Moving the laptop closer to the WAP or away from possible sources of electromagnetic interference might be solutions to the problem, but they should not be the first thing Alice tries.

152. D. The most likely cause of Alice's problem is that she has selected an incorrect encryption protocol. Wired Equivalent Privacy (WEP) is still provided as an option on many wireless devices, but it has long since been found to be insecure and is almost never used. Alice should try selecting the other security types that enable her to enter her passphrase, such as WiFi Protected Access II (WPA2). Although the other options are possible causes of the problem, encryption protocol mismatch is the most likely cause.

153. D. Wireless Local Area Network (WLAN) equipment built to the 802.11a standard can only use the 5 GHz frequency. However, an 802.11g AP can only use the 2.4 GHz frequency. Therefore, the network adapters cannot connect to Ralph's AP.

154. B. The 802.11b and 802.11g standards do not support 5 GHz communications. Configuring the AP to support 2.4 GHz is the only way for the 802.11g computers to connect to the network. The 5 GHz band does support automatic channel selection, so there is no need to configure the channel on each laptop manually. The 5 GHz band does support MIMO, and the 802.11n laptops should be able to connect. Replacing the adapters with 802.11g will prevent them from connecting, as that standard does not support 5 GHz communications. The 802.11a standard does support the 5 GHz band, and those laptops should be able to connect.

155. D. As wireless computers move farther away from the AP, their signals attenuate (weaken), their Received Signal Strength Indicators (RSSIs) go down, and the maximum speed of their connections drops. If the computers were using a different encryption protocol than the AP, there would be no connection at all, not a diminished connection speed. A SSID mismatch would cause the computers to connect to a different network, not necessarily connect at a slower speed. If the computers had 802.11a adapters, they would fail to connect to the AP at all, because 802.11a requires the use of the 5 GHz frequency band, and 802.11g uses 2.4 GHz.

156. B. Replacing the AP with an 802.11n model is not going to have any effect at all unless you upgrade the computer's network adapter as well. Installing a higher gain antenna on the AP can improve its range, enabling the computer to connect more readily. Moving the computer closer to the AP can strengthen the signal and raise its Received Signal Strength Indicator (RSSI), enabling it to connect more reliably. Changing the channel on the AP to a lesser used one can enable the computer to connect more easily.

157. C. Disabling Service Set Identifier (SSID) broadcasts will not defeat dedicated attackers, but it can prevent casual intruders from accessing the network. Media Access Control (MAC) filtering would require Ed to configure the AP with the MAC addresses of all devices that will access the network, which would be impractical in this case. The network is unsecured, so there is no passphrase to change, and a frequency change will have no effect on the problem.

158. D. Absorption is a type of interference that occurs when radio signals have to pass through barriers made of dense materials, such as concrete or cinderblock walls. The density of the material's molecular structure causes the radio signals to be partially converted to heat, which weakens them. Reflection is when signals bounce off of certain surfaces, such as metal. Refraction is when signals bend as they pass through certain barriers, such as glass or water. Diffraction is when signals have to pass around barriers to reach a particular destination. All of these phenomena can weaken the radio signals used in wireless networking, but absorption is the primary problem for Alice in this case.

159. A. The closer the users are to the AP, the stronger the signals will be. Installing an additional AP nearer to the executive offices will likely enable the signals to pass through the barriers more efficiently. The channel used by the AP, the standard on which the AP is based, and the broadcasting of Service Set Identifier (SSID) signals have no effect on the strength of the signals reaching the executive offices and will not resolve Ralph's problem.

160. D. Absorption is a type of interference that occurs when radio signals have to pass through barriers made of dense materials, such as walls and doors. In this case, the construction of the barriers has made them more formidable. Reflection is when signals bounce off of certain surfaces, such as metal. Refraction is when signals bend as they pass through certain barriers, such as glass or water. Diffraction is when signals have to pass around barriers to reach a particular destination. All of these phenomena can weaken the radio signals used in wireless networking, but absorption is the primary problem for Ralph in this case.

161. B, D. Attenuation is the tendency of signals to weaken as they travel through a network medium. In the case of a wireless network, the medium is the air, and the farther away a wireless device is from the Access Point (AP), the weaker the signal will be. Refraction is when signals bend as they pass through certain types of barriers, such as the glass walls of conference rooms. The bending changes the direction of the signals, possibly causing them to weaken in the process. Reflection is when signals bounce off of certain surfaces, such as metal. Diffraction is when signals have to pass around barriers to reach a particular destination. All of these phenomena can weaken the radio signals used in wireless networking, but attenuation and refraction are likely to be the primary problems for Ralph in this case.

162. A, C. The 802.11ac and 802.11g wireless networking standards are fundamentally incompatible. The 802.11g AP uses the 2.4 GHz band, and the user's 802.11ac laptop uses the 5 GHz band. Therefore, the only possible solutions are to install an 802.11ac AP or an 802.11g network adapter. Changing channels on the WAP and moving the user will have no effect on the problem.

163. D. The use of an incorrect wireless security protocol is a well-known source of errorless connection failures, so checking this will most likely enable Ed to locate the source of the problem. Channel overlap is a problem that Ed would check and resolve at the Access Point (AP), not the users' workstations. It is not possible to change the frequency on the WAP because the 802.11g standard only supports the 2.4 GHz frequency. Although signal interference could conceivably be the cause for a connection failure, the users can see the network, so this is probably not the problem.

164. A, B, C. Moving the Wireless Access Point (WAP) to the center of the building will keep as much of its operational range inside the structure as possible. If the signals still reach outside the building, Ed can reduce the power level of the WAP until the network is only accessible inside. Disabling SSID broadcasts will not defeat dedicated attackers, but it can prevent casual intruders from accessing the network. MAC filtering would require Ed to configure the WAP with the MAC addresses of all devices that will access the network, which would be impractical in this case. Installing a captive portal would not block outside users unless Ed configures the portal to require user authentication, which defeats the purpose of the guest network.

165. B, C. The first steps Alice should take are the simplest ones: make sure that the wireless interface in the user's laptop is turned on and that she is attempting to connect to the correct SSID for the company network. Changing the channel would not be necessary unless other users in the area are also having problems due to interference. The 802.11n wireless networking standard is backward compatible with 802.11g, so it should not be necessary to provide the user with a new network adapter.

166. C. If the users are losing their connections due to interference from other types of devices, changing the channel alters the frequency the network uses and can enable it to avoid the interference. The other options are not likely to affect any condition that would cause users to drop their connections.

167. B, D. Of the options provided, the ones most likely to be causing the problem are the use of an incorrect Service Set Identifier (SSID) or encryption protocol. Although signal interference could possibly be a cause, it is more likely that the new users have devices that are incorrectly configured for Ed's network. Channel overlap is a problem that Ed would check and resolve at the Access Point (AP), not the users' workstations.

168. D. WPA has been found to be vulnerable, and WPA2 was designed to address those vulnerabilities, so Ralph should use WPA2 instead of WPA. Suppressing SSID broadcasts does not prevent users from connecting to the network, and MAC filtering strengthens security without exposing MAC addresses to undue risk.

169. C. The 2.4 GHz band used by Wireless Local Area Networks (WLANs) consists of channels that are 20 (or 22) MHz wide. However, the channels are only 5 MHz apart, so there is channel overlap that can result in interference, possibly causing long AP association times and degraded performance. Channels 1, 6, and 11 are the only channels that are far enough apart from each other to avoid any overlap with the adjacent channels. This is why they are often recommended. However, in Ralph's case, these channels are too crowded with other networks. Ralph should therefore use a channel that is as far as possible from the crowded ones. Channels 2, 5, and 10 are all immediately adjacent to a crowded channel, but channel 9 is at least two channels away from the nearest crowded channel. Therefore, Ralph should configure his equipment to use channel 9.

170. B. Effective Isotropic Radiated Power (EIRP) is a measurement of the signal strength generated by an access point (or other radio transceiver) with a particular antenna. Received Signal Strength Indicator (RSSI) is a measurement of the strength of the signal received by a device from an access point. Service Set Identifier (SSID) is a designation assigned to a specific wireless network, which appears in the Available Networks list of a WiFi client. Multiple Input, Multiple Output (MIMO) is a technology used by some IEEE wireless networking standards to increase throughput by using multiple antennae.

171. C. Because the customer can access the other two computers in the house, Ed knows that her Internet Protocol (IP) address and subnet mask are properly configured, that the network cable is plugged in and functional, and that a switching loop is not preventing access to the Internet. Ed also knows that the computer's Domain Name System (DNS) record does not play a role in outgoing connections. The problem is most likely in the default gateway because the gateway address the customer specified is on another network, 172.16.43.0, rather than on her own network, 172.16.41.0.

172. D. The problem is most likely incorrect Access Control List (ACL) settings. Because the computers are all able to access the Internet, their Transmission Control Protocol/Internet Protocol (TCP/IP) settings, including their IP addresses, subnet mask, and default gateway address, must be correct. However, if the users do not have the correct permissions in the ACLs of the filesystem shares, they will not be able to access the shares over the network.

173. B. Because Alice is able to access the server and open the spreadsheet file, the problem is not related to blocked ports, firewall settings, or an untrusted certificate. The problem is most likely that though she has the necessary filesystem ACL permissions to open and read the file, she does not have the permissions needed to modify it.

174. D. The address 169.254.199.22 is from the 169.254.0.0/16 network address assigned to Automatic Private Internet Protocol Addressing (APIPA), a standard for the assignment of IP addresses to DHCP clients when they cannot obtain an address from a DHCP server. 127.0.0.1 is the standard IP loopback address. 240.15.167.251 is from the 240.0.0.0 network address, which is reserved for experimental use. Neither of these is ever assigned by DHCP. 255.255.255.0 is not an IP address at all; it is a subnet mask.

175. B. The Default Gateway setting should contain the address of a router on the local network that provides access to other networks, such as the Internet. In this case, therefore, the Default Gateway address should be on the 192.168.4.0 network, but it contains an address on the 192.18.6.0 network, which is not local. Therefore, the user can only access systems on the 192.168.4.0 network. The Subnet Mask setting must be correct, or the user would not be able to access any other systems. Unlike the default gateway, the Domain Name System (DNS) server does not have to be on the local network, so the address shown can be correct. Dynamic Host Configuration Protocol (DHCP) is not necessary to access the Internet.

176. C. The 169.254.203.42 address assigned to the workstation is from the 169.254.0.0/16 network address assigned to Automatic Private Internet Protocol Addressing (APIPA), a standard for the assignment of Internet Protocol (IP) addresses to Dynamic Host Configuration Protocol (DHCP) clients when they cannot obtain an address from a DHCP server. Since no one else is experiencing a problem, the DHCP server is presumably functioning. The Subnet Mask value is correct for an APIPA address, and APIPA does not provide Default Gateway or Domain Name System (DNS) server addresses. Therefore, an exhausted DHCP scope is the only one of the explanations provided that could be the cause of the problem.

177. B. For a computer connected to the 192.168.32.0/20 network, the Subnet Mask value should be 255.255.240.0, not 255.255.255.0, as shown in the ipconfig output. The IPv4 Address, Default Gateway, and Domain Name System (DNS) Servers settings are appropriate for the network. The workstation apparently has Dynamic Host Configuration Protocol (DHCP) disabled, so it has not retrieved appropriate Internet Protocol (IP) address settings from the DHCP server.

178. B. The Dynamic Host Configuration Protocol (DHCP) client on the workstation is enabled, but the Internet Protocol (IP) address assigned to the workstation is not from the 192.168.4.0/24 network. The assigned address is not an Automatic Private Internet Protocol Addressing (APIPA) address, nor is it expired, so the only conclusion is that there is a rogue DHCP server on the network assigning addresses from a wholly different subnet.

179. D. The autonegotiation mechanism is not the problem, nor is the pinout standard or Ralph's wire pair selection. The speed autonegotiation mechanism in Gigabit Ethernet uses only two wire pairs, so although the Light-Emitting Diodes (LEDs) do light up successfully, a functional Gigabit Ethernet data connection requires all four wire pairs.

180. D. Cable runs are traditionally wired "straight through"; that is, with the transmit pins at one end wired to the transmit pins at the other end. It is the switch that is supposed to implement the crossover circuit that connects the transmit pins to the receive pins. Cable runs wired using T568A at one end and T568B at the other end create a crossover circuit in the cable run. At one time, this would have been a serious problem, but today's switches automatically configure crossover circuits as needed, so they will adjust themselves to adapt to the cable runs. All of the other options would correct the problem, but doing nothing is certainly the easiest and best option.

181. A. The problem is unlikely to be a bad hub port or a bad cable, so moving the cable from port 4 to port 2 will not help. The problem is the crossover circuit between the two computers. The two systems were once connected directly together, which means that Ralph was using a crossover cable. The hub also provides a crossover circuit (except in the X port), and old hubs often do not autonegotiate crossovers. Therefore, the connection has two crossovers, which is the equivalent of wiring transmit pins to transmit pins, instead of transmit pins to receive pins. All of the other options eliminate one of the crossover circuits, enabling the computers to be wired correctly.

182. B. Older Ethernet hubs do not autonegotiate crossovers. Instead, they have an X (or uplink) port that provides a connection without a crossover circuit, so you can connect one hub to another. If both of the cables had been standard straight-through Ethernet cables or if both had been crossover cables, then plugging them into two regular ports should have worked. Because plugging one cable into the X port worked, this means that only one of the cables must be a crossover cable. The problem, therefore, was the cable, not the port. The X port does not provide extra strength to the signals.

183. B. A bent pin on one of the 12th computer's connections would cause a break in the bus, essentially forming two networks that operate independently. The failure to terminate or ground the network would not produce this type of fault. Reversing the transmit and receive pins is not possible on a coaxial connection, due to the architecture of the cable.

184. A, B. An open circuit is caused either by a break in the wire somewhere inside the cable or a bad connection with the pin in one or both connectors. A short is when a wire is connected to two or more pins at one end of the cable or when the conductors of two or more wires are touching inside the cable. In this instance, the damage to the cables could have resulted in either condition. A split pair is a connection in which two wires are incorrectly mapped in exactly the same way on both ends of the cable. Having transposed pairs is a fault in which both of the wires in a pair are connected to the wrong pins at one end of the cable. Both of these faults are the result of incorrect wiring during installation; they are not caused by damaged cables.

185. A. Crosstalk is a type of interference that occurs on copper-based networks when a signal transmitted on one conductor bleeds over onto another nearby conductor. Twisted-pair cables, which have eight or more conductors compressed together inside one sheath, are particularly susceptible to crosstalk. Twisting each of the separate wire pairs tends to reduce the amount of crosstalk to manageable levels. Twisting the wire pairs does not prevent signals from being affected by electromagnetic interference (EMI) or attenuation. Latency is a measurement of the time it takes for a signal to travel from its source to its destination.

186. D. Either the T568A or the T568B pinout standard is acceptable. The patch cables will function properly as long as both ends are wired using the same pinout standard.

187. C. Crosstalk is a type of interference that occurs on copper-based networks when in a signal transmitted on one conductor bleeds over onto another nearby conductor. Twisted-pair cables, which have eight or more conductors compressed together inside one sheath, are particularly susceptible to crosstalk. Twisting each of the separate wire pairs tends to reduce the amount of crosstalk to manageable levels. Untwisting the pairs leaves them more susceptible to crosstalk. Jitter, attenuation, and electromagnetic interference (EMI) are all conditions that can affect the performance of a wired network, but they are not directly related to untwisted wire pairs.

188. A, C. In this scenario, the user was previously able to connect to the network. There have been no hardware or software changes to the computer. These factors indicate that there is possibly a physical layer problem, such as a loose cable, a faulty cable, a bad switch port, or a bad network interface adapter in the computer. Since the user's cable previously worked, there is no need to verify that it is pinned and paired properly, and crossover cables are not used to connect workstations to switches. The first thing Ed should do is verify that all cable connections are secure. If he finds a loose cable and the link pulse

LED lights up when he reseats it, then the cable was the problem. If the link pulse LED does not light, Ed should replace the existing cable with a straight-through cable that is known to be good. If the LED lights up, the existing cable was probably faulty. If the LED does not light up, Ed should suspect a faulty network interface adapter or switch port and try moving the cable to a port on the switch that is known to function. If the connection works, the problem is probably a failed switch port. If the connection still does not work, then the fault is probably the network interface adapter in the user's computer.

189. C, D. Option A is the T568B pinout, and option B is the T568A pinout. Both of these are correct and may be used. Options C and D are both incorrect and can result in excessive amounts of crosstalk.

190. C. In this scenario, some, but not all, users on VLAN2 cannot connect to local and remote resources. Since users connected to other switches within the same VLAN and on other VLANs are not reporting any problems, the router is not the issue. This also excludes a VLAN2 configuration problem because this would affect the VLAN2 users on all of the switches. VLAN3 and VLAN4 users can communicate through the router, so they are also not the problem. The likeliest problem is the common component, which is the switch to which the VLAN2 users experiencing the outage are connected.

191. A. In this scenario, only users on one LAN are experiencing problems connecting to the Internet and other internal LANs. This isolates the problem to a component within that LAN only. Since users can connect successfully to local resources, the problem does not lie within the individual computers, the switch that connects the users to the network, or the backbone network cable. The likeliest problem is in the router connecting problem LAN to the backbone network. Since users on the other internal LANs are not reporting problems connecting to the Internet, the problem most likely does not involve the Internet router.

192. D. Internet Group Management Protocol (IGMP) snooping is a switching technique that prevents network hosts from receiving multicast packets when they are not members of the multicast group. The multicast traffic will still appear on the network, but only the members of the multicast group will process the packets. Asymmetric routing and multipathing all affect the route that the packets take through the network, and flow control only affects the speed at which transmitting systems send packets. None of these can control which hosts process the incoming packets.

193. B. In this scenario, all of the internal users are experiencing problems connecting to the Internet, so the router that provides access to the Internet is the suspected component. Since users can connect to resources on the internal LANs, the problem probably is not in any of the routers connecting the LANs to the backbone or the backbone cable itself. This also eliminates the probability that the switches on the LANs are the problem.

194. A, B, C. Ed will first have to change the Internet Protocol (IP) addresses. This is because the computers on the other side of the router, on the screened subnet, must use an IP network address that is different from the internal network's address. Next, Ed will have to change the default gateway address setting on the internal network computers to the address of the router so that traffic can be directed to the screened subnet. Finally, Ed will have to update the resource records on the Domain Name System (DNS) server to reflect the IP address changes. Media Access Control (MAC) addresses are hard-coded into network interface adapters and are not easily changed.

195. C. The problem is most likely the default gateway address, which directs all traffic intended for the Internet to the cable modem/router. If that address is incorrect, the traffic will never reach the router. Because the computer can access the other two systems on the local network, the Internet Protocol (IP) address and subnet mask are not the problem. It is not necessary (and not always possible) to change the Media Access Control (MAC) address on a Windows workstation.

196. D. Because Ed can connect to WebServ1 successfully, the problem is not an unresponsive service or blocked ports on the server. The problem is not a name resolution failure because Ralph can successfully ping WebServ1 by name. Therefore, of the options listed, the only possible problem must be that the firewall on Ralph's workstation is not configured to allow the remote desktop client's traffic out.

197. C. When a Dynamic Host Configuration Protocol (DHCP) client is offered an Internal Protocol (IP) address by a DHCP server, the client broadcasts Address Resolution Protocol (ARP) requests using that address before accepting it. If another computer on the local network is using the offered address, the computer responds to the ARP request, and the DHCP client declines the address. The DHCP server then offers another address. Domain Name Service (DNS) queries and routing table checks are not reliable means of checking for duplicate IP addresses. It is possible to have two DHCP servers on the same local network, but they must be configured with scopes that do not overlap.

198. C. If someone on the network is spoofing the Media Access Control (MAC) address of Ed's workstation, the MAC address table in the switch handing the network traffic might be continually changing as packets from each computer reach the switch. This could cause some of the response packets to be forwarded to Ed's workstation and some to the spoofer's workstation. Duplicate IP addresses would not cause this problem, because they would be detected by the operating system. Blocked Transmission Control Protocol/User Datagram Protocol (TCP/UDP) ports, incorrect firewall settings, or a flood of multicast transmissions could prevent Ed from receiving responses, but they would not be sent to another workstation.

199. B. Operating systems detect duplicate IP addresses immediately and display error messages or notifications on the computers involved. Therefore, the user with the problem would have been informed immediately if another system were using her IP address. All of the other options are possible causes of the problem that are more difficult to troubleshoot.

200. B. The users' browsers are failing to resolve the hostnames of the requested websites into Internet Protocol (IP) addresses, which they must do before they can connect to the web servers. By asking where the company's DNS server is located, Ralph can determine if the problem is the DNS server itself or the router that provides access to the Internet. If the DNS server is located on Adatum's company network, then the DNS server could be failing to resolve the website names. However, the DNS server could be located on the Internet Service Provider's (ISP's) network, in which case the problem might be in the router that provides access to the ISP's network.

201. B. Attenuation is the weakening of the signals as they traverse the network medium. In this case, the problem is most likely the result of cable runs that exceed the 100 meter maximum defined in the Ethernet twisted-pair specification. Therefore, shortening the cable runs will be likely to solve the problem. All of the Ethernet twisted-pair specifications have a 100 meter maximum length, so running the network at a slower speed, installing a higher grade cable, and installing higher end network adapters might have no effect if the runs are overly long.

202. A. Elevator machinery, fluorescent light fixtures, and other electrical devices in an office environment can generate magnetic fields, resulting in electromagnetic interference (EMI). When copper-based data cables are located too near to such a device, the magnetic fields can generate an electric current on the cable that interferes with the signals exchanged by network devices. If the network users experience a problem every time the elevator machinery switches on, EMI is a likely cause of the problem. Near-end crosstalk (NEXT), far-end crosstalk (FEXT), and attenuation can all cause intermittent network communication problems, but they cannot be caused by elevator machinery.

203. B, D. It is common practice on many networks to disable switch ports that are not in use so that unauthorized individuals cannot plug devices into them. Some networks also use port security, in which switches are configured with Access Control Lists (ACLs) that specify the Media Access Control (MAC) addresses of devices that are permitted to use them. Either of these could be the source of Ralph's problem. Because there are no other network users reporting problems, malfunctioning services such as Network Address Translation (NAT) and Domain Name System (DNS) are not likely to be the cause.

204. A. A duplex mismatch is the most likely of the options. Ethernet running over twisted-pair cable, in its original half-duplex mode, detects collisions by looking for data on the transmit and receive pins at the same time. In full-duplex mode, data is supposed to be transmitted and received at the same time. When one side of a connection is configured to use full duplex and the other end is configured to use half duplex, the full-duplex communications on the one side look like collisions to the half-duplex side. The half-duplex adapter transmits a jam signal as a result of each collision, which causes the full-duplex side to receive an incomplete frame. Both sides then start to retransmit frames in a continuing cycle, causing network performance to diminish drastically. If the problem were a crossover cable or a disabled switch port, the link pulse LED would not light. Outdated drivers would not be likely to slow network performance, and if they did, the slowdown would be minor.

205. C. Green LEDs indicate the device is running at the full speed supported by the switch, whereas orange LEDs indicate that the device is running at a reduced speed. If no device is connected, the LED does not illuminate at all. The LED does not indicate the occurrence of collisions or the type of device connected to the port.

206. A. If the time on the domain controller at the new office is more than five minutes off of the time held by domain controller at the home office, then the new domain controller will not sync. Duplicate Internet Protocol (IP) addresses or an incorrect default gateway address would prevent the new domain controller from connecting to the home office network. A server hardware failure would manifest as an outage far more serious than a domain controller synchronization issue.

207. C. Ralph's new computer is probably equipped with a network adapter that supports at least Fast Ethernet (100Base-TX). Fast Ethernet and newer network adapters support autonegotiation of the connection speed, but 10Base-T does not. Therefore, if the computer tries to negotiate a connection speed with the 10Base-T hub, it will fail and run at its default speed, which the hub does not support. By manually configuring the adapter in the computer to run at 10 Mbps, it should be able to communicate with the network. Setting the computer's adapter to run at 100 Mbps will not change anything. It is not possible to change the speed of a 10Base-T hub.

208. A. Only Domain Name System (DNS) servers perform FQDN resolutions, so that is likely to be the source of the problem. It is possible to ping a device on the local network using its computer name without the use of DNS. Electromagnetic interference (EMI) would inhibit all network communication, and Access Control Lists (ACLs) have no effect on ping tests. Dynamic Host Configuration Protocol (DHCP) assigns IP addresses to clients; it does not resolve FQDNs.

209. D. Since only one user is reporting the problem, the user's computer is the likeliest source of the problem. The user has probably changed or removed the WINS server address. If the user is working with an incorrect WINS address, he can access local network resources but not resources on another internal LAN. Also, he can access resources on the Internet, which means the Internet router and the DNS server are not the problem.

210. C. The 169.254.0.0/16 network is used by Automatic Private Internet Protocol Addressing (APIPA), a standard that provides Dynamic Host Configuration Protocol (DHCP) clients with an Internet Protocol (IP) address when they cannot contact a DHCP server. Unknown to Ralph, the DHCP server on his network has been down for over a week, and the users' IP address leases have begun to expire. This causes them to revert to APIPA addresses. Multiple users changing their IP addresses would not result in them all using the same network address. A rogue DHCP would not be likely to deploy APIPA addresses to clients. Malware infections that modify IP addresses are rare.

211. D. For the link pulse LED on the switch port to light up, there must be a completed connection between the switch and a computer at the other end. None of the other options will cause the LED to light.

212. B. Because Ed knows that the network workstations should be using DHCP to obtain their IP addresses, the best thing to do is to enable the DHCP client and close the ticket rather than configure the system with another static address. There is no indication that there is a rogue DHCP server on the network since the workstation's DHCP client is disabled. This is not the first time that Ed has had a user lie to him, nor will it be the last. He should just let it go and work on addressing the problem.

213. B, D. The solution should call for Ralph to create a VLAN on the ADSL router that matches the Virtual Local Area Network (VLAN) that the network switch port is using. Therefore, he should create a VLAN4 on the router and assign a port to it, which will be the port Ralph uses to connect the router to the network switch. There is no need to create a VLAN1 on the network switch, because all switches have a default VLAN called VLAN1. Modifying the VLAN assignments on the network switch is not a good idea, because it might interfere with the existing VLAN strategy in place.

214. A, B. Ralph could purchase a license upgrade for the router that would enable him to create a VLAN4. However, the simpler and less expensive solution would be to create a VLAN2 on the switch. As long as both ends of the cable are plugged into ports using the same Virtual Local Area Network (VLAN), the router should be able to service the network. Configuring the devices to use the default VLAN1 might interfere with the existing VLAN strategy.

215. A. For the website's Secure Socket Layer (SSL) certificate to be trusted, it must be signed by a source that both parties in the transaction trust. Many security firms are in the business of providing SSL certificates to companies that have provided them with confirmation of their identities. This is what Ralph must do to prevent the error message from appearing to the company's clients. Creating a self-signed certificate or installing a certification authority in-house are not sufficient and are probably already the cause of the problem. Users are not likely to be convinced that everything is all right.

216. B, D. The `route` tool, with the `print` parameter, displays the contents of the routing table on a Windows computer. So does the `netstat -r` command. The `nbtstat` and `nslookup` tools cannot display the routing table.

217. D. To access the Internet, the workstation's routing table must include a default gateway entry. To create a default gateway entry in the routing table, you use the `route add` command with a Network Destination value of 0.0.0.0, a MASK value of 0.0.0.0, and the address of a router on the local network (in this case, 192.168.2.99). The entry must also have a METRIC value that is lower than the other entries in the table so that it will be used first.

218. A. The most likely cause for the slowdown is a broadcast storm. DHCP relies on broadcast messages to assign IP addresses to users, so 500 users all turning on their computers at 9:00 a.m. can generate an abnormally high number of broadcast packets. This can degrade network performance until all of the users have completed their DHCP address assignments. Routing loops, switching loops, and asymmetric routing can degrade network performance, but the degradation would not be limited to the early morning hours. A rogue DHCP server can cause problems but not the one described here.

219. C. Alice's calculations are called an optical link budget. By adding up the various loss factors in decibels (dB), she can determine whether the budget is low, resulting in communication problems over the link. Protocol analysis is an examination of network packet contents. A routing loop is a condition in which packets are circulating endlessly around a network. RSSI is a wireless networking statistic that does not apply to fiber-optic connections.

220. D. On all of the servers, NTP uses the well-known User Datagram Protocol (UDP) port 123 for its communications with a Coordinated Universal Time (UTC) server. If a server's firewall is blocking that port, it cannot synchronize its clock time. If the domain controllers have clocks that are not synchronized, their data synchronization processes can be affected. The problem is not a name resolution failure, an unresponsive database service, or incorrect Transmission Control Protocol/Internet Protocol (TCP/IP) settings because other server functions are not affected.

Chapter 6: Practice Exam 1

1. A, C, D. The three-tier hierarchical architecture for datacenters consists of core, distribution, and access layers. The access layer in a datacenter contains servers, the distribution layer contains redundant switch connections, and the core layer provides high-speed transport between the switches. There is no intermediate layer in the architecture.

2. B. An Acceptable Use Policy (AUP) specifies whether and how employees can use company-owned hardware and software resources. AUPs typically specify what personal work employees can perform while on the job, what hardware and software they can install, and what levels of privacy they are permitted when using company equipment. This is the document that will most likely include the information you seek. A Service Level Agreement (SLA) is a contract between a provider and a subscriber. A Non-Disclosure Agreement (NDA) specifies what company information employees are permitted to discuss outside the company. Bring Your Own Device (BYOD) is a policy that specifies how employees can connect their personal devices to the company network.

3. A. There are many possible causes for the problem that are more likely than a router configuration error, so this is not something you should check first. Asking if the user can access the local network attempts to isolate the problem. If she cannot, the problem could be in her computer; if she can, then the problem lies somewhere in the Internet access infrastructure. If other users are experiencing the problem, then the issue should receive a higher priority, and you will know for sure that the problem does not lie in the user's computer. While the user's job title might not be the first thing you check, it is a political reality that higher ranking users get preferential treatment.

4. B. Biometric scans, identification badges, and key fobs are all mechanisms that are designed to distinguish authorized from unauthorized personnel. Motion detection cannot make this distinction and is therefore not a means of preventing unauthorized access.

5. C. The problem is most likely the result of a duplex mismatch. There should be no collisions on a full-duplex network, so the problem is clearly related to the duplexing of the communications. A twisted-pair Ethernet adapter, running in its original half-duplex mode, detects collisions by looking for data on both the transmit and receive pins at the same time. In full-duplex mode, however, data is supposed to be transmitted and received at the same time. When one side of a connection is configured to use full duplex, as the new computers are, and the other end is configured to use half duplex (as the network switches must be), the full-duplex communications on the one side look like collisions to the half-duplex side. The half-duplex adapter transmits a jam signal as a result of each collision, which causes the full-duplex side to receive an incomplete frame. Both sides then start to retransmit frames in a continuing cycle, causing network performance to diminish alarmingly. The ping tests do not detect a problem, because ping transmits only a small amount of data in one direction at a time. All of the other options would likely cause the ping tests to fail. The solution to the problem is to configure the new computers to autonegotiate their speed and duplex modes.

6. B. An ad hoc topology (also known as an independent basic service set) is one in which wireless computers communicate directly with one another without the need for an access point. A Wireless Access Point (WAP) is a device with a wireless transceiver that also connects to a standard cabled network. Wireless computers communicate with the access point, which

forwards their transmissions over the network cable. This is called an infrastructure topology. Star and bus topologies are not used by wireless networks; they require the computers to be physically connected to the network cable.

7. C. A multilayer switch is a network connectivity device that functions at both layer 2 and layer 3 of the Open Systems Interconnection (OSI) model. At layer 2, the data link layer, the device functions like a normal switch, providing an individual collision domain to each connected node and enabling you to create multiple VLANs. At layer 3, the network layer, the device also provides routing capabilities by forwarding packets between the VLANs. Virtual routers, load balancers, and broadband routers are strictly layer 3 devices that can route traffic but cannot create VLANs.

8. B, C, D. *Data at-rest* is a data loss prevention term that describes data that is currently in storage while not in use. *Data in-motion* is the term used to describe network traffic. *Data-in-use* describes endpoint actions. *Data on-line* is not one of the standard data loss prevention terms.

9. C. WiFi Protected Access (WPA) is the wireless security protocol that was designed to replace the increasingly vulnerable Wired Equivalent Privacy (WEP) protocol. WPA added an encryption protocol called Temporal Key Integrity Protocol (TKIP) that was more difficult to penetrate. However, over time, TKIP too became vulnerable, and WPA2 was introduced, which replaced TKIP with the Advanced Encryption Standard protocol (CCMP-AES).

10. A. The device shown in the figure is a tone generator and locator, which you can use to test twisted-pair wiring and detect certain basic wiring faults. By connecting the tone generator to each wire in turn and locating the tone at the other end, you can determine whether each wire is attached to the appropriate pin in the connector. This tool is not capable of performing any of the tasks described in the other options.

11. C. The term *something you have* refers to a physical possession that identifies a user, such as a smartcard. This type of authentication is nearly always used as part of a multifactor authentication procedure because it is possible for a smartcard or other physical possession to be lost or stolen. A fingerprint would be considered something you are, a password is something you know, and a finger gesture is something you do.

12. A, C, D. Port number 1433 is used by SQL Server; port 1521 is used by SQLnet, and port 3306 is used by MySQL. The port number 3389 is used by the Remote Desktop Protocol (RDP) and is not involved in SQL communications.

13. D. Wireless Local Area Network (WLAN) equipment built to the 802.11a standard can only use the 5 GHz frequency band. However, an 802.11g access point can only use the 2.4 GHz frequency band. Therefore, the network adapters cannot be made to connect to your access point by any means.

14. C, D. RAID is a technology for storing data on multiple hard disk drives, providing fault tolerance, increased performance, or both. The various RAID levels provide different levels of functionality and have different hardware requirements. RAID 5 and RAID 6 both combine disk striping with distributed storage of parity information. RAID 5 enables recovery from a single disk failure. RAID 6 uses redundant parity to enable recovery from a double disk failure. RAID 1 and RAID 10 both use disk mirroring to provide fault tolerance, which does not require parity data. RAID 0 uses data striping only (blocks written to each disk in turn), which does not provide any form of fault tolerance.

15. A, C, E. The 2.4 GHz band used by Wireless Local Area Networks (WLANs) consists of channels that are 20 (or 22) MHz wide. However, the channels are only 5 MHz apart, so it is possible for channel overlap to occur between the access points, which can result in interference. Channels 1, 6, and 11 are the only channels that are far enough apart from each other to avoid any overlap with the adjacent channels. Channels 4 and 8 are susceptible to overlap.

16. B, C, D. Disabling services and ports that are not in use is a server hardening technique that reduces the attack surface of a server. Creating privileged user accounts that are only used for tasks that require those privileges reduces the chance that the administrative accounts will be compromised. These, therefore, are all forms of server hardening. Upgrading the UEFI or BIOS firmware on a server typically does not enhance its security, so it cannot be considered a form of server hardening.

17. C. The Default Gateway setting should contain the address of a router on the workstation's local network that provides access to other networks, such as the Internet. In this case, therefore, the Default Gateway address should be on the 192.168.23.0 network, but it contains an address on the 192.168.216.0 network, which is not local. Therefore, the user can only access systems on the 192.168.23.0/24 network. The Subnet Mask setting must be correct, or the user would not be able to access any other systems. Unlike the default gateway, the DNS server does not have to be on the workstation's local network, so the address shown can be correct. DHCP does not have to be enabled for the computer to access the Internet.

18. C, D, E. A smartphone app that can adjust your thermostat, a remotely monitored cardiac pacemaker, and a camera-equipped refrigerator are all examples of IoT devices because they all have IP addresses and use the Internet to communicate with a controller or monitoring station. Key fobs that unlock cars and TV remote controls are typically short-range radio or infrared devices that do not use the Internet for their communications.

19. A. Windows networks that use Active Directory Domain Services (AD DS) authenticate clients using the Kerberos protocol, in part because it never transmits passwords over the network, even in encrypted form. Remote Authentication Dial-In User Service (RADIUS) is an authentication, authorization, and accounting service for remote users connecting to a network. Windows does not use it for internal clients. WiFi Protected Access II (WPA2) is a security protocol used by Wireless Local Area Networks (WLANs). It is not used for AD DS authentication. Extensible Authentication Protocol - Transport Layer Security (EAP-TLS) is a remote authentication protocol that AD DS networks do not use for internal clients.

20. C, D. The solution requires you to create a Virtual Local Area Network (VLAN) on the ADSL router that matches the VLAN the network switch port is using. Therefore, you should create a VLAN4 on the router's switch module and assign an Ethernet port to it, which will be the port you use to connect the ADSL router to the network switch. There is no need to create a VLAN1 on the network switch because all switches already have a default VLAN called VLAN1. Modifying the VLAN assignments on the network switch is not a good idea, because it might interfere with the existing VLAN strategy in place.

21. A, D. Changing the length of the Service Set Identifier (SSID) will be no help in preventing a war driving attack. The SSID is just an identifier; its length has no effect on security. Wired Equivalent Privacy (WEP) is a security protocol that has been found to have serious weaknesses that are easily exploitable. It is not a satisfactory way to avoid attacks. On the other hand, configuring the access point not to broadcast its SSID will prevent a war driving attacker with standard equipment from seeing the network. Configuring your equipment to use WiFi Protected Access II (WPA2) security will make it difficult for a war driver who detects your network to connect to it.

22. A, D. Infrastructure as a Service (IaaS) provides consumers with processing, storage, and networking resources that they can use to install and run operating systems and other software of their choice. In the public cloud model, one organization functions as the provider, and another organization—in this case, you—consumes the services of the provider. Platform as a Service (PaaS) provides consumers with the ability to install applications of their choice on a server furnished by the provider. Software as a Service (SaaS) provides consumers with access to a specific application running on the provider's servers, but the consumers have no control over the operating system, the servers, or the underlying resources. In a private cloud, the same organization that uses the cloud services is also the sole owner of the infrastructure that provides those services. A hybrid cloud is a combination of public and private infrastructure so that the consumer organization is only a partial owner of the infrastructure.

23. D. The plier-like device is a crimper, which cable installers use to attach RJ45 connectors, like those in the bag, to lengths of bulk cable. This is the process of creating patch cables, which are used to connect computers to wall plates and patch panel ports to switches. Your boss is telling you to start making patch cables in five- and ten-foot lengths. You do not use a crimper to attach keystone connectors, and the boss has not given you the tools and components needed to pull cable runs or install a patch panel.

24. B. The default port for the Post Office Protocol 3 (POP3) is 110, but that is used for incoming mail. Outgoing mail uses the Simple Mail Transfer Protocol (SMTP), which uses the well-known port number 25 by default. Port number 143 is the default port for the Internet Message Access Protocol (IMAP), a different email mailbox protocol that clients never use with POP3. Port number 80 is the default port for the Hypertext Transfer Protocol (HTTP), which is not used by email clients.

25. B. The cable type used for thin Ethernet segments is a coaxial cable called RG-58. RG-8 coaxial is used exclusively on thick Ethernet segments. RJ45 is a type of connector used in twisted pair cabling for data networks. RJ11 is a connector type used in twisted-pair cabling for telecommunications networks.

26. A. A rollover cable is a type of null modem cable, usually flat and light blue in color, with the pinouts reversed on either end, to enable a terminal to communicate with a router or switch through the device's dedicated console port. It cannot connect a workstation to the network. A straight-through cable is the standard network cable used to connect a workstation or other device to an Ethernet network. A crossover cable is designed to connect network adapters to each other directly, creating a two-node network. A plenum cable is a type of cable intended for use within air spaces that has an outer sheath that does not produce toxic fumes when it burns. A shielded cable is intended to protect signals from electromagnetic interference. Both plenum and shielded cables can connect a workstation to a network.

27. A. Authentication Header (AH) is a protocol in the TCP/IP suite that provides digital integrity services, in the form of a digital signature, which ensures that an incoming packet actually originated from its stated source. Encapsulating Security Protocol (ESP) provides encryption services for IPSec. Secure Sockets Layer (SSL) is a security protocol that provides encrypted communications between web browsers and servers. Remote Desktop Protocol (RDP) is a component of Remote Desktop Services, a Windows mechanism that enables a client program to connect to a server and control it remotely.

28. B. VLANs are virtual layer 2 (data link layer) LANs defined within switches. As with physical LANs, only devices in the same VLAN can communicate with each other until a layer 3 device, such as a router or a layer 3 switch, is added to the network. Re-creating and reconfiguring the VLANs will not correct the problem. Traffic filters are usually implemented on routers, not switches. Once a router is in place, VLANs do not have to use the same data link protocol to communicate with each other.

29. A, C. The term for an IPv4 address and port number in combination, which identifies an application running on a specific host, is *socket*. A Media Access Control (MAC) address is an address hard-coded into a network adapter. It is not a TCP/IP element. A subnet mask is not needed to identify a host or an application running on it.

30. A, B, C, D. A cable modem must function as a broadband router to provide access to the cable provider's network. Many cable modems are also Wireless Access Points (WAPs), enabling users to construct a Local Area Network (LAN) without a cable installation. Many cable modems have switched Ethernet ports for connections to wired devices, such as printers and computers. Most cable modems use Dynamic Host Configuration Protocol (DHCP) to assign IP addresses to devices on the home network. Cable modems for home use typically do not function as proxy servers or Remote Authentication Dial-In User Service (RADIUS) servers, which are devices generally used on large networks.

31. A. Like A and AAAA records, which are used for forward name resolution, Pointer (PTR) records contain hostnames and IP addresses. However, PTR records are used only for reverse name resolution—that is, resolving IP addresses into hostnames. A Mail Exchange (MX) record specifies the mail server that the domain should use. Canonical Name (CNAME) records specify aliases for a given hostname. An AAAA resource record maps a hostname to an IPv6 address for name resolution purposes. All of these records except PTR are used for forward name resolution.

32. C, D. Protocol analyzers capture packets from the network and interpret their contents, which can include displaying the application layer payload. Depending on the application, the payload can conceivably include confidential information, such as passwords. Protocol analyzers also display the IP addresses of the systems involved in packet transmissions. Although this in itself might not be a great security threat, intruders might use the IP address information to launch other types of attacks. Protocol analyzers cannot decrypt the protected information they find in captured packets. Vulnerability scanners detect open ports and launch attacks against them; protocol analyzers do not do this.

33. B, D, E. A Remote Authentication Dial-In User Service (RADIUS) server, also known as an AAA server, provides centralized authentication, authorization, and accounting for other network services. Assistance and attenuation are not functions provided by RADIUS or AAA servers.

34. C. Only Domain Name System (DNS) servers perform FQDN resolutions, so that is likely to be the source of the problem. It is possible to successfully ping a device on the local network using its computer name without the use of DNS. Dynamic Host Configuration Protocol (DHCP) cannot be the problem, or you would not be able to ping the server at all. Electromagnetic interference (EMI) would inhibit all network communication, and Access Control Lists (ACLs) are an authorization mechanism that has no effect on `ping` tests.

35. B. Proxy servers provide network users with access to Internet services, and the unregistered IP addresses on the client computers protect them from unauthorized access by users on the Internet, which satisfies the primary objective. The proxy servers also make it possible for network administrators to monitor and regulate users' access to the Internet, which satisfies one of the two secondary objectives. However, proxy servers are not capable of assigning IP addresses to the client computers, and the proposal makes no mention of a Dynamic Host Configuration Protocol (DHCP) server or any another automatic TCP/IP configuration mechanism. Therefore, the proposal does not satisfy the other secondary objective.

36. C. Software as a Service (SaaS) provides the least amount of control. Consumers receive access to a specific application running on the provider's servers, but they have no control over the operating system, the servers, or the underlying resources. The Infrastructure as a Service (IaaS) model provides the consumers with the most control, as the provider furnishes processing, storage, and networking resources that the consumer can use as needed. Platform as a Service (PaaS) provides consumers with the ability to install applications of their choice on a server furnished by the provider, but they have only limited control over the server and no control over the underlying resources.

37. A. Ethernet uses jumbo frames at the data link layer to transfer large amounts of data more efficiently. Ethernet typically restricts frame size to 1,500 bytes, but jumbo frames enable Ethernet systems to create frames up to 9,000 bytes. PPP does not support the use of jumbo frames. Frames are protocol data units associated only with the data link layer, so they do not apply to IP and TCP, which operate at the network and transport layers, respectively.

38. C. The first step in the troubleshooting protocol involves identifying the problem by questioning the user and creating a trouble ticket. You complete the other steps in the troubleshooting protocol after the trouble ticket has been created and prioritized.

39. C. The user has experienced a ransomware attack. Ransomware is a type of attack in which a user's access to his or her data is blocked unless a certain amount of money is paid to the attacker. The blockages can vary from simple screen locks to data encryption. War driving is an attack method that consists of driving around a neighborhood with a computer scanning for unprotected wireless networks. Denial-of-Service (DoS) is a type of attack that overwhelms a computer with traffic, preventing it from functioning properly. Address Resolution Protocol (ARP) poisoning is the deliberate insertion of fraudulent information into the ARP cache stored on computers and switches.

40. B, C. The word *asymmetric* in Asymmetric Digital Subscriber Line (ADSL) means that the service provides different amounts of bandwidth in each direction. In nearly all cases, asymmetric WAN services provide more downstream bandwidth than upstream. Cable television (CATV) networks are also asymmetrical. The word *symmetric* in Symmetric Digital Subscriber Line (SDSL) means that the service provides equal amounts of bandwidth in both directions. Fibre Channel over Ethernet (FCoE) is also symmetrical.

41. B, C. A large enterprise network will—at minimum—have demarcation points for telephone services and a connection to an Internet Service Provider's (ISP's) network. In many cases, these services enter the building in the same equipment room that houses the backbone switch, which enables all the devices on the network to access those resources. This room is then called the Main Distribution Frame (MDF). An Intermediate Distribution Frame (IDF) is a place where localized telecommunications equipment, such as the interface between the horizontal cabling and the backbone, is located. For example, an enterprise network housed in a single building might have its MDF in the basement and an IDF on each floor. Mean Time Between Failures (MTBF) and Remote Desktop Protocol (RDP) are not network cabling locations.

42. B. A plenum space is an area of a building that provides air circulation as part of its ventilation system, such as a heating or air-conditioning duct. Plenum cables have a sheath made of a fire-retardant material that does not outgas toxic fumes when it burns. When network cables are installed in plenum spaces, many local building codes require that installers use plenum-rated cables conforming to specific standards. Plenum cables provide no benefit when installed near other cables, or EMI sources, or when they exceed specified lengths.

43. D. Clustering refers to the combination of multiple servers—not network adapters—into a single unit to enhance performance and provide fault tolerance. Bonding, link aggregation, port aggregation, and NIC teaming are all terms for the same basic technology, in which the bandwidth of multiple network adapter connections is joined to speed up transmissions. The technology also enables the network communication to continue if one of the adapters fails or is disconnected.

44. C, D. Secure Shell (SSH) and Telnet are both remote terminal programs, but Telnet clients pass instructions (including passwords) to the target server in clear text, whereas SSH uses encrypted transmissions. In the same way, Hypertext Transfer Protocol Secure (HTTPS) is the encrypted version of HTTP. In both of these cases, the substitute is more secure and should be suggested to the director. However, Temporal Key Integrity Protocol (TKIP) provides encryption that is less secure than Advanced Encryption Standard (AES), and Wired Equivalent Protocol (WEP) is less secure than WiFi Protected Access II (WPA2).

45. A. A Management Information Base (MIB) is the database on an SNMP agent in which ASN.1 information about the properties of the managed device is stored. The other three options do not perform this function. A trap is an alert message that SNMP agents send to the network management console when an exceptional event occurs. Syslog is a standard for message logging components. Security Information and Event Management (SIEM) is a combination tool that uses information gathered from logs and network devices to provide a real-time analysis of the network's security condition.

46. A, D. Secure Sockets Layer (SSL) is a now-deprecated security protocol that provides encrypted communications between web browsers and servers. Transport Layer Security (TLS) is an updated security protocol that is designed to replace SSL. Datagram Transport Layer Security (DTLS) is a security protocol that provides the same basic functions as TLS but for User Datagram Protocol (UDP) traffic instead of TCP. Secure Shell (SSH) is a character-based tool that enables users to execute commands on remote computers; it does not provide web server/browser security.

47. B. Another term for a screened subnet is a DMZ, or demilitarized zone. They are also known as perimeter networks. A Virtual Local Area Network (VLAN) is a logical network segment created within a switch. Protected Extensible Authentication Protocol (PEAP) is an authentication protocol, and Temporal Key Integrity Protocol (TKIP) is an encryption algorithm. These three options are not terms for a screened subnet.

48. D. RDP is a component of Remote Desktop Services, a Windows mechanism that enables a client program to connect to a server and control it remotely. RDP does not carry actual application data; it just transfers keystrokes, mouse movements, and graphic display information.

49. D, F. Of the options shown, only the 802.11n and 802.11ax standards define WLAN devices that can support both the 2.4 GHz and 5 GHz frequencies. The 802.11a and 802.11ac standards support only 5 GHz, and the 802.11b and 802.11g standards support only 2.4 GHz.

50. B. Multitenancy does not call for tenants to have individual virtual machines. Multitenancy is a software architecture in which multiple tenants share a single instance of an application running in the cloud. Because tenants share a single application, there is a chance that data could be compromised. Because a single application instance is running in the cloud, the operational overhead is reduced compared to the use of individual virtual machines. Tenants share a finite amount of bandwidth, so the possibility exists for competition to occur, such as when one tenant is the target of a Denial-of-Service (DoS) attack.

51. A, C. Secure Hash Algorithm (SHA) and Message Digest 5 (MD5) are file hashing algorithms used to test data integrity by calculating a hash value before transmitting a file over the network. After the transmission, the receiving system performs the same calculation. If the values match, then the data is intact. RC4 and Advanced Encryption Standard (AES) are both cryptographic algorithms, but they are not used for file hashing.

52. B. Least privilege is the practice of only providing users with the permissions they need to perform their designated tasks and no more. For her standard activities, Alice is given an account that does not have administrative permissions because she does not need those permissions to perform standard tasks. The administrative account has the additional permissions needed for Alice to perform administrative tasks. The intention is for Alice to use that account only for those administrative tasks. Zero day is a type of vulnerability; multifactor authentication calls for users to supply two identifying factors; defense in depth refers to the use of multiple security mechanisms to provide additional protection. None of these other three options refers to the use of multiple user accounts.

53. E. After you have established a theory of probable cause, you can try to test the theory by replacing hardware components one by one until you find the faulty device. All of the other options are steps that come either earlier or later in the troubleshooting process.

54. D. An insider threat by definition originates with an authorized user. Therefore, smartcards, motion detection, and biometrics will only detect the presence of someone who is authorized to enter sensitive areas. Video surveillance, however, can track the activities of anyone, authorized or not.

55. D. All of these occurrences are malfunctions on a full-duplex Ethernet network, but colli-sions are normal and expected on a half-duplex network. Runt frames occur when a network interface generates packets that are smaller than the 64-byte minimum allowable length. Giants occur when frames are larger than the 1518-byte maximum allowable length. Late collisions occur when network cables are too long, and frames collide after leaving the send-ing system.

56. B. The Unix/Linux `tcpdump` utility is a protocol analyzer. It is a command-line tool that captures network packets and displays their contents. The `iptables`, `nmap`, and `pathping` utilities cannot capture and analyze packets. `iptables` manages Unix/Linux kernel firewall rules, nmap is a port scanner, and `pathping` is a Windows route tracing tool.

57. A, B. NAS devices are self-contained file servers that connect directly to a standard IP network. A NAS device provides file-level access to its storage devices, and it includes an operating system and a filesystem. NAS devices are typically not iSCSI targets. SANs pro-vide block-level storage and typically function as iSCSI targets, but they do not include an operating system or filesystem.

58. C. Penetration testing is a type of network security evaluation in which a client engages an outside consultant who attempts to penetrate the network's security and gain unauthorized access to protected network resources. Testing by an internal administrator familiar with the security barriers would not be a valid test. Although having a consultant examine the net-work's security from within can be useful, it is not a penetration test. Computers or networks that are alluring targets for intruders are called honeypots or honeynets. Implementation of a new security protocol can only come after the current security situation has been evaluated.

59. C. All of the mechanisms listed are designed to make any attempts to tamper with or physi-cally compromise the hardware devices immediately evident. These mechanisms are therefore various forms of tamper detection. Asset tracking is for locating and identifying hardware. Geofencing is a wireless networking technique for limiting access to a network. Port security refers to network switch ports. These options do not apply to the specified mechanisms.

60. B. The various types of wavelength division multiplexing use different spacing of the wave-lengths they carry, which enables them to fit different numbers of channels on a single medium. WDM (or BWDM) carries two wavelengths for bidirectional communication. CWDM can carry up to 16 channels, and DWDM can carry 40 or 80 (depending on the spacing used). Various amplification technologies (including EFDA and Raman) can expand the amounts of usable wavelength in each type.

61. A, B, C. Layer 2 Tunneling Protocol (L2TP), Internet Protocol Security (IPSec), and Multi-point Generic Routing Encapsulation (MGRE) are all protocols that encapsulate packets in an encrypted form within another protocol to secure their contents. Network Address Trans-lation (NAT) enables workstations on private networks to access the Internet by substituting a public IP address in packets generated with private addresses. NAT does not use tunneling.

62. C. To create a network with 8 subnets and 30 hosts per subnet, you must allocate 3 of the 8 bits in the last octet for use as a subnet identifier. This results in a binary value of 11100000 for the last octet in the subnet mask, which converts to a decimal value of 224. Therefore, the correct subnet mask value is 255.255.255.224. Values for the last octet that are lower than 224 would not enable you to create 8 subnets. Values higher than 224 would not enable you to create 30 host addresses.

63. B. Media Access Control (MAC) filtering takes the form of an Access Control List (ACL) on the wireless network's access points, listing the MAC addresses of all the devices that are permitted to access the network. If the MAC address of your laptop is not included in the ACL, you will be unable to connect to the network. Geofencing is intended to prevent users outside the office from accessing the network. You are inside, so this should not be the problem. You have been given the passphrase for the network, so you should be able to configure the WiFi Protected Access II (WPA2) protocol on your laptop. You have been given the SSID of the network, so you should be able to connect by manually entering it, even if the access points are not broadcasting the SSID.

64. D. For the link pulse LED on the switch port to light up, there must be an active connection between the switch and a functioning network device at the other end. Plugging a running computer into the wall plate will enable the Ethernet adapters at both ends of the connection to communicate, causing the LED to light. None of the other options will cause the LED to light.

65. B. The Ethernet (or IEEE 802.3) protocol at the data link layer uses MAC addresses to identify computers on the local network. MAC addresses are coded into the firmware of physical network interface adapters by the manufacturer. The physical layer deals with signals and is not involved in addressing. The IP at the network layer has its own addressing system. The transport layer protocols are not involved in addressing.

66. C. The Cisco symbol shown in the figure is used in network diagrams to represent a router, as symbolized by the arrows pointing both in and out. This symbol is not used to represent a hub, a switch, or a gateway.

67. B, D. By inserting modified entries into a device's ARP cache, an attacker can cause traffic to be diverted from the correct destination to a system controlled by the attacker. This can enable the attacker to intercept traffic intended for another destination. In a man-in-the-middle attack, the attacker can read the intercepted traffic and even modify it before sending it on to the correct destination. In a session hijacking attack, the attacker can use the intercepted traffic to obtain authentication information, including passwords. Neither of the other two options is facilitated by ARP poisoning. An evil twin is a fraudulent access point on a wireless network. Social engineering is a form of attack in which an innocent user is persuaded by an attacker to provide sensitive information via email or telephone.

68. D. A honeypot is a computer configured to function as bait for attackers, causing them to waste their time penetrating a resource that provides no significant access. This is also a technique that enables the target to gather information about the attackers. A demilitarized zone (DMZ), also known as a screened subnet or perimeter network, is a network segment on which administrators locate servers that must be accessible from the Internet but that are separated from the internal network by a firewall. A root guard provides protection to switch ports. Spoofing is an attack technique in which an intruder modifies packets to assume the appearance of another user or computer.

69. A. A repeater is a physical layer device that regenerates incoming signals and retransmits them. A hub is a type of repeater that receives data through any one of its multiple ports and retransmits the data out through all of its other ports. Bridges and switches are data link layer devices, and routers are network layer devices. None of these three can be described as a multiport repeater.

70. D. A port scanner examines a system for open ports or endpoints that are accessible from the network using the TCP or UDP protocol, which intruders can conceivably exploit to gain access to the system. Port scanners do not list user processes, hardware ports, numbers of packets, or IP addresses.

71. A, E. A Storage Area Network (SAN) is a network that is dedicated to carrying traffic between servers and storage devices. SANs can use specialized network protocols, such as Fibre Channel in this case, or standard Gigabit Ethernet. A Local Area Network (LAN) is a connected group of computers, usually inside a single room or building. In this case, the cluster has one LAN connecting the nodes together and another providing other users with access to the cluster. A Personal Area Network (PAN) provides communication among devices associated with a single person, such as smartphones. A Wide Area Network (WAN) is a network that connects devices or networks at different geographic locations. A Metropolitan Area Network (MAN) is a type of WAN that connects devices within a limited geographic area. The cluster is not connected to a PAN, WAN, or MAN.

72. C. Since only one user is reporting the problem and he has admitted to making changes to his IP configuration, you should start by checking the workstation configuration using the `ipconfig` command. If the routers, the switches, or the DNS server were causing the problem, more than one user would be affected, and there would be additional users calling the help desk.

73. C. Because your colleague can connect to WebServ1 successfully, the problem is not an unresponsive service or blocked ports on the server. The problem is not a name resolution failure, because you can successfully ping WebServ1 by name. Therefore, of the options listed, the only possible problem must be that the firewall on your workstation is configured to block the remote desktop client's traffic.

74. C. The device shown in the figure is a punchdown tool, which you use to connect unshielded twisted-pair cable ends to the keystone connectors used in modular wall plates and patch panels. After lining up the individual wires in the cable with the connector, you use the tool to press each wire into its slot. The tool also cuts the wire sheath to make an electrical contact and trims the end of the wire. This tool is not capable of performing any of the tasks described in the other options.

75. A, B, C. The 5 GHz frequency has 23 channels available in the United States, whereas the 2.4 GHz frequency has only 11. Many household devices, such as cordless telephones, use the 2.4 GHz frequency band, but relatively few devices use the 5 GHz band. Higher frequencies typically support faster transmission speeds, because with all other conditions equal, they can carry more data in the same amount of time. The 5 GHz frequency typically has a shorter range than 2.4 GHz, because it is less able to penetrate barriers.

76. C. The device shown in the figure is a butt set, a basic tool of telephone installers and line workers. By connecting the clips to pins in a punchdown block, you can access telephone circuits in order to test them or place telephone calls. The device shown is not a crimper, a tone generator and locator, or a punchdown tool.

77. A. The File Transfer Protocol (FTP) uses two port numbers. It uses the first, port 21, for a control connection that remains open during the entire client-server session. The second port, 20, is for a data connection that opens only when the protocol is actually transferring a file between the client and the server. Network Time Protocol (NTP), Simple Network Management Protocol (SNMP), and Hypertext Transfer Protocol (HTTP) all use a single port on the server.

78. A. The 13-bit prefix indicated in the network address will result in a mask with 13 ones followed by 19 zeroes. Broken into 8-bit blocks, the binary mask value is as follows:

11111111 11111000 00000000 00000000

Converted into decimal values, this results in a subnet mask value of 255.248.0.0.

79. B. The failure to detect a tone on the eighth wire indicates that there is either a break in the wire somewhere inside the cable or a bad pin connection in one or both connectors. This type of fault is called an open circuit. None of the other three options are faults that manifest as described. A short circuit is when a wire is connected to two or more pins at one end of the cable. A split pair is a connection in which two wires are incorrectly mapped in exactly the same way on both ends of the cable. Crosstalk is a type of interference caused by signals on one wire bleeding over to other wires.

80. B, D. The session layer is responsible for creating and maintaining a dialog between end systems. This dialog can be a two-way alternate dialog that requires end systems to take turns transmitting, or it can be a two-way simultaneous dialog in which either end system can transmit at will. The session layer functions are called dialog control and dialog separation. Data encryption is performed at the presentation layer, and datagram routing occurs at the network layer.

81. A. When individual packets in a data stream are delayed, due to network congestion, different routing, or queuing problems, the resulting connectivity problem is called jitter. While this condition might not cause problems for asynchronous applications, real-time communications, such as VoIP or streaming video, can suffer interruptions from which the phenomenon gets its name. Latency describes a generalized delay in network transmissions, not individual packet delays. Attenuation is the weakening of a signal as it travels through a network medium. A bottleneck is a condition in which all traffic is delayed, due to a faulty or inadequate component. None of these three options would account for the problems reported by the users.

82. C. The 802.11ac standard defines a wireless LAN running at speeds of up to 1.3 gigabits per second (Gbps). None of the other 802.11 standards define networks running at speeds beyond 600 Mbps. There is no currently ratified IEEE 802.11 standard that enables speeds of 2.6 Gbps.

83. B, D. Network Address Translation (NAT) is a network layer service, typically integrated into a router, that converts the private IP addresses in all of a client's Internet transmissions to a registered IP address. NAT therefore works for all applications. A proxy server is an application layer device that performs the same type of conversion but only for specific applications. A Remote Authentication Dial-In User Service (RADIUS) server can provide authentication, authorization, and accounting services for remote access servers, but it does not convert IP addresses. A unified threat management (UTM) appliance typically performs Virtual Private Network (VPN), firewall, and antivirus functions. It too does not convert IP addresses.

84. A, B. 1.1.1.0 and 9.34.0.0 are both valid IPv4 network addresses. IPv4 addresses with first byte values from 224 to 239 are Class D addresses, which are reserved for use as multicast addresses. Therefore, the user cannot use 229.6.87.0 for his network. 103.256.77.0 is an invalid address because the value 256 cannot be represented by an 8-bit binary value.

85. B. Distance vector protocols rely on hop counts—that is, the number of routers between a source and a destination—to evaluate the efficiency of routes. Link state protocols use a different type of calculation, usually based on Dijkstra's algorithm. The terms *interior gateway protocol* and *edge gateway protocol* do not refer to the method of calculating routing efficiency.

86. A, C. Any type of fiber-optic cable will satisfy the client's requirements. Fiber-optic cable supports the required 1000 Mbps data rate and can connect networks that are 500 meters apart. Fiber-optic cable is also immune to EMI. Although both multimode and single-mode fiber would meet the corporation's general needs, multimode is substantially less expensive than single-mode fiber. Twisted-pair wiring (STP or UTP) meets the data rate, but it does not support connections longer than 100 meters. Thin coaxial cable does not support the data rate or distances longer than 185 meters.

87. C, D. An incorrect frequency, Service Set Identifier (SSID), or WiFi Protected Access II (WPA2) passphrase would prevent the user's laptop from ever connecting to the network, so these cannot be the cause of the problem. Greater distance from the access point or interference from intervening walls can both cause a weakening of wireless signals, which can result in the intermittent connectivity that the user is experiencing.

88. A, C, E. Static routes are not automatically added to the routing table by routing protocols and do not automatically adapt to changes in the network. They are therefore not recommended for large internetworks with redundant paths between networks. Administrators must manually add, modify, or delete static routes when a change in a network occurs. For this reason, static routes are recommended only for use in small networks without multiple paths to each destination.

89. C. Network layer protocols specify logical addresses, such as IP addresses, for end system communication. They also use those addresses to route packets to destinations on other networks. The physical layer defines standards for physical and mechanical characteristics of a network. The data link layer uses Media Access Control (MAC) or hardware addresses, not logical addresses. The transport layer uses port numbers, not logical addresses. Session layer protocols create and maintain a dialog between end systems. Presentation layer protocols are responsible for the formatting, translation, and presentation of information. The application layer provides an entry point for applications to access the protocol stack and prepare information for transmission across a network.

90. C. The use of an incorrect wireless security protocol is a well-known source of errorless connection failures, so checking this will most likely enable you to discover the source of the problem. Channel overlap is a problem that you would check and resolve at the access point, not at the users' workstations. It is not possible to change the frequency on the access point, because the 802.11g standard only supports the 2.4 GHz frequency. Although signal interference could conceivably be the cause for a connection failure, the users can see the network's SSID, so this is not likely to be the problem.

91. A, B, C. iSCSI does not include its own flow control mechanism, so this option is incorrect. It runs over a TCP connection, which is the protocol responsible for flow control. Fibre Channel requires a dedicated network using fiber-optic cable. iSCSI traffic can coexist with standard LAN traffic on a single network, although some type of Quality of Service (QoS) mechanism is frequently recommended. Because it runs on any IP network, iSCSI traffic is routable, and it is far less expensive to implement than Fibre Channel.

92. B, C, E. The client's DNS server uses iterative queries when sending name resolution requests to root domain servers and to the authoritative servers for the com and adatum.com domains. In an iterative query, the server replies immediately with the best information it possesses, and the transaction ends. When a client sends a name resolution query to its DNS server, it uses a recursive request so that the server will assume the responsibility for resolving the name. The only other use of recursive requests is in the case of a forwarder, which is configured to pass that responsibility on to another DNS server.

93. D. To access the Internet, the workstation's routing table must include a default gateway entry. The default gateway is a router on the local network that provides access to other networks, such as the Internet. To manually create a default gateway entry in the routing table, you use the route add command with a Network Destination value of 0.0.0.0, a MASK value of 0.0.0.0, and the address of a router on the local network (in this case 192.168.2.99). The entry must also have a METRIC value that is lower than the other entries in the table so that it will be used first.

94. A, B, D. Thin Ethernet networks use BNC connectors. Thick Ethernet networks use N-type connectors. All Unshielded Twisted Pair (UTP) Ethernet networks use RJ45 connectors. You will not need F-type or DB-9 connectors. F-type connectors are used with coaxial cable but are typically used for cable television installations. DB-9 connectors are commonly used for serial communications ports.

95. A. *Geofencing* is the generic term for a technology that limits access to a network or other resource based on the client's location. It is therefore best described as somewhere you are. A finger gesture would be considered something you do, a password is something you know, and a smartcard is something you have.

96. A. Hot, warm, and cold backup sites differ in the hardware and software they have installed. A cold site is just a space at a remote location. The hardware and software must be procured and installed before the network can be restored. It is therefore the least expensive and takes the most time. A warm site has hardware in place, but it still must be installed and configured. A hot site has all of the necessary hardware already installed and configured. A warm site is more expensive than a cold site, and a hot site is the most expensive of all and takes the shortest amount of time to be made operational.

97. A. A host-to-site VPN is a remote access solution, enabling users to access the corporate network from home or while traveling. A site-to-site VPN enables one network to connect to another, enabling users on both networks to access resources on the other one. This is usually a more economical solution for branch office connections than a Wide Area Network (WAN) link. A host-to-host VPN enables two individual users to establish a protected connection to each other. An extranet VPN is designed to provide clients, vendors, and other outside partners with the ability to connect to your corporate network with limited access.

98. B, C, D. The leaf and spine topology uses a full mesh topology in its two layers of switches. This is more expensive than the three-tier topology, but it reduces latency by requiring the same number of hops in the path between any two routers. The use of software-defined networking provides adaptive path determination without the use of the Spanning Tree Protocol (STP) for layer 2 port blocking.

99. D. Performance Monitor is a Windows application that can create logs of specific system and network performance statistics over extended periods of time. Such a log created on a new computer can function as a baseline for future troubleshooting. Event Viewer is a Windows application for displaying system log files; it cannot create a performance baseline. Syslog is a log compilation program originally created for Unix systems; it does not create performance baselines. Network Monitor is a protocol analyzer. Although it can capture a traffic sample that can function as a reference for future troubleshooting efforts, this cannot be called a performance baseline.

100. C. Although a DoS attack typically involves traffic flooding, any attack that prevents a server from functioning can be called a DoS attack. A permanent DoS attack is one in which the attacker actually damages the target system and prevents it from functioning. This can be a physical attack that actually damages the server hardware, or the attacker can disable the server by altering its software or configuration settings. Flood-based attacks include the Distributed Denial-of-Service (DDoS) attack, in which the attacker uses hundreds or thousands of computers, controlled by malware and called bots or zombies, to send traffic to a single server or website in an attempt to overwhelm it and prevent it from functioning. An amplified DoS attack is one in which the messages sent by the attacker require an extended amount of processing by the target servers, increasing the burden on them more than simpler messages would. A reflective DoS attack is one in which the attacker sends requests containing the target server's IP address to legitimate servers on the Internet, such as DNS servers, causing them to send a flood of responses that overwhelm the target.

Chapter 7: Practice Exam 2

1. B, D, E. Bluetooth, Z-Wave, and near-field communication (NFC) are all short-range wireless technologies that are capable of providing communications between PAN devices. The other options are not suitable for PAN communications. Radio-frequency identification (RFID) uses tags containing data, frequently embedded in pets, which can be read using electromagnetic fields. Integrated Services Digital Network (ISDN) is a wide area networking technology that uses the telephone infrastructure to provide a high-speed dial-up service.

2. E. Each port on a router defines a separate network segment. Because routers do not forward broadcast transmissions, each of the three segments forms a separate broadcast domain. Hubs forward all traffic to all of the connected nodes, so the network segment with the hub forms a single collision domain. Switches forward traffic only to the destination node, so each workstation connected to one of the switches forms a separate collision domain. The switch-to-router links count for two more collision domains. There are six switched workstations, plus the hub segment and the two switch-to-router links, for a total of nine collision domains.

3. D. A. Remote Authentication Dial-In User Service (RADIUS) server can provide authentication, authorization, and accounting services for remote access servers. Intrusion Detection Systems (IDSs), Next-Generation Firewalls (NGFWs), and Network Attached Storage (NAS) devices do not provide this type of authentication services.

4. B. A multilayer switch is a network connectivity device that functions at both the data link layer (layer 2) and the network layer (layer 3) of the Open Systems Interconnection (OSI) reference model. At layer 2, the device functions like a normal switch, creating an individual collision domain for each connected node and enabling administrators to create multiple VLANs. At layer 3, the device also provides routing capabilities by forwarding packets between the VLANs. Virtual routers, load balancers, and broadband routers are strictly layer 3 devices that can route traffic but cannot create VLANs.

5. C. The value after the slash in a Classless Inter-Domain Routing (CIDR) address specifies the number of bits in the network identifier. An IP address has 32 bits, so if 19 bits are allocated to the network identifier, 13 bits are left for the host identifier.

6. D. On a TCP/IP network, the Internet Protocol (IP) at the network layer is the protocol responsible for the delivery of data to its final destination, using IP addresses that can be routed through an internetwork. Data link layer protocols are only concerned with communication between devices on a Local Area Network (LAN) or between two points connected by a Wide Area Network (WAN). The transport, session, and application layers are not involved in the actual delivery of data over the network.

7. C, D. The iSCSI protocol runs on a standard IP network, and the Fibre Channel over Ethernet (FCoE) variant runs on a standard Ethernet network. Both of these protocols can share a network with LAN traffic, although the use of a Quality of Service (QoS) mechanism is usually recommended. The original Fibre Channel implementation and InfiniBand both require a dedicated network medium that does not support LAN traffic.

8. B, D. SMTP and DNS are both application layer protocols, but neither one includes a character-based program. Both Telnet and FTP are protocols that include command-line client applications, with Telnet providing terminal emulation and FTP file transfer functionality.

9. B. The Cisco symbol shown in the figure is used in network diagrams to represent a switch, as symbolized by the multiple arrows pointing outward. This symbol is not used to represent a hub, a router, or a gateway.

10. D, E, F. DHCP servers use well-known port numbers 67 and 68. TFTP uses port number 69. Neither protocol uses port 64, 65, or 66.

11. C, D. The change management team is usually not responsible for tasks directly involved in the implementation of the changes they approve. Therefore, they would not be the ones to notify users exactly when the change will take place or document the procedure afterward. They would, however, be responsible for providing a maintenance window, during which the change must occur, and authorizing any downtime that would be needed.

12. C. A server with dual power supplies can run in one of two modes: redundant or combined. In redundant mode, each of the power supplies is capable of providing 100 percent of the power needed by the server. Therefore, the server can continue to run if one power supply fails, making it fault tolerant. In combined mode, both power supplies are needed to provide the server's needs, so a failure of one power supply will bring the server down. Individual mode and hot backup mode are not terms used for this purpose.

13. B. The word paris is the name of the bottommost domain in the given FQDN. paris is a subdomain within mydomain, and mydomain is a second-level domain registered by a particular organization. The topmost layer in the DNS hierarchy is represented by org, which is a top-level domain. In this FQDN, www is not the name of a domain; it is the name of a particular host in the paris.mydomain.org domain.

14. B, C. The two main connectionless protocols in the TCP/IP suite are the Internet Protocol (IP) and the User Datagram Protocol (UDP), both of which use the term *datagram* for their protocol data units. Ethernet uses the term *frame,* and Transmission Control Protocol (TCP) uses the term *segment.*

15. D. Data is stored on tape drives in a linear fashion. Once you write backup data to a tape, you cannot selectively replace individual files. When you perform a restore job, you have to restore the most recent full backup, followed by incremental backups, which overwrite some of the full backup files with newer ones. Hard disk drives are random access devices, meaning that individual files can be written to and read from any location on the disk. When you perform incremental backup jobs to a hard disk, the software can restore data using any version of each file that is available. Data capacity, transfer speed, and block size are not relevant to the number of jobs required.

16. B. A patch is a relatively small update that is designed to address a specific issue, often a security exploit or vulnerability. Patches do not add features or new capabilities; they are fixes targeted at a specific area of the operating system. Updates, upgrades, and service packs are larger packages that might include new features and/or many different fixes.

17. A, D. The twisted wire pairs inside twisted-pair cable prevent the signals on the different wires from interfering with each other (which is called crosstalk). The twists also provide resistance to outside EMI. The twists have no effect on collisions. The twists do nothing to facilitate the attachment of connectors. Twists have nothing to do with the bend radius allowance for the cable.

18. D. The top utility displays performance information about the currently running processes on a Unix/Linux system. The other options are tools that do not display running processes. netstat is a tool that enables you to view active network connections and TCP/IP traffic statistics. It does not measure system performance. The dig tool generates Domain Name System (DNS) queries. perfmon is a Windows performance monitoring tool; there no Unix/Linux tool by that name.

19. B. The Software as a Service (SaaS) model provides consumers with access to a specific application, such as email, running on the provider's servers. Infrastructure as a Service (IaaS) provides the consumers with processing, storage, and networking resources that they can use to install and run operating systems and other software of their choice. Platform as a Service (PaaS) provides consumers with the ability to install applications of their choice on a server installed by the provider.

20. D. In SIEM, forensic analysis is a process of searching logs on multiple computers for specific information based on set criteria and time periods. The other three options specify other SIEM functions. Data aggregation is a process of consolidating log information from multiple sources. Correlation is the process of linking logged events with common attributes together. Retention is the long-term storage of log data.

21. A. DHCP clients use broadcasts to transmit DHCPDISCOVER messages on the local network. DHCP servers are then required to respond to the broadcasts. DHCP clients cannot use unicast, multicast, or anycast messages to initiate contact with DHCP servers, because the clients have no way of learning the addresses of the DHCP servers.

22. A. Layer 2 Tunneling Protocol (L2TP) is a VPN protocol that creates the tunnel forming a VPN connection, but it does not encrypt the traffic passing through the tunnel. To do this, it requires a separate protocol that provides encryption, such as IPsec. Point-to-Point Tunneling Protocol (PPTP) and Secure Sockets Layer (SSL) are both capable of encrypting traffic in the tunnels they create.

23. C, D. IEEE 802.11b, 802.11g, and 802.11n networks all can use the 2.4 GHz frequency band for their transmissions, which can experience interference from a wireless telephone using the same frequency. IEEE 802.11a and IEEE 802.11ac, however, use the 5 GHz band, which will not experience interference from a 2.4 GHz phone.

24. C. A switch is a data link layer device that essentially performs the function of a bridge for each device connected to one of its ports. It can therefore be described as a *multiport bridge*. *Multiport repeater* is another term for a hub, and *multihomed router* is a redundancy, as all routers are by definition multihomed—that is, connected to multiple networks. There is no such device as a multicast hub.

25. D. The term *out-of-band* describes any type of management access to a device that does not go through the production network. Plugging a laptop into the console port avoids the network, so it is considered to be an example of out-of-band management. In-band management describes an access method that does go through the production network. Client-to-site is a type of Virtual Private Network (VPN) connection, and Bring Your Own Device (BYOD) is a policy defining whether and how users are permitted to connect their personal devices to the network.

26. A, B, C, D. The longer the password, the more difficult it is to guess. Corporate policies typically require passwords of a minimum length. A larger character set also makes a password more difficult to guess, so requiring uppercase, lowercase, numeric, and special characters is common. Changing passwords forces the cracking process to start over, so policies typically require frequent password changes and require users to create unique passwords at each change.

27. B. The technology that uses human physical characteristics to authenticate users is called biometrics. Biometric devices can identify users based on fingerprints, retinal patterns, voice prints, and other characteristics.

28. B, C, D. Option B contains a *p*, which is a nonhexadecimal digit. Option C contains blocks larger than 16 bits. Option D contains only seven 16-bit blocks (and no double-colon) instead of the eight required for a 128-bit IPv6 address. The address fe00::c955:c944:acdd:3fcb in option A is correctly formatted for IPv6, with the double-colon replacing three blocks of zeroes. Uncompressed, the address would appear as follows: fe00:0000:0000:0000:c955:c944:acdd:3fcb.

29. A. The terms *fail close* and *fail open* refer to the default position of an electric or electronic door lock when there is a power failure. Security is often a trade-off with safety, and in the event that an emergency occurs that results in a power outage, whether secured doors are permanently locked or left permanently open is a critical factor. The terms *fail close* and *fail open* do not apply to motion detectors or video cameras. A honeypot is a computer, application, or website configured to lure potential attackers; it is not a physical security mechanism.

30. C. Video surveillance can monitor the activities of all users in a sensitive area, authorized or not. With properly placed equipment, even specific actions, such as commands typed into a computer, can be monitored. Identification badges, key fobs, and motion detection can indicate the presence of individuals in a sensitive area, but they cannot monitor specific activities.

31. C. The IP address 127.0.0.1 is a dedicated loopback address that directs outgoing IP traffic directly into the incoming IP traffic buffer. A successful `ping` test using that address indicates that the computer's TCP/IP stack is functioning properly, but the traffic never reaches the network adapter or the network, so the test does not confirm that the adapter is functioning or that the computer has a correct IP address for the network.

32. B, C. *Multifactor authentication* combines two or more authentication methods and reduces the likelihood that an intruder would be able to successfully impersonate a user during the authentication process. A password and a retinal scan is an example of a multifactor authentication system. A smartcard and a PIN, which is the equivalent of a password, is an example of multifactor authentication because it requires users to supply something they know and something they have. Multifactor authentication refers to the proofs of identity a system requires, not the number of servers used to implement the system. Therefore, the use of a Remote Authentication Dial-In User Service (RADIUS) server is not an example of multifactor authentication. A system that requires two passwords is not an example of multifactor authentication, because an attacker can compromise one password as easily as two. A multifactor authentication system requires two different forms of authentication.

33. C. To access the Internet, the workstation's routing table must include a default gateway entry, which would have a Network Destination value of 0.0.0.0. A workstation's routing table does not have to specify the address of a Domain Name System (DNS) server. The loopback (127.0.0.1) and multicast (224.0.0.0) addresses are normal routing table entries that do not affect Internet access.

34. A, D. Multimode cables use an LED light source and have a smaller bend radius than single-mode cables. Single-mode cables have a smaller core filament and can span longer distances than multimode cables. Fiber-optic cables are not conductors of electricity, so they do not require a ground.

35. D. Authentication is the process of confirming a user's identity. Smartcards and passwords are two of the authentication factors commonly used by network devices. Authorization defines the type of access granted to authenticated users. Accounting and auditing are both methods of tracking and recording a user's activities on a network, such as when a user logged on and how long they remained connected.

36. B, D. Ethernet has never used a ring or mesh topology. The first Ethernet networks used a physical layer implementation commonly known as Thick Ethernet or 10Base5. The network used coaxial cable in a bus topology. Later Ethernet standards use twisted-pair or fiber-optic cables in a star topology.

37. C, D. Disabling Service Set Identifier (SSID) broadcasting prevents a wireless network from appearing to clients. The clients must specify the SSID to which they want to connect. Media Access Control (MAC) address filtering is a form of Access Control List (ACL) that is maintained in the access point and that contains the addresses of devices that are to be permitted to access the network. Both of these mechanisms make it more difficult for unauthorized devices to connect to the access point. The other two options will not help to prevent unauthorized access. Kerberos is an authentication protocol used by Active Directory, and relocating the access point to a screened subnet (or DMZ) will not resolve the problem.

38. B, D. Bandwidth throttling is a traffic shaping technique that prevents specified data streams from transmitting too many packets. Rate limiting is a traffic shaping technique that controls the transmission rate of sending systems. A broadcast storm is a type of network switching loop. NAT is a method by which private networks can share registered IP addresses. Neither of these last two is a traffic shaping technique.

39. E, F. The primary function of a network switch is to process packets based on their Media Access Control (MAC) addresses, which makes it a data link layer device. However, multiprotocol switches are devices that can also perform routing functions based on IP addresses, which operate at the network layer. Switches are not typically associated with the other layers of the OSI model.

40. B. An SSID that is not being broadcasted is not detectable by clients, so you must type it in manually. Security protocols are also not detectable, so you must select the WPA2 protocol from the list of options provided on the laptop.

41. C. The IEEE 802.11ac standard, like all of the Wireless Local Area Network (WLAN) standards in the 802.11 working group, uses CSMA/CA for media access control. The 802.1X standard defines an authentication mechanism and does not require a media access control mechanism. The IEEE 802.3 (Ethernet) standard uses a different mechanism for media access control: Carrier Sense Multiple Access with Collision Detection (CSMA/CD).

42. D. The place containing the demarcation points and the backbone switch is called the Main Distribution Frame (MDF). An Intermediate Distribution Frame (IDF) is the location of localized telecommunications equipment such as the interface between the horizontal cabling and the backbone. Mean Time Between Failures (MTBF) and Remote Desktop Protocol (RDP) are not network wiring locations.

43. A. *Geofencing* is the generic term for a technology that limits access to a network or other resource based on the client's location. In wireless networking, geofencing is intended to prevent unauthorized clients outside the facility from connecting to the network. By allowing only users with strong signals to connect, you help to prevent access to outside users. Local authentication is an application or service that triggers an authentication request to which the user must respond before access is granted. Port security is a method for protecting access to switch ports. Motion detection is a system designed to trigger a notification or alarm when an individual trespasses in a protected area. None of these other options are related to signal strength.

44. C. Social engineering is the practice of obtaining sensitive data by contacting users and pretending to be someone with a legitimate need for that data. No software or hardware solution can prevent it; the only way is to educate users of the potential dangers and establish policies that inform users what to do when they experience a social engineering attempt. Social engineering is not a virus or other form of malware, so an antivirus product has no effect against it. Social engineering is not implemented in network traffic, so a firewall cannot filter it, and IPsec cannot protect against it.

45. C. A Class B address uses the first two octets as the network identifier, which yields a binary subnet mask of 11111111 11111111 00000000 00000000. In decimal form, the subnet mask is 255.255.0.0. The 255.0.0.0 mask is for Class A addresses, and the 255.255.255.0 mask is for Class C addresses. 255.255.255.255 is the broadcast address for the current network.

46. B. All of the mechanisms that Alice has implemented are designed to make any attempts to tamper with or physically compromise the network hardware devices immediately evident. This is therefore a form of tamper detection. Asset tracking is for locating and identifying specific hardware components. Geofencing is a wireless networking technique for limiting access to a network based on signal strength. Port security refers to the protection of network switch ports from unauthorized access.

47. A. Because the administrative site is encrypted, you must use the `https://` prefix to access it. Because the administrative site uses the nondefault port number 12354, you must append that number to the server name after a colon.

48. C. Disabling SSID broadcasts is a way of hiding the presence of a wireless network, but if an intruder knows that a network is there, it is a simple matter to capture packets transmitted by the wireless devices and read the SSID from them. The other options do not explain the weakness of suppressing SSID broadcasts. It is not possible to connect to a wireless network without the SSID. SSIDs are set by the administrator of the access point; they are not printed on the device's label. SSIDs can be found relatively easily, but guessing them is no easier than guessing a password.

49. A. In a private cloud, the same organization that uses the cloud services is also the sole owner of the infrastructure that provides those services. In the public cloud model, one organization functions as the provider, and another organization consumes the services of the provider. A hybrid cloud is a combination of public and private infrastructure so that the consumer organization is only a partial owner of the infrastructure. There is no such thing as an ad hoc cloud model.

50. B. On-boarding and off-boarding are identity management processes in which users are added or removed from an organization's Identity and Access Management (IAM) system. This grants new users the privileges they need to use the network, modifies their privileges if they change positions, and revokes privileges when they leave the company. On-boarding and off-boarding are not data loss prevention, incident response, or inventory management processes.

51. B, D. A standard VPN typically uses full tunneling, in which all of the system's network traffic is encapsulated and encrypted for transmission. Split tunneling is a variation of this method in which only part of the system's traffic uses the VPN connection; the rest is transmitted over the network in the normal manner. Administrators can select which applications and devices use the VPN. Split tunneling can conserve the Internet bandwidth used by the VPN and provide access to local network services without the need for encapsulation. Split tunneling does not provide additional data integrity protection or improved performance through multiplexing.

52. B, C. If there is no way for unauthorized people to access the datacenter, then there is no danger of someone plugging a device into a port that is left enabled. If the switch uses an Access Control List (ACL) that specifies the Media Access Control (MAC) addresses of systems permitted to connect to it, then there is no need to disable unused ports, because any unknown devices plugged into open ports will not be granted access to the network. The other two options are not valid reasons. Ports that are not patched in can still be compromised at the switch location. Enabling ports is not difficult, so accommodating new users is not a valid reason for leaving them enabled.

53. C. There are no policies that can prevent users from creating easily guessed passwords. The only action that can help is to educate users that attackers are frequently able to guess passwords by using information such as familiar names and dates. Forcing more frequent password changes would not compel users to alter their method for choosing passwords, nor would increasing the minimum password age value. Assigning random passwords would address the issue, but user complaints and forgotten passwords would likely create greater problems than it would solve.

54. A, B, C, E. ACLs restrict access to network devices by filtering user names, Media Access Control (MAC) addresses, IP addresses, or other criteria. Routers, servers, switches, and Wireless Access Points (WAPs) all can use ACLs to control access to them. Hubs are purely physical layer devices that relay electrical or optical signals. They have no access control mechanisms.

55. D. Role separation is the practice of creating a different virtual server for each server role or application. In addition to providing other benefits as well, this forces intruders to mount attacks on multiple servers to disable an entire network. Geofencing is a technique for limiting access to a wireless network. Network segmentation describes the process of creating multiple Virtual Local Area Networks (VLANs) or deploying firewalls to isolate part of a network. VLAN hopping is a type of attack in which an intruder sends command messages to a switch to transfer a port from one VLAN to another. None of these last three options refers to virtual machine deployment.

56. A, C, D. DHCP snooping is a feature found in some network switches that prevents rogue DHCP servers from assigning IP addresses to clients. It can also detect when DHCP release or decline messages arrive over a port other than the one on which the DHCP transaction originated. While DHCP snooping can prevent DHCP clients from being assigned an incorrect IP address, it does not directly prevent the poisoning of Dynamic Name System (DNS) server caches with erroneous information.

57. D. In this scenario, only one user is reporting a problem. Therefore, the likeliest next step is to perform the same task on another computer attached to the same segment. If you can perform the task successfully, the problem most likely lies within the user's computer or the connection to the switch. Since no other users are reporting the same problem, the server and switches on the network are probably up and functioning. Checking the router is not necessary since the user and server are on the same network.

58. D. A captive portal is a web page displayed to a user attempting to access a public wireless network. The user typically must supply identification, submit credentials, provide payment, or accept an end user agreement before access is granted. A captive portal does not refer to a switch port, a secured entryway to a room, or a type of extortionate computer attack.

59. B. After identifying the problem, the next step is to establish a theory for the probable cause of the problem. After that, you can test your theory, establish a plan of action, implement a solution, verify the functionality of the system, and document the entire process.

60. B, D. The well-known port for HTTPS is 443. The port for unsecured HTTP is 80. Neither of the other options are ports used by HTTP or HTTPS by default. Port 25 is used for the Simple Mail Transfer Protocol (SMTP), and Port 110 is used for the Post Office Protocol (POP3).

61. A, C, D. A load balancing router typically works by processing incoming traffic based on rules set by an administrator. The rules can distribute traffic among a group of servers using various criteria, such as each server's current load or response time or which server is next in a given rotation. Load balancers generally do not use the hardware configuration of the servers to direct traffic, as this is a factor that does not change over time.

62. D. Since only one user is reporting difficulty, the problem is most likely to be in the user's computer and its configuration. A DNS server, proxy server, or router problem would affect more than one user.

63. A. VLAN hopping is a method for sending false commands to switches to transfer a port from one VLAN to another. This can enable the attacker to connect his or her device to a potentially sensitive VLAN. VLAN hopping does not modify the switch's patch panel connections, only its VLAN assignments. It is not possible to rename a switch's default VLAN. VLAN hopping does not enable an attacker to change a switch's native VLAN.

64. A. A problem that affects the entire network should be given highest priority. This includes the issue with the mission-critical backbone router. Problems that affect multiple LANs or an entire department are generally given the next highest priority. A problem that affects a shared application server on a LAN should be given the next highest priority. A problem with a single user's computer should be given the lowest priority, compared to the other problems that have been reported.

65. C, D. One possible cause of the problem is that the DNS process on the remote server is corrupted or not running. Another possible cause is that there is a firewall blocking access to the DNS server's UDP port 53. Both of these would render the port unreachable. The TCP/IP client on the server is operating, as verified by the ping utility. This means that the IP host settings on your computer and on the DNS server are both configured properly and functioning. A router does not need to be running DNS to forward datagrams.

66. D. Store-and-forward switches take in the entire frame and verify its contents by performing a CRC calculation before forwarding it. Cut-through switches are faster because they look at only the first 6 bytes (the destination Media Access Control, or MAC, address) when forwarding a frame; they do not perform a CRC on the entire frame. Source route is a bridging technique in which the source host, not the switch, determines the path a frame will take through a network to reach a destination. Packet filtering is a technique used by firewalls. Neither of these is a type of switch.

67. A. A logic bomb is a code insert placed into a legitimate software product that triggers a malicious event when specific conditions are met. It can therefore affect both wired and wireless clients. The other options are all attacks directed at wireless networks. Deauthentication is a type of Denial-of-Service (DoS) attack in which the attacker targets a wireless client by sending a deauthentication frame that causes the client to be disconnected from the network. The object of the attack is often to compel the client to connect to a rogue access point called an evil twin. An evil twin is a fraudulent access point on a wireless network that mimics the Service Set Identifier (SSID) of a legitimate access point, in the hope of luring in users. War driving is an attack method that consists of driving around a neighborhood with a computer, scanning for unprotected wireless networks.

68. B, E. Upgrading all of the wireless devices to 802.11n will enable them to use the 5 GHz band and evade the interfering traffic generated by the surrounding networks. Configuring the devices to use the 5 GHz band will provide many more channels to choose from and will avoid the interference from the surrounding 2.4 GHz networks. The other options will not resolve the problem. The type of encryption that a wireless network uses has no bearing on the ability of the devices to avoid the interference generated by surrounding networks. Suppressing Service Set Identifier (SSID) broadcasts will not help the devices to connect to the network. Upgrading the firmware on the devices is not likely to have any effect on the connection problems when they are the result of interference from other networks.

69. A. Running the arp utility with the -a parameter on a Windows system displays the contents of the Address Resolution Protocol (ARP) cache, as shown here. The cache contains records of the IP addresses on the network that ARP has resolved into Media Access Control (MAC) addresses. The ping, tracert, and netstat utilities are not capable of producing this output.

70. C. The device shown in the figure is a crimper, which is used to create patch cables by attaching connectors to both ends of a relatively short length of bulk cable. This tool is not capable of placing telephone calls, generating a tone on a wire, or measuring electric current.

71. B. The device shown in the figure is a punchdown tool, used to connect unshielded twisted-pair cable ends to the keystone connectors used in modular wall plates and patch panels. After lining up the individual wires in the cable with the connector, you use the tool to press each wire into its slot. The tool also cuts the wire sheath to make an electrical contact and trims the end of the wire. The tool shown is not a crimper, a butt set, or a tone generator and locator.

72. C, E. IEEE 802.11g supports transmission speeds up to 54 Mbps, and it is backward compatible with 802.11b equipment. IEEE 802.11n is also backward compatible with 802.11b, and it can run at speeds up to 600 Mbps. Bluetooth is not compatible with any of the IEEE 802.11 standards. IEEE 802.11 cannot run at 54 Mbps, and though 802.11a can, it is not compatible with 802.11b.

73. A, B. Both Linux and the Cisco IOS operating systems include the traceroute utility. Windows has its own version of the utility, but it is called tracert. The CSU/DSU cannot run a traceroute command.

74. C, E. WLANs can use the ad hoc topology, in which devices communicate directly with each other, or the infrastructure topology, in which the wireless devices connect to an access point. The bus, star, and mesh topologies are used by wired networks only.

75. C. In this scenario, the best solution is for you to use the existing CATV service for the Internet connection. CATV offers faster data rates than standard modem-to-modem service and supports VPN connections. A dedicated fractional T-1 line is expensive and is not typically used for remote user connections. Since your telephone lines are not run through conduit and the distance to the central office is more than 18,000 feet, you probably cannot use DSL technology, because it requires good-quality lines and close proximity to a central office.

76. C. The customer's IP address, subnet mask, and default gateway values are appropriate for her home network. There is nothing wrong with having a zero in the network address. Therefore, of the options presented, the only logical choice is that the workstation's network cable is damaged or unplugged.

77. D. The Spanning Tree Protocol (STP) prevents packets from endlessly looping from switch to switch due to redundant links. Creating redundant links is a good preventive measure against switch failure, but packets transmitted over multiple links can circulate from switch to switch infinitely. STP creates a database of switching links and shuts down the redundant ones until they are needed. None of the other three protocols listed can perform this function. Network Address Translation (NAT) is a routing method that enables private networks to share registered IP addresses. Routing Information Protocol (RIP) propagates routing table information to other routers. A Virtual Local Area Network (VLAN) is an organizational tool that operates within switches by creating multiple broadcast domains.

78. C. In this scenario, only the users on one LAN are experiencing problems connecting to the Internet and the other internal LANs. This isolates the problem to a component within that LAN only. Since users can connect successfully to local resources, the problem does not lie within the individual computers, the switch that connects the users to the network, or the backbone network cable. The likeliest problem is therefore in the router connecting the problem LAN to the backbone network. Since users on the other internal LANs are not reporting problems connecting to the Internet, the problem most likely does not involve the Internet router.

79. B. The agreed upon 99.9 percent guaranteed availability will be part of a Service Level Agreement (SLA), which is a contract between a provider and a subscriber that specifies the percentage of time that the contracted services are available. None of the other three options contain the guaranteed reliability language. Acceptable Use Policies (AUPs) specify whether and how employees can use company-owned hardware and software resources. A Nondisclosure Agreement (NDA) specifies what company information employees are permitted to discuss outside the company. A Bring Your Own Device (BYOD) policy specifies the personal electronics that employees are permitted to use on the company network and documents the procedures for connecting and securing them.

80. A, B. A bridge can split a single network into two collision domains, because it forwards only the packets that are destined for the other side of the bridge. A switch creates a separate collision domain for each port. Both bridges and switches forward all broadcast packets, so they maintain a single broadcast domain for the entire network. A hub maintains a single collision domain and a single broadcast domain. A router creates two collision domains, but it does not forward broadcasts, so it creates two broadcast domains as well.

81. A. Media Access Control (MAC) addresses are hard-coded into network interface adapters and are not easily changeable. There is also no need to change them for this purpose. First, you will have to change IP addresses of the web servers. This is because the computers on the other side of the router, on the screened subnet, must use an IP network address that is different from the internal network's address. Next, you will have to change the default gateway address setting on the internal network computers to the address of the router on the internal network so that traffic can be forwarded to the screened subnet. Finally, you will have to update the resource records on your Domain Name System (DNS) server to reflect the IP address changes.

82. C. A short is when a wire is connected to two or more pins at one end of the cable or when the conductors of two or more wires are touching inside the cable. This would cause a tone applied to a single pin at one end to be heard on multiple pins at the other end. The other three options would not cause this to occur. An open circuit would manifest as a failure to detect a tone on a wire, indicating that there is either a break in the wire somewhere inside the cable or a bad connection with the pin in one or both connectors. A split pair is a connection in which two wires are incorrectly mapped in exactly the same way on both ends of the cable. Crosstalk is a type of interference caused by signals on one wire bleeding over to other wires.

83. B. Elevator machinery, fluorescent light fixtures, and other electrical devices in an office environment can generate magnetic fields, resulting in electromagnetic interference (EMI). When copper-based cables are located too near to such a device, the magnetic fields can generate an electric current on the cable that interferes with the signals exchanged by network devices. If the network users experience a problem every time the elevator machinery switches on, EMI is a likely cause of the problem. Crosstalk and attenuation can both cause intermittent network communication problems, but they cannot be caused by elevator machinery. Latency describes a generalized delay in network transmissions, not intermittent packet delays.

84. B, D. In an active-active configuration, servers can balance the incoming client load between them. Because the active servers are all servicing clients, the overall performance of the cluster is increased. Both active-active and active-passive configurations provide fault tolerance. Data encapsulation is not a factor in either configuration.

85. D. It is possible that the WAP has been configured to not broadcast the network's SSID as a security measure, so you should first attempt to access it by typing the SSID in manually. You cannot type in the WPA2 passphrase until you are in the process of connecting to the SSID. Moving the laptop closer to the access point or away from possible sources of electromagnetic interference might be solutions to the problem, but they should not be the first thing you try in this case.

86. D. The 802.11b and 802.11g standards do not support 5 GHz communications. Configuring the access point to support 2.4 GHz is the only way for the 802.11b and 802.11g computers to connect to the network. The 5 GHz band does support automatic channel selection, so there is no need to configure the channel on each laptop manually. The 5 GHz band does support MIMO, and the 802.11n laptops should be able to connect. The 802.11b standard does support the 2.4 GHz band.

87. D. The Name Server (NS) resource record identifies the authoritative servers for a particular DNS zone. Pointer Records (PTRs) are used to resolve IP addresses into hostnames. Mail Exchange (MX) records identify the mail servers for a particular domain. Service Records (SRVs) identify the designated servers for a particular application. None of these other options identify the authoritative servers for a zone.

88. B. The 2.4 GHz band used by Wireless Local Area Networks (WLANs) consists of channels that are 20 (or 22) MHz wide. However, the channels are only 5 MHz apart, so there is channel overlap that can result in interference. Channels 1, 6, and 11 are the only channels that are far enough apart from each other to avoid any overlap with the adjacent channels. This is why they are often recommended. However, in this scenario, these channels are too crowded with other networks. You should therefore use a channel that is as far as possible from the crowded ones. Channels 2, 5, and 10 are all immediately adjacent to a crowded channel, but channel 9 is at least two channels away from the nearest crowded channel. Therefore, you should configure your equipment to use channel 9.

89. A. Material Safety Data Sheets (MSDSs) are documents created by manufacturers of chemical, electrical, and mechanical products that specify the potential risks and dangers associated with them, particularly in regard to flammability and the possibility of toxic outgassing. A properly documented network should have MSDS documents on file for all of the chemical and hardware products used to build and maintain it. MSDSs can be obtained from manufacturers or the Environmental Protection Agency (EPA). Electrostatic discharges (ESDs), Nondisclosure Agreements (NDAs), and Bring Your Own Device (BYOD) policies are not concerned with the dangers inherent in building contents.

90. C. The Alternative B PoE variant can use the spare wire pair in a CAT 5 or better 10Base-T or 100Base-TX cable to supply power to connected devices. The Alternative A and 4PPoE variants cannot use the spare wire pair in this manner; they supply power using the wire pairs that carry data at the same time. For Gigabit Ethernet or faster installations, Alternative B is also capable of using the data wire pairs.

91. D. The Internet Storage Name Service (iSNS) is an application that provides iSCSI initiators with automated discovery of targets located on the network. iSNS can also function as a discovery service for Fibre Channel devices. Internet Control Message Protocol (ICMP) and Domain Name System (DNS) are not capable of registering iSCSI targets. iDNS does not exist.

92. C. WPA has been found to be vulnerable, and WPA2 was designed to address those vulnerabilities, so you should use WPA2 instead of WPA. Suppressing SSID broadcasts does not prevent users from connecting to the network, and MAC filtering strengthens security without exposing MAC addresses to undue risk.

93. B, D, E. Subscriber Connector (SC), Mechanical Transfer - Registered Jack (MT-RJ), and Straight Tip (ST) are all types of fiber-optic connectors. DB-9 is a D-shell connector used for serial ports. Bayonet-Neill-Concelman (BNC) is a type of connector used with coaxial cable. RJ11 is used with twisted-pair cable for telephone connections.

94. E. The IoT consists of devices that are ordinarily passive, but which have been made intelligent by installing a network client configuring them to participate on an IP network. All of the devices listed are available as "smart" devices that enable remote users to interact with them over the Internet.

95. D. The physical layer defines the mechanical and electrical characteristics of the cables used to build a network. The data link layer defines specific network (LAN or WAN) topologies and their characteristics. The physical layer specification you will implement is dependent on the data link layer protocol you select. The network, transport, and application layers are not concerned with cables and topologies.

96. D. The 169.254.203.42 address assigned to the workstation is from the 169.254.0.0/16 network address assigned to Automatic Private IP Addressing (APIPA), a standard for the assignment of IP addresses to Dynamic Host Configuration Protocol (DHCP) clients when they cannot obtain an address from a DHCP server. The workstation's DHCP client is activated, and since no one else is experiencing a problem, you can assume that the DHCP server is functioning. The Subnet Mask value is correct for an APIPA address, and APIPA does not provide Default Gateway or Domain Name System (DNS) server addresses. Therefore, an exhausted DHCP scope is the only one of the explanations provided that could be the cause of the problem.

97. C. Operating systems detect duplicate IP addresses immediately and display error messages or notifications on the computers involved. Therefore, the user with the problem would have been informed immediately if another system was using her IP address. All of the other options are possible causes of the problem that are more difficult to troubleshoot.

98. C, D. The `ipconfig /release` command terminates the current DHCP address lease. Then, the `ipconfig /renew` command causes the client to begin the process of negotiating a new lease, this time with the authorized DHCP server. `dump`, `lease`, and `discard` are not valid `ipconfig` parameters.

99. C. East-west traffic describes traffic flow within the datacenter, while north-south is traffic between devices inside the datacenter and outside devices. The terms east-west and north-south do not pertain to the OSI model layers or to the specific devices used.

100. B. A logic bomb is a code insert placed into a legitimate software product that triggers a malicious event when certain conditions are met, such as when a specific time or date arrives. All of the other options do not involve software products. Social engineering is the practice of obtaining sensitive data by contacting users and pretending to be someone with a legitimate need for that data. War driving is an attack method that consists of driving around a neighborhood with a computer, scanning for unprotected wireless networks. An evil twin is a fraudulent access point on a wireless network that mimics the Service Set Identifier (SSID) of a legitimate access point, in the hope of luring in users.

Index

J-K

S

W

X-Y-Z

Online Test Bank

Register to gain one year of FREE access after activation to the online interactive test bank to help you study for your CompTIA Network+ certification exam—included with your purchase of this book! All of domain-by-domain questions and the practice tests in this book are included in the online test bank so you can practice in a timed and graded setting.

Register and Access the Online Test Bank

To register your book and get access to the online test bank, follow these steps:

1. Go to www.wiley.com/go/sybextestprep (this address is case sensitive)!
2. Select your book from the list.
3. Complete the required registration information, including answering the security verification to prove book ownership. You will be emailed a pin code.
4. Follow the directions in the email or go to www.wiley.com/go/sybextestprep.
5. Find your book on that page and click the "Register or Login" link with it. Then enter the pin code you received and click the "Activate PIN" button.
6. On the Create an Account or Login page, enter your username and password, and click Login or, if you don't have an account already, create a new account.
7. At this point, you should be in the test bank site with your new test bank listed at the top of the page. If you do not see it there, please refresh the page or log out and log back in.